FOUNDATIONS O]
INTERNATIONAL .

Between the early seventeenth and mid nineteenth centuries, major
European political thinkers first began to look outside their national
borders and envisage a world of competitive, equal sovereign states
inhabiting an international sphere that ultimately encompassed
the whole globe. In this insightful and wide-ranging work, David
Armitage – one of the world's leading historians of political thought –
traces the genesis of this international turn in intellectual history.
Foundations of Modern International Thought combines important
methodological essays, which consider the genealogy of globalisation
and the parallel histories of empires and oceans, with fresh considerations of leading figures such as Hobbes, Locke, Burke and Bentham
in the history of international thought. The culmination of more than
a decade's reflection and research on these issues, this book restores
the often overlooked international dimensions to intellectual history
and recovers the intellectual dimensions of international history.

DAVID ARMITAGE is the Lloyd C. Blankfein Professor of History
at Harvard University where he teaches intellectual history and
international history. His many publications include *The Ideological
Origins of the British Empire* (Cambridge University Press, 2000),
The Declaration of Independence: A Global History (2007) and, as
editor, *The British Atlantic World, 1500–1800* (2nd edn, 2009), *British
Political Thought in History, Literature and Theory, 1500–1800*
(Cambridge University Press, 2006), *Shakespeare and Early Modern
Political Thought* (Cambridge University Press, 2009) and *The Age of
Revolutions in Global Context, c. 1760–1840* (2010).

[I]n all times, Kings, and Persons of Soveraigne authority, because of their Independency, are in continuall jealousies, and in the state and posture of Gladiators; having their weapons pointing, and their eyes fixed on one another ...

Thomas Hobbes, *Leviathan* (1651)

Power or weakness does not in this respect produce any difference. A dwarf is as much a man as a giant; a small republic is no less a sovereign state than the most powerful kingdom.

Emer de Vattel, *Le Droit des gens* (1758)

FOUNDATIONS OF MODERN
INTERNATIONAL THOUGHT

DAVID ARMITAGE

CAMBRIDGE
UNIVERSITY PRESS

CAMBRIDGE
UNIVERSITY PRESS

University Printing House, Cambridge CB2 8BS, United Kingdom

Published in the United States of America by Cambridge University Press, New York

Cambridge University Press is part of the University of Cambridge.

It furthers the University's mission by disseminating knowledge in the pursuit of
education, learning and research at the highest international levels of excellence

www.cambridge.org
Information on this title: www.cambridge.org/9780521001694

First published 2013
Reprinted 2014

Printed in the United Kingdom by Clays, St Ives plc.

A catalogue record for this publication is available from the British Library

Library of Congress Cataloguing in Publication data

Armitage, David, 1965–
Foundations of modern international thought / David Armitage.
p.   cm.
ISBN 978-0-521-80707-4 (Hardback) – ISBN 978-0-521-00169-4 (Paperback)
1. International relations–Philosophy–History.   2. International law–Philosophy–History.
I. Title.
JZ1305.A75 2012
327.101–dc23
2012019500

ISBN 978-0-521-80707-4 Hardback
ISBN 978-0-521-00169-4 Paperback

Contents

List of figures   *page* vii
Preface   ix
List of abbreviations   xii

Introduction: rethinking the foundations of modern
international thought   1

I   HISTORIOGRAPHICAL FOUNDATIONS

1   The international turn in intellectual history   17

2   Is there a pre-history of globalisation?   33

3   The elephant and the whale: empires and oceans
    in world history   46

II SEVENTEENTH-CENTURY FOUNDATIONS:
    HOBBES AND LOCKE

4   Hobbes and the foundations of modern international thought   59

5   John Locke's international thought   75

6   John Locke, Carolina and the *Two Treatises of Government*   90

7   John Locke: theorist of empire?   114

III EIGHTEENTH-CENTURY FOUNDATIONS

8   Parliament and international law in eighteenth-century Britain   135

9   Edmund Burke and reason of state   154

10 Globalising Jeremy Bentham   172

v

Contents

IV BUILDING ON THE FOUNDATIONS: MAKING STATES
    SINCE 1776

11 The Declaration of Independence and international law   191

12 Declarations of independence, 1776–2012   215

Bibliography   233
Index   292

Figures

2.1 Relative frequency of 'globalisation'/'globalization' in
     English-language works, 1980–2008   34
2.2 Relative frequency of the terms 'global', 'international'
     and 'transnational' in English-language works, 1900–2008   43

vii

Preface

I have accumulated a great many debts over the dozen years in which I have been working on the history of international thought. The most fundamental is to Knud Haakonssen for his generous invitation to deliver the 2003 Robert P. Benedict Lectures in the History of Political Philosophy at Boston University; he and Jim Schmidt were exemplary hosts for that stimulating series. My only regret is that a published version of the lectures was so long in coming and that it has not arrived in the form Knud, or indeed I, had originally anticipated. To deliver the Benedict Lectures, I took a semester's leave from my duties at Columbia University: belated but heartfelt thanks to David Johnston and Jim Zetzel for shouldering the extra burdens my absence created.

Three other opportunities allowed me to pursue my themes. The first was a fellowship at the Charles Warren Center for Studies in American History at Harvard University in 2000–1, where Akira Iriye, Jim Kloppenberg and the late Ernest May led a year of unforgettable discussions with a remarkable group of fellow Warren Fellows. The second was the chance to lead a seminar under the auspices of the Center for the History of British Political Thought at the Folger Shakespeare Library in 2002. I am deeply grateful to John Pocock for that invitation and for his penetrating contributions to the seminar, as well as to all the participants for the light they shed on the early modern foundations of international thought. And the third was Barry Hindess's kind suggestion to spend some weeks in 2004 as a Visiting Fellow in the Research School of Social Sciences at the Australian National University, where I enjoyed many memorable exchanges with Barry and his collaborators.

Over the years, parts of my original project took on lives of their own,[1] but I never stopped thinking about the larger whole of which they were part.

---

[1] Grotius (2004); Armitage (2007a); Armitage and Subrahmanyam (2010); Armitage (in press); Locke (in press).

I am especially grateful to the various students, many now colleagues, with whom I have discussed aspects of international intellectual history, among them Greg Afinogenov, Alex Bevilacqua, Paul Cheney, Theo Christov, Elizabeth Cross, James Delbourgo, Phil Fileri, Lisa Ford, Nick Harding, Alison LaCroix, Jamie Martin, Ted McCormick, Mira Siegelberg, Miranda Spieler, Tristan Stein, Phil Stern and Lauri Tähtinen.

For editorial advice and encouragement, the palm goes, yet again and as so often, to Richard Fisher at Cambridge University Press. Richard vigorously supported my initial conception, tactfully stopped asking about the book when all hope of its completion seemed lost and enthusiastically welcomed its unexpected resuscitation. Such patience and trust went well beyond what any author has a right to expect. And special thanks, finally, to Liz Friend-Smith for picking up the editorial baton at the very end of the race, to Phil Fileri for indispensable research assistance, to Elizabeth Spicer for effortlessly shepherding the text through the press and to Caroline Howlett for her vigilant copy-editing.

Apart from the Introduction, all the chapters of this book have appeared in earlier versions, though two are published here for the first time in English. In revising them, I have tried to eliminate repetitions and excessively local references, corrected errors and updated references where necessary. I am grateful to the editors and publishers for permission to reprint and rework the following material:

Chapter 1, from Darrin M. McMahon and Samuel Moyn (eds.), *Rethinking Modern European Intellectual History* (Oxford University Press, 2013).

Chapter 2, Copyright © 2004, from Deborah Cohen and Maura O'Connor (eds.), *Comparison and History: Europe in Cross-National Perspective.* Reproduced by permission of Taylor and Francis Group, LLC, a division of Informa plc.

Chapter 3, from Ruth Ben-Ghiat (ed.), *Gli imperi: dall'antichità all'età contemporanea* (Il Mulino, 2009).

Chapter 4, from Annabel Brett and James Tully with Holly Hamilton-Bleakley (eds.), *Rethinking the Foundations of Modern Political Thought* (Cambridge University Press, 2006).

Chapter 5, from Ian Hall and Lisa Hill (eds.), *British International Thinkers from Hobbes to Namier* (Palgrave Macmillan, 2009).

Chapter 6, from *Political Theory* 32, 5 (October 2004).

Chapter 7, from Sankar Muthu (ed.), *Empire and Modern Political Thought* (Cambridge University Press, 2012).

Chapter 8, from Julian Hoppit (ed.), *Parliaments, Nations and Identities in Britain, 1660–1850* (Manchester University Press, 2003).

Chapter 9, from the *Journal of the History of Ideas* 61, 4 (October 2000). Copyright © 2000 by the *Journal of the History of Ideas.*

Chapter 10, from *History of Political Thought* 32, 1 (Spring 2011).

Chapter 11, from the *William and Mary Quarterly* 3rd ser., 59, 1 (January 2002).

Chapter 12, from Alfredo Ávila, Jordana Dym, Aurora Gómez Galvarriato and Erika Pani (eds.), *La era de las declaraciónes. Textos fundamentales de las independencias en América* (El Colegio de México-UNAM, 2012).

Abbreviations

BL	British Library, London
Bod.	Bodleian Library, Oxford
HRO	Hampshire Record Office, Winchester
HUA	University Archives, Harvard University, Cambridge, Mass.
LC	Library of Congress, Washington, DC
NYPL	New York Public Library, New York
ODNB	*Oxford Dictionary of National Biography*
OED	*Oxford English Dictionary*
SCDA	South Carolina Department of Archives, Columbia, SC
SRO	Somerset Record Office, Taunton
TNA	The National Archives, Kew
UCL	University College London

Introduction: rethinking the foundations of modern international thought

Foundations of Modern International Thought is the third in a loose trilogy of works in international intellectual history.[1] When the first, *The Ideological Origins of the British Empire*, was published in 2000, the field had neither a local habitation nor a name. It had no common agenda, no coherent body of scholarship and no self-identifying practitioners; it therefore occupied no territory on the broader map of contemporary historiography.[2] The very term 'international intellectual history' had hardly ever been used in print, let alone deployed to define a field of academic study.[3] By the time the second instalment, *The Declaration of Independence: A Global History*, appeared in 2007, international intellectual history had already begun to emerge as a self-conscious area of inquiry pursued by intellectual historians with international interests and by international historians with inclinations towards intellectual and cultural history.[4] In the half-decade since then, it has become an identifiable field, with an expanding canon of works, a burgeoning set of questions and a fertile agenda for research. I hope this volume might stand as a partial record of its recent development as well as an inspiration for international intellectual historians in the future.

The chapters collected here represent the fruits of over a decade's work on the intellectual history of conceptions of international relations and international law, mostly in the period before those two modes of inter-action and negotiation had acquired their current names, disciplinary

---

[1] The others are Armitage (2000); Armitage (2007a).

[2] It did not appear in such classic surveys of the state of intellectual history as Darnton (1980); Kelley (1987); Brett (2002); or Grafton (2006).

[3] For an outlying early usage, see Wellek (1955), p. 118, on Francesco De Sanctis's sudden shift to 'international intellectual history' in the eighteenth-century portion of his *Storia della letteratura italiana* (1870–1).

[4] For early assessments of the field's prospects, see Bell (2002a); Armitage (2004); Rothschild (2006).

boundaries and contemporary canons of authorities and ancestors. The selection of subjects is inevitably arbitrary but it was not random. They mostly sprang from invitations to extend my earlier work on the intellectual history of the anglophone Atlantic world into broader contexts and to cover novel themes. But they did so in light of an ongoing effort to reassess historically some of the myths – in the sense of meaningful narratives, not necessarily delusive falsehoods – that had informed international studies in disciplines outside history. This effort directed my attention, as an intellectual historian, to the thought of Thomas Hobbes, John Locke, Edmund Burke and Jeremy Bentham. It also turned my thoughts, as an international historian, to the salience of states and empires, oceanic histories and global connections, over the *longue durée* as settings for the arguments anatomised in other chapters. And it determined my interest, as an Atlantic historian, in the Americas as the matrix for processes of state-making that would recur across the modern world until our own time. The resulting studies are therefore disparate but 'receive an underlying unity from the philosophy of the writer' as well as from the common themes of the chapters that, taken together, I hope will justify republication and reward reading as a single collection.[5]

The very variety of themes and subjects reflects the exploratory nature of international intellectual history itself. At the end of the twentieth century, research on the international dimensions of intellectual history was mostly fragmentary and remained marginal to the broader historical discipline. The history of *political* thought was certainly ascendant – in some quarters even predominant – among intellectual historians on both sides of the Atlantic and increasingly around the world. Yet the history of *international* thought was pursued, if at all, mostly by self-critical students of international relations and international law who had little contact or interchange with those who identified themselves primarily as intellectual historians.

The situation recalled that diagnosed in 1959 by Martin Wight, co-founder of the so-called 'English School' of International Relations, when he asked, in a much-discussed paper, 'Why Is There No International Theory?'. Wight lamented the lack of any 'tradition of speculation about the society of states, or the family of nations, or the international community' that could parallel, in depth or in analytical illumination, 'the body of writings about the state' collectively known as political theory. He concluded

---

[5] Trevor-Roper (1957), p. v, the classic apologia for collected essays, cited Elliott (2007), p. xiv.

a survey of this fragmentary tradition with a notorious assessment: 'international theory is marked, not only by paucity, but also by moral and intellectual poverty'.[6] Nearly fifty years later, intellectual historians could have echoed Wight's original question to ask, 'Why is there no history of international thought?'. That field also lacked a continuous tradition of inquiry or an agreed subject for research. Poverty, whether moral or intellectual, may not have been the problem, but paucity certainly was.

Only three years before Wight delivered his godfather's curse on international theory, the Cambridge historian Peter Laslett had offered an equally notorious judgment in 1956: 'For the moment, anyway, political philosophy is dead.'[7] This premature epitaph turned out to be a salutary provocation, as became eminently clear in the years that followed, marked at one end by Isaiah Berlin's Oxford inaugural lecture, 'Two Concepts of Liberty' (1958), and at the other by the publication of John Rawls's *A Theory of Justice* (1971), which heralded an unparalleled efflorescence of normative political theory which continues to this day. Likewise, the same period witnessed the beginnings of a persistently fertile vein of inquiry into the history of political thought, running from J. G. A. Pocock's *The Ancient Constitution and the Feudal Law* (1957) to Quentin Skinner's *The Foundations of Modern Political Thought* (1978), by way of Laslett's own path-breaking edition of John Locke's *Two Treatises of Government* (1960).

The contextualist historians of political thought – among them, Laslett himself, Pocock, Skinner and John Dunn – understandably concentrated their attention on the history of the theory of the state in its domestic or municipal capacities. This fact reflected the central concerns of political theory itself during the period in which they wrote and helped to facilitate an ongoing dialogue between historians and political theorists. However, their focus on the internal capacities of the state apparently encouraged neglect of the external relations of states, as the revival of the history of political thought was not accompanied by a parallel resurgence of interest in the history of international thought. In this vein, Skinner concluded *The Foundations of Modern Political Thought* with the claim that '[b]y the beginning of the seventeenth century, the concept of the State – its nature, its powers, its right to command obedience – had come to be regarded as the most important object of analysis in European political thought'.

---

[6] Wight (1966). Here, as throughout the book, I use 'International Relations' to denote the academic discipline that studies the phenomena called 'international relations'.
[7] Laslett (1956), p. vii.

Fundamental to this concept was the state's independence from 'any external or superior power'.[8] Apart from a brief but suggestive account of neo-Scholastic conceptions of the law of nations, Skinner's work included no treatment of the state in its nature, its powers or its rights as an international actor: that is, of what I have called in this volume the foundations of modern *international* thought.[9]

The absence of any extended treatment of those foundations was typical for the time at which Skinner's *Foundations* appeared. In the same year that book was published, W. B. Gallie commented that 'thoughts ... about the roles and causes of war and the possibilities of peace between the peoples of the world' had formed 'an enterprise which the ablest minds of previous ages had, with very few exceptions, either ignored or by-passed'. Gallie argued that the foundations of modern international thought were laid much later, during the eighteenth century, 'in the writings of Montesquieu, Voltaire, Rousseau, and Vattel among others'.[10] Taken together, these two accounts implied that the foundations of modern political thought were distinct from those of modern international thought and that each possessed a distinct chronology, genealogy and canon of fundamental thinkers. Two decades of scholarship did little to dispel that impression, as historians of political thought mostly ignored the international dimensions of their subject while students of International Relations remained largely uninterested in historicising the theories invoked in their field.

Yet the ground had already begun to shift by the mid-1990s. Historians of political thought could not remain entirely unaffected by the increasingly obvious turn towards international and global concerns taking place by that time within political theory itself. In the United States, at least, that movement had begun under the shadow of the Vietnam War which fell across both Rawls's *Theory of Justice* and the treatment of international justice in Michael Walzer's *Just and Unjust Wars* (1977).[11] In his discussion of civil disobedience, Rawls turned to the law of nations for guidance on the 'political principles' that 'govern public policies toward other nations', including the 'fundamental equal rights' of peoples organised into independent states; self-determination and its corollary, the duty of non-intervention; the right of self-defence; the necessity to

---

[8] Skinner (1978), II, pp. 349, 351.   [9] Skinner (1978), II, pp. 151–4.
[10] Gallie (1978), p. 1. Gallie immediately preceded Skinner in the Cambridge Chair of Political Science.
[11] Rawls (1999b), pp. 319–43; Walzer (2006).

keep treaties (*pacta sunt servanda*); and restrictions on the conduct of war (the *jus in bello*): in fact, a standard list of the basic principles of modern positive international law which Rawls took from a reigning text in the field, J. L. Brierly's *Law of Nations*.[12] By contrast, Walzer's *Just and Unjust Wars* sprang in part from an apprehension that international law could no longer 'provide a fully plausible or coherent account of our moral arguments', not least because 'legal positivism ... has become in the age of the United Nations increasingly uninteresting'.[13]

The distinction between 'moral arguments' and 'legal positivism' was the legacy of a gulf that had opened up between law understood positively – that is, as the acts of sovereign agents, whether in their capacities as legislators or as the executors of international agreements, conventions and customs – and law understood normatively.[14] That abyss had widened over the centuries in historical discussions of reason of state and with the decline of natural jurisprudence, as Rawls and Walzer – both historically minded theorists, for all their normative ambitions – were certainly aware. The basic dilemmas they had exposed – for example, the gulf separating 'positive' law and 'moral arguments'; the difficulties of applying interpersonal norms on an international scale; the collision between the statist principles enshrined in the Charter of the United Nations and the universalist assumptions of human rights; and the mismatch between the claims of local and global justice – encouraged a theoretical ferment around questions of international ethics that continues unabated to this day.[15] It was only a matter of time before historians of political thought would follow the new paths blazed by contemporary political theorists.[16]

Other straws in the wind were pointing in new directions, both international and global, for intellectual historians, among them a so-called 'post-positivist' orientation among contemporary theorists of International Relations, particularly (but not exclusively) outside the United States.[17] This manifested itself in various ways: in a return to grand historical theorising about international relations;[18] in the rise of 'constructivism', or the study of the mutual self-constitution of international actors through

---

[12] Rawls (1999b), p. 332, citing Brierly (1963), and noting, 'This work contains all that we need here.'
[13] Walzer (2006), p. xxvi.
[14] For a powerful early deconstruction of these oppositions, see Koskenniemi (2005), originally published in 1989.
[15] From Beitz (1999) to Bell (2010) and beyond.
[16] The first major work in this vein was Tuck (1999), based on his Carlyle Lectures delivered in Oxford at the start of the first Gulf War in 1991 (ibid., 'Preface').
[17] Smith, Booth and Zalewski (1996).   [18] For example, Bobbitt (2002).

rules, norms and representations;[19] in the historical study of International Relations as a discipline, whether as a means of explaining present discontents or as a source of renewal for an allegedly faltering intellectual project;[20] and in a heightened interest in the language of international politics as International Relations undertook its own version of the linguistic turn that had swept other parts of the humanities and interpretive social sciences.[21]

These distinct but often mutually supportive movements were accompanied by a similar turn towards language and history among international lawyers,[22] at the moment when a self-consciously 'new international history' attentive to culture and ideas as much as power and interest emerged from a more traditional diplomatic history centred on the archives and activities of states and their formal agents. That history was more transnational than national, more focused on connections across nations than the collisions between states and more attentive to actors and institutions that worked below and above, or ran in parallel with, the states that had been the traditional subjects of international history.[23] Taken together, these developments in political theory, international relations, international law and international history opened novel possibilities for common conversations between practitioners in all these fields.

It was no coincidence that this dizzying sequence of turns – linguistic, historiographical, transnational and cultural, to name only the most prominent[24] – occurred at just the moment when talk of globalisation began to dominate both popular and professional consciousness. The apprehension, whether well-grounded or not, that borders were dissolving, that the state was withering away and that untrammelled flows of people, capital and goods were now sluicing around the globe inevitably excited interest in the origins and development of these processes. Was global interconnectedness a relatively recent feature of world history, a product perhaps of the 1970s with only shallow roots in previous periods?[25] Was there a pre-history – or were there multiple and discontinuous pre-histories – of globalisation, stretching back to the 1870s, the 1770s, the 1570s or possibly even earlier?[26]

[19] Kratochwil (1989); N. G. Onuf (1989); Wendt (1999); Zehfuss (2002); Lebow (2008).
[20] Dunne (1998); Schmidt (1998); Vigezzi (2005); Guilhot (2011).   [21] Bell (2002a); Bell (2002b).
[22] For example, Marks (2000); Koskenniemi (2002); Anghie (2005).
[23] Manela, 'International Society as a Historical Subject' (unpublished). My thanks to Prof. Manela for the chance to read this important essay in advance of publication.
[24] Surkis, Wilder, Cook, Ghosh, Thomas and Perl-Rosenthal (2012).
[25] For critical examinations of that moment, see Ferguson, Maier, Manela and Sargent (2010); Borstelmann (2012).
[26] O'Rourke and Williamson (1999); Rothschild (2001); Flynn and Giráldez (1995); Gruzinski (2004).

When did awareness of the shrinkage of space converge with knowledge of linkage across time: that is, when, and indeed where, did conceptions of world history first emerge?[27] And how should contemporary historians approach the challenge of writing global histories for a self-consciously global age?[28]

The various efforts to answer these pressing questions contributed to the two main bodies of research that now comprise international intellectual history. These are what might be called the intellectual history of the international and an internationalised intellectual history. The first is the field now also sometimes known as the history of international thought or, when more narrowly focused, the history of international political theory. One leading practitioner has recently defined its subject-matter as 'how thinkers of previous generations conceived of the nature and significance of political boundaries, and the relations between discrete communities'.[29] I would go still further, to define international thought as theoretical reflection on that peculiar political arena populated variously by individuals, peoples, nations and states and, in the early modern period, by other corporate bodies such as churches and trading companies. Such reflection treats the nature of the interactions between these actors and the norms that regulate – or should regulate – them. Its central concern in the modern period may therefore be the relations between states, but for longer swathes of history it also treated a multiplicity of non-state relations, as it still does in an era when the individual is now firmly established as a subject of international law and when international institutions and transnational organisations thickly populate the world.

The second corpus of work, of intellectual history on an international scale, has extended intellectual history's ambit to trace the circulation, transmission and reception of texts, ideas and thinkers within and beyond state boundaries, across oceans and among far-flung communities of actors and readers. The two approaches are clearly not identical but they have substantially overlapped and fruitfully converged in their interests. The creation of mutual understandings of international, transnational and global connection and competition often depended upon the intercultural translation of texts of religion, diplomacy and law, just as transnational structures of commerce and international relations facilitated or hindered the movement of books and other vectors of ideas.

---

[27] Subrahmanyam (2005) offers one compelling answer; Tang (2008), another.
[28] Geyer and Bright (1995); Grew (2006); Lang (2006); Neem (2011); Sachsenmaier (2011).
[29] Bell (2007b), in Bell (2007c), p. 1.

At one end of the spectrum, therefore, international intellectual history encompasses the doctrinal history of international law; at the other, it draws upon the irreducible materiality of the history of the book. To paraphrase Kant, in the international realm (as elsewhere), intellectual history without material history will be empty, while material history uninformed by intellectual history will be blind.[30] Accordingly, the chapters that follow all engage, to a greater or lesser degree of explicitness, with the histories of the circulation and reception of international thought across both time and space. Both forms of movement necessarily involve conscious acts of appropriation and dissemination. Without the availability of long-range textual traditions or the later creation of professional canons; without the need of new disciplines, like International Relations, to forge sustaining genealogies; and without the desire of new states and international organisations to justify themselves in the eyes of the world, no body of international thought – however malleable and shifting – could ever have been created. These processes entailed both 'upward' and 'downward' hermeneutics, as the practices of diplomats and parliamentarians, colonists and rebels, shaped normative theories and official genres.[31] At the same time, debates in council-chambers and committee-rooms and the studies of scholars and philosophers attempted to formalise conceptions being thrashed out elsewhere on battlegrounds, in maritime arenas and along imperial frontiers around the world. The formation of modern international thought was in itself a transnational, indeed global enterprise. Demonstrating this will be a major task for the next phase of research in international intellectual history.[32]

Foundations of Modern International Thought concentrates on the period roughly defined by the public careers of Thomas Hobbes and Jeremy Bentham (*c.* 1629–1832). It is on foundations laid in these centuries, I believe and the following chapters attempt to illustrate, that modern international thought rested. In contrast to Quentin Skinner, whose classic study of *The Foundations of Modern Political Thought* inspired the title of this collection, I make no implicit claim exhaustively or comprehensively to excavate all the basic elements which went into the making of modern international thought. My aim is more modest, as I have tried to indicate by calling this volume *Foundations* – rather than

---

[30] Compare the debate between Robert Darnton and Quentin Skinner: Darnton (2005); Skinner (2005).
[31] I am indebted to Bayly (2012), p. 28, for these formulations.
[32] See, for example, Lorca (in press).

The Foundations – of Modern International Thought. The various essays are symptomatic rather than systematic in their effort to trace the emergence and early development of key elements of international thinking as it appeared between the late eighteenth century and the late twentieth century. Some of those elements remain in the early twenty-first century but the book focuses on a dialogue between the history of early modernity and the history of a 'modern' world that is increasingly receding from us, and is seen through an ever thicker scrim of post-modern scepticism about modernity itself.

On the face of it, my decision to locate modern international thought's foundations within early modernity is unexceptionable because a series of prior aetiological narratives, mostly within the disciplines of international law and International Relations, had also found them there. For example, the origins of modern diplomacy have often been located in the late fifteenth or sixteenth centuries.[33] The sixteenth century may also have witnessed the beginnings of modern international relations, even if the theory to account for the practices of sovereignty, warfare, diplomacy and treaty-making lagged by fifty or a hundred years and only emerged in recognisably modern form by the mid seventeenth century.[34] This chronology followed a slightly different trajectory from that informing the history of international law, the origins of which could variously be traced back to the 'School of Salamanca' in sixteenth-century Spain,[35] to the later sixteenth-century Italian jurist Alberico Gentili or to the work of his Dutch successor, Hugo Grotius, the early seventeenth-century 'father of the law of nations'.[36] The year 1625, which saw the publication of Grotius's *De Jure Belli ac Pacis*, was the start of one narrative of the history of international law, but another story, more closely tied to the mythography of International Relations, posited the primacy of 1648 and the Peace of Westphalia as the beginning of 'traditional' international law (1648–1900) or of the international legal order in 'the French age' (1648–1815).[37] Each of these narratives about early modernity appeared first, and somewhat belatedly, in the succeeding age of modernity. They were therefore not stories actors told about themselves or their achievements but foundation myths retailed by later communities of historians and

---

[33] Mattingly (1955); Anderson (1993); Bély (2007).   [34] Holzgrefe (1989).

[35] Scott (1928); Anghie (1996); Koskenniemi (2010a).

[36] Holland (1874); Kingsbury and Straumann (2010); Pagden (2010); Bourquin (1948); Grewe (1984); Bull, Kingsbury and Roberts (1990).

[37] Kennedy (1986), pp. 1–5, 95–8; Grewe (1988), Pt. III, 'Droit public de l'Europe: Die Völkerrechtsordnung des Französischen Zeitalters 1648–1815'.

diplomats, international lawyers and proto-political scientists, seeking historical validation for their ideological projects and infant professions.[38]

At the root of these later just-so stories was the fundamental assumption that there were two distinct realms called variously the internal and the external, the domestic and the foreign or (in a more legalistic idiom) the municipal and the international. That dichotomy remains perhaps the least investigated of all the fundamental divisions in our political lives. This remains so even though it intersected historically and theoretically with such basic oppositions as private and public, female and male, civilian and combatant, as feminist legal and political scholarship has repeatedly demonstrated.[39] Just when the two spheres, domestic and international, separated and what propelled them apart has caused confusion when it has not been shrouded in amnesia. The most common explanation among International Relations theorists hinged on 'the collapse of universalistic accounts of political, religious and metaphysical hierarchies' in the early modern period, which generated 'political community within and international anarchy without'.[40] But perhaps this was too broad-brush an explanation; a single inventor was needed and he could be found in mid-seventeenth-century England: 'Things would definitely change with Hobbes: "outsides" were "invented," policy became "foreign".'[41] Or maybe the separation emerged a century later in Britain, as Jeremy Bentham thought: 'The term *municipal* . . . was taken by an English author of the first eminence [Sir William Blackstone], to signify internal law in general, in contradistinction to international law, and the imaginary law of nature.'[42] On the contrary, asserted Carl Schmitt, it took another century and a half for the distinction to mature: 'After 1910, it became customary to distinguish *internal* and *external*.'[43] Such accounts were not necessarily incompatible: they could all be held to mark discontinuous stages in the development of an unfolding but punctuated story. Taken together, they do suggest a need for further research on this most basic foundation-stone of modern international thought.

We now inhabit a self-consciously *post*-modern world in which 'the distinction between domestic and foreign affairs begins to break down' and where a British Prime Minister and his Foreign Secretary could each

---

[38] Compare Koskenniemi (2010b).
[39] Charlesworth (1992); Charlesworth (1997); Charlesworth and Chinkin (2000); Simons (2003); Elshtain (2008); Kinsella (2011).
[40] Walker (1993), pp. 16, 33.   [41] Cavallar (2002), p. 173.
[42] Bentham (1996), p. 297 n. z.   [43] Schmitt (2003), p. 210.

proclaim that '[f]oreign policy is no longer foreign'. Modern, as opposed to post-modern, international thought had been premised on 'a recognition of state sovereignty and the consequent separation of domestic and foreign affairs, with a prohibition on external interference in the former'.[44] Within the international realm, states were the primary actors, not individuals, corporations or other non-state actors such as churches, missionary organisations or movements for social reform. That realm lacked any sovereign authority capable of enforcing supranational norms: mutually recognising sovereign states policed order within their own borders, but beyond them lay international anarchy. International law was thus positive law – the law of treaties and other interstate instruments – not natural law, which was increasingly consigned to irrelevance or absurdity. The interactions of states took place within an emergent states-system centred on Europe. That states-system was hierarchically ordered according to a standard of civilisation that left some other societies in a potentially permanent state of subjection, and admitted others to international society on terms set by European powers alone.

No single thinker, or school of thinkers, assembled these defining features of modern international thought into a single whole. They developed piecemeal over at least a century and a half but their normative structure and historical mythology was firmly in place in Europe at least by 1836, when the Académie de France held an essay-competition on the development of modern international law. The Académie posed the question in terms set by the positivist conception of the European states-system: 'Quels sont les progrès que le droit des gens a fait en Europe depuis la paix de Westphalie?' ('What progress has the law of nations made in Europe since the Peace of Westphalia?'). The Académie's rapporteur, former foreign minister Joseph-Marie Portalis, confessed that this was an immense task, involving the constitution of the international order, the past and future of the law of nations, deeds and doctrine, history and the philosophy of history.

According to one entrant, 1648 had marked the beginning of a states-system founded on 'national independence, the legitimacy of governments, the faithful observation of treaties ... the balance of power' and the principle of non-intervention. The one enduring contribution to the competition, the entry by the American diplomat and jurist Henry

---

[44] R. Cooper (2003), pp. 29, 22; Tony Blair, quoted in Garton Ash (2007), p. 633 ('Foreign policy is no longer foreign policy'); Jack Straw, 'Foreword', in Foreign and Commonwealth Office (2004), p. 4.

Wheaton, divided the modern history of the law of nations at 1648, 1713 (the Treaty of Utrecht) and 1763 (the Peace of Paris).[45] When Wheaton expanded his *mémoire* into a full-scale *Histoire des progrès du droit des gens en Europe* (1841) he chose 1648 rather than 1625 as 'the epoch from which to deduce the modern science of international law', because '[t]his great transaction marks an important era in the progress of European civilisation'. The competition's winner confirmed this analysis by arguing that 'dating from this era the nations [of Europe] had their *raison écrite*, and the progress of civilisation found itself officially recognized', even though the previous century had been a decadent period in the law of nations as national self-interest rather than natural law gradually dominated the councils of Europe. Portalis did not approve all the victor's conclusions but admitted perfection in such matters was impossible when the problems at stake 'embrace the universality of the thorniest questions of law, of history and of contemporary politics'.[46]

The tradition of modern international thought was consciously shaped and manipulated by a variety of scholars and professionals during the contest of the faculties that played out across the nineteenth and twentieth centuries. As many of the following chapters show, the pivotal moments in the formation of modern international thought were often points of retrospective reconstruction or appropriation. For example, it was in the late eighteenth and early nineteenth centuries, under the impact and in the wake of the American and French Revolutionary Wars, that such terms as 'international law' and 'diplomacy' were domesticated or coined for the first time, at least in English. It was also in the same period that Grotius became identified as the founding father of international law and that the conception of a states-system first began to emerge.[47] Another great forcing-house of modern narratives of international thought was the inter-War period of the twentieth century, when internationalists of differing stripes, on both sides of the Atlantic, compiled a canon of 'classics' in the history of international law, created the modern discipline of International Relations, and assembled the first traditions of international thought.[48] They were followed in turn by the members of the 'English School' of International Relations, especially Herbert Butterfield and Martin Wight, who drew eclectically on intellectual

[45] Portalis (1841), pp. 400, 408–9, 410–12, 414, 426, 440, 444.
[46] Wheaton (1845), p. 69: Portalis (1841), p. 453.
[47] Macalister-Smith and Schweitzke (1999); Orakhelashvili (2011); Keene (2002), pp. 14–22.
[48] Various works – among them, Dunne (1998); Schmidt (1998); Sylvest (2009); Coates (2010) – have begun to map these movements.

resources from international law, political thought and diplomatic writings to forge factitious but enduringly influential traditions of international thought identified with such thinkers as Grotius, Hobbes and Kant, and exalting the status of a figure like Edmund Burke within the canon of international theory.[49] More recent scholarship has critically deconstructed those invented traditions, and it is to that salutary ongoing enterprise that much of this book is dedicated.[50]

Foundations of Modern International Thought does not attempt to replace earlier narratives with any one point of origin or single continuous, unfolding tradition of discussion. Its various chapters question conventional narratives by critically examining figures who became enshrined within later disciplinary canons, such as Hobbes, Burke and Bentham, as well as those who conspicuously did not, most notably Locke. They also re-examine other historical stories, such as the long-drawn-out transition from a world of empires to a world of states and the emergence of modern statehood itself, from the perspective of intellectual history. The central problem for historians of the foundations of modern political thought was long supposed to be, 'How did we' – whoever 'we' may be – 'come to acquire the concept of the state?' The fundamental concern for historians of the foundations of modern international thought should, by contrast, be, 'How did we – all of us in the world – come to imagine that we inhabit a world of states?' That act of collective human imagination may be the single most important shift in political consciousness of the last 500 years. Understanding it is one, but only one, of the major research agendas for the flourishing field of international intellectual history.

---

[49] Wight (1991).   [50] For a parallel effort, see Christov (2008).

PART I

Historiographical foundations

The international turn in intellectual history

[I]deas are the most migratory things in the world.[1]

On croit souvent que la vie intellectuelle est spontanément internationale. Rien n'est plus faux.[2]

For most of the life-span of the historical profession, in most parts of the world, historians were committed to methodological nationalism. Like most other social scientists, they assumed that self-identifying nations, organised politically into states, were the primary objects of historical study.[3] Their main task was accordingly to narrate how nation-states emerged, how they developed and how they interacted with each other. Even those whose work consciously crossed the borders of national histories espoused similar assumptions. Diplomatic historians used national archives to reconstruct relations among states. Historians of immigration tracked the arrival and assimilation of new peoples into existing states.[4] And imperial historians studied empires as the outward extensions of national histories even as they generally maintained a strict separation between the histories of (mostly European) metropoles and their (mostly extra-European) colonies. The matter of history accordingly concerned stability not mobility, what was fixed not what was mixed.

Only the most self-critical historians noted the irony that it was thanks to the global circulation of ideas of nationhood and to the transnational reception of linear conceptions of history that 'evolutionary nationalist historicism' became 'the dominant form of historical understanding across much of the world'.[5] Post-colonial theorists were among the first and most acute critics of nationalist narratives but they have not been

---

[1] Lovejoy (1940), p. 4. [2] Bourdieu (1990), p. 2.
[3] '[A] nation is a community of sentiment which would adequately manifest itself in a state of its own; hence, a nation is a community which normally tends to produce a state of its own': Weber (1991), p. 176.
[4] Wimmer and Schiller (2003). [5] Hill (2008); Bayly (2011b), p. 13 (quoted).

alone in questioning the primacy of the nation as the consistent container of history.[6] In response to such challenges, historians in all fields have been moving rapidly towards studies variously described as 'international', 'transnational', 'comparative' and 'global'. Their efforts have not been identical in scope, in subject-matter or in motivation, nor is there any consensus on how the various non-national approaches to history can be distinguished from each other. International historians often take for granted the existence of a society of states but look beyond state boundaries to the various relationships between them, from diplomacy and finance to migration and cultural relations. Transnational historians examine processes, movements and institutions that overflow those boundaries: for example, the environment, organised crime, epidemics, corporations, religions and international bodies such as the United Nations. Comparative historians deal with distinct historical subjects – often, but not always, nationally defined – in conjunction, although not always on the basis of actual historical connection. And global historians study the history and pre-histories of globalisation, the histories of objects that have become universalised and the links between sub-global arenas such as the Atlantic, Indian and Pacific Oceans. The family resemblance between their projects is the desire to go above or beyond the history of nationally defined states and state-bounded nations, thereby to take an international turn.[7]

This international turn in the writing of history is perhaps the most transformative historiographical movement since the rise of social history in the 1960s and the linguistic turn of the 1970s. Why it has taken place simultaneously across so many areas of historical work would be a good question for intellectual history. However, it also poses a challenge to intellectual historians, who have not written widely about the internationalisation of their field. This absence of engagement can be attributed in part to the reigning materialism of many of the strains of history that make up the international turn. Historians of capital, empire and migration, alongside sociologists and archaeologists with global ambitions, have led debate on this movement and produced many of the major works of synthesis. To them, intellectual history has seemed immaterial, in both senses of the term: a kind of history from the neck up dealing with the insubstantial imaginings of disembodied beings from inner space. A major challenge for intellectual historians is to combat such scepticism without succumbing to reductionism or dissolving the identity of their field.

---

[6] For example, Duara (1995); Chakrabarty (2008).
[7] Clavin (2005); Bayly, Beckert, Connelly, Hofmeyr, Kozol and Seed (2006).

In this case, the best way to go forward may be to look backwards, to the cosmopolitan roots of intellectual history itself in the period before historiography had been institutionalised as an adjunct of national states.

Intellectual history can justifiably claim to have been international history *avant la lettre*. As Donald Kelley has shown, the first practitioners of the history of ideas, from the Englishman Thomas Stanley in the mid seventeenth century to Victor Cousin in post-Napoleonic France, produced works that were strikingly cosmopolitan in character and content. Their histories sprang from traditions of philosophical eclecticism stretching back to Diogenes Laertius but arose most immediately from early modern epistemological debates in which ideas were held to be independent of their origins, whether national or otherwise.[8] These early forms of the history of ideas were characteristic products of a Republic of Letters that was supranational in its affiliations and the nature of its scholarly exchanges. The *Respublica literarum* 'embraces the whole world and is composed of all nationalities, all social classes, all ages and both sexes', wrote one of its citizens, the French scholar and litterateur Bonaventure d'Argonne in 1699: 'All languages, ancient as well as modern are spoken.' Within this cosmopolitan community that extended from China to Peru, 'ideas were colorless, ageless, raceless, genderless' – and, it might be added, placeless and stateless.[9]

Intellectual history was born international and remained so long after the rise of nationalism within and beyond the historical profession. Accordingly, the logic of territorial statehood marked it much less than other areas of historical inquiry. It became an article of faith among historians of ideas that their objects of study escaped national boundaries. For example, the 'New History' pioneered in the United States in the late nineteenth century by Frederick Jackson Turner and James Harvey Robinson questioned nationalist historiography at the moment of its birth and drew inspiration instead from those historical phenomena that evaded its clutches. As Turner noted in 1891, two years before he proposed his famous 'frontier thesis' of the development of the United States, 'Ideas, commodities even, refuse the bounds of a nation . . . This is true especially of our modern world with its complex commerce and means of intellectual connection.'[10] Half a century later, the founding father of the history of

---

[8] Kelley (2002), chs. 1–2.
[9] Bonaventure d'Argonne, quoted in Anthony Grafton, 'A Sketch Map of a Lost Continent: The Republic of Letters', in Grafton (2009), p. 9; Kelley (2002), p. 117.
[10] Turner (1938), p. 57; Novick (1988), pp. 89–95.

ideas, Arthur O. Lovejoy, might have been recalling Turner's words when he asserted in 1938, 'Ideas are commodities which enter into interstate commerce.' How these ideas were manufactured and how they travelled, who trafficked them and who consumed them, were not questions the classical historians of ideas thought to ask: that was a task for specialists in comparative literature, 'understood to be the study of international intellectual relations'.[11] Only with the rise of the social history of ideas and the history of the book would such material concerns inform the work of intellectual historians. This new strain of intellectual history also proclaimed its internationalism, as a history of *livres sans frontières* joined a history of ideas without borders.[12] 'By their very nature, books refuse to be contained within any discipline', Robert Darnton argued in 1994, before echoing both Turner and Lovejoy: 'They also refuse to respect national boundaries.'[13]

Intellectual history's innate resistance to nationalism may have had the paradoxical effect of making it harder for the field to take an international turn. Because intellectual historians, unlike practitioners of other nationally inflected approaches, have not needed to reject national categories or to embrace cosmopolitan alternatives to them, they might be methodologically underprepared for such a movement. Indeed, the international turn has lately come to intellectual history by the academic equivalent of technological leapfrogging, as the field shifts from the non-national to the supranational without ever having fully inhabited the national frameworks that have traditionally structured most professional history-writing. This move entails facing up to some of the shortcomings of intellectual history as it has traditionally been practised, especially its resistance to considering the spatial dimensions of context. And it demands greater insistence on the distinctive contributions intellectual history can make to the international turn more generally. Yet, as I hope to show, intellectual historians possess some of the best available tools for historicising categories such as the international and the global, for tracing the international circulation of ideas, and for tackling the challenges of idealism, presentism and the redefinition of context raised by the international turn. Intellectual history may therefore have as much to offer the international turn as the international turn has to offer to intellectual history.

The international turn has revived interest in conceptions of space by attending to arenas that were larger than nations, unconfined by the

---

[11] Lovejoy (1948), pp. 3, 1.   [12] Howsam and Raven (2011), p. 1.
[13] Darnton and Daskalova (1994), p. 2.

political boundaries of states, and connected by transnational linkages and circulations. Most of the world's population, for most of recorded history, lived not in nation-states but in empires, those far-flung, stratified polities that projected various kinds of universalism in order to suspend differences among populations without striving for uniformity between them. For a relatively brief period, between the early sixteenth and early twentieth centuries, some of those empires were the outgrowths of confidently national cultures, particularly in Europe and Asia, but most were pre-national or supranational in composition. Oceanic spaces connected elements of these empires in the modern period, but maritime arenas such as the Mediterranean, the Indian Ocean, the Atlantic and the Pacific also segmented sovereignties and became cockpits of inter-imperial rivalry.[14] In light of the long history of empire, the eternal world of states posited by modern conceptions of international relations seems fleeting, even marginal. Indeed, if by some estimates a world of true nation-states, detached from empire, emerged only with the zenith of decolonisation, soon to be swept away by the wave of transnationalism that erupted after the end of the Cold War, then the heyday of the state lasted less than a generation, from about 1975 to 1989.[15] All history, before and after, was pre- or post-national.

By simultaneously uniting and dividing, empires spurred conceptual competition and facilitated the circulation of ideas among diasporic peoples and across commercial routes.[16] From such collisions and transmissions emerged 'competing universalisms' of empire, religion and political economy, for instance, as well as the expansive ideologies that countered or subsumed them, such as pan-Islamism, pan-Africanism, nationalism, anti-colonialism and other forms of 'colored cosmopolitanism'.[17] Most of these movements remained invisible as long as history was viewed through nation-shaped spectacles. They returned to view only when older experiences of space – more extensive, more fluid and less confined by territorial boundaries – again framed questions about the past.

Space may be the final frontier for intellectual history. The field is rife with spatial metaphors – of ideas as 'migratory' and of books refusing the bounds of nations; of 'horizons' of understanding and the public 'sphere'; of 'localism' and 'provincialism' as determinants of an idea's

---

[14] Benton (2002); Benton (2010); ch. 2 below.   [15] F. Cooper (2005); Cooper and Burbank (2010).
[16] On the intellectual history of empire, see especially Pagden (1995); Armitage (1998); Ben-Ghiat (2009); Pitts (2010); Muthu (2012).
[17] Bose (2006); Bose and Manjapra (2010); Aydin (2007); Manela (2007); Slate (2011).

position in a theoretical 'field'; and conceptions of hermeneutic 'containment' and critical 'movement', for example – but such figures of speech do not indicate any substantive engagement with questions of space and place. They are instead shorthand indications that ideas lack material determinants and that they need to be placed into contexts construed almost entirely as temporal and linguistic not physical or spatial.[18] Michel Foucault might have been speaking for intellectual historians when he said in an interview that 'space was that which was dead, fixed, non-dialectical, immobile. On the other hand, time was rich, fertile, vibrant, dialectical.'[19]

Space can be understood intensively as well as extensively. In this regard historians of science may have much to teach both international historians and intellectual historians. A 'spatial turn' in the history of science put in doubt the universality of truth and insisted upon local knowledge: there could be no view from nowhere when every view sprang from somewhere. Ideas emerged from tightly defined spaces, from littoral beaches as well as laboratory benches, and from public houses as well as royal academies. When viewed microscopically in this way, the seamless web of abstract knowledge turned out to be a brittle mosaic of contingent concerns.[20] If one aim of this literature was to debunk the presumed universality of scientific reason, another was to show just how fragments of knowledge were accumulated and collected and how their credibility was secured. 'We need to understand not only how knowledge is made in specific places but also how transactions occur between places': that is, how ideas *travel*, who transports them, what baggage they carry on their journeys and how they become domesticated and naturalised upon arrival.[21]

This approach revealed the intricate mechanisms of information-gathering that made scientific knowledge both possible and plausible. Even the most physically isolated of thinkers, like the land-locked Isaac Newton, could act as 'a fundamental link between the colonial information order and the empiricist knowledge regime forged in the final decades of the seventeenth century' without ever seeing the sea.[22] Corporate bodies such as the Society of Jesus and the English and Dutch East India Companies facilitated big science, in the sense of the

---

[18] On context, see Burke (2002); Felski and Tucker (2011); Gordon (2013).

[19] 'L'espace, c'est ce qui était mort, figé, non dialectique, immobile. En revanche, le temps, c'était riche, fécond, vivant, dialectique': Foucault (1976), p. 78.

[20] Ophir and Shapin (1991); Finnegan (2008); Withers (2009). More generally, see Guldi (2011).

[21] Tresch (2013); Shapin (1998), pp. 6–7 (quoted).   [22] Schaffer (2009), p. 247.

long-distance production of knowledge.[23] And later 'webs of empire' dissolved distinctions between centres and peripheries as each alleged periphery earned a central place in accumulating imperial archives, testing hypotheses and generating ideologies through inter-colonial exchanges.[24] In these ways, extensively elaborated connections linked intensively cultivated locations to create new maps of knowledge through the transmission of ideas and information across continents and oceans.

These studies in what Pierre Bourdieu called the 'science of international relations with regard to culture' offer replicable models for intellectual history more generally.[25] When conceptions of space expand, webs of significance ramify and networks of exchange proliferate to create novel contexts and unanticipated connections among them. Shifting patterns of sociability and correspondence, of the distribution of books and the spatial organisation of knowledge – in rooms and buildings, streets and squares, cities and regions, countries and continents, empires and oceans – force thinkers to reconceive the nature of their audiences, the potential impact of their arguments and the extent of their spheres of action. For example, to answer the question, '*What* was Enlightenment?', intellectual historians attuned to space must now also ask, '*Where* was Enlightenment?'.[26]

Changing conceptions of space expanded the contexts for ideas and, with them, the very possibilities for thought. The most familiar example for European intellectual historians might be the broader contexts that transoceanic exploration and colonisation generated for thinkers in early modern Europe, as intercultural encounters and the proliferation of empires around the Indian Ocean, the Atlantic world and later the Pacific tested conceptions of nature, civilisation, political community, property, religious diversity and toleration, among other questions.[27] For instance, John Locke, a voracious reader of travel literature, confronted instances of diversity and belief and practice drawn from accounts of five continents;[28] Thomas Hobbes, a more modest consumer of Americana, shaped his understanding of international relations by reference to ethnographic descriptions of the state of nature;[29] and David Hume's political economy

---

[23] Harris (1998); Cook (2007); Clossey (2008); Winterbottom (2009).
[24] Ballantyne (2002), pp. 1–17.
[25] '[U]ne science des relations internationales en matière de culture': Bourdieu (1990), p. 1.
[26] Livingstone and Withers (1999); Withers (2007); Manning and Cogliano (2008).
[27] Pagden (1986); Brett (2011).   [28] Carey (2006); Talbot (2010).
[29] Noel Malcolm, 'Hobbes, Sandys, and the Virginia Company', in Malcolm (2002), pp. 53–79; Aravamudan (2009); Moloney (2011).

owed much to his Atlantic connections.[30] Truly global possibilities for thought opened up for the generations of thinkers writing after the mid eighteenth century, among them Smith, Kant, Herder, Burke and Bentham, with consequences for their constructions of universalism and cosmopolitanism as well as for their conceptions of culture and difference.[31] Moving into the later nineteenth century, the compression of space by technology – above all, the steamship, the railway and the telegraph – made new forms of political community imaginable over the expanses of empire and across the world. *Pace* Foucault, space was dynamic, not static. The contexts for thinking expanded to encompass the entire globe. Modern intellectual historians accordingly have to track ideas on ever-larger scales: continental, inter-regional, transoceanic and ultimately planetary. As Heidegger, Schmitt and Arendt were among the first to note in the mid twentieth century, *outer* space may be the truly final frontier for intellectual history.[32]

The movement away from national and towards the transnational passes through the international, the space of human life which has been organised politically into states and nations. A few years ago, I suggested that 'a renaissance in the history of international thought' was beginning that might 'open up new conversations between historians, political theorists, International Relations scholars and international lawyers'.[33] That renaissance is now well under way and has produced the first fruits of the international turn in intellectual history. Nationalists assume that their communities are natural, but nations have no navels; their construction has a history, and a relatively recent one at that.[34] Over the past two centuries, states have given birth to nations at least as often as nations gave rise to states. How these states came to form an international society, what norms governed their behaviour and what traditions of philosophical inquiry and political thinking generated those norms are all questions for the intellectual history of the international.

The revival of the history of international thought marks the most recent of three phases of relations between intellectual history and international history: an age of engagement that lasted from roughly the end of the First World War until the 1950s, an age of estrangement running from the early 1960s to the mid-1990s and an age of rapprochement which

---

[30] Rothschild (2009).   [31] Marshall and Williams (1982); Muthu (2003); Pitts (2005a).
[32] Lang (2003); Bell (2007a), pp. 63–91; Lazier (2011); Bell (2013).
[33] Armitage (2004), pp. 108–9.   [34] Gellner (1996).

is still ongoing. In the initial age of engagement, historians of ideas were often methodologically cosmopolitan and politically internationalist in outlook, while historically minded students of International Relations dealt openly in ideas rather than abstract models or theories. Thinkers otherwise as diverse as Hannah Arendt, Raymond Aron, Herbert Butterfield, Hans Morgenthau, Reinhold Niebuhr, Carl Schmitt, Kenneth Waltz and Martin Wight drew upon shared historical canons even though they disagreed profoundly over such matters as the balance between national sovereignty and the authority of international institutions or the ethics of war and peace.

During the succeeding age of estrangement, intellectual historians and international historians drew further apart. Disciplinary boundaries hardened and were more fiercely defended. The refinement of methodologies and the acceleration of professional specialisation made conversations between fields harder. The separation between the domestic and the international sharpened. 'Theory' – whether political or international – lost ground to positivist models which excluded ideas and ethics from the realms of politics and International Relations, particularly in the United States. In retrospect, the May 1954 Conference on International Politics convened in New York by the Rockefeller Foundation, in which Morgenthau, Niebuhr and others participated, now looks like the high-water mark of an ethical approach to international affairs before the triumph of behaviouralist social science in the United States.[35] Over the next quarter-century, intellectual historians moved ever further away from international historians as a resurgent social history pressed both fields to the margins of the historical profession. What one clerk said to another clerk was evidently as unfashionable as what one philosopher wrote about another philosopher. As Robert Darnton observed gloomily in a 1980 collection published on behalf of the American Historical Association, 'a malaise is spreading among intellectual historians ... after a realignment of research during the last two decades, [intellectual history] now sits below the salt'. In the same volume, Charles Maier offered a similarly downbeat assessment of international history: 'The history of international relations ... [has] little sense of collective enterprise, of being at the cutting edge of historical scholarship.'[36]

As so often, such intimations of obsolescence proved to be spurs to innovation. The age of rapprochement beginning in the 1990s saw revivals in both intellectual history and international history as well as

---

[35] Hoffmann (1977); Guilhot (2011).　　[36] Darnton (1980), p. 327; Maier (1980), p. 355.

the increasing entanglement of the two fields with each other. At least some scholars of International Relations found themselves in a 'post-positivist' phase and renewed their interest in theory, in the history of international affairs and the history of their own discipline. International historians were also becoming more interested in culture, ideology and institutions, 'champions of the international turn as well as vigorous proponents of intellectual and cultural history'. At the same time, intellectual historians were beginning to treat the norms and interactions between peoples, states and other corporate bodies in the world beyond the domestic sphere under the rubric of the history of international thought.[37]

The term 'international thought' was originally an invention of British publicists and litterateurs sympathetic to the League of Nations and nascent international institutions in the years between the two World Wars. In this vein, Thomas Hardy had written in 1923 to his fellow-novelist John Galsworthy, 'The exchange of international thought is the only salvation for the world'; its original purpose had thus been to denote a usable past rather than to create a critical history.[38] It received support from equally committed internationalists across the Atlantic, such as the American international lawyer James Brown Scott who began the creation of the earliest historical canon of works of international thought from Balthazar Ayala to Richard Zouche in the series sponsored by the Carnegie Endowment for International Peace, 'Classics of International Law' (1911–50).[39] The recent revival of the history of international thought has seen it emerge as a robust field in its own right, with a more expansive and less teleological canon of authors, problems and movements, and not just as a subset of the history of political thought.[40] International thought now means less a body of authoritative doctrine to be deployed for present purposes than the past tense of international thinking as the activity of theoretical reflection upon international affairs. In this, it has paralleled the contextualist history of political thought as practised in the past fifty years.

A humanistic return to the sources of international thought revealed the distance between what thinkers like Grotius, Hobbes and Kant were

---

[37] Ashworth (2009); Bell (2009a); Zeiler (2009), p. 1053 (quoted).

[38] Thomas Hardy to John Galsworthy, 20 April 1923, in Hardy (1978–88), VI, p. 192; Galsworthy (1923); Stawell (1929).

[39] Hepp (2008); Coates (2010), pp. 101–5.

[40] Boucher (1998); Jackson (2005); Keene (2005); Jahn (2006); Bell (2007b); Bell (2009b); Covell (2009); Hall and Hill (2009); Behr (2010); Walker (2010); Cavallar (2011).

doing – or, just as often, not attempting to do – and the uses made of them within later disciplinary histories. Grotius could have had no intention of 'founding' international law. Hobbes was no 'Hobbesian', at least as far as that term has been used as a term of art in discussions of international relations. And Kant was rather more than the theorist of the 'democratic peace' to which he has been reduced by the teleological internationalists since the early twentieth century.[41] For the twentieth century, we now have historical studies of international thinkers of all stripes from Norman Angell and Hannah Arendt to Leonard Woolf and Alfred Zimmern, with an especially vigorous cottage industry devoted to the work of Carl Schmitt.[42] At the same time, autocritical disciplinary historians of International Relations and international law have exposed how a 'discourse of anarchy' generated in the inter-War years became a timeless truth for the later Realist school of International Relations and have shown the complicity of idealistic international lawyers with imperial enterprises from the Belgian Congo to the Bay of Pigs.[43]

Intellectual historians have been well placed to assist self-critical historians of the international in questioning some of the basic building-blocks of their disciplines. For example, no date was more foundational for International Relations than 1648 and the Peace of Westphalia. The demolition of the 'myth of 1648' as the origin of a world of mutually recognising, non-interfering sovereign states was a relatively straightforward process. It relied on a reading of the treaties of Munster and Westphalia, the recognition that empires, federations and other kinds of layered or divided sovereignty were more characteristic of political authority than any alleged 'Westphalian' sovereignty, and attention to the world beyond northern Europe to see how little respect was paid to the putative sovereignty of many of the world's peoples under the regime of empire.[44] The Westphalian myth had in turn underpinned a set of assumptions that defined modern international thought: that states, not individuals, were the primary actors in international affairs; that the spheres of the domestic and the foreign, the inside and the outside of the state, were distinct and separate; that positive law trumped natural law; that a hierarchical standard of civilisation applied across the globe; and that the

[41] Tuck (1999); van Ittersum (2006); Noel Malcolm, 'Hobbes's Theory of International Relations', in Malcolm (2002), pp. 432–56; Muthu (2003); Easley (2004); ch. 4, below.
[42] Long and Wilson (1995); Owens (2007); Morefield (2005); Odysseos and Petito (2007); Hooker (2009); Legg (2011).
[43] Schmidt (1998); Koskenniemi (2002).
[44] Osiander (2001); Teschke (2003); Beaulac (2004); Straumann (2008); Piirimäe (2010).

international realm was anarchical and hence governed by maxims of reason of state. These fundamental assumptions were neither uniform nor uncontested but they did set the terms of debate for at least a century and a half.

The intellectual history of the international still teems with possibilities for research. For example, what were the media for international thought, and how might they be understood using the methods of history of the book?[45] Starting in the late seventeenth century and continuing to the present, new and persistent genres of writing and publication, among them treaty-collections, diplomatic manuals and histories of international relations and of the law of nations, proliferated amid the clerical, scholarly and humanistic cultures that intersected so often with transnational diplomatic and military communities: further examination of such genres might help us to understand, among other questions, why Kant cast his 'Toward Perpetual Peace' in the form of a treaty.[46] What were the novel philosophical personae adopted by casuistical envoys, literary-minded administrators and intellectuals in office in the burgeoning international institutions of the eighteenth century and beyond?[47] And how was international thought itself internationalised? To take just one example, the translation and circulation in Asia of Henry Wheaton's *Elements of International Law* (1836), a major vector of Euro-American international thought, suggests that the assumptions underlying modern international thought were becoming increasingly trans-regional, if not yet fully global, by the middle of the nineteenth century.[48] In this sense, the receptivity of large parts of the world to 'the contagion of sovereignty' which almost universally affected it still demands explanation, especially by attending to the determinants of its reception and domestication.[49] Only then can we fully understand the energetic co-production of the national and the international around the globe in the nineteenth and twentieth centuries.[50]

The internationalisation of the international can also be approached through the intellectual history of international institutions. Proponents of the new international history had long urged their colleagues to 'internationalise international history' by studying non-state actors in the international realm: corporations, non-governmental organisations,

[45] For a model study of the translation and circulation of economic texts along these lines, see Reinert (2011).

[46] For suggestive work in these directions, see Lesaffer (2004); Ménager (2001); McClure (2006); Hampton (2009).

[47] Compare Hunter (2010).   [48] Liu (2004), pp. 108–39; Liu (1999b); Gluck and Tsing (2009).

[49] Armitage (2007a), pp. 107–12; Bayly (2011a).   [50] Bayly and Biagini (2008); Isabella (2009).

transnational social movements and bodies such as the World Health Organisation or the United Nations.[51] This call has generated new opportunities for archival intellectual histories of the Institut de Droit international, the Carnegie Endowment for International Peace, the League of Nations, the United Nations, UNESCO and the European Union, to name only some of the most prominent. Some of this work has been internalist and celebratory, but much of it has helped to expand the range of actors, archives and institutions open to examination by intellectual historians.[52] One product of this expansion has been the new history of human rights, a field now in its second wave as it has moved from its teleological phase of telling just-so stories into a more critical literature alert to context and to discontinuity.[53] Other subjects of concern to intellectual historians – the history of economic thought, conceptions of war and government, public health and the history of science – can all be researched in the archives of international institutions, companies and corporations. In this regard, modern intellectual historians can learn from those early modernists who have followed historians of science in constructing intellectual histories of the English and Dutch trading companies in the seventeenth and eighteenth centuries.[54] The explosion of interest among political theorists and students of ethics in the international and global dimensions of their concerns has helped to accelerate all these developments, which took place amid an ever-growing public awareness of the transnational dimensions of human affairs captured by the portmanteau-word 'globalisation'. All these movements have in turn encouraged and reinforced internal tendencies within intellectual history to reconstruct arguments dealing with matters beyond the nation or the state that I have called the international turn among intellectual historians.

So far, this account of the international turn in intellectual history has been overwhelmingly upbeat, a *tour d'horizon* of achievements sustained and promises yet to be fulfilled. But every silver lining has a cloud. In what ways could the international turn possibly be a turn for the worse? This movement has not yet entered the phase of well-earned self-criticism, nor

[51] Iriye (2002b); Iriye (2002a).

[52] Koskenniemi (2002); Droit (2005); Sluga and Amrith (2008); Rothschild (2008); Mazower (2009); Jolly, Emmerij and Weiss (2009) and similar works from the United Nations Intellectual History Project.

[53] For the first, see e.g. Borgwardt (2005); L. Hunt (2007); Martinez (2012); for the second, Moyn (2010); Hoffmann (2010); Iriye, Goedde and Hitchcock (2011).

[54] Van Ittersum (2006); Stern (2011).

has it attracted much sustained attention from outsiders. However, some charges have already been arrayed against it, among them reification, presentism, 'classism' and changing conceptions of context.[55] None of these criticisms is peculiar to international intellectual history: all are familiar from debates on the history of ideas over at least the last half-century. Yet they each become sharper when intellectual history extends over greater expanses of space, as new forms of disjunction between ideas and novel analytical demands come to the fore.

Reification is a familiar charge, going back at least as far as the Cambridge School's criticisms of Lovejoy's history of ideas: what appear to be iterations of the same idea turn out to be distinct conceptions in need of disaggregation and disambiguation rather than assimilation into broader narratives over time or across space.[56] For example, liberalism in Britain was not the same as liberalism in India: each developed within its own ecological niche, yet they did not emerge in ignorance of each other, but rather in dialogues mediated by local conditions of the reception, circulation and hybridisation of arguments.[57] After at least the mid eighteenth century, the conditions of reception were inter-regional and increasingly global: Indian 'liberals' like Rammohan Roy saw their own struggles against despotism as part of worldwide movements encompassing British and Portuguese colonies in Asia, the Spanish monarchy in the Atlantic world, and Britain itself. Texts carried ideas but always amid framing paratexts and then into unpredictable contexts for their translation and reappropriation. These conditions generated dissimilitude out of similarity, but rarely to the extent of complete disjuncture and incomparability. With such caveats in mind, the danger of falling into reification may be overblown. With methodological assistance where necessary from, say, *Rezeptionsgeschichte*, the history of the book and post-colonial theory it should be possible to avoid the dangers of an older, less sophisticated, transhistorical history *of* ideas and replace it with a more methodologically robust transtemporal history *in* ideas.[58]

Presentism may offer a more serious danger for the international turn. 'The whole enterprise [of international intellectual history] is itself presentist, in the sense that the transnational turn is influenced, in evident respects, by the late twentieth and early twenty-first century public controversies over "globalization".'[59] Yet we can no more wish away

[55] Rothschild (2006); Goto-Jones (2009).   [56] Skinner (1969).
[57] Bayly (2012); see also Kapila (2010); Kapila and Devji (2010).
[58] McMahon (2013); Armitage (2012).   [59] Rothschild (2006), p. 221.

current arguments than we can deny the presence of debates over cosmopolitan, universal or global connections and conceptions in the past. It is a
truism – and, like all truisms, by definition at least partly true – that our
ever-changing present continually reveals aspects of the past that have
been overlooked or underappreciated. In this case, as in other aspects
of transnational history, two approaches are possible: 'A first would
suggest that connections did exist and were known to past actors, but
have for some reason been forgotten or laid aside. The task of the historian
would then be to rediscover these lost traces. A second view would instead
posit that historians might act as electricians, connecting circuits
by acts of imaginative reconstitution rather than simple restitution.'[60]
The first of these approaches – connective rather than comparative,
reconstitutive rather than restitutive – might be preferable for most intellectual historians but the second is also surely necessary for the creation
of the requisite historical distance between past imperatives and current
concerns. We surely delude ourselves if we imagine we do not see those
concerns through a glass darkly: we will only be able to see them more
clearly if we place them in long-range perspective.

'Classism' – the idea that 'only the high, or the great, or the highly
educated, have been the subject, in general, of histories of the individual
mind, or the individual self' – is a familiar charge against intellectual
history, rather than a failing peculiar to intellectual history with an
international twist.[61] J. S. Mill, for one, rebutted it as early as 1838 in
his defence of Bentham and Coleridge:

speculative philosophy, which to the superficial appears a thing so remote from
the business of life and the outward interests of men, is in reality the thing on
earth which most influences them, and in the long run overbears every other
influence save those which it must itself obey. The writers of whom we speak
have never been read by the multitude; except for the more slight of their works,
their readers have been few: but they have been the teachers of the teachers.[62]

In between the speculative philosophers and the multitude are the
thinkers of what Emma Rothschild has called 'intermediate' or 'medium
thoughts', the reflections of those too undistinguished to be the subjects
of individual intellectual biography but too profuse in leaving their
reflective traces to be subsumed into any history of *mentalités*, especially,

---

[60] David Armitage and Sanjay Subrahmanyam, 'The Age of Revolutions, *c.* 1760–1840: Global
Causation, Connection, and Comparison', in Armitage and Subrahmanyam (2010), p. xxxi.
[61] Rothschild (2006), p. 222. For implied rebuttals of this accusation, see Rose (2010); Hilliard (2006).
[62] Mill (1838), p. 467.

but not exclusively, those engaged in public policy of various kinds.[63] Such people were often globetrotters and go-betweens, members of the massive Asian, European and African migrations that crossed (and re-crossed) the Atlantic and Pacific Oceans and the steppes, but also the intercultural agents who trafficked in local knowledge and the creation of 'global intelligence'.[64] As historians reconstruct their forms of intellection, and the histories of their ideas, we can expect to find even more widespread evidence of forms of transnational thinking than ever before.[65]

The increasingly elastic definitions of context demanded by transnational history should not deter intellectual historians. Some are beginning to ask how precisely can any idea can be understood 'in context' if context is now defined to encompass intercontinental communications, multilingual communities or the expansion of world systems?[66] Here again the opportunities may be greater than the dangers. Canons of relevance must be defined, routes of active (or at least plausible) transmission mapped and scales of reference calibrated according to contemporaries' conceptions of the international or the global; with such boundaries in place, it should be feasible to reconstruct meaningful spatial contexts for the ideas we trace across borders and bounded discursive communities.

Historicising conceptions of space – of the national, the international, the transnational and the global – may in fact be one implied agenda for intellectual history after the international turn, just as historicising conceptions of time was a major project for intellectual history in the nineteenth and twentieth centuries. This agenda leads inexorably to the question what it might mean for intellectual history to take a global turn. Quite what a global intellectual history would comprise, or even what its subject-matter will be, is still far from clear, though vigorous debate has already begun about these matters.[67] Whether the global turn is just one logical extension of the international turn or a distinct endeavour in its own right remains to be seen. With such widening horizons and enticing prospects, it surely cannot be premature to welcome both the international and the global as turns for the better in intellectual history, as they have been for historical writing *tout court.*

---

[63] Rothschild (2005), p. 210; Rothschild (2011b), pp. 774–6.

[64] Schaffer, Roberts, Raj and Delbourgo (2009).

[65] E.g., Bose and Manjapra (2010); Colley (2010); Rothschild (2011a).

[66] Goto-Jones (2009), p. 14 ('historical context does not appear to overlap with spatiocultural context').

[67] Kelley, Levine, Megill, Schneewind and Schneider (2005); Dunn (2008); Sartori (2008); Black (2009); Moyn and Sartori (2013).

CHAPTER 2

Is there a pre-history of globalisation?

'If it is now asked whether we at present live in an *enlightened* age [*aufgeklärten Zeitalter*], the answer is: No, but we do live in an age of enlightenment [*Zeitalter der Aufklärung*].'[1] Immanuel Kant's memorable accounting of the unfolding achievements and unfulfilled promises of his own age in his essay 'What is Enlightenment?' (1784) might stand as the motto for any consideration of globalisation and the writing of history. The difference between 'an enlightened age' and 'an age of enlightenment' suggests a parallel distinction between a 'globalised age' and 'an age of globalisation' and hence between globalisation as a process and globalisation as a condition.[2] The process of globalisation would be the gradual thickening of connections across national boundaries, their increasing penetration into previously untouched localities and the emergence of a common set of concerns that define a universal cosmopolitan community. The condition of globalisation would be a state of complete transnational integration, encompassing all the people of the world within a single network of economic and cultural connections informed by a common global consciousness. Humanity is manifestly far from attaining such a condition: further, surely, than even Kant's Prussia was from enlightenment. That does not mean that there are no processes of globalisation currently under way; equally it does not imply that that process is necessarily the prelude to the achievement of globalisation as a condition.

Like the most optimistic promoters of Enlightenment, globalisation's most enthusiastic advocates assumed both its potential universality and its relative novelty. As the process of worldwide integration and transnational conjunction, globalisation (to be worthy of the name) should be all-inclusive and spatially expansive. Anything less than complete global

[1] Immanuel Kant, 'Beantwortung der Frage: Was ist Aufklärung?' (1784), in Kant (1964), I, p. 59; English translation in Kant (1991), p. 58.
[2] Compare Starobinski (1993), on civilisation as process and condition.

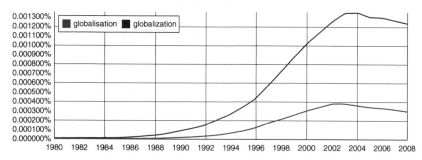

Figure 2.1 Relative frequency of 'globalisation'/'globalization' in English-language works, 1980–2008. Source: Google Ngram Viewer.

coverage would be only a more generous form of internationalism, trans-nationality or even regionalisation, on however grand a scale. Because 'globalise' can be both a transitive and an intransitive verb, 'at once an inexorable material development and a conscious human process',[3] it implies both an inescapable teleology and a congeries of contingent intentions. Those intentions may be consciously directed towards achieving the condition of globalisation; however, like the malign colliding wills that in their 'unsocial sociability' [*ungesellige Geselligkeit*] produce a benign historical trajectory in Kant's vision of a 'Universal History with a Cosmopolitan Purpose' (1784), their consequences are likely to be as unintended as they are unforeseeable.[4] The implied character of globalisation, like that of Kant's universal history, is teleological: maybe not here, maybe not now, but in an increasing number of locales and with ever-gathering velocity.

The character of globalisation, like that of Enlightenment, derives from its future rather than its past. 'The idea of a history of globalisation is at first sight a contradiction in terms. Globalisation or internationalisation has been depicted, for much of the last twenty years, as a condition of the present and the future – a phenomenon without a past.'[5] The relative novelty of the term 'globalisation' (and its cognates in other languages, such as the French term *mondialisation*) encourages the belief that globalisation itself must also be quite recent, if not entirely unprecedented (see Figure 2.1).

An unsophisticated nominalist might argue that without the word itself to affirm its existence neither the process nor the condition of

---

[3] Iriye (2002a), p. 8.
[4] Kant, 'Idee zu einer Allgemeinen Geschichte in Weltbürgerliche Absicht' (1784), in Kant (1964), 1, p. 37; English trans. in Kant (1991), p. 44.
[5] Rothschild (1999), p. 107.

globalisation could exist. A more subtle nominalist would reply that language is an index of social change: vocabulary mutates and neologism occurs to describe the previously indescribable or undescribed. Either way, the lack of the term 'globalisation' before the 1980s would indicate that globalisation is no more than a generation old, whether as a process of market integration and technological innovation or as the proliferating consciousness of globality itself. To call our era 'an Age of Globalization' distinguishes it from any previous epoch only at the cost of the paradox that what is inclusive and extensive in space must be exclusive and intensive in time.[6]

This temporal foreshortening of the global has not gone unchallenged by historians and historically minded social scientists. The three features that distinguish the boosters' vision of globalisation – its teleology, its novelty and its uniformity – have generated critical counterparts in the forms of aetiology, genealogy and multiplicity. The search for the historical origins of globalisation parallels the examination of its localisation by demanding contextual specificity and asking exactly which features – and what definitions – of globalisation are at stake.[7] The results of that search have pushed the chronology of globalisation ever deeper into the past, well beyond the horizon of the generation now living in the present age of globalisation. Most fruitfully, the historical examination of globalisation has disaggregated a seemingly homogeneous (and homogenising) process into a variety of disparate processes that have moved at different speeds across space and time and that appear to be frequently intermittent rather than inevitably linear.

'The chronology of globalisation has generated the most sterile controversy in history today', remarked Felipe Fernández-Armesto dyspeptically.[8] Though we can probably all think of equally apt candidates for that dubious honour, the fertility and the growth of the historical study of globalisation give the lie to the assertion that controversy over its chronology is sterile: inconclusive, circular and frequently whiggish, perhaps, but hardly sterile. On the contrary, research on the pre-history of globalisation – on the origins, the antecedents and the analogues of the global integration of the last twenty years – has been among the liveliest areas of recent historical inquiry. Fernández-Armesto himself mischievously suggested pushing back the pre-history of globalisation to pre-history

[6] Mazlish (1993), p. 1.
[7] As in the penetrating critiques by Tsing (2000); F. Cooper (2005), pp. 91–112.
[8] Fernández-Armesto (2002), p. 76.

itself. 'Strong-sense globalisation – world-wide cultural conformity – last happened in the Paleolithic period': the whole of subsequent human history has since been the record of the divergence of humankind from this primal uniformity.[9] The editor of the essay-collection that inspired his scepticism proposed instead a four-stage theory of globalisation, 'categorized as archaic, proto, modern and post-colonial', to encompass a range of phenomena from before the pre-industrial and the pre-national to the post-industrial and post-national eras.[10]

The diversity of definitions of globalisation determines the variety of globalisations, their origins and trajectories, to be found in the prehistoric – that is, pre-1980 – past. For example, if globalisation is taken to mean 'the integration of international commodity markets' defined by commodity price convergence (as in the work of Kevin O'Rourke and Jeffrey Williamson), then it 'did not begin 5,000 years ago, or even 500 years ago. It began in the early nineteenth century. In that sense, it is a very modern phenomenon.'[11] A more expansive definition of globalisation backdates its origins by 350 years to the beginnings of a global economy in the sixteenth century. The origins of globalisation might only be found at the point where the links in the emergent world economy were joined, specifically at the moment when the silver bullion that was drawn from the Spanish American empire into China created a link between the Atlantic world and the Asian trade: that is, in Manila in 1571.[12] In this sense, it is an *early* modern phenomenon.

Versions of this genealogy have a distinguished history, stretching back through Marx and Engels's judgment that the voyages of Vasco da Gama and Christopher Columbus had 'opened up fresh ground for the rising bourgeoisie' to Adam Smith's identification of '[t]he discovery of America, and that of a passage to the East Indies by the Cape of Good Hope' as 'the two greatest and most important events recorded in the history of mankind' because they marked the origins of a worldwide trading system.[13] The more drastically foreshortened recent histories of globalisation compress into the space of little more than a generation developments Smith and Marx traced over nearly half a millennium.

[9] Fernández-Armesto (2002), p. 76; compare Chase-Dunn and Hall (2002).
[10] A. G. Hopkins, 'Introduction: Globalization – An Agenda for Historians', in Hopkins (2002), p. 3.
[11] O'Rourke and Williamson (2002), pp. 25, 47; compare Rodrik, Obstfeld, Feenstra and Williamson (1998); O'Rourke and Williamson (2004).
[12] Flynn and Giráldez (1995); Flynn and Giráldez (2002); Flynn, Giráldez and von Glahn (2003); Flynn and Giráldez (2010).
[13] Marx and Engels (2002) p. 220; Smith (1976), I, p. 448, II, p. 626.

So long as there is no agreement about the defining features of globalisation – commodity price convergence, intercontinental trading linkages or the emergence of a 'world-system', for example – there is unlikely to be consensus about whether globalisation has a pre-history, let alone how long its history may have been.

If, as most definitions of globalisation agree, the fact of globalisation (however defined) must be accompanied by the consciousness of globality, when did that consciousness emerge?[14] Was it the product of economic convergence or its cause? And did it emerge globally or was it a phenomenon local to particular places and peoples? The most persuasive answers to these questions locate the origins of a consciousness of globality in Europe in the late eighteenth century, as the earlier quotations from Smith and Kant have already implied. This is not to say that such synchronic conceptions of globality had no antecedents before that time. Cartographers since the early sixteenth century had been able to see the world (almost) whole.[15] Cosmographers in the later sixteenth century had speculated about the potential human habitability of the planet.[16] As early as 1658 the English physician Sir Thomas Browne provided a precocious intimation of time-space compression when he compared his own bedtime in England with that of other peoples in more distant time-zones: 'The Huntsmen are up in *America,* and they are already past their first sleep in *Persia.*'[17] However, a diachronic conception of globality, in which universal history was spatialised and universal geography temporalised, was the product of the later eighteenth century.[18]

'The growing call, since the century's midpoint, for a new world history testifies to the depth of the experiential shift that global interdependence engendered.'[19] In these words, Reinhart Koselleck speculated that world history was the product of the post-war period: that is, of the aftermath of the Seven Years' War of 1756–63 not of the six years' war of 1939–45, and hence of the late eighteenth century not the late twentieth century. 'Ministers in this country, where every part of the World affects us, in some way or another, should consider the *whole Globe*', wrote the British

---

[14] Compare Bell (2005).   [15] Goldstein (1972).   [16] Headley (2007), pp. 9–62.
[17] Sir Thomas Browne, *The Garden of Cyrus* (1658), in Browne (1977), p. 387; on 'time-space compression' before the Enlightenment see Harvey (1990), pp. 240–52.
[18] Tang (2008).
[19] Koselleck (2004), p. 244. Franco Venturi had earlier pointed to the Seven Years' War – 'a crisis of the whole of Europe' – as pivotal to the development of Enlightened cosmopolitanism: Venturi (1972), pp. 18–20.

minister the Duke of Newcastle in 1758.[20] He could hardly have known that the conflict would encompass theatres of war as far-flung as the Philippines and Bengal, West Africa and the Plains of Abraham. The fact that it did helped to encourage a wider European public and its leading intellectuals, from Edmund Burke and Adam Smith to the abbé Raynal and Immanuel Kant, to think globally about history and to think historically about the globe. On the publication of the Scottish historian William Robertson's *History of America* in 1777, Burke sent a famous letter of congratulation to the author exulting at the possibility that the great Enlightenment project of a history of humanity might finally be in sight: 'The Great Map of Mankind is unrolld at once; and there is no state or Gradation of barbarism, and no mode of refinement which we have not at the same instant under our View.'[21] The decades following the Seven Years' War comprised 'the first age of global imperialism' and this stadial view of history was as much the product of that set of conjunctions as it was the result of the intercontinental encounter of European armies and navies.[22] It would take the dismantling of such hierarchical accounts of 'barbarism' and refinement before histories of humanity as a global community could be envisaged by Kant (in his 'Idea for a Universal History with a Cosmopolitan Intent'), for example.[23]

The history of globalisation shows that it repeatedly generated equal and opposite reactions towards de-globalisation. This can be shown in the late eighteenth-century transformations of two other global discourses which illustrate the limits of universalism within the history of globalisation: the discourses of rights and of international law. Neither was unprecedented, of course: the identification of subjective natural rights as a peculiarly human attribute can be traced back at least to the early seventeenth century and thence to the late Middle Ages.[24] Likewise, if the antecedents of international law are to be found in either the *ius gentium* or the *ius naturale*, then they extend even further back to Roman law and to stoic universalism.[25] The modern theory of rights and natural law fashioned by Hugo Grotius in the early seventeenth century had attempted to bridge the gap between the law of nature and the law of nations by deducing a minimalist core of morality for all human beings

---

[20] Duke of Newcastle to Earl of Holdernesse, 25 July 1758, BL Add. MS 32882, ff. 65–6, quoted in Middleton (1985), p. 77.
[21] Edmund Burke to William Robertson, 9 June 1777, in Burke (1958–78), III, pp. 350–1. On the 'Enlightened narrative' that lay behind Burke's vision, see O'Brien (1997); Pocock (1999b).
[22] Bayly (1998).   [23] Muthu (2003).   [24] Tuck (1979); Brett (1997); Tierney (1997).
[25] Pagden (2000).

which was both universally intelligible and necessarily obligatory, even if God himself had not existed.[26] The law of nations had thus been assimilable to the law of nature because it seemed to be universally observed by all rational creatures, at whatever stage of civil development, savage, barbarous or polite, and without regard to their religious beliefs. As Montesquieu noted, in a frequently quoted passage from the opening of *L'Esprit des lois* (1748), 'All nations have a right of nations; and even the Iroquois, who eat their prisoners, have one. They send and receive embassies; they know rights of war and peace; the trouble is their right of nations is not founded on true principles.'[27] In 1755, the *Encyclopédie* likewise defined 'Droit des gens' as 'a jurisprudence that natural reason has established among all humans concerning certain matters, and which is observed in all nations': it therefore applied equally to Christians and Muslims, barbarians and infidels.[28]

The subsequent histories of both international law and rights talk have been as discontinuous, reversible and irregular as those of globalisation itself. Late eighteenth-century universalism was thus accompanied by an emergent consensus which held that the scope of the law of nations was restricted to something less than the global scope implied by the law of nature. For example, Robert Ward, the author of the first English-language history of the law of nations, argued in 1795 'that what is commonly called the Law of Nations, falls very far short of *universality*, and that, therefore, the Law is not the Law of *all* nations, but only of particular classes of them; and thus there may be a *different* Law of Nations for *different* parts of the globe'.[29] Similarly, in 1798 Sir James Mackintosh concentrated his lectures on the law of nature and nations on 'that important branch of it which professes to regulate the relations and intercourse of states, and more especially, both on account of their greater perfection and their more immediate reference to use, the regulations of that intercourse as they are modified by the usages of the civilized nations of Christendom'. This was manifestly not the law of 'the brutal and helpless barbarism of *Terra del Fuego*, ... the mild and voluptuous savages of Otaheite, ... the tame, but ancient and immoveable civilization of China, ... the meek and servile natives of Hindostan ... [or] the gross and incorrigible rudeness of the Ottomans'.[30]

The transition from the universalist conception of the law of nations found in Montesquieu and the *Encyclopédie* to the law of Christian

---

[26] Tuck (1987); Hochstrasser (2000).   [27] Montesquieu (1989), p. 8.
[28] *Encyclopédie* (1754–72), v, p. 126, *s.v.*, 'Droit des gens'.   [29] R. Ward (1795), i, p. xiv.
[30] J. Mackintosh (1799), p. 25; Pitts (2012).

civilisation has usually been explained as the product of colonialism during the larger transformation from 'truly plural legal orders to state-dominated legal orders' across the globe.[31] The states and princes of the East Indies, who had been treated as equal sovereign agents by the European states in the sixteenth, seventeenth and eighteenth centuries, became unequal subjects of European colonial rule in the late eighteenth and nineteenth centuries; African and North African rulers whose property rights and sovereignty had been respected before the nineteenth century became casualties of the 'Scramble for Africa' in the late nineteenth century as '[i]nternational law shrank into an Euro-centric system which imposed on extra-European countries its own ideas including the admissibility of war and non-military pressure as a prerogative of sovereignty'.[32] However, as the examples from Ward and Mackintosh suggest, the standard of civilisation, and the identification of international law as the law of Christian nations, originated initially within Europe itself, and not within extra-European relations.[33]

Counter-Revolution, rather than colonialism, was the matrix of this conception of international law. Ward began compiling his history of the law of nations at the height of Pittite war-fever against the French Directory. Though he noted that, by the time his book was published in 1795, 'the conduct of this nation [France] is now *somewhat* mended', he repeatedly deplored any contemplated attempt to withdraw from the common consensus of Christendom: any nation that did so 'may indeed conceive its conduct to be lawful, *according to a law of nations of its own* ... Such has been the conduct of the *French Republic*.'[34] Likewise, Mackintosh, in his lectures on the law of nature and nations, had been keen to repudiate his earlier enthusiasm for the French Revolution: 'The Modern Philosophy, counter-scarp, outworks, citadel, and all, fell without a blow ... The volcano of the French Revolution was seen expiring in its own flames, like a bon-fire made of straw ... The havoc was amazing, the desolation was complete.'[35] Counter-Revolutionary fervour demanded a search for new foundations of international obligation in an age of evident secularisation of morality. The appeal to Christian civilisation, and the narrowing of the law of nations to betoken that law of 'the Nations of our own SET, that is, of EUROPE', derived from a defence of embattled orthodoxy in the

---

[31] Benton (2002), p. 28.   [32] Alexandrowicz (1967), p. 235; Alexandrowicz (1973), p. 6.
[33] Gong (1984); Kayaoğlu (2010).   [34] Phipps (1850), I, p. 15; R. Ward (1795), II, pp. 237–8.
[35] Hazlitt (1825), pp. 215, 216; Haakonssen (1996), pp. 278–80.

face of atheistical French republicanism and a consequent nostalgia for the integrative maxims of a united Christendom.[36]

The modern conception of international law therefore sprang from the counter-Revolutionary and counter-Enlightenment ardour of the 1790s. This in turn underpinned the more famous accounts of the European 'states-system' whose 'initial purpose was to stigmatise the French Revolution, and especially the Napoleonic imperial system, as unlawful in terms of the "traditional" principles of European public law and order'.[37] This period also witnessed Edmund Burke's introduction of the terms 'diplomatic' and 'diplomacy' into the English language, the first (in 1787) as a loan-word from French, and the second (in 1797) to describe the conduct of international negotiations, in his *Letters on a Regicide Peace.*[38] French Revolutionary universalism and Napoleonic pretensions to universal monarchy within Europe had not only threatened the European states-system but had dissolved the distinction between domestic and international relations. As the most influential counter-Revolutionary student of that states-system, Arnold H. L. Heeren, put it, 'It was the peculiarity of the age, that the external relations of the states proceeded from the internal.'[39] All later accounts of the European states-system derived from the histories of Heeren and his near-contemporary the Alsatian academic Christoph Wilhelm Koch, thereby providing modern international relations theory with a hidden counter-Revolutionary genealogy.[40] That genealogy would remain fundamental to conceptions of modern international law until the 1960s and the era of decolonisation. At that point, the emergence of a consciously anti-modern – and even post-modern – conception of international law could at last exorcise the remnants of its occult counter-Revolutionary heritage.[41]

The counter-Revolutionary moment had laid the foundation for a conception of international law as the law of a specifically Christian civilisation rather than as the norms of an emergent global society. In the nineteenth century, that law could be extended to non-Christian nations, such as China, Japan and the Ottoman Empire,[42] but only by means of positive agreements (such as treaties, trading compacts, capitulations and other extraterritoriality agreements) not on the grounds of its universality or its derivation from natural law or natural reason. The consequent

[36] R. Ward (1795), II, p. 161; more generally, see Pitts (2007).   [37] Keene (2002), p. 16.
[38] Roberts (2009), p. 5; *OED*, *s.vv.*, 'diplomacy', 'diplomatic'.   [39] Heeren (1857), p. 332.
[40] Marino (1998), pp. 260–5; Keene (2002), pp. 21–6.   [41] Koskenniemi (2002), pp. 511–17.
[42] Kayaoğlu (2010).

standard of civilisation became enshrined in nineteenth-century positivist conceptions of international law, and then circulated globally in such vehicles as the Chinese translation of the American jurist Henry Wheaton's *Elements of International Law* (1836).[43] That standard would remain central to conceptions of modern international law until the 1960s and the era of decolonisation. It is therefore hardly surprising that human rights have also been confounded with imperialism or that public international law itself has been condemned as 'Eurocentric', the product of but one self-regulating and self-regarding 'civilisation' among many, but not therefore the only one to be regarded as a legitimate source of international norms.[44] Resistance to rights talk has thus often taken the form of anti-occidentalism, anti-imperialism or anti-Americanism. Its dissemination and penetration may be 'the products of recent developments – industrialisation, urbanisation, the communications and information revolutions – that are replicable everywhere, even if they have not occurred everywhere at once'.[45] The fact that they have not is no guarantee that they must or ever will, as the various contested histories of globalisation repeatedly confirm.

The example of legal discourse is especially revealing because it is from that discourse that the term 'international' arose and from it, too, that the reigning contemporary conception of the 'transnational' emerged. 'Whereas "international" implies a relationship among nations, "transnational" suggests various types of interactions across national boundaries.'[46] Like all such terms of art, 'international' and 'transnational' are concepts that depend upon broader and more elaborate theories for their analytical precision and utility. Such concepts can migrate from the theories within which they were first located, but they cannot entirely escape their origins.

When used to describe a form of history, a set of political relations or forms of human association, the word 'international' functions as a transferred epithet. It has been transferred from jurisprudence to historiography, diplomacy and politics. 'International' was one of the many coinages introduced by Jeremy Bentham to clarify (though just as often to obscure) the conceptual vocabulary of his benighted contemporaries, like 'maximise', 'minimise', 'terrorist' and 'codification', among others.[47] According to Bentham, writing in 1780 in a work first published in 1789, 'international law' denoted 'that brand of jurisprudence' whose subject is 'the mutual transactions of sovereigns as such', rather than the activities

---

[43] Janis (2010), pp. 49–69; Liu (1999a), pp. 127–8, 136–42, 155–9.
[44] Onuma (2000); Pagden (2003).   [45] Franck (2001), p. 198.
[46] Iriye (2002b), p. 51.   [47] Mack (1963), pp. 191–5.

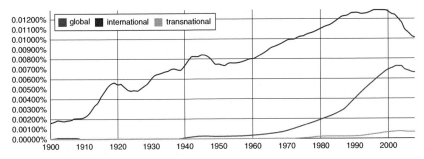

Figure 2.2 Relative frequency of the terms 'global', 'international' and 'transnational' in English-language works, 1900–2008. Source: Google Ngram Viewer.

of individuals who were subject to 'internal' domestic or municipal law.[48] Its concern was therefore the relations between states, in their collective and external capacities, rather than the status of persons with regard to one another or with respect to their governments. Individuals were the subjects, not the objects of such law. It did not treat the transactions of 'nations' in the sense that would generally be understood today, that is, the relation of peoples defined culturally, ethnically or historically. As 'the mutual transactions of sovereigns' it could more clearly be defined as 'inter-state' law. In this sense, it was conceptually continuous with earlier, perhaps less successful, attempts to redefine the law *of* nations (the *jus gentium*, *droit des gens* or *Völkerrecht*) as the law *between* nations, the *jus gentium inter se* (as the Spanish Jesuit Francisco Suárez had called it in the early seventeenth century), the *jus inter gentes* (as the mid-seventeenth-century English jurist Richard Zouche had more systematically analysed it) or the *droit entre gens* (as the French Chancellor D'Aguesseau had termed it fifty years before Bentham).[49] Such forms of law were not shared by all human beings as rational creatures and hence were not considered to be homologous with the natural law; instead, they comprised a novel and increasingly important body of rules, customs and practices that demanded a new word in the course of the eighteenth century to denote and distinguish them from other forms of law and other types of interaction between peoples (see Figure 2.2).

The extension of forms of regulation and interaction beyond those that could be encompassed within the actions of sovereigns alone demanded a further extension of legal vocabulary to denominate 'transnational law'.

[48] Bentham (1996), pp. 6, 296.
[49] Suárez (1612), II, c. 19, n. 8; Zouche (1650), p. 1; D'Aguesseau (1771), II, p. 337, cited Bentham (1996), p. 296 n. x.

In 1956, the Columbia University law professor Philip Jessup took this 'to include all law which regulates actions or events that transcend national frontiers. Both public and private international law are included, as are other rules which do not wholly fit into such standard categories.'[50] Jessup acknowledged that he had not coined the term, though he may have been the first to endow it with its continuing longevity, as a concept whose time had clearly come in the generation after the Second World War, the founding of the United Nations and the promulgation of the Universal Declaration of Human Rights. The earliest usage of the term seems to have been in a philological context, when the Leipzig linguist Georg Curtius used it in 1862 to describe the extra-national extension of languages. The American political essayist Randolph Bourne had nervously celebrated the transcendent multinationalism of the United States in almost Hegelian terms as 'the trans-nationality of all the nations' in 1916, while the British journalist Norman Angell repeatedly applied the term 'trans-national' to the conditions of the post-war economy in Europe in 1921, but only in the last half-century does 'transnational' seem to have taken root as a term of art across the social sciences and, from thence, to the humanities.[51] In the meantime, the map of law has come to encompass not just international and transnational law, alongside domestic, private or municipal law, but also 'supranational', 'global' or 'world' law (dealing with the environment or outer space, for example), in addition to the regional law of such supranational organisations as the European Union, or inter-communal law, regulating relations between different religious or ethnic groups.[52]

The globalisation of law has patently moved at a different speed, along different tracks, from the process of economic globalisation. This should hardly be surprising, in light of the discontinuities evident in the history of globalisation. Globalisation is no more a unitary enterprise than was internationalisation before it; multiple tracks towards globalisation can be discerned, just as multiple movements of resistance to it have arisen. For example, the early nineteenth-century price commodity convergence, though combined later in the century with an ideology of free trade, the lowering of tariff barriers and the consequent free movements of capital and labour, could be seen to have run its course by the 1930s as 'a backlash against globalization' (in the shape of tariff reforms, central banks and immigration controls) 'that had been developing progressively since the

[50] Jessup (1956), pp. 1–2.   [51] Bourne (1916); Angell (1921), pp. 14, 63, 300; Saunier (2009).
[52] Head (1994); Delbrück (1993); Twining (2000), pp. 139–40.

last third of the nineteenth century . . . identified globalism with change
and sin, and held that moral regeneration required national cultures'.[53]
The process of achieving such a global condition in its economic form was
ephemeral and its preconditions had to be constructed afresh for later
moments of globalisation.

Even if economic integration had been smoothly unimpeded since
the early fifteenth or the early nineteenth century, it would not have been
accompanied by the frictionless planetary integration of, say, legal regimes,
cultural norms or religious beliefs. Greater economic convergence
undoubtedly had a mutually sustaining relationship with cultural contact,
for instance, but that led less readily to a convergence of norms than it
did to a collision of competing universalisms – as, for example, in the
Macartney embassy's bruising encounter with the Qing emperor in
Beijing in 1793, which humiliatingly pitted the mercantile and diplomatic
ambitions of the British Empire of George III against the impregnable self-
confidence of the Celestial Empire of Qianlong.[54] Such incommensurable
universalisms could not be combined or negotiated, leaving economic
globalisation as just one – far from uncontested or inevitable – alternative
among many even today.

There is no single universal process of globalisation within which all
forms of human interaction move in lockstep towards an inexorably
globalised condition. Globalisation's histories are multiple and its pre-
histories just as various. It would be fallacious to seek a single pre-history
of globalisation, both because it has had many paths and because none
of those paths has been unbroken. This makes writing the history of
globalisation more difficult, but it should not render it impossible so
long as we recall that the process can be halted or reversed. To live in
an age of globalisation is not the same thing as living in a globalised age:
after all, there have been processes of globalisation before, for example,
in the late fifteenth, late eighteenth and mid nineteenth centuries, none of
which produced a lasting condition of globalisation. The historians'
contribution to the study of globalisation should therefore be to remind
us that we may be living amid only the latest (but probably not the last)
of globalisation's diverse and disconnected pre-histories.

[53] James (2001), pp. 200–1.   [54] Hevia (1995).

CHAPTER 3

The elephant and the whale: empires and oceans in world history

The history of empires and the history of oceans have been two of the most vigorous and fertile strains of historiography in recent years. On the face of it, imperial history and maritime history have much in common. They are both transtemporal, in that they are not tied to any specific period and can be pursued across vast expanses of time. They are also both transnational, because they are not confined to nation-states and must be followed over great tracts of space. Neither has been limited to the study of Europe, or even to the period of European activity in the world beyond Europe. Indeed, some of the most challenging recent oceanic histories have been written by pre- and ancient historians: for example, Peregrine Horden and Nicholas Purcell's wonderfully multi-faceted study of the pre-modern Mediterranean, *The Corrupting Sea: A Study of Mediterranean History* (2000) or Barry Cunliffe's richly expansive *Facing the Ocean: The Atlantic and its Peoples, 8000 BC–AD 1500* (2001).[1] Similarly, the study of empires has been the province of archaeology as much as of history, and extends from some of the earliest human societies in Mesopotamia all the way up to the near-present and the quasi-imperial ventures of contemporary powers in the same region.[2]

The histories of empires and oceans intersect and overlap but they are far from identical. Imperial history treats the complex, often multiethnic, polities in which dominant elites have exerted central control over territory, population and resources.[3] By contrast, oceanic history deals with connections and circulations outside centres of control and calculation and usually beyond the limits set by particular national histories.[4] The competition of empires did shape the histories of the Mediterranean,

[1] Horden and Purcell (2000); Cunliffe (2001); Harris (2004).
[2] For example, Alcock, D'Altroy, Morrison and Sinopoli (2001); Morris and Scheidel (2009).
[3] C. Maier (2006); Cooper and Burbank (2010).
[4] Games, Horden, Purcell, Matsuda and Wigen (2006).

the Atlantic, the Pacific and the Indian Oceans, but so did other forces like commerce, navigation and climate. Oceans were important theatres of imperial activity, but they were not the only such arenas. Even sea-borne empires like the Dutch and the English were territorial entities before they became maritime enterprises, however small the territorial core of the empire was in comparison with the geographical reach of their fleets and settlers. Empires have waxed and waned, but oceanic basins have shifted mostly in the perceptions of the agents who traverse and imagine them.[5] Moreover, empires have tended to operate outward from sovereign cores surrounded by moving frontiers and marchlands. Oceanic arenas, by contrast, have generally been polycentric, without advancing imperial borderlands but with a multiplicity of zones where populations collided and mingled.

The histories of oceans and empires may have become newly fashionable but they also have long pedigrees. They rest upon an old and deep opposition between empires of the land and empires of the sea whose roots can be found in Judaic and Greek, as well as Roman and neo-Roman, traditions. To illustrate that opposition, I here use the biblical image of the elephant and the whale and take as my text to elaborate it chapters 40 and 41 of the Book of Job. In these chapters, the God of the Israelites rebukes the presumptuous Job by reminding him of His two most terrifying and impressive creations: 'Behold now behemoth, which I made with thee', God commands; 'he eateth his grass as an ox ... He moveth his tail like a cedar ... His bones are as strong pieces of brass; his bones are like bars of iron.' Then He asks the quivering Job, 'Canst thou draw out leviathan with an hook? ... Canst thou fill his skin with barbed irons? or his head with fish spears? ... Upon earth there is not his like, who is made without fear' (Job 40:15, 17–18; 41:1, 7, 33).

Behemoth and leviathan, the greatest beasts of land and sea respectively, were sometimes identified in biblical commentary with a bull and a crocodile but, more often, with the elephant and the whale. These two mighty creatures, the one predominant terrestrially and the other oceanically, later became metaphors for power over the land and hegemony over the sea. It was thus in one sense ironic that Thomas Hobbes chose leviathan, the great sea-monster, as the image of sovereign authority in the territorial state.[6] More conventionally, Napoleon Bonaparte compared

---

[5] Steinberg (2001); Klein and Mackenthun (2004); Benton (2010).
[6] Hobbes (1651); compare Hobbes (1679); Schmitt (1996); Malcolm (2007a).

France and Britain to the two great monsters, the French elephant representing Europe's greatest land power, the British whale its – and soon the world's – greatest power by sea.[7]

Like the elephant and the whale, imperial and maritime history are both vast in size and awe-inspiring to contemplate. In this regard, the most important feature they have in common is the scale on which they operate. Imperial history treats the largest, the most variegated and the furthest-flung of all the political communities human beings have constructed for themselves: empires. Similarly, maritime history investigates the broadest, the most fluid and the most all-encompassing of the arenas in which humans have conducted their affairs: the oceans. Yet if both are dizzying in their extent they are also now equally fashionable, even imperative, as units for studying human history.

For much of that history, across most of the globe, most people inhabited political communities rather different from the ones that now seem universal and inescapable to us. The creation of a world of states has been largely the work of the last two centuries and, especially, of the last fifty years.[8] It combined two broad processes: the consolidation of states out of lesser polities or territories and the dissolution of empires into states. The combination of these processes explains the striking pattern of contraction and then expansion in the number of polities observable since the late Middle Ages. A long-term pattern of cultural integration and political centralisation can be discerned in different regions of the world. For example, in Southeast Asia, '[b]etween 1340 and 1820 some 23 independent ... kingdoms collapsed into three'.[9] A similar pattern is obvious in Europe. Roughly 1,000 separate political units in the fourteenth century had become fewer than 500 by the early sixteenth century and then roughly 350 on the eve of the French Revolution, including the pocket-handkerchief principalities of the Holy Roman Empire.[10]

In 1900, Europe had only 25 nation-states at the most generous count. In 1945, 50 states from every part of the world gathered at the San Francisco Conference to found the United Nations. Between 1950 and 1993, more than 100 new states were created by secession, decolonisation or dissolution. By 2012, 193 states (along with Kosovo, Taiwan and the Vatican City) had jurisdiction over every part of the Earth's land surface,

[7] Tombs and Tombs (2006), pp. 253–65.
[8] Frederick Cooper, 'States, Empires, and Political Imagination' in Cooper (2005), p. 190; Strang (1991); Armitage (2007a), pp. 103–7, 137–8.
[9] V. Lieberman (2003), p. 2.   [10] Greengrass (1991), pp. 1–2.

with the major exception of Antarctica. The only states of exception
were the exceptions created by states.[11] At least potentially, states also
have jurisdiction over every inhabitant of the planet: to be a stateless
person is now to wander an inhospitable world in quest of a state's
protection.

What preceded, and also for a long time accompanied, the emergence
of this world of states was a world of empires. Empires are structures of
political and economic interference that organise their component parts
hierarchically. Statehood implies the absence of external interference in
internal affairs as well as formal equality in relations with other states.[12]
In this formal sense, states represent an escape from the conditions of
empire. However, there have been few states that do not share many
imperial features; for this structural reason, states have often been continuous with empires, either as their progenitors or as their legacies.
National histories often overlooked or deliberately suppressed these
continuities between states and empires. Transnational historiography is
the fruit of the reaction against the limitations imposed by conventional
histories focused on nations and states.

The history of empires has received much encouragement from post-
colonial scholarship as well as from more immediate debates over the
question of whether American foreign policy in the early twenty-first
century heralded a revival of neo-imperial ventures across the world.
Likewise, the burgeoning historical interest in globalisation and its antecedents has invigorated the study of oceanic and maritime history.[13] This
is a set of processes that emphasises exchange and interchange, fluidity
and circulation – whether of goods, capital, people or ideas – rather than
the fixity and boundedness associated with the classic conception of
the territorial state. To take only one example: Atlantic history has
been magisterially defined in just these terms as 'the creation, destruction
and re-creation of communities as a result of the movement, across and
around the Atlantic basin, of people, commodities, cultural practices and
ideas'.[14]

These contemporary concerns about imperial legacies and the impact
of globalisation resemble the enduring opposition between empires of
the land and empires of the sea. That opposition is at once among the

---

[11] Agamben (2005).   [12] Keene (2002), pp. 5–6, 97, 143–4.
[13] Hopkins (2002); Hopkins (2006).
[14] Elliott (2009), p. 259; Abulafia (2004), pp. 65, 75–6, 91–2, rightly notes that deserts (e.g., the
Sahara, the Gobi) and lakes (e.g., Victoria) can be the sites of such circulatory histories as well as
oceans.

most basic yet also least investigated themes in western historiography
and political thought, at least from Herodotus in the fifth century BCE
to Carl Schmitt in the mid twentieth century. Indeed, Schmitt seems to
have been the only scholar to have examined the relationship between
empires of land and sea in any depth, first in his brief child's history of
the modern world, *Land and Sea* (1942), and then in his authoritative
study of space in modern history, *The Nomos of the Earth* (1950), in which
he argued that '[w]orld history is the history of the wars waged by
maritime powers against land or continental powers and by land powers
against sea or maritime powers'.[15]

It is possible to go even further than Schmitt to argue that the opposition
of land powers and sea powers, behemoths and leviathans, elephants and
whales, is fundamental both chronologically and ontologically to western
historiography. Indeed, it can be seen to arise simultaneously with historical
thinking itself in the works of Herodotus, Thucydides, Xenophon and,
later, Polybius, where it is connected to such basic oppositions as that
emerging between the 'East' (Asia) and the 'West' (Europe),[16] and the
opposed axes of tyranny (associated with monarchy) and liberty (exemplified by democracy). That opposition was emblematised in the contention
between the Persian land-empire and the Athenian thalassocracy, with
lasting consequences for the figuration of such empires. In this typology,
Athens itself stood at the end of a series of sea powers, just as it would
stand at the head of such a sequence of empires for later observers of
the *translatio imperii*.[17]

Athenian naval victory, most notably over the Persians at the battle
of Salamis, nourished the myth of Athens as a specifically maritime
democracy, whose triremes not only defended Athenian freedom
(*eleutheria*) but may themselves have been a 'school of democracy' for
free Athenians and the slaves who were promised their freedom for rowing
alongside them.[18] Athens exported the values and institutions of democracy in its ships to the archipelago but still remained vulnerable on land,
as other later maritime empires, like Venice, would do. As the fifth
century BCE *Constitutions of Athens*, once attributed to Xenophon, but
now to the 'Old Oligarch', remarked,

[15] Schmitt (1942); Schmitt (2003), p. 5 (quoted); Connery (2001); Derman (2011).
[16] On the importance of the East/West distinction in the classical world, see especially Bowersock
(2004); more generally, see Pagden (2008).
[17] Horden and Purcell (2000), p. 24; compare Momigliano (1944); C. G. Starr (1978). Jonathan Scott
has recently termed this discourse 'maritime orientalism': Scott (2010); Scott (2011), pp. 44–8, 154–5.
[18] Strauss (1996); P. Hunt (2006), pp. 26, 30, 33.

Athens has empire on the sea, but as Attica is on the land, enemies ravage it when it makes expeditions to distant places ... But if the Athenians lived on an island and had also empire on the sea, they would have the power to harm others and no one would be able to harm them, so long as they remained masters of the sea.

Nearly two millennia later, Montesquieu quoted this passage in the *Esprit des lois* (1748) with a contemporary gloss on the continuities between ancient and modern maritime empires: 'You might say that Xenophon intended to speak of England.' Montesquieu also pointed up a major discontinuity by noting that Athens was 'more attentive to extending its maritime empire than to using it', especially for the expansion of its commerce.[19] However, the very vulnerability of Athens on land allowed it to be portrayed as the benign maritime trading empire to Rome's aggressive territorial *imperium*. As Montesquieu's intellectual heir, the abbé Raynal, noted, unlike Athens, Rome 'promoted intercourse between different nations, not by uniting them by the ties of commerce, but by imposing upon them the yoke of subordination'.[20] In this typology, Rome's earlier opposite was Athens, just as its immediate rival for the lordship of the Mediterranean world would be the maritime empire of Carthage.[21]

These oppositions – Persia (or Sparta) and Athens; Athens and Rome; Rome and Carthage – endured through the translations of empire in early modern and modern Europe. They added potent moral and political evaluations to what had begun as historiographical oppositions which were later reinforced by historical examples and self-sustaining myths. Later European conceptions of empire would draw strength from the positive images transmitted through these typologies and would use their negative aspects as ideological weapons in times of war: for example, during the Anglo-Dutch Wars of the seventeenth century, the War of the Spanish Succession and the Seven Years' War, in which both France and Britain liberally deployed the metaphors of Rome and Carthage to promote their respective claims to dominance.[22] Thus, the English political economist Charles Davenant, writing in 1700 against the encroaching territorial monarchy of Louis XIV, argued in favour of English naval supremacy by alluding to the Athenian empire of the seas – 'Their Navy indeed was the occasion of their greatness' – but also warned his

---

[19] Old Oligarch (2008), p. 48 (2. 13–14); Montesquieu (1989), pp. 362–3 (21. 7). For the broader context of this (pseudo-)Xenophontic strain of thought in the eighteenth century, see Ahn (2008); Liddel (2008); Ahn (2011).
[20] Raynal (1777), I, p. 7.   [21] Winterer (2010).   [22] Dziembowski (1998), p. 365.

compatriots that maritime hegemony alone would not be sufficient to ensure other kinds of dominance: 'whatever Nation has the chief Dominion at Land, will in time have the Dominion of the Seas, and they who are strongest at Sea, will have the Trade'.[23]

Davenant spoke here in the political language of modern commercial reason of state. That language had fundamentally redefined the very meaning of the term 'empire' as it had been inherited from Rome. By the time of Julius Caesar and Augustus, an originally juridical language of *imperium* as magistracy had become territorialised, as an abstract conception of *imperium* as authority had become detached from its more precise association with magistrates and generals and then applied to the whole area over which Rome held authority, the *Imperium Romanum*.[24] Though the abstract language of empire as authority or sovereignty would of course endure, the Roman inheritance of the term ineradicably associated it with the power to exclude others (and their authority) from specific spaces. Empire thus came to imply control over territory, that 'bordered political space' over which the leviathan-like power to overawe and frighten (*terreor*) is exercised, and 'from which people are warned off'.[25]

Because this space was fastened in the land, and defined by exclusion, territorial empire was the lineal ancestor of the territorial state, the bounded, exclusive, spatially delimited political community that we now recognise as the primary political unit of the modern world. After 1415, these territorialised polities were gradually joined by the fleets, forts and factories of the Portuguese, Dutch and English empires, as well as by the transoceanic empire of the Spanish Monarchy. The ideological justifications for these modern – meaning post-medieval – empires deepened the older distinction between empires of the land (on the Roman model) and empires of the sea, with their maritime and, increasingly, commercial foundations. However, arguments developed to justify rights of sovereignty and property over land could not readily be transferred to the different medium of the sea.

The *locus classicus* in early modern Europe for the limited application of those territorialist arguments would be Grotius's *Mare Liberum* (1609), in which Grotius determined that land and sea were incommensurable, at least as far as traditional justifications for *dominium* and *imperium* were concerned, because the sea was fluid, not fixed like land. It was indeterminate and unconfinable within identifiable boundaries, again

[23] Davenant (1701), p. 287.   [24] Lintott (1981); Richardson (2008).
[25] C. Maier (2000), p. 808; *OED, s.v.* 'territory'; Baldwin (1992), pp. 209–10.

unlike land, whose boundaries could in theory be firmly inscribed upon the earth. The sea was also inexhaustible, as were its resources (like fish), while land was not. Finally, the sea's fluidity, changeability and lack of plasticity meant that it could not be transformed by human labour, unlike the soil. For all these reasons, no power could claim exclusive dominion over the sea. Instead, in the words of John Locke later in the seventeenth century, 'the Ocean' was 'that great and remaining Common of Mankind'.[26] Movement across territorial borders was becoming increasingly restricted, for both people and goods; by contrast, Grotius argued from the nature of the sea and the activities transacted upon it that travel and commerce across the great common should remain free and undisturbed. It should be open to all humanity to pursue their subsistence and to engage in their natural, even God-given, desire to interact through mutual exchange and interchange.

Grotius's arguments against exclusion from the seas were the product of inter-imperial rivalry between the maritime empires of the Dutch and the Portuguese.[27] They were also marked by the emergence of commerce as a fundamental reason of state for the great territorial monarchies of seventeenth-century Europe when they expanded their activities into the extra-European world. Commercial reason of state added yet another dimension to the opposition of land and sea empires: on the one hand, a vision of free-flowing and unfettered trade that 'establish[es] between two hemispheres, by the happy art of navigation, a communication of flying bridges' (in Raynal's marvellous phrase);[28] on the other, a nightmare of predatory rulers' ambitions for modern universal monarchy on land, in part as the means to secure dominance at sea.

Seen within this context, even the relatively benign pursuit of maritime expansion could become sinister in intent, as the Prussian natural-law theorist Samuel Pufendorf, writing from a mostly landlocked monarchy with few extra-European ambitions in the 1670s, noted:

on the sea, we stretch our empire much farther [than on earth], by the means of ships, now brought to their highest perfection; which are not only serviceable in transporting burdens, but likewise carry Mars through the Kingdoms of Neptune in a far more dreadful array, than he is attended with when he rageth by land.[29]

Yet for a maritime power like England, the association noted by Pufendorf was more likely to be seen as benign rather than threatening. At almost

---

[26] Grotius (2004); Locke (1988), p. 289 (*2nd Treatise*, § 30).
[27] Van Ittersum (2006); van Ittersum (2010); Borschberg (2011).   [28] Raynal (1777), v, p. 473.
[29] Pufendorf (1729), p. 380 (IV. v).

the same moment, the Irish political economist Sir William Petty looked back to the Athenian sea-empire, with the help of a Dutch naval architect, for a more positive assessment of the role of naval technology: 'Such as Desire Empire & Liberty says Aristotle let Them Encourage the Art of Ship-Building.'[30]

Both Pufendorf and Petty wrote on the eve of an epochal struggle between Britain and France for imperial dominance, first within Europe and then in the extra-European world. That 'Second Hundred Years War' (1688–1815) would lend greater ideological urgency to the evaluative distinction between empires of the land and empires of the sea. In the course of that long war, especially within the context of a self-affirming navalist ideology in Britain, commerce would be counterposed to conquest, the virtues of navies pitted against the dangers from armies, and sailors mythologised as vectors of liberty even as soldiers were distrusted as agents of absolutism. This ideology would be fundamental to a conception of the British Empire as a non-territorial, commercial empire of the seas, defended by ships not armies, engaged primarily in commerce not conquest, and whose anthem would be 'Rule, Britannia!'.[31]

The limitations of that British self-image would become starkly clear during and after the Seven Years' War. Propagandists on both sides of the English Channel had cast the conflict between Britain and France as a struggle between a new Carthage and a new Rome. 'The intolerance of the Tyrians and the Carthaginians in commercial matters hastened their destruction', wrote the French critic Élie Fréron early in the War. 'The English should fear the same fate, for all Europe reproaches them for the same principles, the same views and the same vices.'[32] French defeat in the War disconfirmed such predictions, but British territorial conquests in North America and South Asia, and the consequent militarisation of the imperial frontier across the globe, saddled Britain with all the responsibilities of a land-empire while trying to maintain an uneasy dominance at sea. At this moment, 'language and terminology began to change, as those associated with the dominion of the seas based on liberty no longer seemed appropriate'.[33]

The period between the end of the Seven Years' War and the defeat of Napoleon would be a heyday both for imperial historiography and for a renewed attention to the importance of sea power in history. The two

[30] BL Add. MS 72854, f. 106v, quoting Witsen (1671), sig. *3r; McCormick (2009), pp. 268–70.
[31] Armitage (2000), pp. 142–5, 170–4.   [32] Élie Fréron, cit. David A. Bell (2001), p. 103.
[33] P. J. Marshall (1998), p. 10.

greatest imperial histories from that time – Raynal's *Histoire des Deux Indes* and Edward Gibbon's *Decline and Fall of the Roman Empire* – are the most obvious monuments to these immediate concerns.[34] Gibbon's account would stand as the greatest contemporary history of land-empire, while Raynal's *Histoire* (in its various unfolding versions) offered the first history of commercial globalisation, cast in the form of a sequence of sea-empires beginning with the Athenian thalassocracy and progressing through its Phoenician, Carthaginian, Norman and Arab successors until it reached the present-day consequences of the great revolution wrought by the rise of commerce as a reason of state. 'It is since this revolution', stated Raynal, 'which hath, as it were, submitted the earth to the sea, that the most important events have been determined on the ocean.'[35] This vision would also be shared by Adam Smith in the *Wealth of Nations*, the most enduring of all the histories of commerce hatched in the long shadow of the Seven Years' War.[36] Like Raynal and his collaborators, Smith recognised that fierce interstate rivalry for markets and goods had created a single worldwide economic system held together by interoceanic communication but threatened by the imperial ambitions of short-sighted companies and land-hungry states.

According to Carl Schmitt, writing in the immediate aftermath of the Second World War, the triumph of the British 'whale' over the French 'elephant' in 1815 confirmed the final emergence of '*two* separate and distinct global orders within the Eurocentric world order' whose separation had begun in the sixteenth century: a terrestrial order of the land and an oceanic order of the sea.[37] Schmitt wrote in a time when he believed even that fundamental order had been superseded by a novel world order premised on airpower that threatened to dissolve the specifically European ordering of the globe based on the division of land and sea. Even if Schmitt's anxiety now seems incomprehensible, and his defence of that early modern world-order indefensible, both his typology and his genealogy of the competing and exclusive orders of land and sea are immensely suggestive. They are recognisable as but one version of an ancient (and modern) opposition of sea-empires and land-empires, and that the most fully worked-through of the twentieth century both as a theoretical construct and as a historical narrative.

---

[34] Pocock (2005), part IV.
[35] Raynal (1777), IV, p. 419. On the broader French context for Raynal's historiography, see Cheney (2010).
[36] Muthu (2008).   [37] Schmitt (2003), p. 172 (Schmitt's emphasis).

The resilience of this fundamental opposition between empires of land and sea underpinned the long narrative of the succession of empires since at least the fifth century BCE. The brief sketch I have attempted here may draw attention to a comparative framework so deeply buried as to be almost unremarked in the burgeoning historiography of empire. Yet it also points to the deeper roots of perhaps the most profound division in contemporary conceptions of global history. The two leading versions of that history might be described as *inter*-national and *trans*-national, a history of competitive but mutually recognising territorial nation-states pitted against and alongside a narrative of globalisation predicated, like oceanic history, on borderlessness, fluidity, the absence of overarching sovereignty and a lack of territorial fixity. By being alert to the continuity of the fundamental opposition between empires of land and sea that informs these histories, we may be better able to see the ways in which the opposition of these elephants and whales continues to inform post-modern conceptions of world history, just as it had earlier shaped its early modern and modern antecedents.

PART II

Seventeenth-century foundations:
Hobbes and Locke

Hobbes and the foundations of modern international thought

Profecto utrumque verè dictum est,
Homo homini Deus, & Homo homini Lupus.
Illud si concives inter se; Hoc, si civitates comparemus.

(Hobbes, *De Cive*)[1]

For most political theorists and historians of political thought, Thomas Hobbes was the 'first . . . modern theorist of the sovereign state'.[2] This was the state as sovereign over its subjects rather than as a sovereign among sovereigns. The balance of Hobbes's own writings justified this focus on the internal dimension of the state. Hobbes had much less to say about the relations between states than many scholars – particularly theorists of international relations – would like him to have said. In comparison with his treatment of the domestic powers and rights of the sovereign, his reflections on the law of nations, on the rights of states as international actors and on the behaviour of states in relation to one another were scattered and terse. For this reason, students of Hobbes's political theory have generally seen his international theory as marginal to the central concerns of his civil science: 'The external relations of Leviathan are for them on the fringe of Hobbes' theory.'[3]

The relative silence of Hobbes and of his philosophical commentators on this matter contrasts starkly with his canonical position among the founding fathers of international thought: 'No student of international relations theory, it seems, can afford to disregard Hobbes's contribution to that field.'[4] Within the conventional typologies of international

---

[1] Hobbes (1983), p. 73; 'There are two maxims which are surely both true: *Man is a God to man*, and *Man is a wolf to Man*. The former is true of the relations of citizens with each other, the latter of relations between commonwealths': Hobbes (1998), p. 3. On this passage see Tricaud (1969).

[2] Quentin Skinner, 'From the State of Princes to the Person of the State', in Skinner (2002b), II, p. 413.

[3] Forsyth (1979), p. 196. For an early exception, see Gauthier (1969), pp. 207–12.

[4] Malcolm (2002), p. 432.

relations theory, Hobbes stands between Hugo Grotius and Immanuel Kant as the presiding genius of one of three major theoretical traditions: the Hobbesian 'Realist' theory of international anarchy, the Grotian 'Rationalist' theory of international solidarity and the Kantian 'Revolutionist' theory of international society.[5] There is clearly a problem here for historians, political theorists and international relations theorists alike. If Hobbes's contribution to international thought was so fundamental, how could it have been overlooked for so long? And how did he come to be accepted as a foundational figure in the history of international thought if his reflections on the subject were so meagre?

Amid the vast amount of commentary on Hobbes as an international theorist there is little that could be described as being of a genuinely historical character.[6] Accordingly, the first part of this chapter lays out Hobbes's conceptions of the relation between states across the course of his career.[7] As this survey will show, the full range of Hobbes's writings provides a more expansive and nuanced set of reflections on the state in its international capacity than could be inferred from most treatments of the subject. No previous attempt has been made to trace the afterlife of Hobbes's reflections, in large part because there has been little study of the reception of his works more generally in the period since the mid eighteenth century.[8] The second part of the chapter will then survey the afterlife of Hobbes's international thought from the seventeenth century to the twentieth in order to show just how recent is the adoption of Hobbes as a – if not *the* – theorist of international anarchy.

---

[5] Wight (1987); Wight (1991).

[6] As well as Forsyth (1979) and Noel Malcolm, 'Hobbes's Theory of International Relations', in Malcolm (2002), pp. 432–56, see especially Heller (1980); Bull (1981); Navari (1982); Hanson (1984); Airaksinen and Bertman (1989); Caws (1989); Johnson (1993); Malnes (1993); M. W. Doyle (1997), pp. 111–36; Boucher (1998), pp. 145–67; Hüning (1999); Tuck (1999); Akashi (2000); Cavallar (2002), pp. 173–91; Schröder (2002); H. Williams (2003); Covell (2004); Sorell (2006); M. C. Williams (2006); Christov (2008), pp. 30–84; Patapan (2009); Warren (2009); Prokhovnik and Slomp (2011); Moloney (2011).

[7] This chapter deals only with Hobbes's firsthand statements; any full survey of his knowledge and conceptions of international relations would also have to include his early translations of Fulgenzio Micanzio's letters to the second Earl of Devonshire on foreign affairs (1615–26), BL Add. MS 11309 and Chatsworth Hobbes MS 73.Aa, on which see Micanzio (1987) and Coli (2009); Thucydides (1629); and the *Altera secretissima instructio* (1626; English trans., 1627), on which see Malcolm (2007b).

[8] There is as yet no comprehensive survey of Hobbes's late eighteenth- and nineteenth-century reception comparable to Parkin (2007); Noel Malcolm, 'Hobbes and the European Republic of Letters', in Malcolm (2002), pp. 457–545; or Glaziou (1993), though see Francis (1980); Tuck (1989), pp. 96–8; Crimmins (2002).

The earliest statement on the subject of international relations possibly attributable to Hobbes comes from the 'Discourse of Laws' contained in the *Horae Subsecivae* (1620), a volume of essays credited to Hobbes's pupil, William Cavendish, later the second Earl of Devonshire. There the author (who stylometric analysis has suggested may have been Hobbes)[9] provided the following entirely conventional definition of the 'three branches that mens Lawes do spread themselves into, every one stricter then other':

> *The Law of Nature*, which we enjoy in common with al other living creatures. The *Law of Nations*, which is common to all men in generall: and the *Municipall Law* of every Nation, which is peculiar and proper to this or that Country, and ours to us as Englishmen.
> That of *Nature*, which is the ground or foundation of the rest, produceth such actions amongst us, as are common to every living creature, and not only incident to men: as for example, the commixture of severall sexes, which we call *Marriage*, generation, education, and the like; these actions belong to all living creatures as well as to us. The *Lawes of Nations* bee those rules which reason hath prescribed to all men in generall, and such as all Nations one with another doe allow and observe for just.[10]

This definition was conventional because drawn almost word for word from the opening pages of the *Digest* of Roman law, a fundamentally important text for early modern political thought in general.[11]

The first paragraph of the *Digest* distinguished public law (which concerned religious affairs, the priesthood and offices of state) from private law. It then divided private law into three parts: the *ius naturale*, the *ius gentium* and the *ius civile* [*collectum etenim est ex naturalibus praeceptis aut gentium aut civilibus*]. In words that would be followed exactly by the author of the 'Discourse of Laws', it stated that the *ius naturale* is common to all animals and out of it comes marriage, procreation and child-rearing, while the *ius gentium*, 'the law of nations, is that which all human peoples observe'. The source of the *ius naturale* was instinct; that of the *ius gentium*, human agreement. They therefore obliged human beings in different ways. It could thus be concluded of the *ius gentium*: 'That it is not co-extensive with natural law can be grasped easily, since this latter is common to all animals whereas *ius gentium* is common only to human beings among

[9] Reynolds and Hilton (1993); Fortier (1997).
[10] Cavendish (1620), pp. 517–18 (contractions expanded).
[11] Skinner (1998), pp. 39–41; Quentin Skinner, 'John Milton and the Politics of Slavery', and 'Liberty and the English Civil War', in Skinner (2002b), II, pp. 289–91, 313; Skinner (2002a).

themselves.'[12] Though both could be distinguished from the *ius civile*, the internal law of particular communities, the *ius gentium* could not be assimilated to the *ius naturale*. The medieval and early modern theory of natural law would thereafter rest on this trichotomy with its fundamental distinction between the law of nature and the law of nations.[13]

The definitions of the laws of nature and of nations in the *Horae Subsecivae* stand in marked contrast to what would become Hobbes's standard account in the successive versions of his civil science from the *Elements of Law* (1640) through *De Cive* (1642) to the English and Latin versions of *Leviathan* (1651, 1668). If the passage from the 'Discourse of Laws' can be attributed to Hobbes, then his later treatments of the law of nature and of nations represented a clear break with that early triadic definition.[14] Hobbes's mature conception of the law of nations differed in three basic ways from the account offered in the 'Discourse of Laws': first, it derived the law of nature from reason alone; second, it distinguished firmly between the law of nature and the right of nature (a distinction that later writers, such as Samuel Pufendorf, would not observe as scrupulously as Hobbes); and, third, it collapsed the law of nations into the law of nature.

Hobbes's later statements were much closer to the jurist Gaius's definition, also found in the first chapter of the *Digest*, which distinguished the *ius civile* proper to each particular society from 'the law which natural reason has established among all human beings ... among all observed in equal measure ... called *ius gentium*, as being the law which all nations observe'.[15] This produced a dichotomous taxonomy of law in which the law of nature applied both to individuals and to commonwealths and the civil law was distinguished from it as the positive commands of sovereigns. Hobbes's use of the distinction between the law of nations and the civil law would help to create two competing afterlives for Hobbes as a foundational figure both for the seventeenth- and eighteenth-century discipline of the

---

[12] *Digest* (1985), I. I. I, §§ 2–4: 'Ius gentium est quo, gentes humanae utuntur. quod a naturali recedere facile intellegere licet, quia illud omnibus animalibus, hoc solis hominibus inter se commune sit'; Kaser (1993), pp. 64–70. This passage is usually attributed to Ulpian.

[13] Scattola (2003), pp. 10–11.

[14] The fact that the passage is such a literal paraphrase of the *Digest* makes it inapt for the kind of analysis applied in Reynolds and Hilton (1993). Hobbes (1995) supplies little information on the sources of the discourses and, hence, no indication of whether other passages might also be paraphrases. For further evidence of such borrowing in the text, see Huxley (2004), drawing on Chatsworth Hardwick MS 51, printed in Neustadt (1987), pp. 247–71.

[15] Gaius, *Institutiones*, I. 3: 'quod vero naturalis ratio inter omnes homines constituit, id apud omnes populos peraeque custoditur vocaturque ius gentium, quasi quo iure omnes gentes utuntur' (also in *Digest*, I. I. 9); Kaser (1993), pp. 20–2.

law of nature and nations and for nineteenth-century legal positivism. His later reputation as a denier of international law and as a theorist of international anarchy would spring from these competing conceptions of him as at once a naturalist and a positivist, depending on whether he was considered as an international theorist or as a political theorist.

In his first mature account of the law of nations, Hobbes noted in the *Elements of Law* that previous writers on the law of nature could not agree whether it represents 'the consent of all nations, or the wisest and most civil nations' or 'the consent of all mankind' because 'it is not agreed upon, who shall judge which nations are the wisest'. He concluded instead that '[t]here can be ... no other law of nature than reason, nor no other precepts of NATURAL LAW, than those which declare unto us the ways of peace'. Later in the work, he asserted that 'right [*ius*] is that liberty which law leaveth us; and laws [*leges*] those restraints by which we agree mutually to abridge one another's liberty' before applying that distinction to a tripartite division of law crucially different from that found in the *Digest* and in the *Horae Subsecivae*: 'whatsoever a man does that liveth in a commonwealth, *jure*, he doth it *jure civili, jure naturae*, and *jure divino*'. This division omitted the law of nations as strictly impertinent to the internal affairs of a common-wealth and irrelevant to its citizens as individuals and substituted instead the *ius divinum* as the third source of obligation in civil society. Individuals are not the subjects of the *ius gentium*; commonwealths in their capacity as artificial persons are. The *ius gentium* therefore only appeared as an after-thought in the very last sentence of the *Elements of Law*: 'And thus much concerning the elements and general grounds of law natural and politic. As for the law of nations, it is the same with the law of nature. For that which is the law of nature between man and man, before the constitution of com-monwealth, is the law of nations between sovereign and sovereign after.'[16]

Hobbes elaborated this rather cursory statement in *De Cive*, a work whose central themes – 'men's duties, first as men, then as citizens and lastly as Christians' – he defined as constituting 'the elements of the law of nature and of nations [*iuris naturalis gentiumque elementa*], the origin and force of justice, and the essence of the Christian Religion'.[17] After once more distinguishing law from right, Hobbes elaborated his definition of natural law in its application first to individuals and then to states:

Natural law can again be divided into the natural law of *men*, which alone has come to be called the *law of nature*, and the natural law of *commonwealths*, which

[16] Hobbes (1969), pp. 75, 186, 190.   [17] Hobbes (1983), p. 77; Hobbes (1998), p. 7.

may be spoken of as the *law of nations* [*lex Gentium*], but which is commonly called the *right of nations* [*ius Gentium*]. The precepts of both are the same: but because commonwealths once instituted take on the personal qualities of men, what we call a *natural law* in speaking of the duties of individual men is called the *right of Nations*, when applied to whole commonwealths, peoples or nations. And the Elements of *natural law* and *natural right* which we have been teaching may, when transferred to whole *commonwealths* and *nations*, be regarded as the Elements of the *laws* and of the *right of Nations* [*Et quae legis & iuris naturalis Elementa hactenus tradita sunt, translata ad civitates et gentes integras, pro legum et iuris Gentium Elementis sumi possunt*].[18]

This was the clearest statement Hobbes would ever give of his rationale for identifying the law of nations with the law of nature. In the *Leviathan*, he would say only, 'Concerning the Offices of one Sovereign to another, which are comprehended in that Law, which is commonly called the *Law of Nations*, I need not say any thing in this place; because the Law of Nations, and the Law of Nature, is the same thing' in so far as 'every Sovereign hath the same Right, in procuring the safety of his People, that any particular man can have, in procuring his own safety'.[19] This left implicit what Hobbes had made explicit in *De Cive*: that the commonwealth once constituted as an artificial person took on the characteristics and the capacities of the fearful, self-defensive individuals who fabricated it. However, he did not necessarily imply that individuals in the state of nature could be understood reciprocally as possessing 'the characteristics of sovereign states'.[20] The analogy between pre-civil individuals and commonwealths was imperfect and only made sense for Hobbes once states had been constituted as persons; to describe individuals as possessing the characteristics of states would beg the question of just what characteristics a state in fact possessed.

When Hobbes came to offer the final version of his account of the relation between the law of nature and the law of nations in the Latin *Leviathan* (1668), he repeated that they are the same [*idem sunt*] and expanded on his definition in the English *Leviathan* by asserting that 'whatever a particular man could do before commonwealths were constituted, a commonwealth can do according to the *ius gentium*'.[21] What

[18] Hobbes (1983), pp. 207–8 (*De Cive*, XIV. 4); Hobbes (1998), p. 156.   [19] Hobbes (2012), II, p. 552.
[20] Tuck (1999), p. 129.
[21] 'De officiis Summorum Imperantium versus se invicem nihil dicam, nisi quod contineantur in Legibus Naturae supra commemoratis. Nam *Ius Gentium & Ius Naturae* idem sunt. Quod potuit fieri ante Civitates constitutes, à quolibet homine, idem fieri potest per Ius Gentium à qualibet Civitate': Hobbes (2012), II, p. 553.

exactly a commonwealth could do, he said, could be found in the list of the laws of nature earlier in his work. Hobbes left it to his readers to provide an account of the rights of commonwealths in the state of nature, though without any recognition that his account had changed over time. For example, in the *Elements of Law*, Hobbes had specified (as the twelfth law of nature), '*That men allow commerce and traffic indifferently to one another*' and illustrated the principle with the example (also used earlier by Grotius in the same connection) of the war between the Athenians and the Megareans.[22]

Hobbes's subsequent enumerations of the laws of nature in *De Cive* and *Leviathan* omitted without explanation this stipulation that commerce must be unhindered. By contrast, the thirteenth law of nature, '*That all messengers of peace, and such as are employed to maintain amity between man and man, may safely come and go*', did recur in those later enumerations, even though in *De Cive* it was one of the very few laws of nature to have no equivalent in the divine law.[23] Hobbes may have come to think that the right of free trade needed no separate stipulation once the general law of treating everyone else equally had been stated, but he clearly came to believe that it was unenforceable in the state of nature, where there is 'no Culture of the Earth; no Navigation, nor use of the commodities that may be imported by Sea'.[24] He thereby accommodated his account of the law of nations to his account of the law of nature: what could not be rightfully (or practicably) claimed by individuals in the state of nature could hardly be claimed by commonwealths in their relations with one another.

It was on the basis of his assimilation of the law of nations to the law of nature that Hobbes identified the international arena as a still-existing state of nature. Indeed, apart from 'the savage people in many places of *America*', commonwealths in their relations with one another provided the most striking and enduring evidence for the existence of that state of nature.[25] Hobbes seems to have made that discovery between writing the *Elements of Law* and *De Cive*. In the *Elements*, his account of the foundations of international relations was as cursory as his treatment of the *ius gentium*. Hobbes there took the *ius in bello* to be a specifically personal matter: '[t]here is ... little to be said concerning the laws that men are to

---

[22] Hobbes (1969), p. 87; Grotius (2004), p. 12, alluding to Diodorus Siculus, *Bibliotheca historica*, XII. 39, and Plutarch, *Pericles*, XXIX.
[23] Hobbes (1983), p. 115 (*De Cive*, III. 19, where diplomatic immunity becomes the fourteenth law of nature); Hobbes (1998), p. 51; Hobbes (2012), II, p. 236 (where it is the fifteenth law of nature).
[24] Hobbes (2012), II, p. 192.   [25] Hobbes (2012), II, p. 194; Moloney (2011).

observe towards one another in time of war, wherein every man's being and well-being is the rule of his actions'. Beyond that, his treatment of commonwealths as international actors was descriptive rather than normative and concerned only 'the means of levying soldiers, and of having money, arms, ships, and fortified places in readiness for defence; and partly, in the avoiding of unnecessary wars'.[26]

In *De Cive*, Hobbes offered for the first time the full range of descriptive and normative characteristics of commonwealths as international actors that would also be found, with some modification and elaboration, in *Leviathan*. Answering the criticism that he had overestimated the primacy of fear as the fundamental motive for human action in the state of nature, Hobbes adduced the evidence of the relations between commonwealths, which 'guard their frontiers with fortresses, their cities with walls, through fear of neighbouring countries'; '[a]ll commonwealths and individuals behave in this way, and thus admit their fear and distrust of each other'. That fearful defensiveness defined the very nature of commonwealths when seen from the outside: 'And what else are countries but so many camps fortified against each other with garrisons and arms [*totidem castra praesidiis et armis contra se invicem munita*], and their state ... is to be regarded as a natural state, i. e. a state of war?'. Thus, Hobbes concluded, 'hostility is adequately shown by distrust, and by the fact that the borders of their commonwealths, Kingdoms and empires, armed and garrisoned, with the posture and appearance of gladiators [*statu vultuque gladiatorio*], look across at each other like enemies, even when they are not striking each other'.[27]

In the *Leviathan*, this image would become even more decisive evidence for the existence of the state of nature: 'though there had never been any time, wherein particular men were in a condition of warre one against another; yet in all times, Kings, and Persons of Soveraigne authority, because of their Independency, are in continuall jealousies, and in the state and posture of Gladiators; having their weapons pointing, and their eyes fixed on one another; that is, their Forts, Garrisons, and Guns upon the Frontiers of their Kingdomes; and continuall Spyes upon their neighbours; which is a posture of War'.[28] On this basis, there could be no hope of peace among commonwealths: as the Lawyer explained in Hobbes's

---

[26] Hobbes (1969), pp. 101, 184.

[27] Hobbes (1983), pp. 93, 180, 277–8 (*De Cive*, I. 2, X. 17, XV. 27); Hobbes (1998), pp. 25, 126, 231–2. The source of information on gladiators most readily accessible to Hobbes would have been Lipsius (1585) and later editions; Enenkel (2001).

[28] Hobbes (2012), II, p. 196.

Dialogue Between a Philosopher and a Student of the Common Laws of England (1666), 'You are not to expect such a Peace between two Nations, because there is no Common Power in this World to punish their Injustice: mutual fear may keep them quiet for a time, but upon every visible advantage they will invade one another.'[29] However, Hobbes did not infer from this posture of hostility that mutual fear would give rise to an international leviathan, to liberate commonwealths from the dangers of the state of nature as the institution of the sovereign freed individuals from those perils. The two cases were incomparable 'because [sovereigns] uphold thereby, the Industry of their Subjects; there does not follow from it, that misery, which accompanies the Liberty of particular men'.[30] The international state of nature was not equivalent to the interpersonal state of nature and was therefore insusceptible to parallel remedies for its inconveniencies.[31]

Hobbes's scattered reflections on the law of nations, on the behaviour of states and on the relations between them, gave rise to two major but distinguishable conceptions with which his name would become associated in later international thought. The first, and most fundamental, was that the law of nations was simply the law of nature applied to commonwealths. The second, and presently the one identified as most characteristically Hobbesian, was that the international realm is a state of nature populated by fearful and competitive actors. These two concepts were not to be found in tandem in Hobbes's works before the composition of *De Cive* in 1641 nor did he elaborate or elucidate them after their appearance in *Leviathan* in 1651, save for their later translation into Latin in 1668. His failure to expound them systematically had three lasting consequences for his reputation and for the reception of his political philosophy. The first, arising initially in the seventeenth century, was to sharpen the division between naturalism and positivism in international law. The second, which emerged in the eighteenth and nineteenth centuries, was to distinguish his conception of the law of nations from his conception of the international state of nature. The third, arising from the previous two in the twentieth century, was to identify Hobbes as the classic theorist of international anarchy. This last is the most recent and the most contingent but remains the basis of Hobbes's reputation as a theorist of international relations.

The positivist response to Hobbes's naturalism originated even before the appearance of *Leviathan* with the publication in 1650 of the *Iuris*

---

[29] Hobbes (2005), p. 12.   [30] Hobbes (2012), II, p. 196.
[31] Heller (1980); Hoekstra (1998), pp. 69–84; Hoekstra (2007).

et Iudicii Faecialis, sive Iuris Inter Gentes by the Royalist professor of civil
law at Oxford, Richard Zouche. Zouche's later reputation as 'the first
real positivist' in the history of international law rests on the distinction
he made in that work between the *ius gentium* and the *ius inter gentes*.[32]
The *ius gentium* comprised all those elements common to the laws of
various nations, such as the distinctions between freedom and slavery
or private property and public property. This law of nations had to be
distinguished from the law between nations, the *ius inter gentes*,
which comprised the laws different peoples or nations observed in their
dealings with one another, such as the laws of war and commerce.[33]
According to this definition, the *ius inter gentes* was the product of
convention and agreement and did not derive from any other source
of law, natural or divine. Yet in an earlier manuscript version of his
treatise, Zouche had originally defined the *ius inter gentes* as that which
is common among diverse sovereigns or peoples and which is derived
from the precepts of God, nature or nations, a definition derived from
Gaius's in the *Digest*.[34] Zouche had clearly changed his mind about the
definition of the *ius inter gentes* before 1650 and found it necessary
to distinguish it from both the *ius gentium* and the *ius naturae*. The
impulse for this shift seems to have been his reading of Hobbes on
the law of nature and nations. There is no sign that Zouche had read any
of Hobbes's works by the time he composed the manuscript version
of the *Iuris Faecialis*, but *De Cive* did appear in the footnotes to the first
chapter of the printed version.[35] Zouche may therefore have been the
first legal theorist to resist Hobbes's conflation of the law of nations with
the law of nature.

Within the later tradition of natural jurisprudence, from Pufendorf to
Vattel and beyond, Hobbes would be acclaimed as a fundamental
innovator on the basis of that conflation. By the late eighteenth century,
the relationship between the two forms of law appeared to be the primary
question in determining the basis of obligation itself. As Robert Ward put
it in 1795: 'Upon the whole ... the great points of difference concerning
the mode of its structure, seem to turn upon this; Whether the Law of
Nations is merely the Law of *nature* as it concerns man, *and nothing
more*; or whether it is not composed of certain *positive Institutions*

[32] Nussbaum (1947), p. 122.   [33] Zouche (1650), p. 3.
[34] 'Ius inter Gentes est quod in Communione inter diversos Principis vel populos obtinet, et
deducitur ab Institutis divinis, Naturae et Gentium': BL Add. MS 48190, f. 14r.
[35] Zouche (1650), p. 3.

founded upon consent.' Ward took Hobbes, Pufendorf and Burlamaqui to be the key proponents of the first position; Suárez, Grotius, Huber, Bynkershoek, 'and in general the more recent authors, declare for the last'.[36] Pufendorf asked, 'Whether or no there be any such thing as a particular and positive *Law of Nations*, contradistinct to the *Law of Nature?*' and immediately answered his own question by quoting *De Cive*, XIV. 4: 'Thus Mr. *Hobbes* divides *natural Law, into the natural Law of Men, and the natural Law of States, commonly called the Law of Nations*. He observes, *That the precepts of both are the same* . . . This opinion we, for our Part, readily subscribe to.'[37] Burlamaqui concurred, after quoting the same passage from *De Cive*: 'There is no room to question the reality and certainty of such a law of nations obligatory of its own nature, and to which nations, or the sovereigns that rule them, ought to submit.'[38] By the time Emer de Vattel published his *Droit des gens* in 1758, Hobbes's contribution had become foundational but not incontrovertible: 'Hobbes was, I believe, the first who gave a distinct though imperfect idea of the law of nations . . . This author has well observed, that the law of nations is the law of nature applied to states or nations. But . . . he was mistaken in the idea that the law of nature does not suffer any necessary change in that application, – an idea from which he concluded that the maxims of the law of nature and those of the law of nations are precisely the same': an idea, Vattel noted, Pufendorf had also endorsed, following Hobbes.[39]

Before the twentieth century, Hobbes's conception of the international state of nature attracted much less comment and approval than his naturalist conception of the law of nations.[40] His early critics had attacked his conception of the interpersonal state of nature on the grounds that it made untenable assumptions about human motivation (as Grotius was the first to charge) or that it imported features of the civil state of humanity back into the pre-civil state (as Montesquieu contended, anticipating Rousseau).[41] However, they did not argue that his account of the

---

[36] R. Ward (1795), I, p. 4.

[37] Pufendorf (1729), pp. 149–50 (*De Jure Naturae et Gentium*, II. 3. 23); compare Sharrock (1660), p. 229; Rachel (1676), p. 306; James Wilson, 'Lectures on Law' (1790–1), in Wilson (1967), I, p. 151 (quoting Pufendorf).

[38] Burlamaqui (1748), pp. 195–6 (*Les Principes du droit naturel*, VI. 5).

[39] Vattel (2008), pp. 8–9; Jouannet (1998), pp. 39–52.

[40] A distinguished early exception was Leibniz, who commented favourably on Hobbes's image of interstate relations as gladiatorial: G. W. Leibniz, *Codex Iuris Gentium*, 'Praefatio' (1693), in Leibniz (1988), p. 166.

[41] 'Putat inter homines omnes a nature esse bellum et alia quaedam habet nostris non congruentia': Hugo Grotius to Willem de Groot, 11 April 1643, in Grotius (1928–2001), XIV, p. 199; 'Hobbes demande *pourquoi, si les hommes ne sont pas naturellement en état de guerre, ils vont toujours armés? et*

relations between states was necessarily incorrect for the same reasons that his account of the relations between atomised individuals was incorrect. In fact, the very exiguousness of Hobbes's empirical account of international relations helped to ensure almost two centuries of silence on the subject. Throughout the nineteenth century, neither the first textbooks on international relations nor the first studies of Hobbes's thought found it necessary to treat him as an international theorist. For example, he did not appear alongside Grotius and Pufendorf in the most widely used American text on international relations of the nineteenth century, Theodore Woolsey's *Introduction to the Study of International Law* (1860), a work that would also be foundational for the emergent discipline of political science in the United States.[42] Similarly, none of Hobbes's nineteenth-century British students so much as mentioned his reflections on international relations or the law of nations,[43] while glancing allusions to his views on '*Völkerrecht*' appeared only in the second edition of Ferdinand Tönnies's study of Hobbes in 1912.[44]

Hobbes was only identified as a theorist of international anarchy once a consensus had emerged that the international realm was indeed anarchic. That consensus was the product of nineteenth- and early twentieth-century developments internal to the emerging modern disciplines of political science and international law.[45] It rested on a series of propositions, each of which had to be established before the 'discourse of anarchy' could be seen as plausible and coherent. First, it had to be accepted that the domestic and the international realms were analytically distinct. Then, the norms relevant to each realm had to be identified and distinguished. On that basis, it could be argued that states in their international capacity were unconstrained by any norms equivalent formally or obligatorily to those that applied to their own subjects. States were accordingly independent not just of one another but of any superior. Because they were atomistic they were agonistic: in the absence of any external authority, their relations were governed only by force. They therefore stood in relation to one another as competitive actors within an international state of nature. Hobbes's conflation of the law of nature with

pourquoi ils ont des clefs pour fermer leurs maisons? Mais on ne sent pas que l'on attribue aux hommes avant cet établissement des sociétés, ce qui ne peut leur arriver qu'après cet établissement, qui leur fait trouver des motifs pour s'attaquer et pour se défendre': Montesquieu (1973), I, p. 10.

[42] Woolsey (1860); Schmidt (1998), pp. 52–4.

[43] Whewell (1852), pp. 14–35; Maurice (1862), pp. 235–90; Robertson (1886); Stephen (1892), pp. 1–70; Stephen (1904).

[44] Tönnies (1896); Tönnies (1912), pp. 165, 169.   [45] Schmidt (1998), chs. 3, 5.

the law of nations would not support such a sharp analytical distinction between the internal and the external spheres. Though he admitted that the insecurity of individuals in the state of nature was strictly incomparable to that created by the competition between sovereigns, Hobbes assumed an essential analogy between the relations between individuals and the relations between states as international persons.

Hobbes's conception of municipal law led to very different conclusions about the separation between the foreign and the domestic and about the nature of international relations. For the second generation of English Utilitarians and their nineteenth-century heirs, Hobbes was not the founder of international legal naturalism; instead, he was the godfather of legal positivism, the theory of law as command 'set by political superiors to political inferiors', as his admirer the analytical jurisprude John Austin put it. Judged according to this strictly anti-naturalist definition of law, what had come to be called 'international law' could not be called law at all because it issued from no superior authority: it was therefore no more than what Austin notoriously described as '*positive* international *morality*'.[46] States in their relations with one another were unconstrained by any higher authority because the norms specific to the international and the domestic spheres were distinct and incommensurable. Within a tradition of juristic positivism that owed more to Hegel than to Austin, Hobbes similarly appeared as a denier of international law and as a proponent of the division between the external and the internal. In the words of Carl Schmitt, writing a century after Austin: 'The state has its order in, not outside, itself . . . Hobbes was the first to state precisely that in international law states face one another "in a state of nature." . . . Security exists only in the state. *Extra civitatem nulla securitas.*'[47]

Hobbes did not directly inspire the conception of the relations between states as fundamentally anarchic. It was instead the proponents of a 'discourse of anarchy' in international relations who co-opted Hobbes to support their theory, and the opponents of that discourse who likewise invoked Hobbes to discredit it.[48] Juristic theorists of that state argued that 'theoretical isolation is the prime condition of its existence as a state, and its political independence is one of its essential attributes. This is what

---

[46] Austin (1995), pp. 19, 112, 171, 229–33 (note).
[47] Schmitt (1996), pp. 47–8. For a succinct account of Schmitt's reading of Hobbes, see Stanton (2011).
[48] Schmidt (1998), pp. 232–3.

Hobbes meant in saying that, in regard to one another, separate states are to be viewed as in a "state of nature".'[49] In such a condition, 'every independent political community is, by virtue of its independence, in a State of Nature towards other communities'.[50] With states thus 'a law unto themselves', it followed that '[t]he condition of the world, from an international point of view, has long been one of polite anarchy'.[51] Pluralist critics of the juristic theory of the state contended that it not only described but in fact created a condition of international anarchy; they, too, invoked Hobbes in support of their contentions.[52] Conformity to the theory of sovereignty as independence ensured that 'the condition of international society would, indeed, be that which Hobbes in his day conceived it to be'.[53] 'The state is irresponsible', Harold Laski concluded, summing up this line of criticism: 'It owes no obligation save that which is made by itself to any other community or group of communities. In the hinterland between states man is to his neighbour what Hobbes says was true of him in the state of nature – nasty, mean, brutish.'[54]

Hobbes assumed his place among the founders of international thought as much in spite of as because of his own statements on the law of nations and the relations between states. Like many later critics of an allegedly 'Hobbesian' account of international relations, he recognised the limited analytical utility of the analogy between individuals and international persons in a state of nature.[55] He acknowledged that, though states could be just as fearful, vainglorious and competitive as individuals in their relations with one another, they were not vulnerable to the same degree nor was their existence as fragile. Agreements and exchanges were possible both in the interpersonal state of nature and the international state of nature. If the Hobbesian theory of international relations rests on a conception of international anarchy characterised by interstate competition without any possibility of cooperation, then Hobbes himself was no Hobbesian.

The standard account of Hobbes as an international theorist arose in conditions not of his own making. Positivists battled naturalists, pluralist theorists of the state criticised juristic theorists, and political scientists defined their discipline against international law and international relations theory. Hobbes could be invoked on both sides of each dispute.

---

[49] Leacock (1906), p. 89; compare Willoughby (1918), p. 207.
[50] Bryce (1922), p. 5.   [51] Hill (1911), pp. 14, 15.
[52] Schmidt (1998), pp. 164–87; on the pluralists and their debts to Hobbes, see Runciman (1997).
[53] Garner (1925), pp. 23–4.   [54] Laski (1927), p. 291.
[55] E. Dickinson (1916–17); Bull (1977), pp. 46–51.

The naturalists pointed to his conflation of the law of nations with the law of nature as a foundational insight, while the positivists invoked Hobbes's command theory of law to deny the validity of international law as law. Anglo-American juristic theorists turned to Hobbes for their conception of legal personality much as their German counterparts turned to Hegel; critics of their monistic theory of sovereignty invoked Hobbes to warn against the consequences of invoking such a theory when describing the relations between states. Among political scientists, Hobbes's concept of the state would earn him a canonical place as one of the founders of modern political thought. Among international relations theorists, he would be baptised retrospectively as one of the founders of modern international thought, as he had once been hailed by the natural lawyers as a pivotal figure for their discipline.

Hobbes's successors identified him as the originator of the fundamental division between the domestic and the foreign, the inside and the outside of the state. That division rested on a further distinction, also endowed with a Hobbesian pedigree, between the internal realm of positive law and the external realm governed by the law of nature and nations. With the rise of international positivism in the era after the Vienna settlement of 1815, Hobbes came to be identified as one of the first theorists of what would later be called the 'Westphalian system' of sovereign states: after all, could it have been just a coincidence that *Leviathan* was published in 1651, only three years after the Peace of Westphalia in 1648?[56] It hardly mattered that Hobbes had first laid down the major elements of his conceptions of international relations and the law of nations in the *Elements of Law* and *De Cive*, well before 1648, or that he never displayed any knowledge of the terms or consequences of the Peace of Westphalia, unlike Pufendorf, for example.[57] Even if he had, he would hardly have inferred from them the emergence of a positive system of mutually recognised sovereign states: that would be the product of a much later 'myth of 1648', which preceded by almost a century the myth of Hobbes the theorist of international anarchy.[58]

Post-modern international thought has deconstructed the opposition of naturalism and positivism and has collapsed the distinction between the internal and the external dimensions of the state.[59] It has demolished the historical and conceptual foundations of the Westphalian order and

---

[56] For a recent example, see H. Williams (2003), p. 1: 'Hobbes's publication of the justification for the modern state coincided with what is often regarded as the birth of the "Westphalian system".'

[57] Pufendorf (1690), pp. 135–96; Schröder (1999).

[58] Osiander (2001); Teschke (2003).

[59] Koskenniemi (2005); Walker (1993).

has proclaimed the advent of 'post-sovereignty'.[60] This has occurred in tandem with an expansion of the definition of political theory itself to include the international, the global and the cosmopolitan,[61] which in turn inspired a redefinition of the boundaries of the history of political thought to take account of that expansion.[62] The contingent conditions and overdetermining theories that gave rise to the 'Hobbesian' theory of international relations in the early twentieth century have therefore been either unsettled theoretically or discredited historically. The paradoxical but salutary effect of this revision may be to expel Hobbes from the canon of international relations theory and to admit him instead to the history of international thought.

---

[60] Bartelson (1995); Krasner (1999); Kalmo and Skinner (2010).
[61] For example, Beitz (1999); H. Williams (1990); Schmidt (2002).
[62] Brown, Nardin and Rengger (2002).

CHAPTER 5

John Locke's international thought

At first sight, John Locke would be an even less likely candidate than Thomas Hobbes for inclusion in the canon of the history of international thought. None of his major published writings, among them the three *Letters* on toleration (1689, 1690, 1692), the *Essay Concerning Human Understanding* (1689/90), the *Two Treatises of Government* (1689/90), *Some Thoughts Concerning Education* (1693) and *The Reasonableness of Christianity* (1695), was primarily or even substantially concerned with any of the subjects that would now be considered under the rubrics of International Relations or international law. Most of Locke's attempts in these works to theorise the relations between peoples and states, to derive norms for international relations or to describe and analyse the international society of his times, were relatively brief and episodic. And the various reflections on England's foreign affairs scattered throughout his correspondence and manuscripts were not widely circulated in his lifetime and remain little known even today. In short, the question of Locke's international thought seems to be like the puzzle of the dog that did not bark in the night.

Locke's biography, at least, gives the lie to any suspicion that he was indifferent to, or inexperienced in, international matters. In the 1670s, he spent almost four years in France (1675–9) and later lived for nearly six years in Holland (1683–9). In his early thirties, he had been secretary to the English envoy Sir Walter Vane during his mission to the Elector of Brandenburg at Cleves from December 1665 to February 1666. The aim of that embassy had been to prevent the Elector from allying with the Dutch and to join the English instead during the Second Anglo-Dutch War, but the Elector strung the English along and a frustrated Vane left without any firm assurances. The inconclusive negotiations gave Locke an intimate view of the workings of international diplomacy as he stayed alert for information and handled the mission's official correspondence.[1] Yet Locke was modest about his own capacities: 'If my intelligence be not soe considerable as you may expect you will pardon it to my want of experience and language not of will and endeavour', he protested to Sir William Godolphin in 1665. His superiors did not share this low estimation of his talents. As soon as he returned to England in February 1666, he was offered the secretaryship to an English embassy to Spain; he declined that opportunity, as he did the chance later the same year to be secretary to an English mission to Sweden.[2] Over the following decades, Locke accrued knowledge of English colonial and commercial activity in North America, from New York to Carolina, in the Caribbean, Ireland and Africa and could claim a practical cosmopolitanism paralleled among few Englishmen of his time.[3]

After the Glorious Revolution of 1688–9, Locke was able to return from exile in Holland, and a new monarch presented him with novel possibilities. According to Lady Masham, in the spring of 1689, William III offered Locke three diplomatic postings, at the Imperial court in Vienna, at the Electoral court at Brandenburg 'or a third place which I remember not'. He declined them all because of the acuteness of the ongoing crisis for 'Protestant and English interest through out Europe' and what he protested was his incapacity for the Germans' 'warme drinking'. And in 1698, he could have become secretary to the ambassador in Paris, or even Secretary of State, but he again demurred, with elaborate politeness: 'I am too much a novice in the world for the imployment proposed.'[4] The time he had spent living in Europe, the offers he received and his administrative experience meant that Locke had more extensive international experience and diplomatic opportunities than any British political thinker before David Hume, the erstwhile secretary in the 1740s to General James St Clair and attendant to the British ambassador to France in the aftermath of the Seven Years' War.[5]

Few of these biographical details were widely known until historical scholarship on Locke's biography and editorial labour on his writings put the study of his life and works on a more secure footing. This might

[1] Letterbook of Sir Walter Vane, December 1665–February 1666, BL Add. MS 16272 (in Locke's hand); Locke (1976–), I, pp. 225–7; Woolhouse (2007), pp. 60–6.

[2] Locke to William Godolphin, 12/22 December 1665; Locke to John Strachey, 22 February 1666, and 28 February 1666; Charles Perrott to Locke, 21 August 1666, in Locke (1976–), I, pp. 233, 263, 289–90.

[3] See below, chs. 6–7.

[4] Woolhouse (2003), pp. 182–3; Locke to Charles Mordaunt, 21 February 1689; Locke to Sir John Somers, 28 January 1698, in Locke (1976–), III, p. 575, VI, p. 308.

[5] On Hume's experience *en mission*, see Rothschild (2009), pp. 410–12, 415–17; on his international thought, Jeffery (2009); Koskenniemi (2009), pp. 27–30, 64–7.

help to explain why even the most historically minded of international theorists were almost silent on the matter of Locke's contribution to their field. For example, the founding members of the English School of International Relations mentioned him only in passing. For Martin Wight, Locke exemplified the richness of political theorising which could be used to show up the poverty of international theory: 'the student of International Relations cannot, it seems, be ... directed to classics in his branch of politics, of the stature of Aristotle or Hobbes or Locke or Rousseau. Is it because they do not exist?'[6] And for Hedley Bull, Locke offered little more than an alternative to the Hobbesian account of international anarchy: 'Locke's conception of the state of nature as a society without government does in fact provide us with a close analogy with the society of states': anarchic, to be sure, because the members of that society must enforce their own laws, yet still minimally social. This hardly amounted to a robust or distinctive vision of international society and Bull devoted only a few sentences to noting it. On such a slender basis, no 'Lockean' tradition of international theory emerged alongside its Grotian, Hobbesian and Kantian forms.[7] A conception of the international realm as a 'Lockean culture', in which states are the bearers of rights, respect one another's sovereignty and view each other as rivals rather than enemies under 'the live and let live logic of the Lockean anarchical society', later emerged from American constructivism as a new third way between Hobbesianism and Kantianism. However, it did not find general acceptance after its introduction by Alexander Wendt in 1999.[8]

Perhaps as a consequence, the critical literature on Locke as an international theorist has been as incoherent as it is sparse. One strand indebted to the work of the political theorist Leo Strauss argued, *pace* Bull, that Locke was in fact a Hobbesian. In the words of Richard Cox, the leading exponent of this view, 'contrary to the surface impression ... Locke deliberately seeks to convey, his conception of the state of nature – whether with regard to individuals or states – is in fact fundamentally Hobbesian in character': that is, he assumes the primacy of foreign over

[6] Wight (1966), p. 17. Compare Wight's review of Raymond Aron, *Peace and War* (1962; English trans., 1966), quoted in I. Hall (2006), p. 110: 'So much has been written about [international relations], but where are its Hobbes and Locke, its "Wealth of Nations"?'

[7] Bull (1977), p. 48; compare Bull (1966), p. 44: 'Locke's speculations about life of men in anarchy will leave us dissatisfied.' Menozzi (1974) offers a brief elaboration of Locke's theory of international relations along these lines.

[8] Wendt (1999), pp. 279–97. For a sceptical account of Wendt's 'Lockean culture', see Suganami (2002).

domestic policy and espouses a mercantilist vision 'which attaches overriding importance to the right of self-preservation'.[9] Another interpretation influenced by the historian of American liberalism Louis Hartz discerned a distinctively 'Lockean' tradition in American foreign policy consisting of an attachment to the balance of power, a commitment to multilateral organisations and 'a self-confident pragmatism' exercised in the international state of nature as well as through westward expansion and Indian removal.[10] This last feature also foreshadowed a more recent tendency to interpret Locke's main contribution to international thought as a theory of property that could justify colonisation through the cultivation of waste land: 'The American settlers and their frontiersmen have their natural spokesman in Locke.'[11]

Yet if any consensus emerged about what constituted a distinctively 'Lockean' theory of international relations, it was that his account of the rights of individuals in the state of nature, and the laws of nature that constrained them, were reproduced in an international state of nature where states took on the moral characteristics of such individuals and acted according to the same laws.[12] As we shall see in the conclusion to this chapter, that analysis of Locke was shared by John Rawls, the only major philosopher to have taken Locke seriously as an international thinker. And this account also underpins a recent attempt to show that 'Locke ... provides the firmest foundations for an international law open to all states willing to abide by it' and 'devises an international law resting on sovereign equality'. However, other recent literature on Locke's international thought has rejected such a conception of Lockean 'Liberal Legalism'.[13] It has been suggested instead that Locke 'shows little confidence that the natural law principles of morality can be effectively embodied in international institutions' and questioned whether he 'takes the situation of states to be symmetric to that of individuals in the state of nature and permits states to use the executive power of the law of nature altruistically' on the grounds that '[a]lthough Locke does permit individuals to engage in altruistic punishment, he does not allow states to use their coercive power to do the same'.[14]

---

[9] Cox (1960), pp. xix–xx; yet see Dunn (1969), pp. 158–64. For Locke (and Montesquieu) as providing 'less frank and more edifying versions of the Hobbist-Spinozist political teaching', see Pangle and Ahrensdorf (1999), pp. 153–7.

[10] Masters (1967a); also in Masters (1967b), pp. 289–305.

[11] H. Williams (1996), p. 100 (quoted); Boucher (2006).

[12] Tuckness (2008), pp. 470–1; Covell (2009), pp. 120–30.

[13] Doyle and Carlson (2008), pp. 660–6, 649.

[14] L. Ward (2006), p. 704; L. Ward (2010), pp. 266–71; Tuckness (2008), p. 471. Compare Moseley (2005).

In light of such fundamental disagreement about Locke's basic principles and the conclusions that can be drawn from them, there is clearly a need to revisit Locke's international thought in his major political work, the *Two Treatises of Government*, as well as in writings that have not generally been considered in this context.

What then were the broadly characteristic features of Locke's international thought as they emerge from across his writings? He argued that the norms for states were to be found in the law of nature and the law of nations, but that the two could not be identified with each other: in this, as we shall see, Locke was quite distinct from Hobbes. His vision was developmental, if not necessarily progressivist; it could be seen to have moved in stages but without any determining teleology, save perhaps towards putting the world's land under cultivation and turning nature towards human self-preservation. However, these natural imperatives were not sufficient to justify the dispossession of non-European peoples whom Locke knew to be international actors capable of entering into diplomatic relations and positive agreements. Indeed, the 'federative' capacity such peoples possessed was a distinctive property of any well-constituted commonwealth. And, lastly, the English commonwealth in particular could only be properly reconstituted in the face of Catholic threats from within and without by rededicating it to the Protestant cause spearheaded by William of Orange.

Locke had travelled a long way from his earliest remarks at Oxford in the 1650s on England's foreign relations to the Williamite position he promoted in 1689–90. His very first publications were in fact on matters of peace and war: a congratulatory poem addressed to Oliver Cromwell ('You rule in peace that world, you gain'd by war') and another in celebration of the Treaty of Westminster that concluded the first Anglo-Dutch War in 1654 ('to make a world's but to compose / The difference of things, and make them close / In mutual amity').[15] His first extensive reflection on the practical relations between commonwealths and the normative foundations that underpinned them appeared in the 'Essays on the Law of Nature' (*c.* 1663–4) which he delivered as lectures in his capacity as Censor in Moral Philosophy at Christ Church. In the fifth of the lectures, he asked whether the law of nature could be known from the general consent of men and answered that it could not. One reason was the contingency of the customs that arise from positive consent 'prompted

---

[15] John Locke, 'Verses on Cromwell and the Dutch War' (1654), in Locke (1997), pp. 201–3.

by the common interests and convenience of men, such as the free passage of envoys, free trade, and other things of that kind; or from an expressly stated contract, such as the fixed boundary-lines between neighbouring peoples . . . and many other such things'.[16]

At first blush, this might sound like Hobbes's enumeration of the laws of nature in *The Elements of Law* (1640), *De Cive* (1641) or *Leviathan* (1651).[17] Although what Hobbes included among those laws changed across his major works, his grounds for identifying them did not: 'As for the law of nations, it is the same with the law of nature. For that which is the law of nature between man and man, before the constitution of the commonwealth, is the law of nations between sovereign and sovereign after.' Hobbes consistently maintained this identification of the law of nations with the law of nature: many later writers would judge this to be his most original contribution to the natural-law tradition.[18]

Locke would not have been among them. He argued that 'the agreement about envoys having safe passage . . . is positive and does not imply a law of nature' and did so on anti-Hobbesian grounds: 'according to the law of nature all men alike are friends of one another and are bound together by common interests, unless (as is maintained by some) there is in the state of nature a general war and perpetual and deadly hatred among men [*quod aliqui volunt, in statu naturae commune sit bellum et hominibus inter ipsos perpetuum et internicinum odium*]'. The law of nature does not assume humans are inflamed by such hatred or that they must 'be divided into hostile states [*in hostiles civitates divisos*]'. Locke took the examples of the peoples of Asia and America to show that they were not bound by the same positive laws as the inhabitants of Europe: 'Therefore, all this general consent derived from contract does not prove a natural law, but should rather be called the law of nations [*jus gentium*], which is not imposed by the law of nature but has been suggested to men by common expediency [*communis utilitas*].'[19] Locke would develop his political thought greatly in the decades that followed his early Oxford lectures, but he would never have agreed with Hobbes that 'the Law of Nations, and the Law of Nature, is the same thing'.[20]

When Locke laid out his mature political theory in the *Two Treatises of Government*, he attributed much more weight than Hobbes had to

---

[16] Locke, 'Essays on the Law of Nature' (*c.* 1663–4), in Locke (1997), p. 107.
[17] Hobbes (1969), p. 87; Hobbes (1998), p. 51; Hobbes (2012), II, p. 236.
[18] Hobbes (1969), p. 190; see above, pp. 68–9.
[19] Locke, 'Essays on the Law of Nature', in Locke (1997), pp. 107–8; Locke (1954), p. 162.
[20] Hobbes (2012), II, p. 552.

agreements among the 'several States and Kingdoms' of the world
(II. 45).[21] Such positive acts determined the difference between the state
of nature and the state of war, the latter 'not consisting in the number of
Partysans but the enmity of the Parties, where they have no Superior to
appeal to' (I. 131). Locke's acknowledgement that the state of nature and
the state of war were quite distinct left more room even than Hobbes had
done for the continuing operation of the law of nature after civil societies
had been instituted. Indeed, the interactions of commonwealths were
proof, if any were needed, that the state of nature was not simply a
conjectural assumption but for many a continuing empirical condition:
'all Princes and Rulers of *Independent* Governments all through the
World, are in a State of Nature', and hence ''tis plain the World never
was nor ever will be without Numbers of Men in that State' (II. 14).

Treaties and other positive acts might distinguish this state of nature
from a state of war but their presence or absence did not abolish the state
of nature even among commonwealths bound together by alliances:

> For 'tis not every Compact that puts an end to the State of Nature between Men,
> but only this one of agreeing together mutually to enter into one Community,
> and make one Body Politick; other Promises and Compacts, Men may make
> with one another, and yet still be in the State of Nature. (II. 14)

Commonwealths did not suffer 'the Inconveniences of the State of
Nature' to the same degree as individuals (II. 13), and so they do not
enter into regional or global bodies politic but remain in an enduring
international state of nature. As such, 'the whole Community is one Body
in the State of Nature, in respect of all other States or Persons out of its
Community' (II. 145).

Apart from the rulers of states, aliens also remained beyond the reach of
positive law and were subject only to the natural law found in the state
of nature, by which '*every man Hath a Right to punish the Offender, and be
Executioner of the Law of Nature*' (II. 8). How else, Locke asked, could
rulers execute or punish foreigners in their dominions? 'Those who have
the Supream Power of making Laws in *England, France* or *Holland,* are to
an *Indian,* but like the rest of the World, Men without Authority' (II. 9).
Only by virtue of the natural right to preserve humanity, and hence to
punish an offender in a pre-civil state by executing the law of nature,
could sovereigns condemn strangers for their transgressions.

---

[21] Locke (1988). All references to the *Two Treatises* are to this edition by *Treatise* and paragraph
number.

Migrants, like aliens, also found themselves in an international state of nature whenever they left an established commonwealth. Locke argued that the commonwealth's jurisdiction over any individual is derivative, 'since the Government has a direct Jurisdiction only over the Land, and reaches the Possessor of it . . . only as he dwells upon, and enjoys that', by virtue of which he gives tacit consent to the government. Jurisdiction was thus territorial rather than personal. Anyone could leave if they, 'by Donation, Sale, or otherwise, quit the said Possession', to become 'at liberty to go and incorporate himself into any other Commonwealth, or to agree with others to begin a new one, *in vacuis locis*, in any part of the World, they can find free and unpossessed' (II. 121; compare II. 115). Locke imagined large swathes of land, especially in 'some in-land, vacant places of *America*', might be available for cultivation and settlement by such migrants (II. 36).[22]

On Locke's account, commonwealths claimed the Earth's surface through positive agreements in which they mutually recognised each others' exclusive territorial rights. Such agreements had emerged gradually over time. The trajectory of human interaction with nature had begun with individual appropriation to satisfy the need for self-preservation. This permitted in turn the aggregation of property by individuals, who sought the protection of commonwealths for their holdings. Only after the invention of money could humans first accumulate and then exchange the profits of their labour and move from a condition of natural community to a regime of private property (II. 34–44). After that momentous development,

the several *Communities* settled the Bounds of their distinct Territories . . . and so, by *Compact* and Agreement, *settled the Property* which Labour and Industry began; and the Leagues that have been made between several States and Kingdoms, either expressly or tacitly disowning all Claim and Right to the Land in the others Possession, . . . have by *positive agreement, settled a Property* amongst themselves, in distinct Parts and parcels of the Earth. (II. 45; compare II. 38)

However, these positively delimited territorial tranches were surrounded by two remnants of the primitive commons that had been universal in the state of nature: namely, 'the Ocean, that great and still remaining Common of Mankind' (II. 30) and the '*great Tracts of Ground* . . . which (the Inhabitants thereof not having joyned with the rest of Mankind, in the consent of the Use of their common Money) lie *waste*, and are more

---

[22] Klausen (2007).

than the People, who dwell on it, do, or can make use of' (II. 45). In the absence of sovereignty, law and money, Locke implied, the latter commons could not be construed as particular to the indigenous commoners who cultivated them.[23]

These commons were open to all those who could make a claim on their products without depriving others of the means of their subsistence. However, this did not mean that they were entirely outside the ambit of positive acts by sovereigns. For example, immediately after describing the ocean as a common, Locke noted that 'what Ambergriese any one takes up here, is *by* the *Labour* that removes it out of that common state Nature left it in, *made* his *Property* who takes that pains about it' (II. 30). The unusual choice of ambergris – the fragrant intestinal secretion of a sperm whale, often found floating at sea – was likely indebted to Locke's involvement with settlement and trade in the Americas. He knew that ambergris was found in both Carolina and the Bahamas: indeed, in the *Fundamental Constitutions of Carolina*, the Proprietors claimed right of trover over half of the ambergris 'by whomsoever found' in Carolina.[24] The ocean may have been a 'great . . . common' but such a positive claim could still trump the natural rights of those who recovered its produce by their labour.

Locke's 'agriculturalist' argument for a right of possession, as derived from the application of labour to the fruits of nature or to land lying waste, has often been taken to be a charter for the dispossession of native peoples by the allegedly more 'Industrious and Rational' Europeans (II. 34). Yet Locke did not assume that indigenous peoples were irrational, nor did he argue that they could be dispossessed on account of their beliefs, or lack of them.[25] As we have seen, Locke derived the authority of the commonwealth from the property rights of the individuals who made it up; one index of the existence of such authority was the capacity to enter into engagements with other similar authorities. Twice in the *Fundamental Constitutions of Carolina*, the Proprietors acknowledged 'treaties, with the neighbour Indians or any other' and the power 'to make peace and war, leagues and treaties, etc., with any of the neighbour Indians'.[26] In this regard, the Proprietors, and presumably also

---

[23] On Locke and indigenous commons, see Greer (2012), pp. 366–70, 385–6.
[24] As Locke knew, ambergris was found in Carolina and in the Bahamas: *Fundamental Constitutions*, § 104, 'one half of all ambergreece by whom soever found shall wholy belong to the Proprietors': TNA, PRO 30/24/47/3, f. 68r, printed in Locke (1997), p. 180; TNA, PRO 30/24/49, f. 58, endorsed by Locke, 'Ambra Grisia 74'.
[25] See below, pp. 120–3.
[26] *The Fundamental Constitutions of Carolina*, §§ 34, 46, in Locke (1997), pp. 169, 171.

Locke, recognised the rights and authority of 'the neighbour Indians',
through specifying their capacity to employ what in the *Second Treatise*
he would call the 'Federative' or treaty-making power.

Locke's analytical isolation of the capacity to enter into agreements
external to the commonwealth would be his most conspicuous innovation
with regard to international affairs in the *Two Treatises*; it was also the
least successful in the long run. In ch. 12, 'Of the Legislative, Executive,
and Federative Power of the Commonwealth', he proposed a division
of powers that was novel in light of English constitutional analysis.
The legislative power had the authority to make laws for the preservation
of the community but would only be in session intermittently; it was
therefore necessary to have *'a Power always in being'* to enforce the laws
continuously: this would be the executive power (II. 143–4). The one
remaining power 'answers to the Power every Man naturally had before
he entred into Society': namely, the federative power, containing 'the
Power of War and Peace, Leagues and Alliances, and all the Transactions,
with all Persons and Communities without the Commonwealth'. Locke
knew that this division was unfamiliar and sheepishly introduced it with
a neologism: it 'may be called *Federative*, if any one pleases' (II. 145–6),
meaning the power to enter into treaties, or *foedera*. Because this power
could not be exercised according to precedent, it was 'left to the Prudence
and Wisdom of those whose hands it is in, to be managed for the publick
good' and should therefore be exercised by the holder of the executive
power (II. 147–8). In English constitutional terms, Locke was simply
describing the royal prerogative to engage with foreign powers.[27] He
had not in fact defined a new power, nor embodied the 'federative'
authority in any unprecedented agent, such as Parliament. His coinage
had no immediate afterlife and later thinkers ignored his distinction
when discussing of the separation of powers.[28]

The *Two Treatises of Government* had contingent purposes tied to
the national and international politics of their own time. When they
were published in November 1689, Locke hoped that they would be
'sufficient to establish the Throne of our Great Restorer, Our present
King *William* ... And to justifie to the World, the People of *England*,
whose love of their Just and Natural Rights, with their Resolution to
preserve them, saved the Nation just when it was on the very brink of

[27] *Halsbury's Statutes* (1985–), XVIII, pp. 720–1.
[28] *OED*, *s.v.*, 'federative'. Montesquieu's 'république fédérative' was only related etymologically, not
genealogically, to Locke's 'Federative' power.

Slavery and *Ruine*.[29] If that had been their sole aim, of course, the *Treatises* would have been consigned to oblivion along with a hundred other Williamite pamphlets. Locke presented the bulk of his argument in the *Two Treatises* as applicable to all rights-bearing adult humans in those parts of the world that possessed monetised economies, regimes of private property and governments to protect the inheritances of their subjects or citizens. From that argument, they could infer a right of resistance to tyranny and recover their original natural rights to self-preservation and punishment on the rare occasions that that might be justifiable. This amounted, in short, to a political theory about the rights and obligations of rulers and ruled, about the legitimation of domestic authority, and the possibilities for the internal reform of a commonwealth. Locke's brief references to the world beyond the commonwealth – the external arena where sovereigns traded, collided or colluded – and to the people outside the commonwealth – aliens, migrants and 'Indians', for example – were mostly overlooked by subsequent commentators who found little or nothing in Locke's work that could approximate to an international theory.

Locke wrote his only essay devoted solely to international affairs in the spring of 1690, just a few months after the *Two Treatises* had appeared in print. In this untitled and unpublished piece he defended William of Orange's 'delivery [of England] from popery and slavery' and warned that if James II 'ever returne, under what pretences soever, Jesuits must governe and France be our master'. He presented the diplomatic options available to England in stark terms: either an 'alliance for the security of Christendom' against France, or 'expos[ing] it to popish rage and revenge'. Internal divisions could be disastrously exploited by England's enemies and everyone who acknowledged that William had restored security should affirm 'the justice, as well as generosity' of 'his glorious undertaking'. He painted a lurid picture of 'a war upon our hands of noe small weight' which could bring in 'blood, slaughter, and devastation'. For all these reasons, he urged 'every protestant, every Englishman amongst us' to consider 'what mortal quarrell he has to any of his country men' when 'the religion, liberty, safety of himself and his country . . . are at stake and will be lost if we hold not now togeather'.[30] This was the voice of an international thinker definitely not our contemporary, but thoroughly English, Protestant and Whig.

---

[29] John Locke, 'The Preface', in Locke (1988), p. 137.
[30] Bod. MS Locke e. 18 in Farr and Roberts (1985), pp. 395–8; printed as Locke, 'On Allegiance and the Revolution', in Locke (1997), pp. 307–13.

It is a frequent complaint in the emergent field of the history of international thought that there has been an imbalance, both philosophical
and historical, between the study of political theory and that of international theory. At least one major task for the history of international
thought is to correct that imbalance by finally giving due attention to
reflection on international affairs by past thinkers like Locke. I end this
chapter with one precocious effort to do just that, made over forty years
ago by John Rawls in the spring of 1969. Rawls took as the theme for his
regular Harvard lecture-course on 'Moral Problems' the topic of 'Nations
and War'. The aim of the series – delivered amid violent campus protests
against the Vietnam War, a conflict whose justice Rawls vehemently
denied – was, he insisted, to treat 'the moral basis of the law of nations'
as a philosophical matter rather than as a commentary on current events.
As Rawls noted in the opening lecture, 'This part of moral and pol[itical]
phil[osophy] has been *relatively* neglected. The great classics of political
thought concern for the most part the nation state – its inst[itution] and
their moral basis. (Consider Hobbes and Locke, Rousseau and Kant,
Hegel and Marx, etc.) Of course, they have had *something* to say on these
matters, but not as much.' Rawls suggested that the reason for this neglect
'might spring from the greater relative success in being able to change
and reform the national political system' while the international system
had remained mostly unchanged: 'a multi-state sys[tem] regulated, if at
all, by the so-called balance of power'.[31]

Rawls's expressed aim in these lectures was to work towards a full social
contractarian theory of the law of nations, in line with the principles of
A Theory of Justice, which he would soon publish in 1971. It is usually
assumed that Rawls only turned systematically to the international applications of his theory in the last decade of his life, with the successive
iterations of what he called in publications of the 1990s 'the law of
peoples'; however, these lectures from 1969 show that his international
theory developed immediately alongside his political theory, even if it
would not be prepared for publication until two decades later.[32] As in *The
Law of Peoples* (1999), Rawls wrestled with the question of justice between
societies with very different moral principles – Christian *versus* infidel or,
later, liberal peoples *versus* 'decent hierarchical peoples' – and argued that
a doctrine similar to the one he had elaborated for domestic society in
accordance with 'justice as fairness' was also necessary for international
society: 'In order to work in to this, let's turn to Locke for a moment.'

---

[31] HUA, Acs. 14990, box 12, letter file 4 (contractions expanded).   [32] Rawls (1993); Rawls (1999a).

And with this Rawls produced only the second attempt – after Richard Cox's in 1960 – to reconstruct Locke's international thought.[33]

Rawls presented Locke as 'a sort of half-way house' between a natural-law theory of the law of nations exemplified by Aquinas and the thoroughgoing social contract theory Rawls himself wished to offer. He argued that Locke's social contract applies only within societies but not between them. The people within it create the commonwealth as a sovereign body to protect the common good but this '*artificial* person' remains in a state of nature with regard to other commonwealths 'because there is *no* political power to which they as artificial persons are subject'. Rawls took Locke to be saying that 'the Law of Nations is simply, for practical purposes, the N[atural] L[aw] as a body of *ethical* principles ... applying to the moral rights and duties of nations'; he admitted that Locke recognised the fundamental principle of *pacta sunt servanda* behind the making of treaties between commonwealths, 'but he does not, it seems, think of these as comprising a body of positive law'.[34] As an exposition of the *Second Treatise*, this surely underestimates the importance of positive agreements in Locke's international thought, especially as those agreements secured the territorial integrity of commonwealths derivatively from the accumulated property of their citizens. As Rawls's language of 'artificial persons' also indicates, it might also have too closely assimilated Locke to Hobbes, especially in assuming his belief in the homology between the law of nature and the law of nations.[35]

Rawls was nonetheless correct in seeing that for Locke the commonwealth could not take on any powers that had not been possessed by the individuals who had constituted it. Just as individuals in the state of nature were equal, free and independent, so are states in the international arena; just as individuals have the executive power of the law of nature, so have states. 'In external affairs in the community of nations, the *rights of nations* are derived from those of ind[ividual]s. As the basic rights of ind[ividual]s are equal, so are those of nations.' At this point in his lectures, Rawls moved on to defining 'nations' in his quest for a social

---

[33] HUA, Acs. 14990, box 12, letter file 4, 'Lecture VI – Natural Law and Rights: Aquinas and Locke.' Cox is the only writer on Locke whom Rawls cites in the lectures.

[34] HUA, Acs. 14990, box 12, letter file 4, 'Lecture VI – Natural Law and Rights: Aquinas and Locke.' Rawls's annotated copy of Peter Laslett's edition of the *Two Treatises* is preserved in HUA, HUM 48.1 Box 1.

[35] Though elsewhere Rawls firmly distinguished the 'problems' and 'assumptions' of Hobbes and Locke: Rawls (2007), p. 105.

contractarian account of the law of nations that left Locke behind as a
suggestive, but incomplete, forerunner, perhaps helpful as a foil but not
the exponent of a plausible theory: 'our problem is this: Locke takes the
fundamental N[atural] L[aw] as *given* (along with the original state of
equality, of equal right). It is based eventually on the right of creation.
What we want to do is to work out a *full* S[ocial] C[ontract] theory from
the idea of the O[riginal] P[osition].'[36] Locke would never bulk large
among Rawls's philosophical inspirations. Rawls erased most of the traces
of history, as well as the international applications of his theory, from
the *Theory of Justice*. He did not consider the international dimensions
of Locke's political philosophy in his later lectures on the subject.[37]
When Rawls did return to the law of peoples in the last years of his
life, Locke would not be among the sources he considered when framing
his realistic utopia.

Rawls was not alone in failing to find in Locke's writings a coherent
international theory. Like almost all the handful of subsequent scholars
who have sought such a theory, he confined himself to searching the
Second Treatise alone, as if to confirm the apprehension that international
thought can only be excavated from within the canon of political thought
rather than by supplementing it with other sources of reflection and
debate. In this chapter, I have tried to follow recent historical students
of Locke in ranging across his work, both systematic and occasional,
printed and unpublished, to suggest other sources for recovering his
international thought.

Many of Locke's direct interventions were closely tied to immediate
circumstance and to the imperatives of a Protestant power within the
European states-system with expansive interests in the Atlantic world and
in burgeoning global commerce. When Locke had addressed foreign
relations directly, it was often as a 'lover of his King and country, a lover
of peace and the protestant interest': a specifically *English* international
thinker who was also committed to 'the common interest of Europe'
against the Catholic Bourbon threat.[38] His one innovation – the proposal
that the 'Federative' be considered a separate power – did not take root.
And the later use of his works to justify dispossession of indigenous
peoples around the world from Connecticut to New South Wales left

[36] HUA, Acs. 14990, box 12, letter file 4, 'Lecture VII – The Full S[ocial] C[ontract] Theory Law of
Nations (I) (How to set up).'
[37] Rawls (2007), pp. 103–55.
[38] Farr and Roberts (1985), p. 395; Locke to Edward Clarke, 29 January 1689, in Locke (1976–), III, p. 546.

him exposed, perhaps unfairly (as we shall see in the next two chapters) to post-colonial criticism. For all these reasons, it may be understandable that Locke contributed little to later international theory. However, the range of his concerns, and the evidence of his engagement with foreign affairs, should justify his admission to any historical canon of international thought.

CHAPTER 6

John Locke, Carolina and the Two Treatises of Government

It is now a commonplace in the history of political thought that there has long been a mutually constitutive relationship between liberalism and colonialism.[1] That relationship might not extend in time quite to the fifteenth-century origins of European settlement beyond Europe but it can now be seen to go back at least as far as the origins of liberalism within the tradition of subjective natural rights. From the early seventeenth century, European theorists who were later variously canonised as liberal elaborated their political theories to address contexts at once domestic and colonial.[2] As Richard Tuck has argued, 'the extraordinary burst of moral and political theorising in terms of natural rights which marks the seventeenth century, and which is associated particularly with the names of Grotius, Hobbes, Pufendorf and Locke, was primarily an attempt by European theorists to deal with the problem of deep cultural differences, both within their own community (following the wars of religion) and between Europe and the rest of the world (particularly the world of the various pre-agricultural peoples encountered around the globe)'.[3] The successors of these seventeenth-century natural-rights theorists extended their interests beyond Europe, the East Indies and the Americas to South Asia, North Africa and Australia in following centuries. Not all liberals were complicit with colonialism and colonialism was not defended only by liberals. The rollcall of liberal theorists who were employed by overseas trading companies or who possessed specialised knowledge of extra-European

---

[1] Both 'liberalism' and 'colonialism' are, of course, anachronistic and imprecise terms to apply to any period before the nineteenth century (if then); however, they provide a convenient conceptual shorthand and have the virtue of familiarity as terms of art.

[2] See especially Parekh (1994b); Parekh (1994a); Parekh (1995); Tully (1995); Leung (1998); Mehta (1999); Ivison (2002); Pagden (2003); Muthu (2003); Pitts (2005a); Sylvest (2008); Mantena (2010); Fitzmaurice (2012).

[3] Tuck (1994), p. 163; compare Tuck (1999), pp. 14–15, 232–4.

settlement and commerce is nonetheless distinguished and diverse and
runs from Grotius and Hobbes to Tocqueville and Mill.

John Locke has become a crucial link in the historical chain joining
liberalism with colonialism. The reasons for this are primarily biographical.
From 1669 to 1675, the Proprietors of the infant colony of Carolina –
among them his patron Anthony Ashley Cooper, later the first Earl of
Shaftesbury – employed Locke as their secretary.[4] Between 1672 and 1676,
he followed the Earl of Shaftesbury in becoming a stockholder and
co-proprietor in a company set up to trade between the Bahamas and
the American mainland.[5] In September 1672, he was also named in the
charter of the Royal African Company, the English monopoly for trading
in slaves.[6] From October 1673 to December 1674, he was secretary and
then also concurrently treasurer to the English Council for Trade and
Foreign Plantations.[7] Two decades later, from 1696 until ill-health forced
him to relinquish office in 1700, Locke was among the first Commissioners appointed to the English Board of Trade, the main administrative
body which oversaw the commerce and colonies of the Atlantic world.[8]
While in that post, he assured a correspondent in Virginia that '[t]he
flourishing of the Plantations under their due and just regulations [is]
that which I doe and shall always aim at', and he was always as active
in its counsels as his fragile health would permit.[9] His administrative
duties and financial investments over the course of four decades earned
Locke practical experience of English colonial and commercial activity
in North America, from New York to Carolina, in the Caribbean, Ireland
and Africa.[10]

By the time Locke resigned from the Board of Trade in June 1700, he
had become one of the two best-informed observers of the English
Atlantic world of the late seventeenth century: only his rival on the Board
of Trade, the career administrator Sir William Blathwayt, had a more
comprehensive command of English colonial administration by that
time.[11] His service in both private and public colonial administration

[4] Bod. MS Locke c. 30; TNA PRO 30/24/47, 30/24/48; *Shaftesbury Papers* (2000); L. Brown (1933),
     chs. 9–10; Haley (1968), ch. 12; Leng (2011).
[5] HRO, Malmesbury Papers 7M54/232; BL Add. MS 15640, ff. 3r–8v, 9r–15r; Haley (1968), pp. 232–3.
[6] TNA C 66/3136/45, CO 268/1/11 (27 September 1672).
[7] LC, Phillipps MS 8539, pt. 1; Bieber (1925).
[8] TNA CO 391/9, 391/10, 391/11, 391/12, 391/13; Cranston (1957), ch. 25; Kammen (1966); Laslett
     (1969); Ashcraft (1969); Turner (2011).
[9] Locke to James Blair, 16 October 1699, in Locke (1976–), VI, p. 706.
[10] Most of his practical writings relating to colonial matters will appear in Locke (in press).
[11] Murison (2007), pp. 33–4.

had provided him with a more thorough understanding of his country's commerce and colonies than that possessed by any canonical figure in the history of political thought before Edmund Burke. No such figure played as prominent a role in the institutional history of European colonialism before James Mill and John Stuart Mill joined the administration of the East India Company. Moreover, no major political theorist before the nineteenth century so actively applied theory to colonial practice as Locke did by virtue of his involvement with writing the *Fundamental Constitutions* of the Carolina colony. For all these reasons, Locke's colonial interests have been taken to indicate that 'the liberal involvement with the British Empire is broadly coeval with liberalism itself'.[12]

Locke's colonial activities would nonetheless be irrelevant to the interpretation of his political theory if they had left no traces in his major writings. Such traces are especially abundant in the *Two Treatises of Government* and have been sufficient to sustain a well-developed 'colonial' reading of Locke's political theory.[13] The references to '*America*' or to the '*Americans*' (meaning the indigenous peoples of America not the Euro-American settlers) almost all appear in the *Second Treatise*.[14] For example, when 'a *Swiss* and an *Indian*' encounter each other 'in the Woods of *America*' (II. 14) they meet as if in the state of nature. The reader can infer that the Indian's family structure is as loose as his political arrangements: 'in those parts of *America* where when the Husband and Wife part, which happens frequently, the Children are all left to the Mother, follow her, and are wholly under her Care and Provision' (II. 65); 'And if *Josephus Acosta*'s word may be taken … in many parts of *America* there was no Government at all' (II. 102), especially in those parts 'out of the reach of the Conquering Swords, and spreading domination of the two great Empires of *Peru* and *Mexico*' where 'the People of *America* … enjoy'd their own natural freedom' (II. 105). Such peoples have 'no Temptation to enlarge their Possessions of Land, or contest for wider extent of Ground', meaning that 'the *Kings* of the *Indians* in *America*' 'are little more than *Generals of their Armies*' (II. 108). Their medium of exchange, 'the Wampompeke of the *Americans*', would be as valueless to European rulers as 'the Silver Money of *Europe*' would have been formerly to an *American*' (II. 184).

[12] Mehta (1999), p. 4.
[13] See especially Lebovics (1986); Castilla Urbano (1986); Tully (1993); Arneil (1996); Pagden (1998), pp. 42–7; Michael (1998); Ivison (2003); Farr (2009); Turner (2011).
[14] Locke (1988). All references are to this edition by *Treatise* and paragraph number.

The references to America and its inhabitants appear in seven of the eighteen chapters of the *Second Treatise* but more than half of them cluster within a single chapter, Chapter 5, 'Of Property'. The most cursory survey of that chapter's argument reveals two key figures: that of 'the wild *Indian*' who feeds on fruit and venison (II. 26), the same '*Indian*' who, by killing his deer, is endowed with property in it by the law of reason (II. 30), and that of the planter who with his family is heading for 'some in-land, vacant places of *America*' (II. 36). Locke describes the 'several Nations of the *Americans* . . . who are rich in Land, and poor in all the Comforts of Life', whose 'King of a large and fruitful Territory there feeds, lodges, and is clad worse than a day Labourer in *England*' (II. 41). He compares '[a]n Acre of Land that bears here Twenty Bushels of Wheat, and another in *America*, which, with the same Husbandry, would do the like' for their same intrinsic value but differing worth or benefit (II. 43). He remarks the futility of a man's owning 'Ten Thousand, or an Hundred Thousand Acres of excellent *Land*, ready cultivated, and well stocked too with Cattle, in the middle of the in-land Parts of *America*, where he had no hopes of Commerce with other Parts of the World' (II. 48) and draws his famous conclusion that 'in the beginning all the World was *America*, and more so than that is now; for no such thing as *Money* was any where known' (II. 49). All these references from across the whole of the *Second Treatise* refute the contention that 'America belongs only at the margins of [Locke's] main concerns in the *Two Treatises*.'[15]

Locke's *Second Treatise* cannot be reduced to its colonial references nor can its meaning be determined by a colonial reading alone.[16] However, the frequency and prominence of those references still require explanation. James Tully has suggested that 'in arguing for the superiority of commercial agriculture over Native American hunting, trapping and gathering, Locke may also have been arguing for the superiority of English colonization over the French fur-trading empire', but concluded that '[m]ore research on the colonial documents is needed to test this hypothesis'.[17] However, there is little evidence among those documents of Locke's interest in the French fur-trade and none of any comparative treatment of its productivity or legitimacy relative to English colonial models. Richard Tuck has argued instead that Locke's target was even more specific: the Pennsylvania colony which Charles II had chartered to William Penn in 1681. Tuck argues that Pennsylvania 'represented all the things which Locke was attacking in the *Second Treatise*: that is, the

---

[15] Buckle (2001), p. 274.   [16] Ivison (2003), p. 87.   [17] Tully (1993), pp. 165, 166.

absolutism of Penn's frame of government and his treatment of the Indians as the rightful possessors of their land, which even chartered colonists had to buy from them'.[18] In this case, there is some evidence of Locke's concern in the form of his manuscript commentary on Penn's 1682 *Frame of Government* for Pennsylvania. Though Locke did criticise the balance of power between proprietor and assembly in Pennsylvania, he nowhere mentioned Penn's method for acquiring property in land. Moreover, Locke's comments on Penn's frame of government can be dated no earlier than November 1686: that is, four years later than even the latest date (of 1682) that has been suggested for the composition of the *Second Treatise*.[19]

If Locke's references to America in the *Second Treatise* derived from a particular and definable colonial context, then it would be essential to know just when those references made their way into the text of the work. The explanation for those references thus depends in part on the intricate question of the dating of the work as a whole. The *Two Treatises* first appeared in print in late 1689, with a date of 1690 on the title-page, thereby encouraging for almost 300 years the belief that they were composed as a retrospective justification of the Glorious Revolution of 1688–9. Peter Laslett overturned that dating in 1960 with his argument that Locke composed the *Second Treatise* during the Exclusion Crisis in the winter of 1679–80 and then followed it with the *First Treatise* early in 1680.[20] More recent research has generally questioned Laslett's argument that the *Second Treatise* preceded the *First Treatise* and has gradually pushed the date of composition of the *Second Treatise* farther forward into the 1680s.[21] For example, J. R. Milton has argued that Locke began work on the *Second Treatise* late in 1680 or early in 1681, laid it aside after the Earl of Shaftesbury's arrest in July 1681 and then took it up again in February 1682 before completing the manuscript later that year.[22] Richard Tuck has independently confirmed this later dating by his observation that the *Second Treatise* contains Locke's implicit critique of Pufendorf's *De Jure Naturae et Gentium* and *De Officio Hominis et Civis*, works which

---

[18] Tuck (1999), pp. 177–8.
[19] Bod. MS Locke f. 9, ff. 33–7, 38–41, Locke's journal 1686–8, between entries for 8 and 22 November 1686; Ashcraft (1986), pp. 518–20.
[20] Locke (1988), pp. 65, 123–6.
[21] Locke (1989), pp. 49–89; J. Marshall (1994), pp. 222–4 n. 25, 234–58; J. R. Milton (1995); J. Marshall (2006), pp. 50–4.
[22] Milton (1995), p. 389.

Locke only obtained and read in 1681.[23] Milton has further argued that three chapters of the *Second Treatise* (4, 'Of Slavery'; 5, 'Of Property'; and 16, 'Of Conquest') contain biblical citations in a style different from that in the remaining chapters and only known to have been used by Locke relatively late in his career. On this evidence, he concluded that these chapters were composed (or, at least, revised) apart from the rest of the *Second Treatise* and specifically that 'chapter V is an intruder ... either earlier or later than its surroundings'. He decided that it must be earlier precisely because the chapter contains so many allusions to America, which must derive from Locke's interest in Carolina: 'the period of his main involvement was considerably earlier, while he was acting as Secretary to the Lords Proprietors between 1669 and 1675'.[24] This is a defensible inference (albeit one at odds with the logic of the rest of Milton's argument for Chapter 5's later date) only so long as it is assumed that Locke's relationship with Carolina had effectively ended by 1675 and that he did not resume any active involvement with colonial administration until his appointment to the Council of Trade in 1696, long after the composition of the *Two Treatises*.

To accept both the conventional chronology of Locke's colonial activities and even the most expansive range of dates proposed for the composition of the *Two Treatises* is to be left with an explanatory conundrum. The earliest date, of 1679, and the latest, of 1682, proposed for the original composition of the *Two Treatises* both fall squarely within the twenty-one years from 1675 to 1696 when Locke was apparently unconnected with English colonial administration. The frequency of the American references in the *Second Treatise* and their insistent clustering in Chapter 5 would support the argument that there was an elective affinity between liberalism and colonialism as the twin offspring of capitalism and modernity.[25] A more exacting historical account would still remain troubled by the apparent disjuncture between Locke's periods in the service of English colonialism and the moment when he produced one of the founding texts of liberalism. If it were possible to produce evidence that Locke had not ceased to be directly interested in the affairs of Carolina after 1675 and that he continued to be concerned

---

[23] Tuck (1999), p. 168. This *terminus a quo* of 1681 would also fit with Locke's citation of Robert Knox's 'late Relation of *Ceylon*' (II. 92), which he bought on 29 August 1681: Locke (1988), pp. 55, 327 n. 12; Knox (1680).

[24] J. R. Milton (1995), pp. 372–4.   [25] Mishra (2002).

about the government and prospects of the colony, not only after 1679
but even as late as 1682, then it might also be possible to confirm the
persistent suspicion that there must have been some urgent reason for
Locke to have elaborated the American example as the basis for the
argument of Chapter 5 of the *Second Treatise*. The next section of this
chapter will offer just such evidence of this continued colonial activity,
while its concluding section will investigate some interpretive implications of the novel contextualisation of the *Second Treatise* (in particular,
of Chapter 5) that this evidence makes possible.

At least since the early eighteenth century, the *Fundamental Constitutions
of Carolina* (1669) have been central to understanding the relationship
between Locke's political theory and his colonial interests.[26] To Locke's
admirers, his presumed authorship of a constitution that granted uniquely
broad religious toleration was a source of genuine pride. Thus Voltaire
advised: 'Cast your eyes over the other hemisphere, behold Carolina,
of which the wise Locke was the legislator.'[27] Locke's hand in the *Fundamental Constitutions* was also taken to vindicate the role of theory in
the world of governmental practice: after all, who better than such a
'great philosopher' to design a new commonwealth?[28] Locke's enemies
were not quite so sanguine. The *Fundamental Constitutions* assumed the
existence of slavery and affirmed the absolute powers of life and death
of slave-holders. They also erected the first hereditary nobility on
North American soil. What worse commonwealth for a philosopher to
have designed than this anti-democratic slave society dominated by a
'tyrannical Aristocracy'?[29]

The *Fundamental Constitutions* were drafted initially in 1669 during
the period of Locke's secretaryship to the Lords Proprietors of Carolina.
The secretaryship was an executive as well as administrative position; this
fact, combined with Locke's closeness to Anthony Ashley Cooper, the
Proprietor most intimately associated with the *Fundamental Constitutions*,
makes it inconceivable that he would not have played at the very least a

[26] Most recently in Kidder (1965); McGuinness (1989); Hallmark (1998); Hsueh (2010), pp. 55–82.
[27] 'Jetez les yeux sur l'autre hémisphère, voyez le Caroline, dont le sage Locke fut le législateur':
Voltaire (2000), p. 152.
[28] Locke (1720), sigs. A3r–A4v; Lee (1764), p. 28; Butel-Dumont (1755), p. 279; Hewatt (1779), I, p. 44
(quoted).
[29] Defoe (1705), p. 8; Tucker (1783), p. 92 (quoted); John Adams, *Defence of the Constitutions of
Government of the United States of America* (1788), in Adams (1850–6), IV, pp. 463–4; Boucher
(1797), p. 41.

major supervisory role in their drafting.[30] Though frequently revised and just as often ignored by the settlers, the *Fundamental Constitutions* did formally provide the frame of government for the colony until they were overthrown by the settlers forty years after they had first been promulgated.[31] They were repeatedly published in Locke's lifetime, both in manuscript copies for the settlers and in a variety of printed versions, from deluxe large-paper printings (presumably for the Proprietors) to abbreviated summaries designed to encourage emigrants.[32] Indeed, the *Fundamental Constitutions* were the only printed work with which Locke's name could be associated before the *annus mirabilis* of 1689–90, when both the *Essay Concerning Human Understanding* and the *Two Treatises of Government* first appeared in print. After Locke's death, the *Fundamental Constitutions* appeared in the first posthumous collection of his fugitive writings; they have remained among his miscellaneous works ever since.[33] The attribution of the *Fundamental Constitutions* to Locke earned him the distinction of having created the constitution for an actually existing society, an honour shared alone among post-classical political philosophers with Jean-Jacques Rousseau, author of the unrealised constitutional project for Corsica (1765) and the *Considérations sur le gouvernement de Pologne* (1772).[34]

Generations of scholars have mistakenly believed the manuscript of the *Fundamental Constitutions* (21 July 1669) found among Shaftesbury's papers to be in Locke's own hand. Apart from numerous revisions throughout the document, only the first two paragraphs were written by Locke.[35] This fact in itself would not argue against his composition of the whole text: it seems to have been his practice, at least later in his career, to begin a manuscript in his own hand before passing the rest to an amanuensis for transcription.[36] None of the surviving printed copies of the *Fundamental Constitutions* attributes them to Locke; indeed, the

---

[30] Haley (1968), pp. 242–8; J. R. Milton (1990); P. Milton (2007b), pp. 260–5.

[31] Roper (2004), pp. 99–101; Moore (1991).

[32] *Fundamental Constitutions* ([1672?]), Houghton Library, Harvard University, call-number *f EC65 L7934 670f, is a unique large-paper copy; *Carolina Described* (1684), pp. 12–16, 33–56, summarises and reprints the *Fundamental Constitutions* of 12 January 1682.

[33] Locke (1720), pp. 1–53; Locke (1823), x, pp. 175–99; Locke (1989), pp. 210–32; Locke (1997), pp. 160–81.

[34] Rousseau (2005); Putterman (2010), pp. 122–45.   [35] TNA PRO 30/24/47/3.

[36] P. Long (1959), p. ix; for example, 'Of seeing all thing [*sic*] in God' (1693); 'Des Cartes's proof of a god from the Idea of necessary existence examined' (1696); 'Some of the Cheif Greivances of the present Constitution of Virginia with an Essay towards the Remedies thereof' (1697); 'Queries to be put to Colonel Henry Hartwell or any other discreet person that knows the Constitution of Virginia' (1697), Bod. MSS Locke d. 3, f. 1; c. 28, f. 119; e. 9, ff. 1, 39.

only copy with any ascription of authorship accords them to the Earl of
Shaftesbury.[37] Locke's contribution was nonetheless apparently extensive
enough to justify the elevation in April 1671 of this country attorney's
son to the hereditary noble rank of landgrave of Carolina, in recognition
of 'his great prudence, learning and industry both in settling the form
of government and in placing colonies on the Ashley River' (*magna sua
prudentia, eruditione et industria tam in stabilienda regiminis forma, quam
in Coloniis ad Flumen Ashleium collocandis*), as his landgrave patent put
it.[38] This tribute failed to define his role precisely but at least it derived
from a moment close to the initial drafting of the *Fundamental Constitutions* in 1669 and had the endorsement of those who had most reason
to know and to value Locke's achievement, the Carolina Proprietors
themselves.[39] It also gave him a larger claim to land in the Americas than
that possessed by any other comparable thinker: 48,000 acres of territory
in Carolina, which he never took up, but which he also never repudiated.

Locke never explicitly acknowledged responsibility for the composition of the *Fundamental Constitutions* but that reticence is not in itself
evidence against his involvement. Locke's reluctance to admit to the
authorship of any of his major works apart from the *Essay* is as notorious
as his solemn protest in 1684 'that I am not the author, not only of any
libell, but not of any pamphlet or treatise whatsoever in print good bad
or indifferent'.[40] In 1673, the Proprietor Sir Peter Colleton credited
Locke with 'that excellent forme of Government in the composure
of which you had soe great a hand' and later in the 1670s two of Locke's
French correspondents wrote to him of 'vos constitutions' and 'vos
loix'.[41] Locke neither confirmed nor denied these statements which, in
themselves, provided no evidence of the nature of his role in framing the
Fundamental Constitutions. Yet if Locke never claimed credit for the
Fundamental Constitutions, neither did he ever attempt to distance himself from their provisions *tout court*. He does seem to have disassociated
himself particularly from the provision for an Anglican establishment
which first appeared in the 1670 revision of the *Fundamental*

---

[37] *Fundamental Constitutions* ([1672?]); Bod. Ashmole F4 (42): 'made by Anth: Earle of Shaftesbury'.
[38] Bod. MS Locke b. 5/9 (another copy in SCDA, Recital of Grants, AD120, pt. II (15 November
1682), f. 18). Comparison with other contemporary landgrave patents – e.g., for James Colleton
(16 March 1671), John Yeamans (5 April 1671) and Sir Edmund Andros (3 April 1672) – shows that
this form of words was unique to Locke's grant.
[39] Compare the list of landgrave patents in TNA CO 5/286, f. 42v.
[40] John Locke to Thomas Herbert, Earl of Pembroke, 28 November 1684, in Locke (1976–), II, p. 664.
[41] Sir Peter Colleton to Locke, October 1673; Nicholas Toinard to Locke, 2 July 1679; Henri Justel to
Locke, 17 September 1679, in Locke (1976–), I, p. 395, II, pp. 47, 105.

Constitutions; this might be taken to indicate that he saw no compelling reason to repudiate any of the *Constitutions'* other articles.[42]

The *Constitutions* apportioned land and provided the legal and institutional framework for the infant colony. Plantation by English migrants had languished in the first five years under the Proprietors' first grant of 1663 and an initial settlement on the Cape Fear River (in present-day North Carolina) had collapsed by 1668. The 1669 *Constitutions* signalled a fresh start to the Proprietors' plans. They were explicitly designed to 'avoid erecting a numerous Democracy' and placed all authority perpetually in the hands of 'the true and absolute Lords and Proprietors of the province'.[43] Beneath them would be the hereditary nobility composed of landgraves and cassiques who would have jurisdictional authority over a further hereditary class of perpetual serfs or leet men. 'Thus was a cast [*sic*] to be formed among the Whites – a constitution worthy of Hindoo superstition', complained a defender of Locke in 1807 who acknowledged such a flaw in the *Fundamental Constitutions* to be 'very unworthy of the author of the "Treatises of Government".'[44]

The Proprietors owned one-fifth of the land in Carolina; the nobility, a further fifth. The rest was set aside for the freemen of Carolina who would be barred from residence and landholding if they did 'not acknowledge a God and that God is publickly and solemnly to be worshiped'. That minimal qualification for residence was also the maximal qualification for religious toleration, in order that 'heathens, Jews and other dissenters from the purity of Christian Religion may not be scared and kept at a distance'. Grace did not confer dominion any more than theism alone could justify possession: 'the Natives of that place ... are utterly strangers to Christianity whose Idollatry Ignorance or mistake gives us noe right to expell or use them ill'. Religious toleration would also be extended to slaves, 'yet noe slave shall hereby be exempted from that civill dominion his Master hath over him but in all other things in the same state and condicion he was in before'. Therefore (as the *Fundamental Constitutions'* most notorious article put it): 'Every Freeman of Carolina shall have absolute power and Authority over his Negro slaves of what opinion or Religion soever.'[45] The presence of this article in the *Fundamental Constitutions* only confirmed the suspicion of Locke's later detractors that 'the most eminent Republican Writers, such as LOCKE, FLETCHER of

---

[42] Locke (1720), p. 42.   [43] TNA, PRO 30/24/47/3, f. 1, printed in Locke (1997), p. 162.
[44] [J. T. Rutt,] 'Defence of Locke Against Lord Eldon' (9 February 1807), in Goldie (1999), IV, p. 391.
[45] TNA, PRO 30/24/47/3, ff. 58r, 59r–60r, 58r–59r, 65r, 66r, ptd. in Locke (1997), pp. 177, 178, 179–80.

Saltown, and ROUSSEAU himself, pretend to justify the making Slaves of others, whilst they are pleading so warmly for Liberty for themselves'.[46]

The apparent biographical distance between the Locke of the *Fundamental Constitutions* and the Locke of the *Two Treatises* came as something of a relief to Locke's defenders. Whatever the degree of his involvement in the composition of the *Fundamental Constitutions* – whether as a political philosopher cutting his teeth on the creation of a political society *de novo*, or simply as a hired hand taking dictation from his master – Locke could not be entirely exculpated from responsibility for their harsher and more illiberal provisions. If 'Locke's dealings with Carolina show that he was a social conservative in the 1670s', how can this be reconciled with the allegedly more egalitarian, democratic, liberal Locke of the 1680s found in the *Two Treatises of Government*?[47] In 1776, Josiah Tucker (a distinctly hostile witness) ventriloquised one defensive answer to this question: '"Mr. LOCKE was then a young Man, as appears by the Date of this Code of Laws [1669] And as he lived under the Reign of a *Tyrannical* STUART [Charles II] it is no Wonder, that he should be a little tainted with the Vices of the Times".'[48] Any disquiet about the relationship between the supposedly 'conservative' Locke of the 1660s and 1670s and the more 'liberal' Locke of the 1680s and 1690s could thus be laid to rest by appealing to the chronological disjuncture between Locke the dependent client of Shaftesbury and Locke the independent philosopher.

The evidence of Locke's formal activities on behalf of the Carolina Proprietors does not greatly narrow that gap. A set of temporary laws for Carolina supplementary to the *Fundamental Constitutions* – including a notable provision against the enslavement of Indians – exists in Locke's handwriting from December 1671.[49] He continued to act as secretary to the Proprietors until he left England for France in November 1675, at which point he is usually assumed to have effectively resigned his position and thus to have terminated his direct involvement with the affairs of the colony. However, such an assumption not only makes the American references in the *Second Treatise* harder to explain; it also overlooks much evidence that Locke's interest in the prospects for Carolina generally, and his attachment to the provisions of the

---

[46] Tucker (1781), p. 168.   [47] Wootton (1992), p. 79 (quoted), pp. 82–7.
[48] Tucker (1776), p. 104; compare [Rutt,] 'Defence of Locke Against Lord Eldon', in Goldie (1999), IV, p. 393. Locke was thirty-seven in 1669 and thus middle-aged by the standards of his time.
[49] TNA, CO 5/286, f. 41r, printed in Rivers (1856), p. 353; Hinshelwood (in press).

Fundamental Constitutions specifically, lasted well beyond the formal conclusion of his secretaryship to the Proprietors in 1675.

Locke's private correspondence and notebooks belie the impression that his initial period of colonial activity was discontinuous with the period of his mature philosophy. He sought copies of the *Fundamental Constitutions* on three occasions, once in the summer of 1674 and twice in the autumn of 1677.[50] Many of the running notes on social discipline, marriage law and settlement patterns which Locke entitled 'Atlantis' (1676–9) referred explicitly or implicitly to Carolina.[51] In 1679–81, he corresponded regularly with his French friends Nicholas Toinard and Henri Justel regarding the details of the *Fundamental Constitutions*, the future of 'une fort bonne isle . . . qu'on ma fait lhoneur d'appeller de mon nom' (that is, Locke Island, now Edisto Island, in present-day South Carolina) and his supposed plans to flee a corrupt England for his Carolinian utopia or even the French island of Réunion.[52] In 1681, he recorded his possession in Oxford of two copies of the *Fundamental Constitutions*; he left at least three copies with James Tyrrell when he fled to Holland in 1683 (including one sealed by the Proprietors); an unbound copy was among a list of his books made in June 1699; he was promising to show a copy to Anthony Collins in March 1704; and he still possessed two copies, one of which may have been the copy he left to Francis Cudworth Masham, at his death in 1704.[53] Locke's interest in the *Fundamental Constitutions* was thus enduring, albeit intermittent. In the absence of other evidence, it would not indicate any lasting attachment to their provisions or even commitment to the colony's prospects. For that, other evidence of Locke's continuing involvement with the Carolina colony and its *Fundamental Constitutions*, up to and even beyond the time when he can be presumed to have first drafted the *Two Treatises*, would be necessary.

There is circumstantial evidence of Locke's concern for the future of Carolina during his travels in France after 1675.[54] One of the two longest

---

[50] TNA, CO 5/286, f. 125v, 29 July 1674: 'Memd send Mr Locke into the Country a Coppy of the F. Constitutions'; Thomas Stringer to Locke, 7 September 1677; Stringer to Locke, 5 October 1677, in Locke (1976–), I, pp. 516, 518.

[51] John Locke, 'Atlantis' (1676–9), in Locke (1997), pp. 253–9; de Marchi (1955); Bellatalla (1983).

[52] Locke (1976–), I, p. 590, II, pp. 19, 27, 32 (quoted), 34, 40, 47, 68, 95, 105, 132, 141, 147, 441, 444; Bod. MS Locke f. 28, f. 19.

[53] Bod. MS Locke f. 5, f. 93; MS Locke c. 25, f. 31r; MS Locke f. 10, f. 98; MS Locke b. 2, f. 124; MS Locke f. 17, f. 46r; MS Locke b. 2, f. 172v; Locke to Anthony Collins, 6, 9, 13 March 1704, in Locke (1976–), VIII, pp. 232, 234, 238; Bod. MS Locke c. 35, f. 49v.

[54] On Locke's French travels, see especially Locke (1953); Locke (2005).

manuscripts he produced during these years was the 'Observations on Wine, Olives, Fruit and Silk' (1 February 1680).[55] It has attracted little commentary and has remained largely inassimilable to the traditional picture of Locke's intellectual biography.[56] Yet, if seen as a piece of 'agricultural espionage' undertaken on Shaftesbury's behalf with the needs of the Carolina colony in mind, the 'Observations' comes into much clearer focus.[57] Throughout his journeys in France, Locke took special notice of viticulture, arboriculture and sericulture. He meticulously noted every variety of grape, olive and fig, for example, and lengthily questioned his informants about every aspect of wine, silk and olive-oil production. His notebooks for 1677–8 reveal that these were not disinterested inquiries but instead concerned whatever might be 'fit', 'good' or 'usefull in Carolina'.[58] The 'Observations' should thus be read as a sketch for a practical economic future for Carolina in the business of Mediterranean import-substitution growing fruit and producing wine, silk and olive-oil. Shaftesbury received Locke's manuscript in February 1680 'with great joy' and 'perused it greedily'.[59] It was therefore no coincidence that the party of French Huguenots who reached the colony in April 1680 were 'many of them skilfull & practiced in the manufacture of Wines, Silkes and Oyles'.[60] Locke had clearly been acting on Shaftesbury's instructions during his travels in France and was still contributing to the material prospects of the colony when he presented the 'Observations' to his patron.

The 1680 'Observations' provide evidence that Locke was still thinking practically about the prospects for Carolina after the very earliest date, of 1679, that has been proposed for the composition of the *First Treatise* and that he was doing so in his capacity as a client, if not still formally a servant, of the Earl of Shaftesbury. At the very least, the 'Observations' show that agrarian improvement not only provided an enduring common interest between Locke and Shaftesbury but also part of the explanatory context for the *Two Treatises*.[61] However, this manuscript is not enough in

---

[55] TNA, PRO 30/24/47/35; Locke (1766); Locke (1823), x, pp. 323–56. Locke's other major (and still unpublished) work of these years was Bod. MS Locke c. 34, transcribed in Stanton (2003), II.

[56] The main exception is a series of studies by Tim Unwin: Unwin (1998); Unwin (2000); Unwin (2001).

[57] Compare Unwin (1998), pp. 143–5, 150, with the account in Unwin (2001), pp. 83–4.

[58] Bod. MS Locke f. 15, ff. 26, 42, 91; Woolhouse (2007), pp. 122–3.

[59] John Hoskins to Locke, 5 February 1680, in Locke (1976–), II, p. 154; Gray and Thompson (1941), I, pp. 52–4, 184–5, 188–90.

[60] Childs (1942); Committee of Trade and Plantations, 20 May 1679, printed in Rivers (1856), p. 392; Haley (1968), p. 533.

[61] Wood (1984), pp. 21–71.

itself to explain why America should have been on Locke's mind when he came to compose the *Second Treatise*. After all, wines, silks and oils are not prominent among the products alluded to in 'Of Property'. Many of those products were colonial not domestic, as when Locke compared 'an Acre of Land planted with Tobacco, or Sugar, sown with Wheat or Barley; and an Acre of the same Land lying in common' (II. 40). Likewise, the prominence of venison in the diet of the 'wild *Indian*' (II. 26, 30) suggests that deer were the main example of profitable local game, indicating that Carolina – where the deerskin trade was a commercial staple peculiar to Anglo-Indian commerce in North America – was Locke's specific example when writing Chapter 5, 'Of Property'.

The conventional chronology of Locke's involvement with Shaftesbury and with the Carolina colony gives no grounds to explain why Carolina should have been on his mind when composing the *Two Treatises*. Richard Ashcraft argued instead that the explanatory context that links Locke with Shaftesbury at this point was not Carolina but rather the Rye House Plot. Ashcraft's case for Locke's involvement in Shaftesbury's insurrectionary plans, especially in the summer of 1682, was necessarily inferential and speculative.[62] However, there is more reliable evidence from just the same period that ties Locke to Shaftesbury via Carolina and the *Fundamental Constitutions* rather than treason and assassination-plots. After Shaftesbury had been released from imprisonment in the Tower of London in 1681, his major publicly expressed concern was the future of Carolina and specifically the revision of the *Fundamental Constitutions* to attract potential immigrants, particularly French Huguenots and Scottish dissenters.[63] Ashcraft thought that those Scottish Whigs who associated with Shaftesbury in 1682 were engaged in 'a pretense of consulting about . . . colonial interests in Carolina' as a cover for Shaftesbury's rebellious designs in Scotland. In fact, they were seriously planning emigration and demanded changes to the *Fundamental Constitutions* as well as other political concessions to make it possible.[64] The success of those concessions helps to explain the ethnographic precision in Locke's only reference to Carolina anywhere in his published works (save for the *Fundamental Constitutions* themselves): 'in Peopling of *Carolina*, the *English*, *French*, *Scotch*, and *Welch* that are there, Plant

[62] Ashcraft (1986), pp. 354–5, 372; P. Milton (2000), pp. 647–68; P. Milton (2007a).
[63] Haley (1968), pp. 705–7; Sirmans (1966), pp. 35–43.
[64] Ashcraft (1986), p. 354; *Letters Illustrative of Public Affairs* (1851), pp. 58–60; Karsten (1975–6); Fryer (1998); Roper (2004), pp. 72–82.

themselves together, and by them the Country is divided *in their Lands after their Tongues, after their Families, after their Nations*' (I. 144).[65]

In January 1682, the Proprietors revised the *Fundamental Constitutions* for the first time in ten years and subsequently issued a printed version.[66] In March 1682, they began an energetic new pamphlet campaign on behalf of the colony, and Shaftesbury himself – despite old age and illness – reportedly attended the Carolina coffee-house in London to respond to emigrants' queries.[67] The campaign was so vigorous that it became the subject of anti-Whig satire by John Dryden later that year:

> Since faction ebbs, and rogues grow out of fashion,
> Their penny-scribes take care t'inform the nation
> How well men thrive in this or that plantation;
> How Pennsylvania's air agrees with Quakers,
> And Carolina's with Associators:
> Both e'en too good for madmen and for traitors.[68]

In early May 1682, the Proprietors revised the *Fundamental Constitutions* 'for the greater Liberty Security & quiet of the people' by proposing new measures to appoint the Palatine and members of the Grand Council, to allow both the Grand Council and grand juries to make proposals to the Carolina Parliament and (as a sop to the Scots) to release new settlers from their duty to pay rents to the Proprietors.[69] And some time between late May and mid-August 1682, they overhauled the *Fundamental Constitutions* yet again, this time much more thoroughly.[70]

Where was John Locke during this flurry of renewed activity on behalf of Carolina? He left Oxford for London on 30 May 1682 and did not leave London again until 8 August; he spent the weeks between at Thanet House, Shaftesbury's London residence.[71] He could not therefore have been present for the first review of the *Fundamental Constitutions* which took place three weeks before his arrival; but he would have been on hand

[65] This passage must date from after the first Scots settlement in 1684; however, no sizeable Welsh community in Carolina is recorded before the early eighteenth century: Sirmans (1966), p. 168.
[66] *Fundamental Constitutions* ([1682]).
[67] *The True Protestant Mercury*, 15–18 March 1682, 18–22 March 1682; R. F. (1682); *True Description* ([1682]); Wilson (1682).
[68] Dryden, 'Prologue to the King and Queen' (1682), in *Poems on Affairs of State* (1968), pp. 372–3. Dryden wrote the prologue between 14 May and 16 November 1682: see headnote, ibid., p. 372.
[69] TNA, CO 5/286, ff. 91v–92v (10 May 1682), printed in Rivers (1856), pp. 395–6. No copy of the *Constitutions* incorporating these changes seems to have survived.
[70] TNA, PRO 30/24/48, ff. 335–51, provides a detailed list of the changes from the 'Third' *Constitutions* (12 January 1682) to the 'Fourth' *Constitutions* (17 August 1682), TNA, CO 5/287, ff. 24–32.
[71] Bod. MS Locke f. 6, ff. 63, 83.

for consultation during the second revision which produced a new version of the *Fundamental Constitutions* dated 17 August 1682, nine days after he left London. In the absence of any other evidence, Locke's part in the revision of the *Fundamental Constitutions* would remain as circumstantial and speculative as the grounds for believing he was immersed in Shaftesbury's plans for insurgency. Very little of Locke's correspondence survives from the summer of 1682 (fuelling the suspicion that it may have contained evidence of his complicity with Shaftesbury's alleged insurrections which had to be destroyed). What little does survive suggests no interest in Carolina, nor can any such interest be detected in his notebook for the same period.

The previous autumn, in September 1681, Locke's French friend Nicholas Toinard had alerted him to 'many things embarrassing and quite contrary to the tranquility that subordinates look for in those kinds of country' in the *Fundamental Constitutions* and urging him to 'consider seriously the reform of the laws of Carolina'.[72] Although Toinard seems to have believed that Locke still had influence with the Proprietors, the letter was only the latest in a lighthearted exchange he and Locke had been conducting about their own fantastical plans to flee Europe for Carolina. The revision of the *Fundamental Constitutions* was a task that Locke could not have undertaken at his own initiative. However, his presence in Shaftesbury's household over the summer of 1682 provided him with the opportunity to take part in just such a reform of the Carolina laws.

The survival of the printed copy of the January 1682 'Third' *Fundamental Constitutions* that was used to draw up revisions for the 'Fourth' *Fundamental Constitutions* in August 1682 reveals Locke at work, for the first time since 1671, refining the provisions of the frame of government for Carolina.[73] Emendations fill the margins, excisions score through the printed pages, and manuscript sheets bound into the book extend the sprawling discussions and contain further basic revisions. Three different people added their remarks and changes. Shaftesbury was not among them, presumably because he was sick with the diseases that would kill him little more than six months later in January 1683: in July 1682, he had mortgaged his lands in England and Carolina to his

---

[72] Nicholas Toinard to Locke, 24 September 1681 ('nous [i.e., Toinard and Henri Justel] avons trouvé bien des choses embarassantes, et tres contraires à la tranquillité que des subalternes cherchent dans ces sortes de païs'), Toinard to Locke, 24 September 1681 ('Songez serieusement à la reformation des loix de la K.'), in Locke (1976–), II, pp. 441, 444.

[73] *Fundamental Constitutions* (1682), New York Public Library, call-number *KC + 1682.

bankers, presumably to escape confiscation but perhaps also as an intimation of mortality.[74] Instead, the bulk of the revisions are in the formal hand of an unknown writer: neither one of the Proprietors, nor a prominent member of Shaftesbury's household, nor a known correspondent of Locke. The other two writers are more readily identifiable. One was the Proprietor Sir Peter Colleton, a former Whig member of Parliament, Exclusionist and absentee owner of one of the largest slave-plantations on Barbados. He had been associated with Carolina, and with Shaftesbury, since he had joined the Proprietors in 1667 and had been present at the time of the initial composition of the *Fundamental Constitutions* in 1669. He had also been closely associated with Locke when they had attended meetings of the Proprietors together from 1669 to 1672. Colleton and Locke corresponded regularly and intimately until Shaftesbury's fall from grace with Charles II in 1674 and it had been Colleton in 1673 who had praised 'that excellent forme of Government in the composure of which [Locke] had soe great a hand'.[75] It need come as no surprise, then, that the third writer who had a hand in revising the *Fundamental Constitutions* during the summer of 1682 was John Locke.[76]

Locke, Colleton and their companion seem to have scrutinised every provision of the January 1682 *Fundamental Constitutions* before amending or replacing more than a quarter of the existing articles. Locke then renumbered them all to reflect the plan of revision. Locke's and Colleton's interventions were roughly equal in extent though not quite in intent: Colleton queried many of the changes but Locke was more decisive. For example, when Colleton queried whether turning out the Proprietors' deputies in Carolina for misdemeanours might not encourage the Proprietors back in England to 'make them surrender the government to the crown', Locke laid his fears to rest: 'Agreed that the Proprietors Deputys are not to be turned out.' He provided for the Palatine's choice of any landgrave or cassique to be his deputy. He proposed secret balloting in the Grand Council, a minimum number of members (sixty) who had to be present in Parliament for any sentence or judgment to be passed against anyone and a 'box' out of which a ten-year-old child would draw lots to determine jury-duty.

---

[74] Haley (1968), p. 725.
[75] Buchanan (1989), chs. 1–6; Henning (1983), II, p. 106, *s.v.*, 'Colleton, Sir Peter'.
[76] The NYPL card-catalogue; Powell (1964), p. 94; and Lesser (1995), p. 28, all note the presence of Locke's hand but without further investigation.

He also provided revision of the supposedly 'sacred and unalterable' *Fundamental Constitutions* whenever 'the variety of human affairs' demanded it.[77]

Locke was clearly an equal partner in the discussions around the revision of the *Fundamental Constitutions*. The degree of detail to which he descended in considering legal and parliamentary procedures (including prorogation and adjournment, those critical questions during the Exclusion Crisis) demonstrates that he remained an interested party and not merely a hired hand: Locke was, after all, still a landgrave of Carolina, as he had been for more than a decade, since April 1671. His contributions were also evidently taken seriously, for all made their way into the revised 'Fourth' *Fundamental Constitutions* of August 1682 which remained in force until their fifth and final revision of 1698. It is also possible that he retained the very copy of the 'Third' *Constitutions* containing the 1682 revisions: in 1686, a friend in the West Country wrote to Locke concerning a 'copy of Carolina Laws with marginall notes of your hand and also some leaves put in of your handwriteing' which Locke spent six months trying to recover.[78] Once again, his solicitude for the *Constitutions* was evident: as well it might have been, because he seems to have been the only person (apart from Sir Peter Colleton) who had responsibility for them both in 1669 and in 1682.

The discovery of Locke's role in the 1682 revision of the *Fundamental Constitutions of Carolina* goes a long way towards explaining the presence and the prominence of the American examples in the *Second Treatise*, especially in Chapter 5. There is no longer any need to invoke the French fur-trade or the frame of government for Pennsylvania to support historically the 'colonial' reading of Chapter 5. Instead, Carolina, the colony with which Locke had been most closely and continuously associated, can be shown to have been among his identifiable political concerns in the summer of 1682. This fact would be consistent with the evidence of Locke's reading, which suggests a date of 1681 at the earliest for large parts of the *Second Treatise*. It would also be consistent with the unconscious evidence offered by Locke's practices of biblical citation. It would also corroborate the speculation that Locke was still working on the

---

[77] *Fundamental Constitutions* (1682), pp. 11, 22, ff. 1v, 2v, 3r, 3v; Locke amended articles 14, 34, 39, 40, 52, 59, 67, 70, 73, 75, 116 and 120 in this copy.
[78] David Thomas to Locke, 25 November 1686, Thomas to Locke, 26 December 1686, note on letter from Edward Clarke, 25 April 1687, in Locke (1976–), III, pp. 74, 90, 166; Mary Clarke to Edward Clarke, 30 April 1687, SRO, Sanford (Clarke) Papers.

Second Treatise that summer, and in particular that 'Of Property' was one of the last sections of the work that he drafted.

Further evidence for the independent composition of Chapter 5 comes from Locke's correspondence regarding manuscripts he had left in England before leaving for Holland in the autumn of 1683. Three years later, in a coded letter to his relative in Somerset, Edward Clarke, Locke expressed particular concern about three manuscripts contained in a 'red trunk'. Locke advised Clarke that he would 'finde in the least parcel marked 2. if he examine it, nuts, acorns, shineing pebles ambergris and such other things of natures production as she her self offers to humane use'. 'In an other bigger parcel (carying the figure 1. as I remember)', Clarke would 'finde things relateing to the animal Kingdome as it is divided in the begining of Gen: into the three great provinces viz. Fishes of the sea fouls of the air and beast cattle and creepeing things that creepe upon the earth'. The third and 'bigest parcell made up in long bundle is all of artificiall things more exalted and refined into spiritality [*sic*] by art'. Locke warned Clarke that the various parcels were 'trifles some whereof are not very safe to be medled with' and urged him not to 'keepe them altogeather unseparated in the terrible posture they are now' but to order them according to specific instructions Locke had earlier given to him.[79]

These three manuscripts can be tentatively identified with works Locke can be presumed to have completed before the end of 1683. The largest 'bundle' has usually been taken to be the manuscript of the 'Critical Notes' on Stillingfleet (1681).[80] The second largest, which carried 'the figure 1.' and dealt with 'the animal Kingdome as it is divided in the begining of Gen:' would seem to refer to the *First Treatise* alone, with its refutation of Filmer's scriptural arguments for Adam's primal dominion over the brute creation (I. 16, quoting Genesis 1:26). The alleged contents of the smallest parcel – 'nuts, acorns, shineing pebles ambergris and such other things of natures production as she her self offers to humane use' – all appear in Chapter 5 of the *Second Treatise*, and they appear together only in that chapter: nuts (II. 46); acorns (II. 28, 31, 42, 46); 'a sparkling Pebble' (II. 46); ambergris (II. 30); and 'the Fruits ... and Beasts ... produced by the spontaneous hand of Nature ... for the use of men' (II. 26).[81] It seems

---

[79] Locke to Edward Clarke, 26 March 1685, in Locke (1976–), II, pp. 708–9.
[80] Locke (1976–), II, p. 709 n. 1.
[81] The only other commentator to have noticed this passage seems to have been Ashcraft (1986), p. 463 n. 221.

likely, then, that this parcel contained a relatively short free-standing manuscript treating property and its acquistion that can be substantially identified with what we now know as Chapter 5, 'Of Property'.

This evidence might confirm the suspicion that Chapter 5 was an intruder composed independently of the rest of the *Second Treatise* and then inserted into the text at a late stage in its cumulative composition.[82] The subject of Chapter 5 is conspicuously different from what comes before in Chapter 4 ('Of Slavery') and after in Chapter 6 ('Of Paternal Power'). Those two chapters both concern different forms of power and authority, whether of masters or parents, and the corresponding varieties of liberty and equality. Read sequentially, they form a seamless discussion of forms of non-political authority. By contrast, the language of power and authority, liberty and equality, is strikingly absent from Chapter 5, whose key terms are instead 'labour', 'industry' and 'property.' This discontinuity in vocabulary suggests that 'Of Property' was composed independently and that Locke inserted it where he had opened a seam in an already existing argument.[83] The evidence of textual discontinuity also corresponds with a crucial shift in Locke's theory of the acquisition of property. As late as 1677–8, Locke had offered a broadly Grotian account of the process by which the primal positive community in the world had given way to the regime of exclusive private property. Locke argued that that process was contractual and that it was designed to prevent a state of anarchic competition for resources:

Men therefor must either enjoy all things in common or by compact determine their rights[.] if all things be left in common want rapine and force will unavoidably follow in which state, as is evident happynesse cannot be had which cannot consist without plenty and security. To avoid this estate compact must determin peoples rights.[84]

Such a contractual account of the origins of property could only refer to the agreements made between parties equally capable of entering into compacts with each other.

The 'colonial' reading of the *Second Treatise* has established that Locke's argument in Chapter 5 addressed both American and English contexts. In the seventeenth-century context of relations between Native Americans and Anglo-Americans, the incomers did not always recognise

---

[82] As suggested independently by Ashcraft (1986), p. 463 n. 221; J. R. Milton (1995), p. 372.
[83] Compare J. H. Hexter's classic account of Thomas More 'open[ing] a seam' to insert the 'Dialogue of Counsel' into the text of *Utopia*: Hexter (1952), pp. 18–21.
[84] Bod. MS Locke c. 28, f. 140, printed in Locke (1997), p. 268; Tuck (1979), pp. 168–9.

the indigenes' equal capacity with Europeans to determine rights by compact. For example, the *Fundamental Constitutions* (§ 112) expressly banned settlers in Carolina from holding or claiming any land by 'purchase or gift' from the natives, a clear sign that contracts there could only hold among Anglo-Americans and not between Anglo-Americans and Native Americans.[85]

The presence of an argument from contract in the account of property in the *Second Treatise* would therefore have been an indication that Locke intended that account either for domestic purposes alone, or to govern relations between subjects of the English Crown. No such argument is to be found in the *Second Treatise*; instead, Locke contends that 'God gave the World to Men in Common; but ... it cannot be supposed he meant it should always remain common and uncultivated' (II. 34).

This argument from divine command to cultivate those '*great Tracts*' of unappropriated land became the classic theoretical expression of the agriculturalist argument for European *dominium* over American land. Precisely that argument underlay the rights claimed by the Proprietors over the land of Carolina, according to the terms of their grants from the English Crown. The original 1629 grant had called Carolina a region '*hitherto untilled* ... But in some parts of it inhabited by certain Barbarous men', and this description had been reaffirmed in Charles II's grant to the Lords Proprietors in 1663 which had charged the Lords Proprietors 'to Transport and make an ample Colony of our Subjects ... unto a certain Country ... in the parts of AMERICA *not yet cultivated or planted*, and only inhabited by some barbarous People who have no knowledge of Almighty God'.[86] The agriculturalist argument was the best justification that could be given for dispossession after arguments from conquest and from religion had been gradually abandoned.[87] As the English learned from the Spanish, the argument from conquest could only justify *imperium* over the native peoples but not *dominium* over American land. Nor could Native American unbelief alone provide a justification for dominion. As we have seen, in 1669 the authors of the *Fundamental Constitutions* had specified that 'Idolatry Ignorance or mistake gives us noe right to expell or use [the Natives of Carolina] ill', and that article remained in all later versions of the *Fundamental Constitutions*. Locke himself later upheld

---

[85] TNA, PRO 30/24/47/3, f. 66r, printed in Locke (1997), p. 180. This provision remained unaltered in all subsequent revisions of the *Fundamental Constitutions*.

[86] Charter to Sir Robert Heath (30 October 1629) and Charter to the Lords Proprietors of Carolina (24 March 1663), in *North Carolina Charters and Constitutions* (1963), pp. 64, 76 (my emphases).

[87] On arguments from conquest in early English colonial ideology, see Macmillan (2011).

just that same argument in the *Letter Concerning Toleration* (1685): 'No man whatsoever ought ... to be deprived of his Terrestrial Enjoyments, upon account of his Religion. Not even *Americans*, subjected unto a Christian Prince, are to be punished either in Body or Goods, for not imbracing our Faith and Worship.'[88] The only remaining argument was the contention (first propounded in its modern form by Thomas More in *Utopia*) that dominion fell to those best able to cultivate the land to its fullest capacity, not least to fulfil the divine command to subdue the earth (Genesis 1:28, 9:1). The peculiar form of Locke's argument therefore had identifiably colonial origins, though not exclusively colonial applications.[89]

The same might be said of the references to the '*West Indies*' – meaning either the English Caribbean, or English settlements in the western hemisphere more generally – in the *Two Treatises*. They are less precisely datable than the American references in Chapter 5 of the *Second Treatise* but just as suggestive. Both occur in the same chapter of the *First Treatise*, and each refers to the legitimacy of a 'Man in the *West-Indies*' making war, leading his sons, friends, soldiers 'or Slaves bought with Money' 'out against the *Indians* to seek Reparation upon any Injury received from them' (I. 131, 130).[90] Locke there argued, *contra* Filmer, that such a planter would not need absolute monarchical dominion, descending from Adam, to pursue his vengeance but instead derived authority from his role as father of his sons, friend of his companions or owner of his slaves. He would thus be like the '*Master of a Family*' portrayed in the *Second Treatise*, uniting '*Wife, Children, Servants and Slaves*' under his domestic rule, save for the all-important proviso that the master possessed power of life and death only over his slaves and not over the rest of his extended household (II. 86).

The paterfamilias's 'Legislative Power of Life and Death' was the same power and authority possessed by '[e]very Freeman of Carolina over his Negro slaves of what opinion or Religion soever' (§ 110). That article was missing from what seems to be the very earliest manuscript of the *Fundamental Constitutions* but its first appearance was idiomatically Lockean in its insistence on the slave-holder's 'absolute arbitrary Power, over the Lives, Liberties and Persons of his Slaves, and their Posterities'.[91]

---

[88] John Locke, *A Letter Concerning Toleration* (1685), in Locke (2010), p. 39.
[89] Armitage (2000), pp. 49–50, 92–9.
[90] On *First Treatise*, § 130, see Drescher (1988); Farr (1989).
[91] Compare SCDA, Recital of Grants, AD120, pt. II, ff. 41–6 (MS copy of the 'Fundamental Constitutions' [1669]) with 'Coppy Of the modell of Government prepared for the Province of Carolina &c', (unfoliated), NYPL, Ford Collection, article 73.

It also went untouched in the 1682 revisions even as Locke renumbered it with all the rest. There is therefore no mistaking either his tacit commitment to this brutal provision or the hold the master-slave relationship had over his political imagination both before and during the composition and revision of the *Two Treatises*.[92] This perhaps becomes less surprising once we know he had collaborated with the Barbadian planter Sir Peter Colleton on the revisions to the *Fundamental Constitutions* in 1682.

As early as 1776, Locke's conservative critic Josiah Tucker had noted the consistency between the *Fundamental Constitutions'* attribution of the power of life and death to slave-holders and the portrait in the *Second Treatise* of slaves taken in a just war being 'subjected to the Absolute Dominion and Arbitrary Power of their Masters'. Tucker noted that in the *Fundamental Constitutions*, Locke 'lays it down as an invariable Maxim ... "That every Freeman of *Carolina* shall have ABSOLUTE POWER AND AUTHORITY over his Negro Slaves."' How could this be reconciled with the statement in the opening lines of the *Two Treatises of Government* that 'Slavery is so vile and miserable an Estate of Man ... that 'tis hardly to be conceived, that an *Englishman*, much less a *Gentleman*, should plead for 't'? So much for 'the humane Mr. LOCKE! the great and glorious Assertor of the natural Rights and Liberties of Mankind'. Tucker thought that in this regard Locke was just like all 'Republicans', or what we would call liberals: in favour of levelling all hierarchies above themselves while 'tyrannizing over those, whom Chance or Misfortune have placed below them'.[93] This might be seen as an ancestor of the argument that liberalism as a 'creed' is exclusionary by its very nature. Just over fifty years later, during the British debate on the abolition of slavery in June 1829, Jeremy Bentham assailed Locke for making private property the foundation of both liberty and happiness: 'Property the only object of care to Government. Persons possessing it alone entitled to be represented. West Indies the meridian for these principles of this liberty-champion.' His proof came from the *Fundamental Constitutions of Carolina*, 'a performance which from that day to this has never been more spoken of in any other character than that of a failure'.[94] The complicity of Lockean liberalism with English colonialism was thus

---

[92] For a range of treatments of Locke on slavery, see Dunn (1969), pp. 108–10, 174–7; Farr (1986); Glausser (1990); Welchman (1995); Uzgalis (1998); Waldron (2002), pp. 197–206; Farr (2008).

[93] Tucker (1776), pp. 103–4; Tucker (1781), p. 168.

[94] Jeremy Bentham, 'Article on Utilitarianism' (8 June 1829), UCL Bentham XIV. 432 (marginal note), XIV. 433.

not first exposed by liberal self-scrutiny nor was it originally unearthed by an effort of post-colonial critique. Tucker and Bentham's assaults on Locke may have been malevolent but they were theoretically acute; little did they know that, in light of Locke's political activities in the summer of 1682, their attacks were also historically accurate.

CHAPTER 7

John Locke: theorist of empire?

Even twenty-five years ago, it might have been eccentric to ask whether John Locke was a theorist of empire. Within the shorthand histories of political thought, Locke was the grandfather of liberalism; in the standard histories of philosophy, he was the exemplar of empiricism. Liberalism had long been assumed to be inimical to empire, and the main links between empiricism and imperialism were found in the work of Francis Bacon and the seventeenth-century Royal Society. However, as the preceding chapter has shown, a generation of recent scholars have fundamentally revised understandings of liberalism's relation to empire and in particular of Locke's relationship to settler colonialism in North America and beyond.[1] The impact of their work has been so widespread that, alongside Locke the founder of liberalism and Locke the pivotal empiricist, we now find the figure of 'Locke, the champion of big property, empire, and appropriation of the lands of Amerindians'.[2] Locke has finally joined the canon of theorists of empire: but how much does he deserve his place there?

What it might mean to be a theorist of empire was profoundly shaped by the experience and practices of imperialism in the two centuries after 1757: that is, from the beginnings of European military dominance in South Asia to the first great wave of formal decolonisation outside Europe. James Tully has succinctly summarised Europe's imperial vision in this period:

It is 'imperial' in three senses of this polysemic word. It ranks all non-European cultures as 'inferior' or 'lower' from the point of view of the presumed direction of European civilisation towards *the* universal culture; it serves to legitimate European imperialism, not in the sense of being 'right' . . . but, nevertheless, in

---

[1] See especially Tully (1993); Arneil (1996); Ivison (2003); Farr (2008); Farr (2009).

[2] Israel (2006b), p. 529; however, see Israel (2006a), pp. 546, 603–5, for a more moderate admission that 'it is perhaps not entirely fair to depict Locke as an ideologist of empire': ibid., p. 604.

being the direction of nature and history and the precondition of an eventual, just, national and world order; and it is imposed on non-European peoples as their cultural self-understanding in the course of European imperialism *and* federalism.[3]

Tully's immediate example here was Immanuel Kant viewed through the lens of Edward Said's *Culture and Imperialism* (1993), but accounts of the relationship between Locke and empire have shared many of the same assumptions. He has been held to be an 'imperial' thinker in all three senses: allegedly because he placed the world's peoples in a hierarchical order with Europeans at the top of the scale; because he legitimated European imperialism within a progressivist vision of history; and because he proposed European capacities – specifically, the rationality of Europeans – as a universal standard against which other peoples were to be judged and towards which they were to be led.[4] On these grounds, there would now be widespread agreement that Locke has as much claim to be a theorist of empire as any other proponent of the 'self-consciously universal ... political, ethical and epistemological creed' of liberalism, whether Bentham, the Mills or Macaulay (to take only British examples).[5] Yet the philosophical distance between Locke and Kant, or between Locke and Mill, should give pause before affirming that consensus. So should the very different forms and conceptions of empire found in the seventeenth and nineteenth centuries.[6] This chapter's argument will be that the label 'imperial' cannot be aptly applied to Locke because he did not espouse or elaborate a hierarchical ordering of populations, least of all one that placed Europeans above or even apart from other groups, because he saw rationality itself as evenly distributed among human populations and the usual markings of civilisation as contingent and fragile.

JOHN LOCKE, COLONIAL THINKER

Locke's experience in colonial administration had both widened his intellectual horizons and focused his practical interests on the Atlantic world. During the closing decades of the seventeenth century, when he

---

[3] Tully (2008), p. 27 (italics Tully's).
[4] See especially Parekh (1995); Mehta (1999). For acute questionings of the assumptions summarised here, see Carey and Trakulhun (2009); Hsueh (2010), pp. 1–24.
[5] Mehta (1999), p. 1. For an illuminating critique of this reading of liberalism, see Pitts (2005a).
[6] On Kant and empire, see especially Muthu (2003), ch. 5; on the varieties of empire, see Armitage (1998); Porter (1999); Tully (2009).

was most involved in colonial affairs, 'there is evidence of sharpening legal distinctions between the Atlantic and the Indian Ocean'. The Board of Trade's activities concentrated almost entirely on the Atlantic world and they considered affairs in the Indian Ocean only when they had implications for that arena, as in the case of global piracy, for example.[7] His economic writings provide evidence that his colonial vision was similarly bounded by the Atlantic. There is a single reference to the Indian Ocean arena in his economic writings, when he implored an antagonist 'please to remember the great Sums of Money ... carried every year to the *East-Indies*, for which we bring home consumable Commodities'.[8] And Locke mentioned the East India Company only once in print, in his *Second Letter Concerning Toleration* (1690), when he taxed an interlocutor with failing to see that 'Civil Society' has different goals from other forms of human association: 'By which account there will be no difference between Church and State; A Commonwealth and an Army; or between a Family and the *East-India* Company; all which have hitherto been thought distinct sorts of Societies, instituted for different Ends.'[9] He did not invest in the New East India Company until after he had left the Board of Trade: even then, he held on to his bonds for less than a year, and sold them at a small loss in the summer of 1701.[10]

Locke's imperial vision was comparatively less wide-ranging than that of many contemporary English political economists. For example, Sir William Petty gradually expanded his range outward from the Three Kingdoms of Britain and Ireland to the Atlantic world and from there to a conception of an economically defined, globally dispersed polity in which all of England's interests – British, American, African and Asian – would be equally represented.[11] No less comprehensive were the analyses of England's East India trade by Charles Davenant and Henry Martyn, who each saw Asian commerce as crucial to England's economic fortunes and to the elaboration of interoceanic and global trade more generally. On their analysis, bullion taken largely from the Americas could be exchanged in Asia both for luxury goods and for more widely affordable

[7] TNA, CO 324/6, ff. 160r–64v, 166v–71r, 175; TNA, CO 5/1116, ff. 1r–17v; compare Bod. MS Locke c. 30, ff. 62–3, endorsed 'Pyracy 97'; Benton (2005), p. 718.

[8] John Locke, *Some Considerations of the Consequences of the Lowering of Interest* (1696), in Locke (1991), I, p. 333.

[9] Locke (1690), p. 51. It is therefore highly unlikely that the distinctive voting procedures of the East India Company inspired his conception of majority rule in the *Two Treatises*, pace Galgano (2007), pp. 327–33, 340–1.

[10] Bod. MS Locke c. 1, ff. 106, 107.   [11] Armitage (2000), pp. 152–3; McCormick (2009), pp. 230–3.

commodities such as the boomingly popular calicoes which were exported from India to England and the American colonies. For Martyn, in particular, the import of cheaper textiles from India may have undercut domestic English industry, but that was an unavoidable side-effect of comparative advantage to which protectionism could provide no solution: 'When we shall be reduc'd to plain Labour without any manner of Art, we shall live at least as well as the Wild *Indians* of *America*, the *Hottantots* of *Africa*, or the Inhabitants of New *Holland*', he remarked sardonically. Martyn drew heavily on Locke's comparison between the productive capacities of England and America in the *Second Treatise* (II. 41) to support his argument, but this debt only pointed up the absence of the Asian trades in Locke's political economy.[12]

The limits of Locke's imperial vision become even clearer when we compare him with other seventeenth-century European contributors to the modern tradition of natural jurisprudence. For example, Grotius's fundamental writings on natural law sprang originally from his defence of the Dutch East India Company's activities in maritime southeast Asia, most notably in his *The Free Sea* (1609), the *locus classicus* for freedom of trade across the oceans of the world and a work Locke certainly knew.[13] Later in the century, Samuel Pufendorf's conception of human sociability implied a potentially global conception of commercial society linking together the peoples of the world through mutually sustaining systems of utility and exchange.[14] This 'neo-Aristotelian' vision of commercial sociability found its closest parallel in late seventeenth-century French Augustinianism, especially in the work of the French theologian and essayist, Pierre Nicole. As Nicole put it in his 'Treatise of Peace' (1671), using the example of Northern European trade with East Asia:

The world then is our citty: and as inhabitants of it, we have intercourse with all man kinde, And doe receive from them advantages, or inconveniencys [*de l'utilité & tantôt du dommage*]. The Hollanders have a trade with Japan, we [the French] with Holland; and soe have a commerce with those people, at the farthest end of the world ... They are linked to us, on one side, or other; & all entre into that chain, which ties the whole race of men togeather by their mutuall wants [*besoins réciproques*].[15]

---

[12] Hont (2005), pp. 201–22, 245–58; Martyn (1701), pp. 58, 72–3.

[13] Van Ittersum (2006); Borschberg (2011); Grotius (2004); Grotius (2006). Locke possessed Grotius's *Mare Liberum* (1609) in an edition of Grotius, *De Jure Belli ac Pacis libri tres* (The Hague, 1680), Bod. Locke 9. 99.

[14] Tuck (1999), pp. 167–72.

[15] Hont (2005), pp. 45–51, 159–84; Nicole (2000), p. 117. See also Cumberland (2005), p. 318.

Nicole's vision of global commerce appeared here only fleetingly but it contrasted starkly with Locke's own conception of commerce, which was by default almost entirely confined to the Atlantic world. Locke certainly knew Nicole's work, for he translated the 'Treatise of Peace' in the mid-1670s. However, his political economy and political theory remained more limited than Nicole's and his universalism more constrained than either Grotius's or Pufendorf's in its range of reference. As we shall see, this combination of cosmopolitanism and regional concentration characterised Locke's universalism, more broadly conceived.

THE LIMITS OF LOCKEAN UNIVERSALISM

Locke sometimes joked with friends about emigrating to New England or Carolina but he never travelled further west than his native county of Somerset. Although he spent almost a decade living outside England, in France and Holland, he did not even see the Atlantic Ocean until he was fifty-six years old, and then only from La Rochelle in France.[16] In this regard, he can be compared to his friend Sir Isaac Newton who became a global centre of communication because he commanded correspondents from the Gulf of Tonkin to the Strait of Magellan.[17] Like Newton's correspondence, Locke's comprised a nearly world-wide web: among the almost 4,000 letters from and to him that survive, there are items from the Caribbean, New England, Virginia and Carolina, as well as from Bengal and China, not to mention extensive exchanges with friends and acquaintances in Scotland, Ireland, France, the Netherlands, Germany and Sweden. Among seventeenth-century correspondence networks, only those of the Jesuit Athanasius Kircher and the philosopher Gottfried Wilhelm Leibniz were both larger in size and comparably far-flung in extent.[18] During his years in Europe, Locke collected numerous accounts of the extra-European world. By the time of his death, Locke's collection of travel literature was one of the largest ever assembled in Britain and it comprised 195 books, many maps and a portfolio of ethnographic illustrations 'of the inhabitants of severall remote parts of the world espetially the East Indies', which included representations of Laplanders, Brazilian 'Cannibal[s]', 'Hottentot[s]'

---

[16] Locke (1976–), I, pp. 379, 590, II, pp. 27, 34, 40, 68, 95, 105, 132, 141, 147, 441, 444; Bod. MS Locke f. 28, f. 19; Locke (1953), p. 232: 'This is the first time I ever saw the Ocean' (7 September 1678).
[17] Schaffer (2009).
[18] Mark Goldie, 'Introduction', in Locke (2002), pp. viii, xviii; Findlen (2004); Lodge (2004).

from the Cape of Good Hope and inhabitants of Java, Amboina, Macassar, Malaya, Ternate, Tonkin, Japan, China and 'Tartary'.[19]

In the course of compiling his major published works, Locke mined his library and pressed his global connections for data about matters medical, theological, ethnographical, social and political. Their greatest impact can be found in the five editions of the *Essay Concerning Human Understanding* (1690–1706), in which information regarding the diversity of human beliefs provided crucial ammunition for his arguments against the supposed innateness of ideas. The key test-case for innatism was the idea of God. If even that seemingly most fundamental of ideas could not be shown to be universal, then surely no other could be said to be inborn, 'since it is hard to conceive, how there should be innate Moral Principles, without an innate *Idea* of a *Deity*'. Locke offered evidence to the contrary from the accounts of what 'Navigation discovered, in these latter Ages'. Not content with one or two examples to combat innatism, he continued to add empirical material to this passage and other similar ones until in the last, posthumous edition of the *Essay* (1706), 'the number of authorities he had cited had risen to 16 ... The locations they described ranged from the Caucasus and Lapland to Brazil, Paraguay, Siam, China, the Cape of Good Hope, and elsewhere.' In this way, Locke made greater use of ethnographic information than any other philosopher in Britain before the eighteenth century.[20]

Locke's knowledge of travel literature, and the information he gathered as a servant of English colonial ventures, encouraged his scepticism about human capacities and his humility about the alleged superiority of Europeans. In the early lectures he gave at Oxford that are now known as the *Essays on the Law of Nature* (*c.* 1663–4), Locke had judged the 'primitive and untutored tribes [*barbaras ... et nudas gentes*]' harshly, 'since among most of them appears not the slightest trace or track of piety, merciful feeling, fidelity, chastity, and the rest of the virtues'. To this extent, he did not distinguish between the peoples 'of Asia and America who do not consider themselves to be bound by the same laws, separated from us as they are by long stretches of land and unaccustomed to our morals and beliefs [*nec moribus nostris aut opinionibus assueti*]'.[21] This recognition of diversity served the purposes of Locke's evolving criticism of innate ideas

---

[19] BL Add. MS 5253; Locke to William Charleton, 2 August 1687, in Locke (1976–), III, p. 240.

[20] Locke (1975), pp. 87–8 (I. iv. 8); Carey (1996), p. 263; Carey (2006), pp. 71–92; Talbot (2010). Locke had earlier invoked the atheism of the inhabitants of Brazil and Soldania Bay in the *Essays on the Law of Nature* (*c.* 1663–4), Locke (1997), p. 113; Locke (1954), pp. 172–4/173–5 (Latin/English).

[21] Locke (1997), pp. 98, 108; Locke (1954), pp. 140/1, 162/3 (Latin/English).

but his evaluation of that diversity would become more complex in his later writings, starting in the late 1660s and early 1670s. His developing arguments in this regard do not easily fit the imperial stereotype of a thinker who ranked the peoples of the world hierarchically and placed some within, but many outside, the pale of liberalism.

It is now a commonplace that liberalism of the kind often traced back to Locke was both inclusive and universal in *theory*, but exclusionary and contingent in *practice*. As the most eloquent and subtle proponent of this view has put it, 'as a historical phenomenon, the period of liberal history is unmistakably marked by the systematic and sustained political exclusion of various groups and "types" of people'.[22] Among the categories of persons denied the benefits and rights that liberalism theoretically promised to all human beings were, variously, indigenous peoples, the enslaved, women, children and the mentally disabled, those whom Locke called 'mad Men' and 'Idiots'. The main criterion used to exclude such persons was their lack of rationality, and it has been argued that '[t]he American Indian is the example Locke uses to demonstrate a lack of reason'.[23]

Yet Locke did not charge Native Americans with irrationality when he convicted them of impiety, mercilessness, infidelity, promiscuousness and other vices in 1663–4. Indeed, a few years later, he wrote of their 'quick rationall parts' when, by virtue of his Carolina connections, he became the first European philosopher since Michel de Montaigne over a century before to meet and interrogate Native Americans in Europe. In 1670, two sons of the 'Emperor' of the Kiawah Creek town of Cofitachequi in Carolina travelled to England by way of Barbados. They were named, by the English at least, Honest and Just. Little is known about their movements before they returned to Carolina in 1672, but it is clear that Locke spoke to them before he had completed the second draft of his *Essay Concerning Human Understanding* in 1671.[24] In what is known as 'Draft B' of the *Essay*, he compared mathematical computation to human language and speculated that all counting consisted of only three operations: addition, subtraction and comparison. If a number becomes so large that it cannot be redescribed using the names of smaller numbers, Locke argued, it becomes impossible to conceive the idea of such an enormous sum:

[22] Mehta (1999), pp. 46–7 (on exclusion, quoted), 52–64 (on Locke); compare Mehta (1990); Sartori (2006); Greene (2010).
[23] Arneil (2007), pp. 209–22, 216 (quoted).
[24] Childs (1963); Vaughan (2006), p. 104; Farr (2008), p. 498; Farr (2009), pp. 50–61.

And this I think to be the reason why *some Indians I have spoken with*, who were otherwise of quick rationall parts could not as we doe count to a 1000. though they could very well to 20 because their language being scanty & accomodated only to the few necessarys of a needy simple life unacquainted either with trade or Mathematiques, had noe words in it to stand for a thousand. soe that if you discoursed with them of those great numbers they would shew you the hairs of their head to expresse a great multitude which they could not number.[25]

When Locke incorporated a revised version of this passage into the published *Essay* (1690), he compared the constraints on the mathematical knowledge of the '*Americans*' with the similar limits on Europeans' rational capacities: 'I doubt not but we our selves might distinctly number in Words, a great deal farther than we usually do, would we find out but some fit denominations to signifie them by.'[26] Such epistemological humility would be characteristic of his later writings. The encounter with Honest and Just helped to shape Locke's conception of Native Americans' rational capacities and prevented him from concluding that Europeans alone possessed any superior cultural self-understanding, 'for by the help of their natural Reason they enjoy that Happiness which the Philosophers could not by their Study and Reading attain to', judged the author of the chapter on Carolina in John Ogilby's *America* (1671), who circumstantial evidence suggests may have been Locke.[27]

Only in the *First Treatise of Government* did Locke ever call indigenous peoples 'irrational', and then just as a means of praising their untutored wisdom in preference to the sophistication of supposedly civilised nations: 'He that will impartially survey the World ... will have reason to think, that the Woods and Forests, where the irrational untaught Inhabitants keep right by following Nature, are fitter to give us Rules, than Cities and Palaces, where those that call themselves Civil and Rational, go out of their way, by the Authority of Example' (I. 58).[28] Locke generally found greater inequalities of capacity *within* particular peoples than he did *between* them. In this vein, he argued in *The Conduct of the Understanding* (1697), 'Amongst men of equall education there is great inequality of parts. And the woods of America as well as the Schools of Athens produce men of severall abilitys in the same kinde.'[29] The more fundamental difference between 'Americans' and Europeans therefore lay not in their

[25] John Locke, 'Draft B' (1671) of the *Essay*, § 50, in Locke (1990–), I, p. 157 (my emphasis).
[26] Locke (1975), p. 207 (II. xvi. 6). [27] 'Carolina', in Ogilby (1671), p. 209; Farr (2009), pp. 67–74.
[28] Locke (1988), p. 183. All references in the text are to this edition, by *Treatise* and paragraph number, unless otherwise noted.
[29] Locke (2000), p. 156.

intellectual abilities but in their contingent circumstances, their education and their needs as shaped by their environment.

Locke argued consistently throughout his works that God sends us into this world without innate ideas or any of the other physical 'conveniencies of life' (to use a favourite Lockean phrase). It was necessary for human beings to exercise their physical and their mental labour upon the otherwise inert creation given to them by God, this being 'the Condition of Humane Life, which requires Labour and Materials to work on' (II. 35).[30] Human beings could neither add to nor subtract from the divine creation but they had a duty to construct it to their own devices, both mentally and physically. What we might call Locke's 'constructivist' understanding of human labour was basic to his epistemology in the *Essay Concerning Human Understanding*:

> The Dominion of Man, in this little World of his own Understanding, being much the same, as it is in the great World of visible things; wherein his Power, however managed by Art and Skill, reaches no farther, than to compound and divide the Materials, that are made to his Hand.[31]

It is up to us to furnish ourselves with a stock of ideas just as we must transform nature into materials for our use: 'it is want of Industry and Consideration in us, and not of Bounty in him, if we have them not' (*Essay*, I. iv. 16). Thus, even the idea of God himself could be lacking, just as physical constructions like bridges or houses will be, if humans do not act industriously, if they fail to seize their God-given opportunities or if they are constrained by their own reduced circumstances like the people of the 'West Indies':

> nature furnish[es] us only with the materials for the most part rough and unfitted to our uses it requires labour art and thought to suit them to our occasions, and if the knowledg of men had not found out ways to shorten the labour and improve severall things which seem not a[t] first sight to be of any use to us we should spend all our time to make a scanty provision for a poore and miserable life. a sufficient instance whereof we have in the inhabitants of that large and fertill part of the world the west Indies who lived a poore uncomfortable laborious life with all their industry scarce able to subsist and that perhaps only for want of knowing the use of that stone out of which the Inhabitants of the old world had the skill to draw Iron.[32]

The presence or lack of adequate tools or commodities could account entirely for the differential productivity of particular peoples. Such conveniences

---

[30] Compare Hundert (1972).   [31] Locke (1975), p. 120 (II. ii. 2).
[32] Bod. MS Locke f. 2, p. 44, printed in Locke (1997), p. 261.

were accidental and external; they bear no relation to the supposedly innate capacities of individuals or groups.

Locke was a thoroughgoing anti-essentialist and did not argue for any inherent ethnic, let alone racial, difference. Any people could go up or down the scale of civility according to the materials nature had given to them: 'were the use of *Iron* lost among us, we should in a few Ages be unavoidably reduced to the Wants and Ignorance of the ancient savage *Americans*, whose natural Endowments and Provisions come no way short of those of the most flourishing and polite Nations'.[33] He also believed firmly in the rationality of Native Americans and that the advantages enjoyed by Europeans, even by philosophers like himself, were accidental: 'had the *Virginia* King *Apochancana* been educated in *England*, he had, perhaps, been as knowing a Divine, and as good a Mathematician, as any in it'.[34] The lack of those advantages could just as easily make the English irrational as Native Americans had become because they lacked certain human inventions: 'perhaps without books we should be as ignorant as the Indians whose minds are as ill-clad as their bodies'.[35]

Locke's sensitivity to contingent differences and interest in the rational capacities of the indigenous peoples of the Americas came under attack soon after his death and was sustained across the course of the eighteenth century. In 1709, the 3rd Earl of Shaftesbury – grandson of Locke's patron, Anthony Ashley Cooper – was already berating 'the credulous Mr. LOCKE, with his *Indian*, Barbarian Stories of wild Nations, that have no such Idea (as Travellers, learned Authors! And Men of Truth! and great Philosophers! have informed him;)'.[36] Later in the eighteenth century, Josiah Tucker, the conservative Anglican dean of Gloucester, argued repeatedly during the American Revolution that the colonists' rebelliousness sprang from their attachment to Locke's political theory. Among his strategies for discrediting American revolutionary ideology was to attack the contractarian theories of 'Mr. LOCKE and his followers' on the grounds that they misleadingly deployed 'the Tribes of Savage *Indians*' as examples of human sociability in a state of nature: 'Let them not din our Ears with the examples of the Savages of *America*, as being any Proofs and

---

[33] Locke (1975), p. 646 (IV. xii. 11). On Locke's anti-essentialism, see especially Anstey and Harris (2006), pp. 151–71; Anstey (2011), pp. 204–18.

[34] Locke (1975), p. 92 (I. iv. 12). In 'Draft B' of the *Essay*, Locke had made the same point using the example of another Virginia Native American leader, Tottepottemay: Locke, 'Draft B', § 12, in Locke (1990–), I, p. 120, drawing on Lederer (1672), 7; Farr (2009), pp. 40–4.

[35] Locke, 'Of Study' (27 March 1677), in Locke (1997), p. 367.

[36] 3rd Earl of Shaftesbury to Michael Ainsworth, 3 June 1709, in A. A. Cooper (1981–), II, pp. iv, 404.

Illustrations of their Hypothesis; – which, when thoroughly discussed, and accurately examined, prove just the contrary.' Locke and his disciples, Tucker continued, were either ignorant of the true nature of the Native Americans, 'or they must have acted a very disingenuous Part' in appealing to them.[37]

During the French Revolution, another Anglican apologist, George Horne, the bishop of Norwich, likewise objected to Locke's appeal to the Native American example: 'This is not a state of *nature*, but the most *unnatural* state in the world, for creatures made in the image of God. And does a polite philosopher, in these enlightened days, send us to study politics under Cherokee tutors!'[38] Shaftesbury, Tucker and Horne shared the prejudices associated with the high imperial vision regarding the capacities of indigenous peoples. The distance between them and Locke is another sign of how only with difficulty can he be assimilated to later imperial theories. Yet, as we have seen, Locke's stress on the contingency and the reversibility of so much that later thinkers took to be the markers of higher civilisation makes it impossible to call him an imperial theorist on the grounds that he ranked cultures within a progressivist vision of human history.

LOCKE AND THE LEGITIMATION OF EMPIRE

Locke can therefore only be described as a theorist of *empire* in a narrowly restricted definition of that term. In early modern usage, the meanings of 'empire' clustered around two main referents: empire as sovereignty (*imperium*), and empire as a composite state.[39] Locke would certainly have recognised the meaning of 'empire' as sovereignty or *imperium* and understood it to be territorial in application, as in the passage in the *Second Treatise* where he described how the 'several States and Kingdoms' of the world 'have, by positive agreement, settled a Property amongst themselves, in distinct Parts and parcels of the Earth' (II. 45). However, there is no evidence he would have understood 'empire' to refer to a composite state: for example, the terms 'English empire' or 'British empire' appear nowhere in his writings. Nor did Locke anywhere conceive of an empire in terms that later theorists might have recognised: as a territorially defined, hierarchically organised polity which suspends

---

[37] Tucker (1781), pp. 200–1; Pocock (1985), pp. 167–79.
[38] George Horne, '*Mr. Locke*, Consideration on His Scheme of an Original Compact' (*c.* 1792), in Horne (1800), II, p. 294.
[39] Armitage (2000), pp. 29–32.

diversity within unity, usually for the benefit of a metropolitan or other central authority.[40] He was, in regard to his strictly political theory (particularly in the *Two Treatises of Government*), a theorist of the commonwealth, or state, and not a theorist of empire. How, then, might he have come to be identified as an imperial theorist?

Two answers might be given to that question, one historical and one more immediately textual. The first would be that his arguments were in fact often used in settler colonies around the world, and by other theorists who promoted European settlement beyond Europe, to justify the expropriation of indigenous peoples. For example, in the early eighteenth-century context of settler claims against the native title of the Mohegans of Connecticut, Locke could be excerpted to argue that the Native Americans were pre-civil peoples who had less right to the lands on which they lived than the more industrious English colonists.[41] This 'agriculturalist' argument gained its greatest purchase in the version inflected by Physiocratic political economy propagated by the Swiss jurist, Emer de Vattel, in his *Droit des gens* (1758), where he argued that peoples who, 'to avoid labour, chuse to live only by hunting, and their flocks', pursued an 'idle mode of life, usurp more extensive territories than ... they would have occasion for, and have therefore no reason to complain, if other nations, more industrious, and too closely confined, come to take possession of a part of those lands'. From this argument, it followed that 'the establishment of many colonies on the continent of North America might, on their confining themselves within just bounds, be extremely lawful'.[42] Vattel's arguments were widely dispersed across the globe by the circuits of empire in the late eighteenth and nineteenth centuries; their force could be felt when, for example, the Sydney *Herald* proclaimed in 1838 that Australia was for the Aborigines only 'a common – they bestowed no labour upon the land – their ownership, their right, was nothing more than that of the Emu or the Kangaroo'.[43] This was a theoretical justification for the foundations of property-holding in an imperial context, and it was idiomatically Lockean in form.

---

[40] Compare C. Maier (2006), pp. 20–1, on empire as 'a system of rule that transforms society at home even as it stabilizes inequality transnationally by replicating it geographically, in the core and on the periphery'.

[41] John Bulkley, 'Preface', in Wolcott (1725), pp. xv–lvi; Tully (1993), pp. 166–8; Yirush (2011).

[42] Vattel (2008), pp. 129–30 (I. vii. 81).

[43] Quoted in Ivison (2006), p. 197; on the persistence of Vattelian arguments in nineteenth-century British imperial thought, see Claeys (2010), pp. 16–18, 108–9, 140, 202, 238, 263, 284–5.

Like these imperial iterations of Locke's arguments, the second answer
to the problem of Locke's identification as a theorist of empire goes back
to the *Two Treatises of Government*. The allusions to non-European
peoples in the *Two Treatises* are almost exclusively drawn from the
Americas. There are only two passing references to Asia in the *Treatises*,
one to the Chinese as 'a very great and civil People' (I. 141), the other to
the deleterious consequences of absolute monarchy Robert Knox had
portrayed in his 'late Relation of *Ceylon*' (1680) (II. 2) which Locke
acquired in 1681.[44] Otherwise, the historical and ethnographic examples
Locke uses referred to '*Americans*', meaning Native Americans, accompanied by occasional references to the creole settlers. Thus, in the *First
Treatise*, Locke drew on examples from Peru,[45] Carolina, the 'little Tribe[s]'
'in many parts of *America*', 'our late Histories of the *Northern
America*' and the '*West*-Indies' to ridicule Sir Robert Filmer's patriarcha-
lism (I. 57, 130, 131, 145, 154). And in the same work, he twice alluded
to the 'Planter', a 'Man in the *West-Indies*, who hath with him Sons of his
own Friends, or Companions, Souldiers under Pay, or Slaves bought with
Money', to disaggregate two forms of authority, political sovereignty
and the power to make war, which Filmer had conflated (I. 130, 131).

The still more frequent allusions in the *Second Treatise* were likewise
almost entirely confined to the Native Americans. As we have seen in the
previous chapter, the prominence of these allusions to America in the *Two
Treatises*, and their accumulation in the chapter 'Of Property', were in
part the product of Locke's continuing relationship with Carolina in the
early 1680s, when he had had to produce a justification of appropriation
which would do double duty, both in England and in America. He
contended that 'God gave the World to Men in Common; but ... it
cannot be supposed he meant it should always remain common and
uncultivated. He gave it to the use of the Industrious and Rational,
(and *Labour* was to be *his Title* to it;) not to the Fancy or Covetousness
of the Quarrelsom and Contentious' (II. 34). Each person has an exclusive
right to his own body and therefore also of the labour of that body:
'Whatsoever then he removes out of the State that Nature hath provided,
and left it in, he hath mixed his *Labour* with, and joyned to it something
that is his own, and thereby makes it his *Property*' (II. 27). Only after land
had been appropriated in this way could it be apportioned 'by compact

---

[44] Knox (1680), pp. 43–7; Locke (1988), p. 327 n. 12; Winterbottom (2009), pp. 515–38.
[45] Locke used the same example of Peruvian cannibalism from Garcilaso de la Vega, in Locke (1975),
    p. 71 (I. iv. 9). On Locke and Garcilaso, see Fuerst (2000), pp. 349–405.

and Agreement' in those parts of the world where a monetary economy had been introduced and land had become scarce, just as the 'several States and Kingdoms … have, by *positive agreement, settled a Property* amongst themselves in distinct Parts and parcels of the Earth', leaving '*great Tracts of Grounds*' waste and lying in common, 'the Inhabitants thereof not having joyned with the rest of Mankind, in the consent of the Use of their common Money' (II. 45).

Locke amplified the relevance of America to his arguments when he made a final set of manuscript revisions to the *Two Treatises* some time after 1698. The most extensive changes and additions he made were to the chapter 'Of Property' and sprang from his experience as a Commissioner on the Board of Trade in the late 1690s. First, he expanded his assessment of the benefits provided by cultivation and enclosure of land: 'he who appropriates land to himself by his labour does not lessen but increase the common stock of Man kind', by a factor of ten to one, or more likely

it is much nearer an hundred to one. For I aske whether in the wild woods and uncultivated wast of America left to Nature, without any improvement, tillage or husbandry, a thousand acres yeild the needy and wretched inhabitants as many conveniencys of life as ten acres of equally fertill land in Devonshire where they are well cultivated?

A few paragraphs later, Locke made a second addition which turned this observation into a tenet of economic reason of state for William III and his ministers. He had originally concluded a brief discussion of the multifarious forms of labour that go into the production of any commodity with a reflection on the relative unimportance of land to value: 'So little, that even amongst us, Land that is left wholly to Nature, that hath no improvement of Pasturage, Tillage, or Planting, is called … wast':

This shews, how much numbers of Men are to be preferd to largenesse of dominions and that the increase of lands [*sc.* hands?] and the right imploying of them is the great art of government. And that Prince who shall be so wise and godlike as by established Laws of liberty to secure protection and incouragment to the honest industry of Mankind against the oppression of power and narrownesse of Party will quickly be too hard for his neighbours.[46]

Such encouragement of industry was for Locke a matter of equal importance at home in Britain and across the Atlantic in America. Labour, he

[46] John Locke, manuscript additions to Locke (1698), pp. 193, 197 (II. 37, 42), Christ's College, Cambridge, call-number BB 3 7a; Locke (1988), p. 297 n. For recent discussions of these passages (but which ignore the evidence of their dating and context), see Andrew (2009) and L. Ward (2009).

wrote in an essay on the English Poor Law for the Board of Trade in 1697, was 'the burden that lies on the industrious'. Genuine relief for the poor 'consists of finding work for them, and taking care that they do not live like drones upon the labour of others'. A strict regimen of labour would have the benefit of providing education for the children of the poor who would be put to work in school, to ensure that they would no longer be 'as utter strangers both to religion and morality as they are to industry', perhaps like those natives of Carolina who, nearly twenty years earlier, the *Fundamental Constitutions* had deemed 'utterly strangers to Christianity' but who were not on that account to be dispossessed or ill-treated.[47]

These links among the *Fundamental Constitutions*, the *Two Treatises* and the 'Essay on the Poor Law' suggest two conclusions regarding Locke as a theorist of empire that reinforce the evidence from his other works treated in this chapter. The first is that his was not a universalistic vision of English, British or European superiority over the rest of the world and its peoples. It did not assume formal equality only for those deemed to be 'civil' peoples. Indeed, as Locke argued in a little-discussed passage in the *Letter Concerning Toleration*, even a Christian people, uprooted from their domestic setting and placed in an unfamiliar and dependent position, would be even more vulnerable than the 'pagans' among whom they settled:

An inconsiderable and weak number of Christians, destitute of every thing, arrive in a Pagan Country: These Foreigners beseech the Inhabitants, by the bowels of Humanity, that they would succour them with the necessaries of life: they all joyn together, and grow up into one Body of People. The Christian Religion by this means takes root in that Countrey, and spreads it self; but does not suddenly grow the strongest. While things are in this condition, Peace, Friendship, Faith and equal Justice, are preserved amongst them.

Charity demands equal treatment for both pagans and Christians, and weakness leads to a fragile tolerance. However, the consequences of dominance and the assumption of religious rectitude bring not just intolerance but dispossession and destruction:

At length the Magistrate becomes a Christian, and by that means their Party becomes the most powerful. Then immediately all Compacts are to be broken, all Civil Rights to be violated, that Idolatry may be extirpated: And unless these innocent Pagans, strict Observers of the Rules of Equity and the Law of Nature, and no ways offending against the Laws of the Society, I say unless they will

---

[47] John Locke, 'An Essay on the Poor Law' (September–October 1697), in Locke (1997), pp. 184, 189, 192; TNA CO 388/5, ff. 232r–48v (26 October 1697); Bod. MS Locke c. 30, ff. 86r–87v, 94r–95v, IIIr–v.

forsake their ancient Religion, and embrace a new and strange one, they are to be turned out of the Lands and Possessions of their Forefathers, and perhaps deprived of Life it self.

The conclusion Locke drew was Atlantic in form yet more general in application: 'For the reason of the thing is equal, both in *America* and *Europe* ... neither Pagans there, nor any Dissenting Christians here, can with any right be deprived of their worldly Goods ... nor are any Civil Rights to be either changed or violated upon account of Religion in one place more than another.'[48]

A second conclusion follows from the first: Locke's theory was non-hierarchical and inclusive to the extent that all adult humans possessed the same rationality because reason is likewise equal 'both in *America* and *Europe*' (and China, for example). As Locke put it in the *Second Treatise*, God gave the earth 'to the use of the Industrious and Rational', with labour as their means to earn title to it; yet the opposite of 'the Industrious and the Rational' in this passage were not the 'idle' and the 'irrational' but rather 'the Quarrelsom and Contentious': that is, anyone who exceeded 'the *bounds*, set by reason of what might serve for his *use*' and unjustly 'desired the benefit of another's Pains, which he had no right to' (II. 31, 34). The rational do have a right to possession, but only if they exercise their industry and do not invade the fruits of another's labour. Locke did not justify dispossession on grounds of any incapacity, whether mental or otherwise: if accumulation were pursued within the bounds set by reason, 'there could be then little room for Quarrels or Contentions about Property so establish'd' (II. 31).[49] Least of all did he associate rationality with Europeans and irrationality with indigenous peoples. If any later settler colonialists sought an argument for indigenous dispossession on the grounds of their assumed innate rational superiority and others' lack of industry, only with some theoretical and historical difficulty could they have extracted such a justification from Locke's *Second Treatise*.

The preceding two chapters have tried to provide an account of Locke's conceptions of empire based on a full survey of his writings, in line with other recent discussions of his views on slavery, for example.[50] I hope to

---

[48] Locke, *A Letter Concerning Toleration* (1685), in Locke (2010), pp. 39–40.
[49] Compare Locke, *Some Considerations of the Consequences of the Lowering of Interest* (1696), in Locke (1991), I, p. 292: 'Nature has bestowed Mines on several parts of the World: But the Riches are only for the Industrious and Frugal. Whomever else they visit, 'tis with the Diligent and Sober only they stay.'
[50] Especially Farr (2008).

have shown that Locke's thought underwent change and that the historical Locke was necessarily more complex and more often conflicted than later Lockeans – whether his followers or those who have analysed his work – have perhaps given him credit for being. The contextual and conceptual limits to Locke's theories should remind us that diverse circumstances generated, and necessitated, differing strains of what has sometimes been aggregated as a single imperial 'liberalism' of which Locke is now held to be the progenitor.

In 1769, Warren Hastings had expressed a hope for 'Lockes, Humes and Montesquieus in Number sufficient for each Department' to govern India through the East India Company. He would have been disappointed, at least in his desire for idiomatically Lockean administrators. There is otherwise very little concrete evidence for the reception of Locke among Britons in Asia before the late eighteenth century. An East India Company official in Sumatra was reading the *Essay* in 1714. Locke's works travelled to India in the baggage of Arthur Wellesley, the future duke of Wellington in 1796. And Philip Francis knew Locke's economic writings well.[51] However, it was not until the Permanent Settlement of Bengal in 1793 that Lockean categories of land-use (and abuse), of waste and productivity, began to be applied by British colonial officials in South Asia.[52] Locke only became an imperial thinker in a region to which he devoted little thought and through an application of his ideas with which he might well have disagreed. He cannot therefore be held responsible for a liberalism he could not have envisaged in the service of an imperial ideology he did not attempt to imagine.

There can be no doubt that the shape of Locke's political theory owed decisive debts to his experiences as a colonial administrator and servant of the English state as it projected its authority into the Atlantic world. Those experiences also placed limits on his universalism and ensured that later appropriations of his arguments would often have to reformulate them to fit later colonial contingencies. If indeed we are to use the anachronistic shorthand 'liberalism' to describe Locke's political theories, then we must be aware that there have been different strains of imperial and colonial liberalism and that they have not

---

[51] Joseph Collet to Richard Steele, 24 August 1714, in Collet (1933), pp. 99–100 ('Mr. Lock who first taught me to distinguish between Words and things'); Guedalla (1931), p. 55; Parkes and Merivale (1867), I, pp. 51–2; Guha (1996), pp. 97–8; Warren Hastings to George Vansittart, 23 December 1769, BL Add. MS 29125, f. 22r. On the trajectory of 'liberalism' in India itself, see Bayly (2012).

[52] Whitehead (2012).

necessarily been continuous with each other. And if liberalism itself is to have the traces of its complicity with empire exposed and expunged, that will have to be undertaken in diverse and historically sensitive ways to create various post-colonial liberalisms, some of which may be able to draw robustly upon other Lockean legacies.[53]

---

[53] See Ivison (2002), for one distinguished attempt.

PART III

Eighteenth-century foundations

CHAPTER 8

Parliament and international law in eighteenth-century Britain

The study of Parliament and international law in the eighteenth century illuminates crucial distinctions among nation, state and empire. For example, after 1603 but before 1707, the Scottish Parliament in Edinburgh represented a nation but aroused English opposition whenever it tried to legislate as if Scotland were an independent state. Before 1801, the Irish Parliament in Dublin represented only a very narrowly defined Irish nation and, prior to the repeal of Poynings's Law in 1782, made no pretence of legislating as if Ireland were a state rather than a dependent kingdom. Only the Westminster Parliament could claim that national representation authorised its legislating for the English – later, British – state and for the British Empire. Across the course of the century, war and revolution tested the limits of that Parliament's sovereignty, especially in the decades succeeding the Seven Years' War. These developments occurred within European, imperial and global contexts, with the imperial setting only gaining primacy in the latter third of the century.[1] As scholars of nineteenth-century British history have shown, most strikingly in relation to the Reform Acts of 1832 and 1867, domestic contexts alone cannot explain the course of parliamentary history.[2]

The defining moments of British parliamentary history in the 'long' eighteenth century have often been associated with a single date: for example, 1688, 1707, 1765, 1776, 1801, 1832. At each of these points, so the story goes, the powers, the capacities or the scope of parliamentary authority changed. In 1688 and 1832 – the conventional boundaries of a long century of revolution and reform – the Glorious Revolution and the Great Reform Act shifted first the balance of power between Crown and Parliament and then that between Parliament and people (however narrowly defined). In 1765 and 1776, the crises following the passage of the

[1] Simms (2007); Ahn and Simms (2010).
[2] C. Hall (1994); Hall, McClelland and Rendall (2000); M. Taylor (2003a); M. Taylor (2003b).

135

Stamp Act and the American Declaration of Independence heralded years of arguments across the Atlantic and British bloodshed before the nature and extent of Parliament's imperial sovereignty could be settled. In 1707, that sovereignty had been extended to encompass Scotland by incorporation; in 1801, it was further expanded to include Ireland, thereby to reach its greatest territorial extent. The process of incorporating the Three Kingdoms into the embrace of the Westminster Parliament extinguished the competing and parallel legislatures in Edinburgh and Dublin just as it also formally abolished the English Parliament in 1707. By 1801, parliamentary sovereignty had apparently been settled exclusively at Westminster in a pan-British and imperial legislature, albeit one with greatly reduced fiscal powers over its dependent territories in the Caribbean and British North America.[3]

The calendar of British parliamentary history does not entirely correspond with the roster of canonical moments in eighteenth-century British international history. Within that chronology, 1688 and 1776 certainly have a place, but 1713, 1748, 1757, 1763, 1802 and 1815, for example, are the more salient dates. These were all moments in the contested history of the British state's positive engagement with other European states or of the involvement of quasi-state agencies like the East India Company with extra-European actors like the Nawab of Bengal.[4] Each date marked a moment of formal cessation of hostilities, cession of territory or the extension of British authority, and each became enshrined within British historical memory. These were events in the international history of the British state: not 'mere parliamentary wrangle', as J. R. Seeley invidiously put it, but rather 'the history of England [*sic*] . . . in America and Asia'.[5]

The Glorious Revolution had changed England's foreign policy and determined its confessional orientation. Louis XIV confirmed that orientation in the eyes of Europe by his recognition of the Protestant succession in the Treaty of Utrecht. The succession itself became a matter of international dispute between Scotland and England in 1703, when the Scottish Parliament expressed its independent ability to determine the succession. The Union of 1707 solved that difficulty (among others) by creating a new political entity – the United Kingdom of Great Britain – and in the process abolished two previously existing states, the kingdoms of England and Scotland. The Anglo-Irish Union did not add to or subtract from the sum of states because Ireland had had no

---

[3] Maitland (1908), p. 339.   [4] Bowen (1991), pp. 30–47; R. Travers (2007); Wilson (2008).
[5] Seeley (1883).

separate or distinct international standing except for a brief period in the 1640s.[6] After 1801, a multinational, multidenominational British state assumed an expanded territorial presence on the international stage.[7]

The relationship between these competing chronologies of parliamentary and international history and the history of 'identities' is conceptually fraught. This is largely because the term 'identity' is an ambiguous one for any period before the closing decades of the eighteenth century. 'Identity' in the sense of individuality (or 'identicality') first appeared in the early seventeenth century, but it did not gain more general acceptance until its philosophical application by John Locke and David Hume. Its meaning of 'identification' – and, more precisely, of 'self-identification' – does not antedate Rousseau and seems to have had little circulation in English before the 1780s, when Edmund Burke employed it in a recognisably modern (though still, for its time, suspiciously avant-garde) sense.[8] Even then, it would have to wait almost a century before it would be qualified by the adjective 'national'. When the term 'national identity' did first appear, in 1872, it was used tentatively, and was immediately trumped by considerations of 'race': 'as personal identity has been affirmed to consist in the consciousness of personal identity, so it might be argued … that national identity consisted merely in the consciousness of national identity. Nevertheless, blood does usually assert itself in greater or lesser degree, and questions of race and descent are therefore well worthy the attention of political students.'[9]

National 'character' or national 'interest', rather than national identity, would be a more aptly idiomatic term for the eighteenth century. Even then, 'loyalty, station, degree, honour, connection, orthodoxy and conformity' – whether applied to individuals or social groups – possessed more imaginative appeal and explanatory power for contemporary Britons than 'identity'.[10] It was indeed possible, at least by the early nineteenth century, to conceive that '[e]very nation, as an organized being, must have a principle of individuality' because '[s]uch a nation is a political person',[11] but this was more comparable to earlier Hobbesian conceptions of the personality of the state than to later transferred metaphors of psychological identity.[12] Any deployment of 'national identity' to apply to periods before the late nineteenth century is, therefore, strictly anachronistic and beset by competing conceptions of ethnic or political community.

---

[6] Ohlmeyer (1995).   [7] Doyle (2000).

[8] Force (1997); Wootton (2000), pp. 148, 152–3; and, more generally, C. Taylor (1989); Brubaker and Cooper (2000); Wahrman (2004).

[9] Beddoe (1872), p. xxvi; Mandler (2006).   [10] Kidd (1999), p. 291.   [11] Pownall (1803), p. 32.

[12] Skinner (2007).

Likewise, to apply the adjective 'national' to the identity or sovereignty of Parliament at any point after the Reformation is also inherently ambiguous. A strict conception could define the nation as that body of people represented in – and hence subject to – Parliament, as Lord Shelburne did in 1775: 'No man can be at a loss to know, that a majority of both Houses, however constituted, are the nation.'[13] However, that did not correspond to the English realm nor, with the expansion of that realm, did it map closely onto the British Empire. Beginning with the Anglo-Welsh union of the 1530s, the English Parliament legislated for more than one nation; with the incorporation of Scotland and Ireland, and later the conquest of territory and subjugation of non-British, non-white and non-Protestant peoples from Québec to Bengal, it included a greater wealth of nations than could be defined by, or identified with, the ambit of parliamentary sovereignty alone. According to Burke's theory of representation, 'Parliament is not a congress of ambassadors from different and hostile interests . . . but parliament is a *deliberative* assembly of *one* nation, with *one* interest, that of the whole.'[14] He therefore distinguished between a homogeneous nation, identifiable with a single interest, and a heterogeneous 'empire . . . the aggregate of many states under a common head; whether this head be a monarch, or a presiding republic'.[15]

Parliament could neither legislate nationhood into being nor expunge conceptions of nationhood that competed with the Anglo-British version propagated from Westminster with increasing force after 1707. It could only determine the internal boundaries of the state by virtue of its capacity for legislation and taxation.[16] As events in British America after the Seven Years' War showed, that capacity (and the resulting determination of boundaries) was essentially contestable. The American Revolution temporarily settled the contest, but only at the expense of confirming the multinational nature of the British Empire and the limits on Parliament's authority to legislate beyond the Three Kingdoms.[17] The English – later, British; still later, imperial – Parliament had been multinational since the 1530s, but it took a crisis of sovereignty to show that nation and state were concentric but still distinct. The American colonists may have claimed membership in a pan-Atlantic British nation but their attempt to capitalise on that nationhood ultimately drove them to declare separate

---

[13] *Parliamentary History* (1806–20), XVIII (1774–7), col. 162.
[14] Edmund Burke, 'Speech to the Electors of Bristol' (3 November 1774), quoted in Sutherland (1968), p. 1005.
[15] *Parliamentary History* (1806–20), XVIII (1774–7), col. 503.   [16] Gunn (1999), p. 117.
[17] Gould (1997); Gould (1999).

statehood for each of the thirteen former colonies. Intra-imperial relations, mediated through Parliament, thereafter became international relations, conducted between the United Kingdom and the United States, the one determinedly unitary (by virtue of common allegiance to the king), the other avowedly plural (at least until 1865, when 'the United States' became a singular entity for all but diehard Confederates and defenders of states' rights).[18]

Parliament's capacity to define and expound the national interest, particularly in an international context, was institutionally and constitutionally limited. 'Parliament could serve as both an institution in which political groups could define their identity and express their views, and one in which ministerial schemes could be expounded and presented as national interests to both domestic and international audiences.'[19] However, that did not mean that it was the only arena for such acts of definition and exposition, which could take place informally in the public prints or formally among lawyers and diplomats, for instance. For as long as foreign affairs remained a matter of royal prerogative and only came before Parliament at the discretion of monarchs and ministries, Parliament's role in sustaining Britain's international standing would necessarily be circumscribed and episodic.[20]

The conception of Parliament's omnipotence in municipal matters contrasted with its relative impotence in foreign affairs. As Sir William Blackstone argued, in an account of parliamentary authority almost Diceyan in its scope:

It hath sovereign and uncontrollable authority in making, confirming, enlarging, restraining, abrogating, repealing, reviving, and expounding of laws, concerning matters of all possible denominations, ecclesiastical, or temporal, civil, military, maritime, or criminal; this being the place where that absolute despotic power, which must in all governments reside somewhere, is entrusted by the constitution of these kingdoms ... It can regulate or new model the succession to the crown ... It can alter the established religion of the land ... It can change and create afresh even the constitution of the kingdom and of parliaments themselves; as was done by the act of union, and the several statutes for triennial and septennial elections. It can, in short, do every thing that is not naturally impossible; and therefore some have not scrupled to call it's power, by a figure rather too bold, the omnipotence of parliament.[21]

---

[18] Pocock (1996), pp. 57–111.   [19] J. Black (2000), p. 47.
[20] J. Black (1991); Black (1992); Black (1993); Black (2004); Black (2011).
[21] Blackstone (1765–9), I, p. 156, 'Of the Parliament' (all further references are to this edition unless otherwise noted); compare Chambers (1986), I, p. 140.

Over domestic matters, Parliament was thus absolute, despotic, even omnipotent; over foreign affairs, its authority depended on the prerogatives of the Crown. These, Blackstone argued, 'respect either this nation's intercourse with foreign nations, or it's own domestic government and civil polity'. 'With regard to foreign concerns', he continued:

> the king is the delegate or representative of his people. It is impossible that the individuals of a state, in their collective capacity, can transact the affairs of that state with another community equally numerous as themselves. Unanimity must be wanting to their measures, and strength to the execution of their counsels. In the king therefore, as in a center, all the rays of his people are united, and form by that union a consistency, splendor, and power, that make him feared and respected by foreign potentates; who would scruple to enter into any engagements, that must afterwards be revised and ratified by a popular assembly. What is done by the royal authority, with regard to foreign powers, is the act of the whole nation: what is done without the king's concurrence is the act only of private men.[22]

The royal prerogative included – indeed, still includes – sending and receiving ambassadors; entering into treaties, leagues and alliances; and making war and peace.[23] The Act of Settlement had demanded parliamentary consent for any war fought to defend non-British interests, though 'not once was this parliamentary control driven home' during the eighteenth century.[24] As Lord Strange warned during the 1754 debate on the East India Mutiny bill, 'Supposing it should become necessary to declare war against some neighbouring potentate: do we not know, that our sovereign may do so by virtue of his prerogative, and without the authority of an act of parliament?'[25] One major theoretical constraint on the prerogative thus proved unenforceable in practice. Yet, if that prerogative encompassed all collective dealings with foreign powers, it did not have exclusive authority over transactions with individual foreigners or with their vessels at sea: 'our laws have in some respect armed the subject with powers to impel the prerogative; by directing the ministers of the Crown to issue letters of marque and reprisal upon due demand' and to grant safe-conducts to distressed foreigners and to

---

[22] Blackstone (1765–9), I, p. 245, 'Of the King's Prerogative'; compare Chambers (1986), I, p. 158, and Alexander Hamilton, '*The Federalist* no. 69' (14 March 1788), in Hamilton, Madison and Jay (1982), pp. 351–2.

[23] *Halsbury's Statutes* (1985–), XVIII, pp. 720–1, §§ 1406, 1407; Richards (1967); Carstairs and Ware (1991).

[24] J. Black (2000), p. 14.   [25] *Parliamentary History* (1806–20), XV (1753–65), col. 275.

'strangers who come spontaneously'.[26] Parliament also limited the prerogative power by preventing foreign enlistment and regulating foreign
loans and, after 1783, commerce with the United States. The division of
labour between Crown and Parliament was therefore not absolute but
relative, though in foreign affairs the balance always tipped decisively
in the Crown's favour.

Municipal affairs took place within the ambit of national law while
foreign affairs were transacted under the law of nations. On these
grounds, Blackstone in the House of Commons during the Stamp Act
crisis and his successor as Vinerian Professor at Oxford, Sir Robert Chambers, both supported Parliament's right to tax the colonies: as Chambers
noted in his Oxford lectures, 'It appears ... reasonable to conclude that
all colonies may be taxed by that state on which they depend for support,
and to which they fly for protection, and that English colonies may ... be
taxed by an English legislature.'[27] Parliament could legislate municipally
but could only apply the law of nations or incorporate it into national
legislation. What then *was* the relationship between a sovereign, imperial
Parliament (as defined by the Henrician Act in Restraint of Appeals of 1533)
and the law of nations, 'a system', according to Blackstone, 'of rules,
deducible by natural reason, and established by universal consent among
the civilized inhabitants of the world'? Blackstone's answer defined the
conventional legal wisdom of the mid eighteenth century:

since in England no royal power can introduce a new law, or suspend the
execution of the old, therefore the law of nations (wherever any question arises
which is properly the object of it's jurisdiction) is here adopted in it's full extent
by the common law, and is held to be part of the law of the land. And those acts
of parliament, which have from time to time been made to enforce this universal
law, or to facilitate the execution of it's decisions, are not to be considered as
introductive of any new rule, but merely as declaratory of the old fundamental
constitutions of the kingdom; without which it must cease to be part of the
civilized world.[28]

Blackstone's judgment affirmed the supremacy of statute and the integrity
of the common law by encompassing the law of nations within them
rather than erecting it as a higher law above them. It did not imply that

---

[26] Blackstone (1765–9), I, pp. 250, 251.   [27] Ryder (1969), p. 268; Chambers (1986), I, p. 292.
[28] Blackstone (1765–9), IV, pp. 66–7, 'Of Offences Against the Law of Nations'. Chambers was more
circumspect: 'in England in particular the municipal law in this instance [regarding diplomatic
immunity from arrest for debt or civil contract], *as in most if not all others*, perfectly conforms itself
to the law of nations': Chambers (1986), I, p. 262 (my emphasis). On Blackstone and the law of
nations, see Janis (2010), pp. 2–10.

the law of nations could be used to overturn English law, nor that explicit references to the law of nations in legislation could be deemed to graft alien principles onto English statutes. (Blackstone's view was, however, strictly English, and contrasted starkly with Scots lawyers' understandings before 1707 of the relationship between municipal and natural law, for whom '[t]heories of sovereignty might stress statutes or customs; natural law had primacy over them'.)[29] If the principles of the law of nations were already enshrined in the common law, and if common law and statute law were necessarily harmonised with one another, then the law of nations must, logically, be in concert with, and intrinsic to, the law made by Parliament itself.

Yet the relationship between the law of nations and municipal law was not quite as straightforward, or indeed as immemorial, as Blackstone would have liked his readers to believe. In 1754, Mansfield, speaking in the case of *Triquet* v. *Bath*, recalled that in the earlier case of *Buvot* v. *Barbuit* in 1737,

LORD TALBOT declared clear Opinion – 'That the *Law of Nations*, in its *full* Extent, was Part of the Law of England.' . . . 'That the *Law of Nations* was to be *collected* from the *Practice* of the different nations, and the Authority of *Writers*.' Accordingly, he argued and determined from such Instances, and the Authority of *Grotius, Barbeyrac, Binkershoek, Wiquefort, &c.*, there being no *English* writer of Eminence, upon the Subject.[30]

Mansfield (when still plain Mr Murray) had acted as counsel in *Buvot* v. *Barbuit*; likewise, Blackstone acted as counsel in *Triquet* v. *Bath*.[31] A clear line of transmission can thus be traced for the doctrine that the law of nations was part of English law, running back from Blackstone through Lord Mansfield to Lord Talbot. However, Mansfield's account of Talbot's ruling was not published until 1771, and the standard report of *Buvot* v. *Barbuit* (first published in 1741) contained no statement to the effect that the law of nations was part of the law of England.[32] The doctrine therefore cannot be traced any earlier in print than Blackstone's *Commentaries*.

---

[29] Cairns (1995), pp. 254 (quoted), 268.
[30] *Triquet and Others* v. *Bath* (1764), in *Reports of Cases* (1771–80), III, p. 1480; Nussbaum (1947), pp. 136–7; D. Lieberman (1989), pp. 105–6. The writers named are Hugo Grotius (1583–1645); Jean Barbeyrac (1674–1744), Swiss editor of Grotius and Pufendorf; Cornelis van Bijnkershoek (1673–1743), Dutch author of *De foro legatorum in causa civili, quam criminali* (1721); and Abraham de Wicquefort (1606–82), Dutch author of *Mémoires touchant l'ambassadeur et les ministères publics* (1676).
[31] Lauterpacht (1940), p. 53; Adair (1928), p. 296; more generally, O'Keefe (2008).
[32] *Buvot* v. *Barbuit* (1737), in *Cases in Equity* (1741), pp. 281–3.

In both *Buvot* v. *Barbuit* and *Triquet* v. *Bath* the point at issue had been the immunity of diplomats from civil and criminal prosecution. In each case, diplomatic immunity was taken to be a recognised principle of the law of nations but not one that had therefore always been enshrined in English law. However, even during the Commonwealth and Interregnum, aggrieved ambassadors appealed to the Council of State or the Protector (as did the brother of the Portuguese ambassador Dom Pantaleone de Sá in 1653–4) rather than to Parliament. Until the early eighteenth century, offenders against diplomatic immunity were punished by prerogative action rather than by the common-law courts.[33] This particular principle of the law of nations, at least, had therefore not been historically part of the common law of England.

Prior to 1709 there had been no formal recognition of the principle that the law of nations was part of the law of England. In that year, Parliament passed the Act of 7 Anne c. 12 which guaranteed ambassadors and their servants immunity from arrest or prosecution, '[t]he deficiency of the laws, to punish insults, in the case of Foreign Ministers being apparent'.[34] Creditors of the heavily indebted Russian ambassador Andrei Artemonovich Matveev had him arrested after his final audience in 1708. In the process, the arresting sheriff and his men beat the ambassador, assaulted his footmen, bundled him into a carriage and briefly detained him. Seventeen men responsible for issuing and enforcing the writ against Matveev were tried and convicted on the facts, though their guilt in law was never determined. The English government admitted that the law of nations had been breached, but no criminal charges could be brought because neither statute nor the common law had been broken.[35] When Peter the Great demanded the culprits' execution, Queen Anne placed a bill before Parliament declaring all writs against accredited diplomats or suits for the seizure of their property to be void because they were '[c]ontrary to the law of nations, and in prejudice of the rights and privileges, which ambassadors, and other public ministers ... have at all times been thereby possessed of, and which ought to be kept sacred and inviolable'.[36]

The opinion that 7 Anne c. 12 'was not an *Alteration* of the Law from what it was before' seems to have originated with Blackstone, when he acted as counsel in *Triquet* v. *Bath*, in which proceedings it then had

---

[33] Adair (1928), pp. 292–4.

[34] 7 Anne c. 12, 'An Act for preserving the Privileges of Ambassadors, and other publick Ministers of Foreign Princes and States'; *Parliamentary History* (1806–20), VI (1702–14), col. 792.

[35] Frey and Frey (1999), pp. 227–9.   [36] *Parliamentary History* (1806–20), VI (1702–14), col. 793.

been approved and elaborated by Lord Mansfield himself.[37] Blackstone noted in 1765 that 'in consequence of this statute, thus enforcing the law of nations, these privileges are now usually allowed in the courts of common law'.[38] By the time the second edition of his *Commentaries* appeared in 1766, this passage had become even more emphatic: 'In consequence of this statute, thus *declaring and* enforcing the law of nations, these privileges are *now held to be part of the law of the land, and are constantly allowed* in the courts of common law.'[39] His first account acknowledged that this was a recent development in the courts ('*now* usually allowed'); his second, that the Act of 7 Anne c. 12 had applied a principle of the law of nations that had acquired increasing force and application ('now ... *constantly* allowed in the courts of common law'). Thus, even Blackstone admitted that there had been historical change in the relationship between English law and the law of nations, both in its incorporation into statute and in its application in the courts. Indeed, when at the conclusion of the *Commentaries* he enumerated '[t]he chief alterations of the moment' in English law, the first he listed was 'the solemn recognition of the law of nations with respect to the rights of embassadors'.[40]

The Act of 7 Anne c. 12 was one of only two statutes during the long eighteenth century that expressly referred to the law of nations.[41] Its enactment had demonstrated that the principle of diplomatic immunity had not been enforceable in English law before 1709, while the almost complete dearth of statutory reference to the law of nations thereafter in the long eighteenth century revealed the distinction between the two species of law. The relationship between English law and the law of nations was evidently not one of explicit declaration or complete incorporation.[42] However, English legal doctrine as Mansfield affirmed in *Heathfield* v. *Chilton* in 1764 did consistently hold the view that an Act of Parliament could not alter the law of nations.[43] This principle implied that natural law could not be affected by a merely human enactment: as

---

[37] *Reports of Cases* (1771–80), III, pp. 1478–79, citing 31 Henry VI c. 4, Grotius, Bijnkershoek and various English court-cases.
[38] Blackstone (1765–9), I, p. 248.
[39] Blackstone (1766–9), I, pp. 256–7 (my emphasis); compare Chambers (1986), I, p. 262. On Blackstone's revisions to the *Commentaries*, see Prest (2008), pp. 246–53.
[40] Blackstone (1765–9), IV, p. 434, 'Of the Rise, Progress, and Gradual Improvements, of the Laws of England'.
[41] The other was 55 Geo. III c. 160, sec. 58, 'An Act for the Encouragement of Seamen': Thomas Erskine Holland, 'International Law and Acts of Parliament', in Holland (1898), p. 193.
[42] Picciotto (1915), pp. 75–108.   [43] Holdsworth (1937–72), X, p. 372.

Burke argued in 1781, '[t]he rights of war were not ... limited by the learning of the schools, by the light of philosophy, by the disquisitions of councils, by the debates of legislatures, or by the sense of delegated assemblies'.[44] It also implied that Parliament could make no laws that did not accord with natural reason, and hence with the law of nations that derived from the universal assent of rational creatures. Though English law and the law of nations remained distinct in their application, they could still be assimilated in principle, so that the law of nations presented no challenge to the supremacy of Parliament and the absolute power of Parliament posed no threat to the highest of all laws. The law of nations could thus be deployed in matters beyond national jurisdiction, as when it was applied in the Court of Admiralty or when the law-merchant was gradually taken up by common-law courts;[45] it could also be adopted selectively by statutory incorporation. Either way, each form of law remained independent, and was thereby no threat to the authority of the other within its own proper sphere.

In light of the preceding discussion, the question of Parliament's relationship to international law in the eighteenth century might seem utterly *mal posée*. After all, Parliament had no formal role in conducting foreign policy and hence in directly negotiating matters subject to the law of nations. The moments at which it exercised its rights of review and debate over inter-national agreements were relatively few and hence particularly notorious, as in the case of the argument over the Anglo-French Commercial Treaty of 1786.[46] The occasions on which parliamentary statute appealed to the law of nations were vanishingly small in number, nor (according to English legal doctrine) could legislation supersede that higher law.

However, even taking these important objections into account, there remain at least three areas in which the question of Parliament's relation-ship to international law can be genuinely illuminating. The first lies in the reconsideration of parliamentary action within the acknowledged context of the law of nations, for example, during the Glorious Revolution, in the course of the Anglo-Scottish Union negotiations or the debate on the recognition of American independence in 1782–3. The second lies in the use of international law in parliamentary debate, where it was always more conspicuous than in legislation, and where it became more noticeable after the Seven Years' War: that is, during the period when imperial and

---

[44] *Parliamentary History* (1806–20), XXII (1781–2), col. 230.   [45] Bourguignon (1987); Baker (1999).
[46] J. Black (1994), pp. 104–11, 491–2.

military matters progressively came to dominate deliberation and discussion at Westminster. The third area is the extra-parliamentary development of the law of nations itself, especially as it came to be reconceptualised in the closing decades of the eighteenth century (and not just in Britain). Out of these discussions on the scope and nature of international law emerged conventional and abiding distinctions between internal and external forms of law which in turn mirrored differences between domestic and international histories and rendered them mutually incomprehensible.

The relevance of the law of nations to English and, later, British definitions of parliamentary legitimacy and authority demonstrates the artificiality of such enduring distinctions and differences. This became especially clear in the period between the Glorious Revolution and the Anglo-Scottish Union of 1707. In contrast to later Whig interpretations of the Revolution, Tories and radical Whigs had understood the Revolution as an event within European history and hence within the categories of the law of nations. William's invasion, whether seen as motivated by the imperatives of his own foreign policy or as a generous response to English concern at dynastic instability, was nonetheless an external intervention into the affairs of a divided country. The presiding authority in international law at the time of the Glorious Revolution was Hugo Grotius. He had enumerated the extenuating conditions under which resistance or intervention might be justifiable, and provided authoritative support for those in England who wished to defend the Revolution on grounds other than that of *force majeure*. According to those who appropriated Grotius's arguments during the Revolution debate of 1689–93, William had defeated James in a just war and could thus claim title to the English throne as a legitimate conqueror.[47] Understood as an invasion of one sovereign by another, the Revolution was an event in the relations between states and hence covered by the law of nations rather than by English law alone. Such arguments found more purchase in pamphlets than they did within Parliament, but even there – or, rather, in the Convention – it was argued that because the nation had been returned to a state of nature by James's dereliction, the law of nature and of nations provided the only guide: a 'gentleman cries, where is the Law? When we cannot find it, we must have recourse to the law of nations.'[48]

The law of nations, and more specifically Grotius's account of it, also provided an explanatory framework for the Anglo-Scottish Union of 1707.

---

[47] Blount (1689); *Parliamentary History* (1806–20), v (1688–1702), col. 69; Goldie (1977).
[48] *Parliamentary History* (1806–20), v (1688–1702), col. 128.

In this context, it was invoked not to supply an absence of law (as in the Convention debates of 1688) but rather as the means to understand the legislative union of two sovereign powers. Proponents of union frequently referred to Grotius's account of the union between the Romans and the Sabines, in which the great jurist argued that the two peoples had not lost their separate rights but had instead communicated them to one another as they made up one new state (Grotius, *De Jure Belli ac Pacis*, II. ix. 9).[49] Because the union of England and Scotland was negotiated between two separate states (albeit two states sharing a single monarch), the negotiations occurred within the terms set by the law of nations. However, the commissioners who negotiated the terms of the treaty of union had been appointed by the English and Scottish Parliaments and not by the royal prerogative, and thus the treaty of union was not procedurally equivalent to a treaty as defined in public international law. Moreover, acceptance of the terms of the treaty by the two Parliaments extinguished each of them, created a new British legislature at Westminster and introduced a wholly new state, the United Kingdom of Great Britain. The Treaty of 1707 could not subsequently be challenged or renegotiated under the terms of international law because the parties to it no longer existed as international entities: '[t]he reason ... is that, paradoxically, the Law of Nations is concerned – not with nations [like England and Scotland] – but with states [like the United Kingdom]'.[50] Under the terms of the Treaty, the two nations remained separate in matters of private law, for example, but in the eyes of public law they had become one. With a single legislature to complement a single crown, there need no longer be collisions between two Parliaments pursuing competing foreign and commercial policies (the dangers of which the Scots Darien venture – an attempt promoted by the Scottish Parliament to settle the isthmus of Panama – had magnified in the 1690s), though the constitutional distinction between executive and legislative, and hence between prerogative and Parliament, remained as it had been since 1688: treaties needed only to be laid before Parliament if they necessitated either new fiscal exactions or an Act of Parliament to enforce their provisions.[51]

The prominence of Grotius in the Union debates stemmed, in part, from the centrality of the modern tradition of natural law to legal and ethical education in Scotland and, increasingly, in England.[52] However, prior to

---

[49] J. Robertson (1995a), pp. 18–19; Robertson (1995b), p. 221.   [50] T. B. Smith (1962), p. 8.
[51] Gibbs (1970), pp. 118–24.
[52] Cairns (1995), pp. 258–9; D. Lieberman (1989), pp. 38–9; D. Lieberman (1999a), p. 363.

the Seven Years' War, citations from continental authorities on the law of
nature and of nations appeared mostly in the literature out of doors; only in
the latter half of the eighteenth century do they seem to have become an
essential part of the oratorical arsenal of the well-prepared parliamentary
debater. It was therefore no surprise to see Grotius repeatedly cited in the
Commons' debates at the opening of the Seven Years' War, for example.[53]
Such texts became even more prominent in Parliament as they were more
thoroughly assimilated into the literature of the English common law.
In this regard, one of the more notable features of the later volumes of
Blackstone's *Commentaries* is their reliance on continental legal thought:
not just Beccaria's recently published *Essay on Crimes and Punishments*
(1764; English translation, 1767) but also such writers as Pufendorf,
Bijnkershoek, Montesquieu and Vattel.[54] Likewise, Mansfield's reliance
on '[t]he Roman code, the law of nations, and the opinion of foreign
civilians' in his rulings on commercial law, and his much-admired 1753
memorial on Prussian neutrality (which earned him the plaudits of both
Montesquieu and Vattel), may also have made such authorities more
familiar to British lawyers and parliamentarians.[55]

The debate on the preliminary articles of peace after the American
War provided a test-case for the utility of the law of nations by bringing
to a head debate on the relative authority of Parliament and the
Crown. Unlike the Seven Years' War, the American War entailed the
dismemberment, rather than the augmentation, of the British Empire and
a fundamental reassessment of the authority of the British state, with
consequent reconsideration of British nationhood in a world where
fellow-Britons had become rebels and rebels then became independent
actors within the extended European states-system.[56] Even though the
King had declared the colonists to be in rebellion by the autumn of 1775,
he had not thereby absolved them of allegiance to the British Crown.
According to the principle *nemo potest exuere patriam*, the colonists
could not renounce their British citizenship by their own unilateral
declaration of independence.[57] Recognition of American independence
also demanded the cession of territory formerly part of the Crown's

---

[53] *Parliamentary History* (1806–20), xv (1753–65), cols. 554 (Gilbert Elliot), 556 (Welbore Ellis), 568
(Charles Townshend).

[54] See, for example, Blackstone (1765–9), I, p. 43; II, p. 390; III, pp. 70, 401; IV, pp. 16–17, 66, 185, 238;
D. Lieberman (1989), pp. 205–8.

[55] Murray (1753); 'Junius' (*sc.* Philip Francis), letter 41, to Lord Mansfield (14 November 1770), in
Junius (1978), p. 208; D. Lieberman (1989), p. 112.

[56] Conway (2002).   [57] Plowden (1784); Plowden (1785); Kettner (1976); Martin (1991).

dominions in North America. Because the Crown could not divest itself of territory by prerogative alone, nor could it unilaterally dissolve the acts of Parliament that had comprised the constitution of the empire, Parliament had to intervene in the framing of the peace-treaty. Such an intervention was not, of course, unprecedented: similar questions had arisen with reference to the return of Dunkirk to France in 1662, in relation to Gibraltar in 1720 and with regard to the cessions of territory after the Seven Years' War.[58] Under the terms of a 1782 Act, Parliament had empowered the Crown to cede the former territory of the British colonies to the Americans, 'any Law, Act or Acts of Parliament, Matter or Thing, to the contrary in anywise notwithstanding'.[59] This move was intended to circumvent disquiet regarding 'the right of the crown to dismember the empire without sanction of parliament; and, for the sake of making peace, to resign a territory not acquired during the war', raised by the Earl of Carlisle in the Lords' debate on the articles of peace in the following year.[60] Opponents of the peace-articles argued that the 1782 Act had only authorised the Crown to recognise American independence, not to cede territory in North America to the United States or fishing rights in Newfoundland and the gulf of St Lawrence, for example. Though Parliament ultimately ratified the terms of the treaty, the larger question remained unresolved until the cession by Parliament of Heligoland in 1890, which seemed to settle the matter in favour of statute rather than prerogative.

The debate of 1782–3 on American independence, which Lord North called 'an object of the greatest magnitude that ever came under parliamentary discussion', was partly conducted in the language of the law of nations, and with the aid of the best modern authorities.[61] Those authorities did not agree with one another: Burlamaqui, for one, held that the ruler of a patrimonial kingdom might alienate any part of his territories at will; however, Vattel denied that England was such a kingdom, and argued instead that the Kings of England 'cannot alienate any part of their dominions without the consent of parliament'.[62] Lord Hawke cited

---

[58] Gibbs (1970), pp. 125–9 (on Dunkirk and Gibraltar); A. Smith (1978), pp. 324–5 (report of 1762–3), citing Pufendorf, Cocceius and Hutcheson.

[59] 22 Geo. III, c. 46, 'Act to Enable His Majesty to Conclude a Peace, or Truce, with the Revolted Colonies in North America'.

[60] *Parliamentary History* (1806–20), XXIII (1782–3), col. 378; compare cols. 484, 514–15.

[61] *Parliamentary History* (1806–20), XXIII (1782–3), col. 560.

[62] Marquis of Carmarthen in *Parliamentary History* (1806–20), XXIII (1782–3), col. 379 (citing Burlamaqui (1763), II, pp. 215–16, and Vattel, *Droit des gens*, I. iii. 117); Gibbs (1970), p. 125 n. 40.

Pufendorf to support the Crown's right to cede East Florida; in response to speakers who 'gravely referred their lordships to Swiss authors for an explanation of the prerogatives of the British crown', the Lord Chancellor, Lord Thurlow, scoffed at the 'lucubrations and fancies of foreign writers' and denied the authority of 'Mr. Vattel and Mr. Puffendorf'.[63]

The standard European texts of international law became more readily available in English and French translations, which may partly explain or even excuse the notorious backwardness of British (meaning, mostly, English) lawyers in contributing to contemporary international jurisprudence. European observers, and later historians, discerned only four lasting eighteenth-century British additions to the corpus of international thought: Mansfield's memorial of 1753; Jeremy Bentham's 'Pacification and Emancipation' (better known as his 'Essay for Universal and Perpetual Peace') (*c.* 1786–9); Robert Ward's *Enquiry into the Foundation and History of the Law of Nations in Europe, From the Time of the Greeks and Romans, to the Age of Grotius* (1795); and Sir James Mackintosh's *Discourse on the Study of the Law of Nature and Nations* (1799).[64] Bentham's plans remained among his papers until their publication in the mid nineteenth century, but Ward's *Enquiry* and Mackintosh's *Discourse* gained greater fame in their own time. Ward's *Enquiry* became a standard history of the law of nations for the positivist era. Its author was sceptical of the utility of deriving international norms from conceptions of natural law which were clearly not universal, and instead described the laws of a Christian civilisation clearly confined to Europe and its imperial outposts and successor-states, but also threatened by the atheistical French republican attempt to legislate its own conception of the law of nations.[65] Mackintosh's *Discourse* formed the preface to the enormously successful – but now, unfortunately, lost – set of lectures, eclectically derived from German histories of philosophy, the jurisprudence of Montesquieu and the canon of international law from Grotius to Vattel, which he delivered in Lincoln's Inn Hall in early 1799 to a distinguished audience including six peers and twelve Members of Parliament.[66] However, most prominent of all in bringing 'the elements and principles of the law of nations, the great ligament of mankind' to the

---

[63] *Parliamentary History* (1806–20), XXIII (1782–3), cols. 390 (referring to Samuel Pufendorf, *De Jure Naturæ et Gentium Libri Octo* (1688), VIII. v. 9), 431–2.

[64] UCL Bentham XXV, heavily edited in Bentham (1838–43), II, pp. 546–60; R. Ward (1795); Mackintosh (1799).

[65] Ward (1795), II, p. 338.

[66] BL Add. MS 78781; J. Mackintosh (1835), I, pp. 108, 111–15 (extracts from first lecture); J. Mackintosh (2006), pp. 250–8 ('Appendix to the "Discourse": Extracts from the Lectures').

attention of Parliament was surely Edmund Burke, who drew upon them repeatedly in the Hastings trial and who, like Charles James Fox, argued over the relevance of Vattel to the justification of war with the French Directory.[67]

The prominence of these authorities on the law of nations was symptomatic of burgeoning interest in the definition of international law itself in the last two decades of the century. That interest was not confined to Parliament, or to Britain; it was in the nature of the subject itself to be transnational in scope. Jeremy Bentham coined the term 'international' in 1780 to denote the body of law dealing specifically with the relations between sovereign states, rather than between nations or peoples, whether individually or collectively: 'inter*state* law' might therefore have been a less ambiguous designation.[68] His neologism did not catch on more generally in anglophone usage for a quarter of a century, though the need for the word 'international' was one sign that the law of nations (or, we might say, states) had now to be distinguished from the law of nature (with which it had been traditionally held to be almost entirely homologous). It was therefore more closely identified with customary or positive law, the actions of states and the positive agreements between them. This, in turn, created greater demand for collections of treaties as evidence of international norms. As Charles Jenkinson put it, in the preface to his treaty-collection of 1785, 'The Utility of such a Work is sufficiently obvious to the Gentleman, and the Politician. To the Statesman it is a Code, or Body of Law; since a Collection of Treaties is to him of the same Use, that a Collection of Statutes is to a Lawyer.'[69]

The rise of interest in the decades following the Seven Years' War in the theory and practice of the law of nations paralleled the expansion of imperial and extra-national legislation by the Westminster Parliament. The ratio of legislative activity devoted to imperial and other (including international) legislation – rather than to local, national or 'British' legislation – declined across the course of the century; however, the absolute volume of imperial and international legislation did increase dramatically after 1763.[70] Parliament's willingness to legislate extraterritorially was, of course, no novelty in the late eighteenth century: the Navigation Acts had ring-fenced global trade since the 1650s and laws against piracy had swept non-state

---

[67] Edmund Burke, *First Letter on a Regicide Peace* (20 October 1796), in Burke (1991), p. 240; Charles James Fox, 'Address on the King's Speech at the Opening of the Session' (21 January 1794), in Fox (1815), v, p. 156; Stanlis (1953); Whelan (1996), pp. 287–91; Hampsher-Monk (2005).
[68] Bentham (1996), pp. 6, 296; Suganami (1978); Janis (1984), pp. 408–10.
[69] Jenkinson (1785), i, pp. iii–iv.   [70] Innes (2003), p. 19.

actors from the seas in the half-century before 1720, for example.[71]
The suppression of the slave-trade is, of course, the most spectacular evidence
of Parliament's desire to enforce norms of international law – by treating
slave-traders as enemies of humankind (*hostes humani generis*), as pirates had
traditionally been designated – but it was hardly unique.[72] From the early
nineteenth century, Parliament legislated not just for the nations of Britain
and Ireland and for the territories comprising the realm, but even further
abroad for territories under the protection of the Crown, such as Honduras
or Tahiti (Murders Abroad Act, 57 Geo. III c. 53), the Pacific Islands (9 Geo.
IV c. 83 § 4), Hong Kong (3 & 4 William IV c. 93 §§ 5–16, 6 & 7 Victoria
c. 80) or the Cape (6 & 7 William IV c. 57).[73] 'This was more obviously
an "imperial parliament": a parliament superintending the affairs of several,
interacting but distinct politico-cultural entities': but clearly not just within
the ambit of Britain and Ireland alone.[74]

   The causes of change across the eighteenth century were obvious to
Edmund Burke:

as Commerce, with its Advantages and its Necessities, opened a Communication
more largely with other Countries; as the Law of Nature and Nations (always a
Part of the Law of *England*) came to be cultivated; as an increasing Empire; as
new Views and Combinations of Things were opened . . . antique Rigour and
over-done Severity gave Way to the Accommodation of Human Concerns, for
which Rules were made, and not Human Concerns to bend to them.[75]

The particular prominence of international law in parliamentary debate
and the willingness of Parliament to legislate extraterritorially may however
have helped to harden distinctions between municipal and international
law rather than to relax them. The pre-eminence of statute, and the
evident impossibility of enforcing international norms without the force
of legislation, encouraged theorists of positive law, most notably John
Austin, in their denial that international 'law' was law in any recognisable
sense, precisely because it lacked a sovereign legislator, could not be
construed as a command and carried with it no enforceable sanctions.[76]
This distinction between municipal and international law reinforced the
abiding distinction between domestic and international history.

   Parliamentary history has usually been understood as the history of
municipal legislation and debate, and hence as part of domestic rather

---

71 Pérotin-Dumont (1991), pp. 214–18; Ritchie (1986): Benton (2005).
72 Davis (1998), pp. 113–19; Allain (2007); Keene (2007).   73 Holdsworth (1937–72), XIV, pp. 81–6.
74 Innes (2003), p. 38.   75 Report on the Lords Journals (30 April 1794), in Burke (1998), p. 163.
76 Austin (1995), pp. 123, 160, 171, 175–6.

than international history. In part, such a description of Parliament's capacities derived from the constitutional divisions between executive and legislative; however, in so far as law-making and discussion came ever more to encompass imperial issues and to be conducted in the language of the law of nations, parliamentary debate became more international and even transnational in scope while legislation increasingly regulated actions or events in ways that transcended national frontiers, whether within Britain and Ireland or far beyond them as the British Parliament had to pay increasing attention to the norms of international law in a century of imperial rivalry, global war and republican revolution.

CHAPTER 9

Edmund Burke and reason of state

Edmund Burke has been one of the few political thinkers to be treated seriously by international theorists.[1] According to Martin Wight, one of the founders of the English School of international theory, Burke was '[t]he only political philosopher who . . . turned wholly from political theory to international theory'.[2] The resurgence of interest in Burke as an international theorist did not, however, generate any consensus about how he might be classified within the traditions of international theory. Wight variously divided thinkers into trichotomous schools of Realists, Rationalists and Revolutionaries, Machiavellians, Grotians and Kantians, or theorists of international anarchy, habitual intercourse and moral solidarity;[3] more recent international theorists refined or supplemented these categories to construct similar trinitarian traditions of Realism, Liberalism and Socialism, and of Empirical Realism, Universal Moral Order and Historical Reason.[4] Burke's place within any of these traditions has remained uncertain. Debate over whether he was a realist or an idealist, a Rationalist or a Revolutionist, has concluded variously that he was a 'conservative crusader', or a 'historical empiricist', a belated dualist or a Cold Warrior before the fact, or, most egregiously, 'a proto-Marxist, or more precisely proto-Gramscian' theorist of hegemony.[5] The fact that Burke so obviously eludes definition puts in doubt the analytical utility of closely defined 'traditions' of international theory.[6]

---

[1] For introductions to Burke as an international theorist, see Burke (1999) and Bourke (2009).
[2] Wight (1966), p. 20.
[3] Wight (1991); Wight (1987); Bull (1976), pp. 101–16 (reprinted in Wight (1991), pp. ix–xxiii); Porter (1978).
[4] Doyle (1997), pp. 18–20, and *passim*; D. Boucher (1998), pp. 28–43, and *passim*.
[5] Vincent (1984); D. Boucher (1991); D. Boucher (1998), pp. 308–29; Harle (1990), pp. 59, 72; K. Thompson (1994), p. 100; Halliday (1994), pp. 108–13.
[6] Welsh (1995), pp. 6–9, 172–80; Welsh (1996), pp. 173–7, 183–6; Burke (1999), pp. 38–9, 51–6. On 'traditions' within international theory more generally, see Nardin and Mapel (1992); Dunne (1993); I. Clark (1996); Jeffery (2005).

Burke's relationship to conceptions of reason of state provides a more precise example of the confusion within such taxonomies. According to one historian of international theory, Burke 'laid the foundations' of the 'conservative approach to International Relations . . . informed by the two modern notions of state interest and necessity, by *raison d'état*'; however, in the words of another, 'Burke . . . was vehemently opposed to the idea of Reason of State and did not subscribe to the view that national interests override moral laws.'[7] The assumptions on which each of these judgments rests are clearly incompatible: on the one hand, that a 'conservative approach' in the realm of foreign affairs implies an espousal of reason of state defined as the primacy of 'state interest and necessity', that Burke did, indeed, acknowledge; on the other, that reason of state is defined more exactly as 'the view that national interests override moral laws', and that Burke did not hold such a view, so could not therefore be defined as a reason-of-state theorist. It might, of course, be possible that Burke held various views on such matters at various points in his long literary and political career, or that he argued for differing conceptions of reason of state in differing contexts. To test such a hypothesis demands a historical account of Burke's relationship to the theories of reason of state held by his contemporaries and predecessors.

To place Burke within traditions of reason of state might seem to be a simple category error. After all, he famously scorned 'dashing Machiavelian politicians', deplored 'the odious maxims of a Machiavelian policy', condemned 'the dreadful maxim of Machiavel that in great affairs men are not to be wicked by halves' and identified the *Discorsi* as the inflammatory textbook of French republicanism.[8] His strictures on Machiavelli and Machiavellianism affirmed *avant la lettre* the classic modern account of reason of state offered by Friedrich Meinecke, which counterposed '*raison d'état* on the one hand, and ethics and law on the other' and traced the emergence of this separation to the heathen Florentine who had given the tradition its familiar nickname.[9] Such accounts of reason of state and of Machiavelli reinforced the long-standing interpretation of Burke as the

---

[7] Knutsen (1992), pp. 141, 143; D. Boucher (1998), p. 14.

[8] Edmund Burke, *Reflections on the Revolution in France* (1790), in Burke (1989), pp. 60, 132; Burke, *Fourth Letter on a Regicide Peace* (1795–6), in Burke (1991), p. 69 (alluding to Machiavelli, *Discorsi*, I. 27); Burke, *Second Letter on a Regicide Peace* (1796), in Burke (1991), p. 282.

[9] Meinecke (1998), pp. 28, 29. Meinecke earlier argued that Burke 'struck the first decisive blow against conceptions of the state that the eighteenth century had formed on the basis of natural law' and assimilated him to Machiavelli and later advocates of *Realpolitik* who had also recognised the importance of 'the irrational components of the life of the state, for the power of traditions, customs, instinct, and impulsive feelings': Meinecke (1970), p. 101.

last of the medieval theorists of natural law, for whom no merely human calculations of advantage or interest could override the dictates of divine reason. If reason of state represented the doctrine that political expediency should supersede moral law, then Burke could only have been its (and Machiavelli's) enemy: his 'politics ... were grounded on recognition of the universal law of reason and justice ordained by God as the foundation of a good community. In this recognition the Machiavellian schism between politics and morality is closed, and it is exactly in this respect that Burke stands apart from the modern positivists and pragmatists who in claiming him have diminished him.'[10] To accept otherwise would have allowed him to fall back into the hands of those exponents of expediency, the utilitarians and the secularists.

These accounts of reason of state and of natural law arguably depend upon a misapprehension of the modern natural-law theory to which Burke was heir. That theory, revived initially by Hugo Grotius and elaborated by his successors, took its foundational principle of self-preservation from the Stoics. To determine the limits of self-preservation as a practical principle always demanded calculations of competing goods according to consequentialist criteria.[11] This was true no less for bodies politic and their rulers than for private persons. In the political realm, the fundamental determining factor in any calculation of outcomes would be necessity. In the case of the *res publica*, necessity, as a principle of political action, could only be justified by an appeal to that *salus populi* which was the *suprema lex*, in Cicero's famous words (*De Legibus*, III. 3). Cicero placed severe constraints upon such calculations in the municipal sphere, and restricted them to the ends of self-defence, security or the protection of liberty; any actions taken in pursuit of such ends had also to avoid infamy and to be in accordance with the republican constitution.[12] In their later recensions – shorn of the specifically Roman and republican legal context within which Cicero wrote – such theories could reconcile the principles of natural law with strictly limited appeals to necessity in the interests of the common good; they could also be extended beyond the municipal to the international realm.[13]

This 'modern' tradition of natural jurisprudence, which rested upon the arguments of Stoic ethics, was utilitarian to the extent that it depended upon the calibration of competing goods in relation to specific

---

[10] Burke (1949), p. xv.   [11] Tuck (1987); Tuck (1993), pp. 172–6.   [12] De Sousa (1992), ch. 2.
[13] On the foundations of a 'humanist' tradition of reason of state, stretching back to Cicero, see Tuck (1999), pp. 18–23, 29–31.

ends. To place Burke within the theory of reason of state derived from this tradition implies no inconsistency in his thought. The opponent of 'Machiavellian' expediency could equally well be the proponent of Ciceronian 'necessity': the difference between the two depended upon the criteria deployed, the circumstances that could be appealed to and the consequences that were desired or imagined. To situate Burke within this strain of early modern reason-of-state theory also makes it possible to appreciate just 'how much weight [he] attaches to considerations based on expediency, treated simply as a practical regard for consequences'.[14] Moreover, because reason of state within this tradition was consequentialist precisely because it was grounded in a neo-Stoic conception of natural law, to see Burke as a reason-of-state theorist in this context neatly avoids the sterile dispute about the true character of his political thought as either utilitarian or natural jurisprudential.[15] It could be described as both, so long as the tradition of natural jurisprudence in question was the 'modern' one initiated by Grotius and so long as the utilitarianism in question was of this consequentialist kind. The assertion that 'the natural-law tradition and consequentialism are opposed at a very deep level' is therefore not true of all forms of natural jurisprudence or even of consequentialism;[16] nor is it necessary to choose between them to characterise Burke's political or international thought.

Burke's reason-of-state theory could be applied equally to the internal constitution and the external relations of a state. In this way, its scope extended beyond the internal political determinations laid down by Cicero to the international realm treated by the modern theorists of natural law like Grotius. Reason of state was thus Janus-faced like its conceptual near-neighbours in early modern political thought, sovereignty and the balance of power.[17] Like them, reason of state crossed the boundary between political theory, defined as the theory of legitimacy and distribution of power within the state, and international theory. In both spheres, reason of state acknowledged the compulsions of necessity; its particular theoretical concern was therefore with the contingent, the extraordinary and the unforeseeable. 'A high degree of causal necessity', argued Meinecke, 'which the agent himself is accustomed to conceive as absolute and inescapable, and to feel most profoundly, is ... part of the very essence of all action

---

[14] Winch (1996), p. 196.   [15] Dinwiddy (1974), pp. 107, 123–5.
[16] *Pace* Boyle (1992), p. 119; compare Friedrich (1957), pp. 31–2.
[17] Hinsley (1986), chs. 4–5; Anderson (1993), pp. 150–4.

prompted by *raison d'état*.'[18] Since necessity has no law (*necessitas non habet legem*), reason of state could not be codified or legislated. Reason of state alone could not determine which circumstances were truly cases of extreme necessity, and hence which precise occasions could permit the overriding of custom and law. It could only lay down norms from which such exceptions could be derived, and more generally it provided a consequentialist means of applying the norms of natural law. In these regards, reason of state was close to resistance theory which also dealt with extremity and overwhelming necessity. Resistance theory did, however, lay down stringent conditions under which rebellion might be justified, even if only in retrospect, and offered a wider range of agents the possibility of making judgments of necessity, even to the point of democratic agency. The compulsion of necessity demanded in reason-of-state theory was assumed to be universally recognisable, but only under particular circumstances by specific, usually sovereign, agents. The conditions that would make necessity both evident and compelling could never be defined with any precision; it therefore demanded princely or conciliar discretion for its application. These requirements placed it firmly among the *arcana imperii*, and left it open to the charge (especially from those who were excluded from judging) that it was merely subjective, arbitrary and unconstrainable.

Because reason of state, whether municipal or international, was morally ambivalent, two types might legitimately be inferred, one natural and hence justifiable, the other merely putative and hence reprehensible.[19] The English Whig tradition that preceded Burke, and upon which he drew, contained examples of these two strains of reason of state. For example, the Marquis of Halifax argued in 1684 that 'there is a natural reason of State, an undefinable thing grounded upon the Common good of mankind, which is immortall, and in all changes and Revolutions still preserveth its Originall right of saving a Nation, when the Letter of the Law perhaps would destroy it'.[20] 'Reall Necessity', he later affirmed, 'is not to bee resisted, and pretended necessity is not to bee alleadged.'[21] Since politicians still alleged necessity nonetheless, it would be distrusted as simply one of the '*Arcana Imperii*', complained John Toland in 1701, 'when in reality Reason of State is nothing else but the right reason of managing the affairs of the State at home and abroad, according to the

---

[18] Meinecke (1998), p. 6.   [19] Viroli (1992), pp. 273–4.
[20] George Savile, Marquis of Halifax, *The Character of a Trimmer* (1684), in Halifax (1989), I, p. 191.
[21] Halifax, 'Prerogative' (1685–8?), in Halifax (1989), II, p. 41.

Constitution of the Government, and with regard to the Interest or Power of other Nations'.[22] The difficulty of judging whether reason of state was natural and directed legitimately towards the interest of the community, or contrived for the benefit of the rulers alone, made it both contestable and open to apparently opposing constructions, even within the thought of a single theorist. As Burke himself noted, in his *Third Letter on a Regicide Peace* (1796–7), 'Necessity, as it has no law, so it has no shame; but moral necessity is not like metaphysical, or even physical. In that category, it is a word of loose signification, and conveys different ideas to different minds.'[23]

Burke's engagement with the language of reason of state ran from his first major published political work, the *Vindication of Natural Society* (1756), to the last, the *Third Letter on a Regicide Peace*. In this *Letter*, he remarked in passing that 'reason of state and common-sense are two things';[24] thirty years earlier, in the *Vindication*, he had satirised contemporary consequentialism along the same lines:

All Writers on the Science of Policy are agreed, and they agree with Experience, that all Governments must frequently infringe the Rules of Justice to support themselves; that Truth must give way to Dissimulation; Honesty to Convenience; and Humanity itself to the reigning Interest. The Whole of this Mystery of Iniquity is called the Reason of State. It is a Reason, which I own I cannot penetrate. What Sort of a Protection is this of the general Right, that is maintained by infringing the Rights of Particulars? What sort of Justice is this, which is inforced by Breaches of its own Laws? . . . For my part, I say what a plain Man would say on such an Occasion. I can never believe, that any Institution agreeable to Nature, and proper for Mankind, could find it necessary, or even expedient in any Case whatsoever to do, what the best and worthiest Instincts of Mankind warn us to avoid.[25]

The publication of Bolingbroke's deistical writings in 1754 provided the immediate occasion for the *Vindication*'s ironic attempt to undermine arguments in favour of natural religion by reducing equivalent arguments

[22] Toland (1701), pp. 93–4.
[23] Burke, *Third Letter on a Regicide Peace* (1796–7), in Burke (1991), p. 344.
[24] Burke, *Third Letter on a Regicide Peace*, in Burke (1991), p. 300.
[25] [Edmund Burke,] *A Vindication of Natural Society* (1756), in Burke (1997), p. 154. Compare Jean-Jacques Rousseau's almost exactly contemporaneous remarks in 'The State of War' (*c.* 1755–6), in Rousseau (1997), p. 163: 'according to the ideas of princes about their absolute independence, force alone, speaking to citizens in the guise of law and foreigners in the guise of reason of state, deprives the latter of the power and the former of the will to resist, so that everywhere the vain name of justice only serves as a shield for violence'.

for natural society *ad absurdum*.[26] However, Burke's target in this passage of the *Vindication* was not Bolingbroke but David Hume. In the *Treatise of Human Nature* (1739–40), Hume had argued that the laws of nations did not supersede the laws of nature. Both persons and bodies politic were bound by the same duties to uphold property and promises; however, the obligation is weaker for princes than for private persons: 'the morality of princes has the same *extent*, yet it has not the same *force* as that of private persons', in proportion to the advantages to be gained by nations rather than individuals from security of property, the administration of justice and the adjudication of equity, he argued.[27] When Hume returned to this question in the *Enquiry Concerning the Principles of Morals* (1751), he restated the distinction in the language of reason of state and provided the immediate occasion for Burke's satire in the *Vindication*:

> The observance of justice, though useful among [nations], is not guarded by so strong a necessity as it is among individuals; and the *moral obligation* holds proportion with the *usefulness*. All politicians will allow, and most philosophers, that REASON OF STATE may, in particular emergencies, dispense with the rules of justice, and invalidate any treaty or alliance, where the strict observance of it would be prejudicial, in a considerable degree, to either of the contracting parties. But nothing less than the most extreme necessity, it is confessed, can justify individuals in a breach of promise, or an invasion of the properties of others.[28]

Burke's ironic recension of Hume left the theoretical foundations of this argument for acting in accordance with reason of state unscathed. Only if civil society itself were illegitimate would such reason of state be unconscionable. If – as Burke later argued in the *Reflections* – government was a necessary 'contrivance of human wisdom to provide for human *wants*' and that 'men have a right that these wants should be provided for by this wisdom', it followed that government was empowered to provide for those wants by any necessary means: the individual members of civil society had already resigned to the government their 'right of self-defence, the first law of nature', and had therefore ceded adjudications of necessity to their governors.[29]

---

[26] Weston (1958); Burke (1993), pp. 4–6. Hampsher-Monk (2010), pp. 245–66, persuasively questions the traditional identification of Rousseau's Second *Discourse* as Burke's other target in the *Vindication*.

[27] Hume (2000), pp. 362–4 (III. ii. 11, 'Of the Laws of Nations').

[28] Hume (1998), p. 100 (Section IV, 'Of Political Society').

[29] Burke, *Reflections on the Revolution in France*, in Burke (1989), p. 110. On the deep background of Burke's suspicion of rationalism in politics, and hence inferentially of any widely distributed power to make rational judgments of necessity, see Hampsher-Monk (1998).

Even within the municipal sphere, Burke argued, any law might be suspended, though only under the compulsion of extreme necessity and in the interest of the preservation of the political community. Conor Cruise O'Brien took such an admission to be 'one of those distressing matters, abounding in the Burkean universe, for which some arrangement of veils was normally appropriate'.[30] However, the principle seems to have caused Burke little distress and would hardly have been a revelation to him. As he told the House of Commons in 1780, the great patent offices in the Exchequer could not be swept away in the name of Economical Reform because, as offices held for life, they were a species of property and only necessity could override the principle of legitimate possession. 'There are occasions', he nevertheless admitted, 'of publick necessity, so vast, so clear, so evident, that they supersede all laws. Law being made only for the benefit of the community, . . . no law can set itself up against the cause and reason of all law.'[31] Only such overmastering compulsion, defined in accordance with public necessity (the Ciceronian *utilitas publica* or *utilitas rei publicæ*), could justify an appeal to reason of state. On the same grounds, he charged that the Protestant Association's opposition to Catholic relief, which they 'dignified by the name of reason of state, and security for constitutions and commonwealths', was a mere 'receipt of policy, made up of a detestable compound of malice, cowardice, and sloth', and hence not a legitimate invocation of the principle.[32] Because the appeal to necessity was only justifiable for the benefit of the whole community and ultimately the preservation of society itself, the occasions on which it could legitimately be invoked had to be extraordinary and overmastering: as Burke argued consistently during the impeachment of Warren Hastings, it could therefore not be raised into a regular principle of government.[33]

Burke argued that only the Glorious Revolution fulfilled these exacting conditions in recent English history and hence provided a reliable standard against which to judge later claims of public necessity. Richard Price's assertion that 1688 had made cashiering kings a regular principle

[30] O'Brien (1972), pp. 34–5.
[31] Edmund Burke, 'Speech on Presenting to the House of Commons, a Plan for the Better Security of the Independence of Parliament, and the Œconomical Reformation of the Civil and Other Establishments' (1780), in Burke (1803–27), III, p. 310. He also argued that the patent offices should be protected because 'the reason of state in every country' demands that public service be rewarded by such grants: ibid., III, p. 310.
[32] Edmund Burke, 'Speech at the Guildhall in Bristol, Previous to the Late Election in that City, Upon Certain Points Relative to his Parliamentary Conduct' (1780), in Burke (1803–27), III, p. 418.
[33] Cone (1957–64), II, pp. 205–7; Greenleaf (1975), pp. 549–67; Whelan (1996), pp. 188–93, 199–202.

of the British constitution forced Burke to refine this theory of state necessity. Against Price, Burke argued that the Revolution had been 'an act of *necessity*, in the strictest moral sense in which necessity can be taken', and that it could not therefore be erected into a constitutional precedent. The extremity of the situation showed that it was possible 'to reconcile . . . the use of both a fixed rule and an occasional deviation', and that this was the only way to remedy such an emergency without a complete dissolution of government.[34] This argument resuscitated a Tory means to defend the Whig doctrine of the ancient constitution in the aftermath of 1688; by adopting it, Burke was also following the lead of the nervous Whig prosecutors of Henry Sacheverell in 1712.[35] This particular argument from necessity had first been employed as a justification of the Revolution by Tories such as Edmund Bohun and Thomas Long, as well as by the Whig Charles Blount, who had all relied upon Grotius to justify a limited right of resistance, as had *de facto* theorists like Anthony Ascham earlier in the seventeenth century.[36] In Book I of *De Iure Belli ac Pacis* (1625), Grotius admitted that even some of the laws of God carried a tacit exception in cases of extreme and imminent peril, though in no case would this be defensible if consideration of the common good were to be abandoned. On such minimalist grounds, resistance would be justified against a ruler who had renounced his governmental authority, alienated his kingdom or otherwise made himself an enemy to the people.[37] Stripped of its explicitly Grotian roots, though maintaining the appeal to self-preservation, this argument provided the Whig managers of Sacheverell's impeachment with just the weapon they needed to combat the doctrine of non-resistance without raising the spectre of a general and unrestricted right of rebellion.[38] Burke quoted the transcript of the Sacheverell trial at length in the *Appeal from the New to the Old Whigs* (1791) to show (in Robert Walpole's words) that only 'the *utmost necessity* ought . . . to engage a nation, *in its own defence, for the preservation of the whole*'.[39]

During the debate on the French Revolution, reason of state in the Grotian tradition provided Burke with an argument to show that the events of 1688 (in England) and 1789 (in France) were similar in that

---

[34] Price (1789), p. 34; Burke (1989), pp. 68, 72.   [35] Goldie (1978b), p. 328; Pocock (1987), p. 381.
[36] Goldie (1977); Wallace (1968), pp. 32–5; Ascham (1648), reprinted in 1689 as Ascham (1689).
[37] Hugo Grotius, *De Iure Belli ac Pacis* (1625), I. 4. 7–14, cited for example by Blount (1689); T. Long (1689), pp. 22, 35.
[38] Holmes (1973), p. 139; Miller (1994), pp. 79–87.
[39] Burke, *An Appeal from the New to the Old Whigs* (1791), in Burke (1992), p. 131; for Burke's use of the trial see ibid., pp. 124–44.

each presented a case of imminent danger that justified armed intervention and hence fulfilled the conditions of 'necessity'.[40] This argument
from necessity thereby supplied Burke with a weapon against those
English Jacobins who assimilated the French Revolution to the Glorious
Revolution, and helped him to show that 1789 was indefensible for
just the same reasons that 1688 had been justifiable. Burke could then
argue that the French Revolution was uniquely threatening, because it
jeopardised the true interests of the states of Europe which were the basis
of their natural reasons of state. On these grounds, a crusade against the
French Revolution would be 'the most clearly just and necessary war, that
this or any other nation ever carried on',[41] in accordance with the
principles of the law of nations laid down by Emer de Vattel. For Burke,
the crucial distinction was that England before 1688 was like France *after*,
not before, 1789. Though the English Jacobins wanted to see the French
republicans as the equivalent of the Whigs, for Burke they were not
only the equivalent of the Jacobites, but were in fact more like Louis
XIV in their desire for universal monarchy.

Burke's appeal to necessity revealed the conceptual difference between
the Glorious Revolution and the French Revolution. The former had
been limited, strategic and constrained precisely by the principle of *salus
populi*; the latter set fair to unleash illimitable consequences as a result of
its unprincipled and unrestricted reasons of state that would endanger
the integrity of all states. This, at least, was the direction of Burke's
argument in the years following the publication of the *Reflections* and
marked a shift in his conception of reason of state between 1790
and 1793. However, the fundamental argument, derived from necessity,
and based upon vestiges of the Roman and neo-Roman theory of reason
of state, was contained in the *Reflections* itself. The Glorious Revolution
and the French Revolution could be distinguished according to the
true and false appeals to necessity each had inspired. Within the terms
of the *ius gentium*, England in 1688 and France after 1793 became
conceptually equivalent because each state was internally divided, each
was threatened by or itself threatened an imminent danger and hence
each could justifiably necessitate armed intervention on the side of
justice. The distinction lay in the fact that France after 1793 (under the
militant, oppressive and outwardly aggressive Directory) was equated

---

[40] For a detailed contextual account of Burke's changing arguments for intervention between the
summer of 1792 and the summer of 1796, see Hampsher-Monk (2005).
[41] Burke, *A Letter to a Noble Lord* (1796), in Burke (1991), p. 168.

with England in 1688 (under the rule of the tyrannical James II). As Burke put it in a startling passage of the *Reflections*, thick with classical allusions and founded upon an argument for conquest that was originally Tory, not Whig,

Laws are commanded to hold their tongues against arms; and tribunals fall to the ground with the peace they are no longer able to uphold. The Revolution of 1688 was obtained by a just war, in the only case in which any war, and much more a civil war, can be just. 'Justa bella quibus *necessaria.*'[42]

Burke here alluded to two of the most frequently cited classical mottoes justifying force over law – Cicero's maxim *silent . . . leges inter armas* (*Pro Milone*, IV. 11) and the speech of Pontius the Samnite in which he argued that the Roman rejection of the Samnites' conciliatory overtures after the battle of the Caudine Forks justified them in going to war on grounds of necessity: *iustum est bellum, Samnites, quibus necessarium* (Livy, *Histories*, IX. 1. 10). In *De Iure Belli ac Pacis*, Grotius had similarly argued that only the municipal laws of a particular community are 'silent . . . in the midst of arms' while the natural law remains in force. Grotius further argued that anyone who has given another just cause for war cannot claim to be acting defensively when they are attacked; just so the Samnites were justified in attacking the Romans after the battle of the Caudine Forks.[43] When Roman implacability demanded extreme measures in response, war became a necessity and arms became lawful for those who were deprived of all other hope. In just such terms, Burke concluded that the intransigence of James II had been a similar 'case of war, and not of constitution', 'an extraordinary question of state, and wholly out of law'.[44]

External intervention, in this case by the Protestant Prince of Orange and his army, had been justified in England's internal affairs, as a civil war outside the bounds of municipal law became a public war between two princes under the principles of the *ius gentium*. In such a contest, victory generated a legitimate appeal to conquest; on these grounds, it was conceivable to see William's intervention in 1688 as an example of a just war and his victory over James as a legitimate act of conquest.[45] It is possible that Burke here was thinking primarily as an Irishman: the

---

[42] Burke, *Reflections on the Revolution in France*, in Burke (1989), p. 80.

[43] Grotius, *De Iure Belli ac Pacis*, 'Prolegomena' 26; II. 1. 18. On Grotius's use of classical quotations, especially from Cicero, Livy and Polybius, see Bederman (1995–6), p. 32; more generally, Straumann (2007).

[44] Burke, *Reflections on the Revolution in France*, in Burke (1989), p. 80.

[45] M. Thompson (1977), pp. 33–46; Goldie (1978a).

Jacobite War of 1690–1 that marked the Irish phase of the Glorious Revolution was, indeed, a war of conquest, as the bloodless standoff between James II and the future William III had hardly been in England.[46] However, more easily documented is Burke's debt here to Vattel. In *Le Droit des gens* (1758), Vattel argued that every foreign power had a right to aid an oppressed people if insupportable tyranny had driven them to rebellion, just as '[t]he English justly complained of James II' in 1688. 'Whenever ... matters are carried so far as to produce a civil war, foreign powers may assist that party which appears to them to have justice on its side'; moreover, 'every foreign power has a right to succour an oppressed people who implore their assistance'. On these grounds, William of Orange had justly intervened on the side of the injured parties, the people of England.[47]

Vattel's use of the Glorious Revolution to justify intervention by foreign powers and Burke's argument that the Revolution presented a case of just war were in fact the same argument, each with the conclusion that 1688 had been a just war precisely because intervention from outside had been justified according to Vattel's criteria. Burke used just this argument, with direct support from Vattel, in *Thoughts on French Affairs* (1791) to show that '[i]n this state of things (that is in the case of a divided kingdom) by the law of nations, Great Britain, like every other Power, is free to take any part she pleases'. 'For this', he had earlier counselled his son, 'consult a very republican writer Vattell.'[48] This appeal to Vattel harked back to an earlier debate on the morality of war, when – in the case of British capture of the Dutch island of St Eustatius in 1781 during the American War – Burke had invoked 'Vattel as being the latest and best [exponent of natural law], and whose testimony he preferred; because, being a modern writer, he expresses the sense of the day in which we live'.[49] In the case of the French Revolution, however, the question of justice was more vexed and controvertible. According to Vattel, it was 'a very celebrated question, and of the highest importance', whether the aggrandisement of a neighbouring power could be a sufficient and just

---

[46] The argument that Burke's divided Irishness inflected the whole course of his political thinking is, of course, the burden of C. C. O'Brien (1992).

[47] Vattel (2008), pp. 290–1, 648–9 (II. iv. 56; III. xviii. 296). On Vattel's arguments for and against intervention, see Hampsher-Monk (2005), pp. 75–7; Zurbuchen (2010).

[48] Edmund Burke, *Thoughts on French Affairs* (1791), in Burke (1992), p. 207; Burke to Richard Burke, Jr, 5 August 1791, in Burke (1958–78), VI, p. 317.

[49] Edmund Burke, 'Speech on the Seizure and Confiscation of Private Property in St Eustatius', 14 May 1781, in *Parliamentary History* (1806–20), XXII (1781–2), col. 231; Hurst (1996); Abbattista (2008).

reason for war.[50] Though Grotius and later Wolff had specifically argued that it could never be a just grounds for war 'to take up arms in order to weaken a growing power' simply because it might become a source of danger,[51] Vattel disagreed, and provided Burke with just the reason-of-state argument he needed to justify a holy war against the Directory. Vattel argued that the safety of a state could be so threatened by a looming neighbour that it would be just to anticipate aggression in the interests of the liberty and order of the whole of Europe, as had been the case during the War of the Spanish Succession.[52] He argued further that modern Europe was now a kind of republic, in which all of the formerly separate nations were bound together by the ties of common interest. The balance of power was the safeguard of those common interests, and provided the means of guaranteeing liberty for Europe. A purely utilitarian calculation would not be enough to justify preventive aggression, and only a pre-emptive response to a threatened injury could be sufficient justification for war. Confederacies might be the best means of defending against such injuries, but, if they failed, an evidently aggressive power that threatened the liberties of Europe should be opposed and weakened in the interests of the great commonwealth, and in accordance with justice and probity.[53] Michael Walzer has taken Burke to be the opponent and Vattel the proponent of intervention to uphold the balance of power that maintained the stability of the European 'republic'; however, whatever Burke's views may have been in 1760, by 1793 he had come to agree with Vattel that such intervention in defence of the balance of power was justifiable.[54]

Vattel's key historical example of such justifiable precaution was the War of the Spanish Succession. In that war, as Whigs had argued at the time, and as Vattel agreed half a century later, Louis XIV had presented a dire threat to the whole European order by his designs for universal monarchy.[55] Because Burke similarly saw 1789 in the light of 1688, he judged the war against the Directory to be conceptually equivalent to the War of the Spanish Succession. The Treaty of Utrecht that had ended that war enshrined the balance of power as the central regulating principle of

---

[50] Vattel (2008), p. 491 (III. iii. 42).

[51] Grotius, *De Iure Belli ac Pacis*, II. i. 17; II. xxii. 5; Christian Wolff, *Jus Gentium Methodo Scientifica Pertractatum* (1749), §§ 640, 651–2; Vagts and Vagts (1979), p. 562; Tuck (1999), pp. 189–90.

[52] Vattel (2008), pp. 491–4 (III. iii. 42–4). On Vattel and modern reason of state, see Nakhimovsky (2007); Devetak (2011).

[53] Vattel (2008), pp. 492–4, 496–7 (III. iii. 44, 47–9).

[54] Walzer (1999), pp. 76–80, quoting Burke's *Annual Register* (1760). On Burke and the balance of power, see especially Vincitorio (1969).

[55] Robertson (1993), pp. 356–8.

the international order, in opposition to the threat of universal monarchy from a power such as Louis XIV's France. Reason of state after 1713 therefore made preventive aggression justifiable in defence of the balance against aspiring universal monarchs. The Whiggish idiom of universal monarchy and the memory of the wars that had spawned it clearly lay behind Burke's warning in the *Letters on a Regicide Peace* that 'France, on her new system, means to form a universal empire, by producing a universal revolution.'[56] This was the logical successor to Burke's argument, in the *Reflections*, that the French Revolution and its aftermath should be seen in light of the Glorious Revolution. The analogy was useful precisely because the common maxims of European civilisation and security so menacingly threatened by the 'new system' of the French were those enshrined in the Treaty of Utrecht and upheld by Vattel.[57] Vattel's argument was partly the product of the opening phase of the Seven Years' War, and in it he assumed – as Bolingbroke, Hume, Robertson and Gibbon also did[58] – that the Utrecht balance of power was the basis of European international order. Burke returned to the same origin to argue that, '[i]f to prevent Louis the XIVth from imposing his religion was just, a war to prevent the murderers of Louis XVIth from imposing their irreligion upon us is just'.[59]

The Revolutionary Wars would in due course shatter the European balance of power and, as Paul Schroeder has argued, thereby irreversibly transform European politics.[60] Burke was the prophet of the transformation, and he foresaw it with the help of Vattel, in accordance with post-Utrecht reason of state. In the *Remarks on the Policy of the Allies* (1793), he cited Vattel to show that the right to intervene became a duty in certain circumstances, according to 'whether it be a *bona fide* charity to a party, and a prudent precaution with regard to yourself'. As Burke showed

---

[56] Edmund Burke, *Third Letter on a Regicide Peace*, in Burke (1991), p. 340. Thomas L. Pangle and Peter J. Ahrensdorf argue that 'it is in his loathing of universal empire that Burke stands furthest, in his conception of international relations, from his otherwise favourite authority, the Roman patriot Cicero', though this fails to distinguish between differing conceptions of 'universal empire' (on which see for example Cicero, *De Officiis*, II. 27), Pangle and Ahrensdorf (1999), p. 184.

[57] On the genesis of post-Utrecht reason of state, and the vision of the great commonwealth of Europe that sustained it, see Pocock (1999a), pp. 109–13, 133–4, 138–9; Pocock (1999b), pp. 170, 219, 275–7.

[58] Bolingbroke (1932); David Hume, 'Of the Balance of Power' (1752), in Hume (1987), pp. 338–41; Whelan (1995); Black (1997), pp. 225–8.

[59] Edmund Burke, *First Letter on a Regicide Peace* (1796), in Burke (1991), p. 238; compare Burke, *A Letter to a Member of the National Assembly* (1791), in Burke (1989), p. 306: 'The princes of Europe, in the beginning of this century, did well not to suffer the monarchy of France to swallow up the others. They ought not now, in my opinion, to suffer all the monarchies and commonwealths to be swallowed up in the gulph of this polluted anarchy.'

[60] Schroeder (1994).

with an appendix of extracts from Vattel, intervention against France would be a 'prudent precaution' for all European states precisely because the French republic presented an unprecedented threat to their natural reasons of state – their interests, their security and above all their shared political maxims as partners in the commonwealth of Europe.[61] Proximity, vicinity and legitimate apprehension of danger therefore justified intervention: as Burke crisply summarised this position in 1796, 'I should certainly dread more from a wild cat in my bed-chamber, than from all the lions that roar in the deserts beyond Algiers.'[62]

Burke argued in the *Thoughts on French Affairs* (1791) that, though there had been many internal revolutions within the governments of Europe, none (not even the Glorious Revolution) had effects beyond their own limited territories. However, he added:

The present Revolution in France seems to me to be quite of another character and description; and to bear little resemblance or analogy to any of those which have been brought about in Europe, upon principles merely political. *It is a Revolution of doctrine and theoretick dogma.* It has a much greater resemblance to those changes which have been made upon religious grounds, in which a spirit of proselytism makes an essential part.

The last Revolution of doctrine and theory which has happened in Europe, is the Reformation ... [the] effect [of which] was *to introduce other interests into all countries, than those which arose from their locality and natural circumstances.*[63]

To introduce alien interests – as the Reformation had, and as the Revolution threatened to do – and in particular to introduce alien interests which claimed universal applicability – such as justification by faith, or the rights of man – dissolved the necessary connection between a state's natural situation and the idiomatic interests it generated. Thereby, 'if they did not absolutely destroy, [they] at least weakened and distracted the locality of patriotism'[64] and with it the determinative, organic reasons of state.

Throughout the 1790s, and particularly during the opening years of the war against the Directory, Burke maintained that Britain and its allies were engaged against France in a '*religious war*', 'a moral war' against the

---

[61] Edmund Burke, *Remarks on the Policy of the Allies* (1793), in Burke (1989), p. 474; the 'Appendix' of extracts from Vattel is omitted from this edition. For a fragment of Burke's working notes on Vattel, see Sheffield Archives, Wentworth Woodhouse Muniments, BkP 10/27 (passage transcribed from Vattel, *Droit des gens*, II. xii. 196–7, printed in Burke (1793), pp. 207–9).

[62] Burke, *First Letter on a Regicide Peace* in Burke (1991), p. 259 (arguing against Charles James Fox's claim that the French republic should be tolerated on the same grounds that justified keeping a consul in Algiers).

[63] Burke, *Thoughts on French Affairs*, in Burke (1992), p. 208 (Burke's emphases).

[64] Burke, *Thoughts on French Affairs*, in Burke (1992), p. 209.

'armed doctrine' of 'a sect aiming at universal empire'.[65] He was not alone, of course, in arguing that the war against the Directory was a war of religion; such arguments were a staple of Anglican polemic during the early years of the war. This 'new and unheard-of scheme of conquest and aggrandizement . . . the total subversion of every lawful government, of all order, of all property, and of all established religion' could only be resisted by a '*just* and *necessary* war', argued Walker King at Gray's Inn in 1793. 'The nation with whom we are at war', Charles Manners Sutton told the members of the House of Lords in the following year, 'is professedly a heathen nation; and unless it shall please God to spare his people, our laws, and liberty, and religion, are inevitably lost.' Such 'a war against all Religion, carried on in the very centre of Christendom, by a people hitherto numbered among the most enlightened of nations', George Gordon informed his audience in Exeter on the same day, 'is a novelty in history'; to oppose it would demand 'a war of stern necessity, and consequently of the strictest justice'.[66] However, Burke's charge of universal empire hinted that the French republic was as great a threat to the common maxims of the great republic of Europe as Louis XIV had been almost a century earlier. In his international theory as in his political theory, Burke remained true to the ideological inheritance of English Whiggism, not least because he drew so heavily on Vattel, whose anglophilia was decidedly Whig in complexion,[67] and whose doctrines of the law of nations were directed to the same end as Burke's: that is, to the defence of the European balance of power and the new international reasons of state originally guaranteed by the Treaty of Utrecht.

Burke was more than just a conspiracy theorist of the Revolution, though he did sympathise with those, like the abbé Barruel, who saw free-thinkers, Freemasons and Jews behind the events of 1789 and thereafter;[68] he was also more than simply the most frantic and prominent apologist for Anglicanism in the face of French revolutionary atheism, though there is truth in that view, too. He was, in fact, a classic early modern theorist of reason of state within the natural-law

---

[65] Burke, *Remarks on the Policy of the Allies* (1793), in Burke (1989), p. 485; *Fourth Letter on a Regicide Peace* (1795–6), in Burke (1991), p. 70; *First Letter on a Regicide Peace* (1796), in Burke (1991), p. 199; *Second Letter on a Regicide Peace*, in Burke (1991), p. 267; Ryan (2010).

[66] King (1793), pp. 12, 10–11; Sutton (1794), p. 14; Gordon (1794), pp. 10, 26.

[67] See Vattel (2008), pp. 89–80, 97–8, 127, 131, 132 (I. ii. 24; I. iv. 39; I. vi. 76; I. viii. 85, 87, etc.). On the traditional Whiggism of Burke's reflection on international relations, see also Simms (2011).

[68] J. M. Roberts (1971); Hofman (1988); McMahon (2001).

tradition revived by Grotius and revised by Vattel. Reason of state made
the internal and external realms of state policy mutually intelligible
for Burke; it provided him with an argument to ensure security in
extremity without destroying security, property or law; and it provided
the most persuasive analysis of the collapse of the European states-
system, the failure of the balance of power and the desperate need for
self-preservation compelled by the French Revolution.[69] This strain
within Burke's political thought showed that reason of state had not
lost its rational basis long before 1789 (*pace* Reinhart Koselleck);[70] it
also demonstrated that it was not a necessary consequence of reason-of-
state theory that it should separate a state's domestic maxims from its
foreign policies (*pace* Meinecke);[71] and proved, to Burke's satisfaction
(as it no doubt would have been to Vattel's, too), that reason of state
was not by definition the enemy of 'law or innate moral principles'
(*pace* almost everybody, of course).[72]

Vattel and Burke stood at the end of this tradition of reason of state.
It was, after all, in the context of the same late eighteenth-century wars
that Kant and Bentham produced their respective plans for perpetual
peace, each of which attempted to conceive cooperative, transparent
international norms and institutions that would render such reason of
state inoperable and obsolete.[73] Both also questioned the Whiggishly self-
congratulatory account of the Glorious Revolution on whose historical
foundations Burke's theory rested, Kant because it exemplified both a
'monstrous' appeal to 'a right of necessity (*ius in casu necessitatis*)' and a
tacit, standing right to rebellion without restriction, Bentham because
he could not see it as beneficial for the interest of the nation (rather than
to the 'particular interest of the aristocratic leaders in the revolution').[74]
The Kantian categorical imperative and Bentham's greatest happiness
principle provided competing but equally fatal alternatives to this tradition of reason of state; their anathematisation of it opened up that gulf
between morality and politics out of which Meinecke's instrumentalist
account – and, consequently, almost everyone else's – emerged. To place

---

[69] Onuf and Onuf (1993), pp. 8–9, 188–9.   [70] Koselleck (1988), pp. 17, 39.
[71] Meinecke (1998), p. 13.   [72] In this case, D. Boucher (1991), p. 135.
[73] Immanuel Kant, 'Perpetual Peace: A Philosophical Sketch' (1795), in Kant (1991), pp. 93–130;
Jeremy Bentham, 'Pacification and Emancipation' (1786–9), UCL Bentham XXV, printed (in a
heavily edited version) as 'A Plan for an Universal and Perpetual Peace', in Bentham (1838–43), II,
pp. 546–60; Conway (1987), pp. 803–9.
[74] Immanuel Kant, 'Über den Gemeinspruch: "Das mag in der Theorie rightig sein, taugt aber nicht
für die Praxis"' (1793), in Kant (1964), I, pp. 156, 160; English translation in Kant (1991), pp. 81,
83–4; Jeremy Bentham, 'The Book of Fallacies' (1818), in Bentham (1838–43), II, pp. 447–8.

Burke on one side or the other of this argument has always risked distorting historical accounts of his thought, whether in the political sphere or the international realm; it has also sharpened the distinction between these two arenas in ways which neither early modern theorists of reason of state nor Burke himself would have recognised. Burke's place in the history of international thought should therefore be assimilated more closely to his position in the traditions of political thought, as a standing reproach to procrustean taxonomies and overhasty appropriations.

CHAPTER 10

Globalising Jeremy Bentham

Historians of political thought have lately made two great leaps towards expanding the scope of their inquiries. The first, the 'international turn', was long-heralded and has been immediately fruitful. Histories of international thought that treat reflection on the relations among states, nations, peoples, individuals and other corporate actors in the international arena have idiomatically reconstructed the norms that regulate (or have been supposed to regulate) their interactions. Over the course of barely a decade, this lively historiography has already established a robust canon of thinkers and problems.[1] The second move, towards what might be called a 'global turn' in the history of political thought, is for the moment much less well developed. Political theorists, historians of philosophy and others have variously called for a transnational intellectual history or the globalisation of the history of political thought. Will this be a history of the convergence of intellectual traditions from around the world? Or of the global circulation of ideas? What is certain is that the possibilities for such a history – or even for multiple histories under this rubric – remain enticingly open-ended.

Any global history of political thought will surely have to include the history of political and other forms of thinking about global connections and about the phenomena variously subsumed under the umbrella term 'globalisation'.[2] Past thinkers who attempted to conceive the world, its peoples and its polities holistically will be indispensable to its inquiries. This chapter tackles one such thinker, Jeremy Bentham, with the larger goal of imagining a global history of political thought firmly in mind. Unlike some of his distinguished predecessors and contemporaries, such as Diderot, Turgot, Smith, Herder, Kant or Goethe, Bentham has not

---

[1] For recent work mapping the field see, for example, Keene (2005); Jahn (2006); Bell (2007b); Hall and Hill (2009).
[2] Bell (2009a).

generally been considered in such global terms.[3] Yet only by failing to take seriously his own self-conception have historians managed to overlook the global Bentham.[4] On the day before his 83rd birthday in February 1831, he made the extent of his ambitions evident: 'J. B. the most ambitious of the ambitious. His empire – the empire he aspires to – extending to and comprehending the whole human race, in all places, – in all habitable places of the earth, at all future time ... Limits has it no other than those of the earth.'[5] These were also the dimensions his sympathetic contemporary, William Hazlitt, thought Bentham had attained. The prophet may have been without honour in his own country but distance served to multiply his influence: 'His reputation lies at the circumference; and the lights of his understanding are reflected, with increasing lustre, on the other side of the globe', Hazlitt wrote in 1825. 'His name is little known in England, better in Europe, best of all in the plains of Chili and the mines of Mexico. He has offered constitutions for the New World, and legislated for future times.'[6] It was this Bentham that the Central American reformer José del Valle hailed in 1826 as the 'legislator of the world' (*Legislador del mundo*).[7] And it was this Bentham his American editor, John Neal, diagnosed in 1830 as 'unknown to the great body of English every where' but 'found in every public library in Europe ... circulated in chapters throughout every quarter of the globe – the north striving with the south, the new world with the old, to give them simultaneous publicity'.[8] By the time of his death in 1832, Bentham and his acolytes had spread his influence from the Americas to Bengal, and from Russia to New South Wales, by way of Geneva, Greece and Tripoli.[9] He had therefore achieved an ambition expressed in 1786: 'The Globe is the field of Dominion to which the author aspires. The Press the Engine and the only one he employs – The Cabinet of Mankind the Theatre of his intrigue.'[10]

---

[3] Muthu (2011); Rothschild (2004); Muthu (2003), ch. 5; Muthu (2008); Tang (2008); Bartelson (2009); Cheney (2010).

[4] Some studies have already pointed towards this 'global Bentham': e.g., Niesen (2006); Kaino (2008). Eric Hobsbawm seems to have been the first to use the term: Hobsbawm (1992), p. 27 n. 33.

[5] Jeremy Bentham, 'Memorandum-Book' (1831), in Bentham (1838–43), XI, p. 72, quoted in Twining (2000), pp. 15–16.

[6] Hazlitt (1825), p. 3.

[7] José del Valle to Jeremy Bentham, 21 May 1826, in Bentham (1968–), XII, pp. 217–18; also in Bentham (1998), p. 370.

[8] John Neal, 'Biographical Notice of Jeremy Bentham', in Bentham (1830), p. II.

[9] Bentham (1990); Rosen (1992); Blamires (2008), ch. 9, 'The Impact of the *Traités*: Benthamism Goes Global.'

[10] Jeremy Bentham, 'Pac. & Emanc. – Introd.' (1786), UCL Bentham XXV. 26; Bentham (1838–43), II, p. 546.

Bentham was however notoriously reluctant to employ the press himself and it was mostly left to his earliest editors – Étienne Dumont and John Bowring – to smooth the passage of his works around the world in their versions of his recalcitrant manuscripts.[11] They often did so by excising many of the traces of particular events and contexts that gave rise to Bentham's arguments. The decontexualised 'historical Bentham' created by Dumont, Bowring and, later, John Stuart Mill, appeared more universal because less rootedly local, and it has taken immense editorial effort to recover the more idiomatic 'authenticity Bentham' from his vast *Nachlass*.[12] Excavating the global Bentham from his published and unpublished writings demands attention both to his immediate contexts and his universalist ambitions. His career spanned almost the whole of what his contemporaries were already calling an 'Age of Revolutions' and what more recent historians have termed a 'World Crisis' encompassing the decades from the Seven Years' War to the 1830s.[13] In this chapter, I trace Bentham's universalist ambitions from their roots in his earliest writings to their culmination in one of the last projects of his life, an abortive attempt to codify 'international' law – a term Bentham himself had invented in the 1780s, which spread rapidly ('Witness Reviews and Newspapers', Bentham noted with pride in 1823) and which would be perhaps his most lasting legacy to global thought.[14]

Bentham's generation, born around the mid-point of the eighteenth century, was perhaps the first in European history to grow up with a comprehensively global vision of its place in the world.[15] That vision was the product of many linked developments: maritime exploration; the elaboration of interoceanic commerce; the expansion of European empires in the Atlantic, Indian and Pacific Oceans; the diffusion of maps, histories and travel accounts; and the ties created by the circulation and exchange of goods and ideas. It would find its most lasting monuments in the great global histories of empire and commerce of the 1770s, all of which Bentham consulted: the abbé Raynal's *Histoire des deux Indes*, Adam Smith's *Wealth of Nations* and William Robertson's

---

[11] On Dumont, see de Champs (2006); Whatmore (2007); Blamires (2008); and de Champs and Cléro (2009), pt. II, 'Bentham et Dumont: les premières traductions françaises'. On Bowring, see Conway (1991); Todd (2008).

[12] D. Lieberman (2000), p. 108.

[13] Bayly (2004), ch. 3, 'Converging Revolutions, 1780–1820'; Darwin (2007), ch. 4, 'The Eurasian Revolution'; Armitage and Subrahmanyam (2010).

[14] Bentham (1996), p. 297 n. y; Suganami (1978); Janis (1984).   [15] Bowen (1998).

History of America.[16] Bentham captured this view of the world in the opening lines of his *Fragment on Government* (1776) written in the wake of James Cook's return from his second voyage in 1775: 'Ours is a busy age; in which knowledge is rapidly advancing towards perfection. In the natural world, in particular, every thing teems with discovery and with improvement. The most distant and recondite regions of the earth traversed and explored ... are striking evidences, were all others wanting, of this pleasing truth.'[17]

Bentham's was a war-time generation, raised and schooled during the Seven Years' War. He was up at Oxford during the latter years of the conflict (1760–3) and one of his earliest literary productions treated its conclusion. In search of a topic for some Latin verses in 1763, Bentham settled on the British siege of Havana the year before. Samuel Johnson himself had earlier urged that the precocious scholar tackle some other British victory in the conflict, but Bentham noted that 'the Conquest of North America did not suggest to me any Thoughts', nor was he 'better able to find Matter on the subject of the Manilla's'. He decided instead 'upon the Havannah for the Subject of my Verses' in which he argued that Britain should restore its conquests to Spain, 'and moreover that commerce will afford it [Florida] us by a more peacefull method'.[18]

The fifteen-year-old Bentham may have had doubts about the benefits of British conquests in the war, but his older self would be much more dyspeptic about the long-term consequences of the conflict for both Britain and France. As he later put it in the manuscript 'Cabinet No Secresy' (1789), 'true enough it is that a man who has had his leg cut off, and the stump healed, may hop faster than a man who lies in bed with both legs broke can walk. And thus you may prove that Britain was put into a better case by that glorious war, than if there had been no war, because France was put into a still worse.'[19] This verdict was evidently too harsh for the pacifist Bowring when he came to edit this material as Bentham's 'Plan for an Universal and Perpetual Peace' (1786–9). Bowring rendered the reference to war general rather than specific, just as he struck out most of Bentham's other historical references

---

[16] For Bentham's interest in Smith and Raynal see, for example, UCL Bentham XXV. 121; BL Add. MS 33564, ff. 41v, 43r; for Robertson, UCL Bentham CIX. 1–2.

[17] Bentham (1988), p. 3.

[18] Bentham to Jeremiah Bentham, 6 May and 29 June 1763, in Bentham (1968–), 1, pp. 72, 78–9. The verses have not survived.

[19] UCL Bentham XXV. 58; compare UCL Bentham XXV. 29, f. 12, for a similar judgment on the outcome of the war.

in the surrounding text.[20] Bentham's image as a universal legislator could thereby be affirmed, but only at the cost of suppressing some of the precise contextual evidence – and often the polemical bite – that shaped his arguments, here and elsewhere.

The next great conflict of Bentham's lifetime, the American War, gave rise to his first extended engagement with such key issues in the emerging international order of the late eighteenth century as secession, recognition and the changing structure of the law of nations.[21] In relation to all these topics, 1775–6 was Bentham's *annus mirabilis*. Between the spring of 1775 and the summer of 1776, Bentham wrote, drafted, collaborated on and published a series of legal and political works heralding interests that would shape many of his later considerations of the same subjects. All can be seen to be as at least partly the precipitate of the American War, a conflict as crucial for forming his mature view of the world as the Seven Years' War had been for shaping his earliest conceptions of the global interactions of empires.

Bentham's major publication in 1776 was the anonymously issued *Fragment on Government*, an attack on Sir William Blackstone's account of the origin of government in his *Commentaries on the Laws of England* (1765–9). Blackstone grounded his account in the universalism of natural law: 'This law of nature, being co-eval with mankind and dictated by God himself, is of course superior in obligation to any other. It is binding over all the globe, in all countries, and at all times: no human laws are of any validity, if contrary to this.'[22] Bentham substituted for this his own 'fundamental axiom, [that] *it is the greatest happiness of the greatest number that is the measure of right and wrong*'. This too was a universal principle, especially when placed in the service of what he termed a 'censorial' jurisprudence dedicated – unlike the more pragmatic 'expository' jurisprudence – to generating normative propositions: 'That which *is* Law, is, in different countries, widely different: while that which *ought to be*, is in all countries to a great degree the same. The *Expositor*, therefore, is always the citizen of this or that particular country: the *Censor* is, or ought to be the citizen of the world.'[23] For the rest of his career, Bentham would

---

[20] Bentham, 'Plan for an Universal and Perpetual Peace', in Bentham (1838–43), II, p. 560: 'And thus you may prove that Britain *is* in a better case *after the expenditure* of a glorious war, than if there had been no war; because France *or some other country*, was put by it into a still worse condition' (my emphases). On the editing of these manuscripts, see Hoogensen (2005), pp. 40–54.

[21] Compare Boralevi (1984), pp. 121–3; Valentini (1993); Olivieri (2006); Rudan (2007).

[22] Blackstone (1765–9), I, p. 41. Bentham attacked Blackstone's doctrine of non-repugnancy to natural law in Bentham (1988), pp. 94–5.

[23] Bentham (1988), pp. 3, 8.

project precisely this jurisprudential cosmopolitanism as the foundation of all his major works and, especially in his later years, as the higher wisdom he could offer more parochial legal expositors around the globe.

Blackstone had divided law into various branches – law in general, the law of nature, the law of revelation, the law of nations and municipal law – and in the *Fragment on Government* Bentham paid most attention to municipal law. However, in the context of the American War, questions relevant to the law of nations, such as the division of sovereignty and the legitimacy of secession, could not easily be disentangled from matters of domestic or internal law. Blackstone had famously defined the rights of sovereignty in political society as 'a supreme, irresistible, absolute, uncontrolled authority, in which the *jura summa imperii* . . . reside'. That he applied this definition to the British Parliament's 'absolute despotic power' as it was exercised over the American colonies can be inferred from one of his rare speeches in the House of Commons in which he supported Parliament's authority to tax the American colonies during the Stamp Act crisis: 'If the colonies reject a law of taxation, they may oppose any other, and they will become a more distinct separate dominion under one head. All the dominions of this country have been subject to Parliament', even if only Calais had ever sent representatives to Westminster.[24] Bentham agreed with his adversary that the supreme power should be unbounded, and in 1775 even concurred with the view that the king in Parliament had the right to tax the colonies.[25] However, he argued that 'express convention' could allow other dispositions of divided authority. To assert otherwise would be to deny the positive fact of federalism across Europe and throughout history: 'it would be saying that there is no such thing as government in the German Empire; nor in the Dutch Provinces; nor in the Swiss Cantons; nor was of old the Achaean league'.[26] By implication, it would also be to deny one conceivable solution to the Atlantic crisis of the 1760s and 1770s: a federal distribution of powers between Parliament and the colonial assemblies.[27]

By April 1776, when Bentham published the *Fragment on Government*, any federal solution to the problems of Britain's Atlantic empire was a rapidly vanishing option. Secession was a much more likely outcome to

---

[24] Blackstone (1765–9), I, pp. 39–46, 49, 156; Ryder (1969), p. 268; Prest (2008), pp. 201, 225–6.
[25] [Jeremy Bentham,] 'The Design', in Lind (1775), pp. xv–xvi; compare Bentham, 'Preparatory Principles – Inserenda' (*c.* 1776), UCL Bentham LXIX. 156. Bentham returned to the question of the Crown's right to legislate independently for its colonies in 1803: Bentham (1803), pp. 30–6.
[26] Bentham (1988), p. 101.
[27] On the various proposals for a federal solution to the imperial crisis, see LaCroix (2010), pp. 104–26.

the crisis. That possibility may have been on Bentham's mind when he tested Blackstone's account of the origins of political society by asking:

suppose an incontestable political society, and that a large one, formed; and from that a smaller body to break off: by this breach the smaller body ceases to be in a state of political union with respect to the larger: and has thereby placed itself, with respect to the larger body, in a state of nature – What means shall we find of ascertaining the precise juncture at which this change took place? What shall be taken for the *characteristic mark* in this case?

Bentham took as his example the defection of the Dutch from the Spanish monarchy to become 'independent states'. Exactly when they had ceased to be part of that monarchy and had entered a state of nature with regard to it and every other state 'will be rather difficult to agree upon'. (In a footnote, he suggested that 'the defection of the Nabobs of Hindostan' from the Mughal empire might have been a more exact historical illustration of the same conundrum, though less well known to his readers.) 'When is it, in short', he went on, 'that a *revolt* shall be deemed to have taken place; and when, again, is it, that that revolt shall be deemed to such a degree successful, as to have settled into *independence?*'[28]

Bentham's answer to that question in the context of the American controversy would certainly not have been '4 July 1776'. He would join his friend, the young lawyer and pamphleteer John Lind, in writing the anonymous *Answer to the Declaration of the American Congress* (1776) sponsored by lord North's ministry.[29] Bentham's main contribution to the pamphlet was the 'Short Review of the Declaration',[30] in which he demolished the 'theory of government' expressed especially in the second paragraph of the American Declaration of Independence.[31] The colonists' adoption of incoherent and self-defeating arguments, Bentham concluded, could only aid the British cause, now that the world could see the Americans had been aiming at independence all along: 'the nation will . . . teach this rebellious people, that it is one thing for them to *say*, the connection, which bound them to us, is *dissolved*, another to *dissolve* it; that to accomplish their *independence* is not quite so easy as to *declare* it'.[32]

---

[28] Bentham (1988), pp. 46–7.

[29] [Lind and Bentham] (1776). On Lind, see Avery (1978); Rudan (2007), pp. 11–25.

[30] Jeremy Bentham to John Lind, September 1776, 'American Declaration. Hints B', BL Add. MS 33551, ff. 359r–60v, in Bentham (1968–), i, pp. 341–4; [Jeremy Bentham,] 'Short Review of the Declaration', in [Lind and Bentham] (1776), pp. 119–32; printed in Armitage (2007a), pp. 173–86.

[31] Hart (1982), pp. 63–5; D. G. Long (1977), pp. 51–4; Armitage (2007a), pp. 75–80.

[32] [Bentham,] 'Short Review of the Declaration', in [Lind and Bentham] (1776), p. 131; printed in Armitage (2007a), p. 186.

Bentham's first major missile from the press after the *Fragment on Government* and the *View of the Hard Labour Bill* (1778) was the *Introduction to the Principles of Morals and Legislation*, originally printed in 1780 but held back until 1789, partly in response to William Paley's *Principles of Moral and Political Philosophy*, published four years earlier in 1785.[33] This was a more thoroughgoing application of the principle of utility than he had attempted before, as well as a more comprehensive system of jurisprudence. It was in this work that Bentham first publicly treated the law of nations, though to describe it he introduced one of his most enduring neologisms: the word 'international' to denote 'that branch of jurisprudence' dealing with 'the mutual transactions between sovereigns as such'. Bentham acknowledged the term to be a 'new one, though sufficiently intelligible and analogous', and chiefly useful as an alternative to the traditional 'law of nations', which he judged to be better as a literal description of the law applied to members of the same state rather than to those of different states: that is, what he called 'internal' rather than 'international jurisprudence'.[34]

The distinction between the internal and the international would have been especially salient in 1780 – perhaps even more so than in 1789 – at the height of the American War, before British defeat seemed inevitable as it did after 1781. If the colonists' claims to independence were refutable and ignorable, then relations between them and Great Britain were strictly matters of internal jurisprudence; only with the achievement (and recognition) of independence would they come under the rubric of international law as transactions between distinct peoples inhabiting separate states.

Bentham's earlier attack on the premises of the Declaration of Independence may have helped to sharpen his sense that the term 'international' was needed to denominate an increasingly salient body of law. If the Continental Congress were to be acknowledged as a legitimate executive body, then its Declaration could be construed as a positive act within the ambit of international law. However, it could only be acknowledged in this way if the Declaration itself were recognised as the positive act that had endowed Congress with international personality as a sovereign body. How could independence be declared, except by a body that was already independent in the sense understood by the law of nations?

Yet even after Britain had recognised American independence by the Treaty of Paris in 1783, Bentham could still not accept that the principles

---

[33] Bentham (1996), p. li; Schofield (2006), p. 187.   [34] Bentham (1996), pp. 6, 296.

invoked in the Declaration of Independence and elsewhere would support the conclusions that had been drawn from them.[35] Bentham did not question the legitimacy of what he later called 'our ci-devant colonies; – the now happily independent (and long may they remain!) *United States*', but he strictly separated his admiration for the outcome of American independence from the philosophical arguments on which it had originally rested. As he ruefully put it in conversation at the end of his life, 'The American colonies really said nothing to justify their revolution. They thought not of *utility*, and *use* was against them.'[36]

Bentham's criticism of naturalism as a foundation for law or rights had begun during the American War but continued to be one of the defining features of his political and legal thought. This was despite the fact that, during the American Revolution, he wrote in defence of Britain's right to retain its American colonies, while during the French Revolution he would write urging the French to emancipate theirs: 'Little did I think,' he told John Bowring in 1827, 'that I was destined to write, within fifteen or sixteen years thereafter, an address to the French Commonwealth, for the express purpose of engaging them, by arguments that applied to all mother countries, to emancipate their colonies.'[37] Beneath that shift lay his consistent antipathy to deriving rights from nature. Legislation was the only solid foundation for rights within the municipal sphere of the state; likewise, in the relations between states, the only positive acts were the transactions of sovereigns that made up a body of positive 'international law'.

Bentham's campaign to reform and codify international law is less well known than his assault on natural rights in the cause of utility. However, it too sprang from similarly fundamental concerns and reappeared at various points in his later career, from the 1780s to the 1830s. Bentham stated his basic objection in an unpublished draft preface for the *Introduction to the Principles of Morals and Legislation*:

The Books that have been written on the subject of what is called the Law of Nature are a sort of dull Romance. The business of them is to lay down rules concerning either what is done or what ought to be done in an imaginary state of things, the state of nature. Do they give them as proper to be observed in any one

---

[35] Bentham (1996), p. 311 n. c; Bentham (1838–43), X, p. 63; see below, pp. 204–5.
[36] Bentham (1802), p. 1; 'Bentham's Conversation' (1827–8), in Bentham (1838–43), X, p. 584.
[37] Bentham to John Bowring, 30 January 1827, in Bentham (1968–), XII, pp. 307–9, referring to *Emancipate Your Colonies! Addressed to the National Convention* of France (1793), in Bentham (2002), pp. 289–313.

place upon earth? No, that they don't. Rules that are proper to be enacted – where? In the moon perhaps: not any where upon earth.[38]

The only basis for a truly cosmopolitan, universal law of nations would be the common and equal utility of all nations ('l'utilité commune et egale de toutes les nations'), subject to the expedient constraints of particular circumstances.[39]

Bentham's first attempt to imagine the reform of international law came in the second half of the 1780s, when he drafted a series of proposals under the general headings of 'Law Inter National 1786' and 'Pacification and Emancipation' (*c.* 1786–9). These were the texts that were 'dismembered, reconfigured and arbitrarily sewn together in the sort of "Frankenstein" creation' known as the 'Principles of International Law' fabricated by John Bowring and his co-editor Richard Smith in the 1830s.[40] Bentham's peace proposals have attracted more attention from pacifists (especially in the League of Nations moment after the First World War) and from later international relations theorists than have his writings on international law from this period.[41] The writings on international law provide evidence of Bentham's developing conception of the legislator, and hence derived from the legal philosophy elaborated earlier in the *Fragment on Government* and the *Introduction to the Principles of Morals and Legislation,* while his peace proposals had more contingent applications arising from Bentham's criticism of the younger Pitt's foreign policy in 1789.[42] As early as 1782, Bentham had already drafted a brief 'Projet Forme – Entre-gens' on the codification of duties and rights between sovereigns under international law, the last of his writings on the subject to derive from the period of the American War.[43]

Bentham's international legal writings of the later 1780s applied the principle of utility not only to the relations between sovereigns *as* sovereigns but also to the relations of sovereigns with the rest of humanity taken as an aggregate. This extension of the greatest happiness principle to

---

[38] UCL Bentham XXVII. 143; compare UCL Bentham XXVII. 174, 'Difference between this work & one on the Law of Nature'. On Bentham's invocation of the moon in a parallel context, see Pitts (2005b), p. 82 n. 5.

[39] UCL Bentham XXV. 1; UCL Bentham XXVII. 143.

[40] UCL Bentham XXV. 1–9, 26–49; 'Principles of International Law', in Bentham (1838–43), II, pp. 537–60; Hoogensen (2005), p. 44 (quoted).

[41] Though see Schwarzenberger (1948); Hoogensen (2005), pp. 94–100; Guillot (2011a); Guillot (2011b).

[42] Conway (1987); Conway (1989), pp. 82–6.

[43] UCL Bentham XXXIII. 81–2; Bentham (1838–43), III, pp. 200–1; for the dating see Conway (1989), p. 100 n. 112.

encompass all nations was essential, Bentham argued, if the legislator's duty to promote the welfare of his own people were not to be prosecuted at the expense of the well-being of all others. 'Expressed in the most general manner, the end that a disinterested legislator upon international law would propose to himself, would therefore be the greatest happiness of all nations taken together.' The resulting international code would have as its 'substantive' laws the laws of peace, while the laws of war 'would be the adjective laws of the same code'.[44] Wars could be prevented by dealing more systematically with the various causes of dispute – such as uncertain succession, civil war, boundary disputes or religious hatred – by making unwritten customs explicit, by elaborating new international rules where no such rules exist and, more broadly, '[b]y perfecting the style of the laws of all kinds, whether internal or international'.[45] Though Bentham saw internal and international jurisprudence as equally ripe for reform along utilitarian lines, he firmly separated the two realms and saw no further homology between them. In that separation he was of course definitively distancing himself from the natural jurisprudential tradition of the law of nature and nations which he so frequently denounced in all his legal and political writings.

The originality of Bentham's conception of international law can be briefly illustrated by comparing it with two contemporary works on the law of nations produced in Britain within a decade of Bentham's writings, Robert Ward's *Enquiry into the Foundation and History of the Law of Nations in Europe* (1795) and Sir James Mackintosh's *Discourse on the Study of the Law of Nature and Nations* (1799).[46] Bentham owned Ward's book and Mackintosh acknowledged Bentham's invention of the term 'international law', but there any resemblances ended.[47] For both Ward and Mackintosh, the law of nations was an extension of the law of nature applied to states and sovereigns as international persons in a state of nature. It was thus for them a branch of moral philosophy rather than, as it would be for Bentham, a distinct science of legislation. They both adopted a historicist and developmental account of the law of nations found elsewhere in Europe in German surveys of the public law tradition such as G. F. von Martens's *Summary of the Law of Nations, Founded on the Treaties and Customs of the Modern Nations of Europe* (1785),

[44] UCL Bentham XXV. 2–4; Bentham (1838–43), II, pp. 538–9.
[45] UCL Bentham XXV. 4; Bentham (1838–43), II, p. 540.   [46] R. Ward (1795); J. Mackintosh (1799).
[47] BL Add. MS 33564, f. 39v; J. Mackintosh (1799), p. 6.

D. H. L. von Ompteda's *Litteratur des gesammten sowohl natürlichen als positiven Völkerrechts* (1785) and Karl Gottlob Günther's *Europäisches Völkerrecht in Friedenszeiten* (1787–92). These works offered an account of the law of nations as an aspect of the history of natural jurisprudence: for example, Ompteda divided the law of nations into a series of periods – ancient, medieval, early modern and modern – and further subdivided the modern period into ages defined by the greatest European practitioners, from Grotius to Pufendorf (1625–73), from Christian Wolff to J. J. Moser (1673–1740) and thence to his own times (1740–85).[48]

This periodisation proved lastingly influential well into the nineteenth century, not least because it established the originary contribution of Grotius and his *De Jure Belli ac Pacis* (1625).[49] In giving Grotius such a prominent place, Ompteda showed himself to be heir to the great eighteenth-century German histories of morality that identified the Dutchman as the founder of modern natural-law theory and as the greatest ethical innovator before Kant.[50] It was from just those histories that Mackintosh drew his narrative in the *Discourse*, as amply revealed by Mackintosh's working notes for the public lectures to which the *Discourse* was the introduction.[51]

Similarly, Ward's *Enquiry* traced the law of nations from its barbarous infancy under the Greeks and Romans, through its decline in the feudal era prior to a gradual revival under the combined influences of Christianity and chivalry, until the defining moment when 'the philosopher of *Delft* [Grotius] rose like a star amid the surrounding darkness' and 'gave to the world a Treatise which has stood the test of time'.[52] Ward thereby linked the history of moral philosophy to a broader Enlightened narrative of the progress of manners. 'The law of nations, like the municipal law, follows the progress of manners', argued a British pamphleteer in similar vein in 1790, 'and it is the easiest, as well as a most accurate criterion of rudeness or refinement': the progress of Christianity, chivalry, commerce and civility had ameliorated the murderous individualism of ancient warfare and introduced more humane and just rules of war among states.[53] Mackintosh concurred in his assessment of 'the general mildness of

---

[48] Martens (1795); Ompteda (1785); Günther (1787–92). More generally, see Alexandrowicz (1961); Koskenniemi (2008).

[49] See, for example, Reddie (1842), pp. 7–87.   [50] Hochstrasser (2000).

[51] BL Add. MS 78781; Add. MS 78784A, ff. 1–7, contain notes for some of the early lectures, none of which was published.

[52] R. Ward (1795), II, pp. 614–15.   [53] R. Brown (1790), pp. 11, 20–1, 23–4, 25–7.

character and manners which arose from the combined and progressive influence of chivalry, of commerce, of learning, and of religion'.[54]

Ward and Mackintosh wrote after the French Revolution and in the wake of the wars of the Directory, and their moral and civilisational narrative was deliberately counter-Revolutionary in intent. Ward was a client of Lord Eldon, William Pitt's Solicitor-General, at whose suggestion he began compiling his history; likewise, Mackintosh in his lectures on the law of nature and nations disavowed his earlier *Vindiciae Gallicae* (1791) and went almost as far in the opposite direction towards a corrosive conservatism.[55]

For both Ward and Mackintosh, the only foundation for an obligatory law of nations was revealed (rather than natural) religion; the only revealed religion worthy of the name was Christianity; therefore, the only binding law of nations was the law of Christendom. Such judgments laid the foundation for a conception of the law of nations as the law of civilisation defined specifically as *Christian* civilisation and would in turn underpin the accounts of the European 'states-system' whose 'initial purpose was to stigmatise the French Revolution, and especially the Napoleonic imperial system, as unlawful in terms of the "traditional" principles of European public law and order'. French Revolutionary universalism and Napoleonic pretensions to universal monarchy within Europe had not only threatened the European states-system but had dissolved the distinction between domestic and international relations.[56]

Bentham would have disagreed with almost every aspect of the account of the law of nations found in Ward's *Enquiry* and Mackintosh's *Discourse*. He was as disillusioned as Kant regarding the allegedly ameliorating force of the traditional law of nations. Also like Kant, he wished to interrupt a narrative in which the great masters of natural jurisprudence played the pivotal roles and charged that Grotius, Pufendorf and their ilk were merely visionary, and hence impractical, universalists.[57] As he contemplated his own achievements, in the *Auto-Icon* (1831–2), Bentham imagined Francis Bacon congratulating him for rigorously distinguishing 'between that which ought to be, and that which is. By Grotius, by Puffendorf, by their predecessors, by their successors the Burlamaquis, &c., that which ought to be, and that which is, were continually

---

[54] J. Mackintosh (1799), p. 13.   [55] Panizza (1997), pp. 43–82; J. Mackintosh (2006), pp. 203–49.
[56] Keene (2002), pp. 16, 21–6.
[57] For more extensive comparisons between Bentham and Kant in these regards, see Niesen (2006); Niesen (2007).

confounded: observing what had been the practice of men in power, they inferred, or rather took for granted, that it was right'.[58]

Bentham's universalism would also not accept any narrowing of its application to any single civilisation, nor could he accept the assimilation of jurisprudence to any non-utilitarian moral philosophy. He strove to maintain the separation between internal and the external relations of states, hence his need to distinguish international law from the law of nations as traditionally conceived. Bentham cannot have been unaware of the narrative espoused by his contemporaries but he never expressed his judgment upon it. However, his editor and disciple, Étienne Dumont (to whom Bentham had lent copies of Ward's *Enquiry* and Vattel), did. Dumont's judgment was impeccably Benthamite in its dismissal of Ward's naturalist foundations:

The English work of Mr Ward on the law of nature and nations, is an historical portrait of the revolutions that have taken place in international practices. This way of conceiving the subject would be curious and instructive if the author had borrowed the philosophy of Hume and the elegance of Robertson. However, he argues like Grotius and Vattel on natural law and moral obligations.[59]

Towards the end of his life, Bentham lamented the continuing malignant hold of the natural-law tradition over the law of nations and actively sought a remedy for the malaise. 'Few things are more wanting than a code of international law', he reportedly said in 1827 or 1828: 'Vattel's propositions are most old-womanish and tautological. They come to this: Law is nature – Nature is law. He builds upon a cloud. When he means anything, it is from a vague perception of the principle of utility; but more frequently no meaning can be found. Many of his *dicta* amount to this: It is not just to do that which is unjust.'[60] A few years later, he sought a collaborator for the vital work of codifying international law. He chose for this task Jabez Henry, a barrister of the Middle Temple who had followed a transnational legal career that had taken him from three years in the Presidency of the court of Demerara and Essequibo to being chief judge of

---

[58] Bentham (1842?), p. 14.
[59] 'L'ouvrage anglais de Mr Ward sur le droit de la nature et des gens, est un tableau historique des révolutions qui ont eu lieu dans les coutumes internationales. Cette manière d'envisager le sujet seroit curieuse et instructive, si l'auteur eût emprunté la philosophie de Hume, et l'élégance de Robertson. Mais il raisonne comme Grotius et Vattel sur le droit naturel et les obligations morales': Dumont (1829a), p. 23 (my translation). Bentham lent copies of Vattel and Ward to Dumont on 3 February 1806: BL Add. MS 33564, f. 39v.
[60] 'Bentham's Conversation' (1827–8), in Bentham (1838–43), x, p. 584.

Corfu and the Ionian Islands.[61] Bentham's attention had initially been captured by Henry's treatment of an international bankruptcy case that raised important issues in the conflict of laws.[62] Henry reciprocated that interest by sending Bentham his _Outline of a Plan of an International Bankrupt Code for the Different Commercial States of Europe_ (1825?), in which he rigorously followed the Benthamite conception of an international code for bankruptcy.[63] When Bentham selected Henry 'to undertake a New Vattel', he sent Henry transcriptions of a plan entitled 'International Law' (11 June 1827). Bentham proposed a legislative alliance among 'all civilized Nations', which he admitted 'at present is as much as to say, all Nations professing the Christian Religion', each to be represented by an envoy at a congress with both judicial and legislative authority. He rejected the abbé de St Pierre's plan for such a system as unworkable and likewise judged Vattel to be inadequate as the foundational work for a new international order: only one 'grounded on the greatest happiness principle ... would, if the plan and execution be more moral and intellectual than Vattels, possess a probability of superseding it, and being referred to in preference'.[64]

Bentham's plan for 'a New Vattel' never came to fruition. The effort to codify international law nevertheless remained a leading aspiration of many of his disciples. James Mill had projected such a code in an article on the 'Law of Nations' for the _Encyclopedia Britannica_ on which Bentham took notes, though without any apparent valuation, either positive or negative.[65] Étienne Dumont pointed out the manifold failings of the existing traditions of the law of nations before attempting his own inconclusive and abortive codification of international law. Dumont argued that such a code could be founded on only two forms of sanction: public opinion and the threat of war.[66] The lack of a positive legislator, and of agencies able to enforce punishments for breaches of the code, was however not a deterrent to codification, for him as it was not for Bentham. It would take another of Bentham's disciples, John Austin, to turn a scepticism about available sanctions back upon the idea of law itself to deny that international 'law' was law in any recognisable sense: instead, it could only be a positive international morality, consisting of the

[61] On Henry, see Graham (2001); Graham (2005); _ODNB_, s.v., 'Henry, Jabez (1775–1835)'.
[62] Henry (1823).
[63] Henry ([1825?]), presentation copy to Bentham, BL pressmark C.T. 55 (1); Nadelmann (1961).
[64] BL Add. MS 30151, ff. 15v–16r; Nys (1885).
[65] James Mill, 'Law of Nations', in Mill (1825); UCL Bentham XCVII. 189.
[66] Dumont (1829b); Dumont MSS 60.

'opinions or sentiments current among nations generally. It therefore is not law properly so called.'[67] This was surely a rather un-Benthamite conclusion derived from some idiomatically Benthamite premises.

The 'spectre of Austin' would haunt later attempts to place international law on solid positivist foundations. If Austin's analysis was correct, then many of the same charges that Bentham himself had laid against natural jurisprudence could be applied to international law: that it was non-binding, factually indeterminate and merely hortative. And if international law suffered all these faults, then it needed some other foundation, such as divine revelation or Christian theology, to give it moral efficacy.[68] Contrary to many of the standard narratives twentieth-century international lawyers told themselves about the origins of their discipline, there was no smooth transition from naturalism to positivism in the late eighteenth and nineteenth centuries: indeed, what had been called 'synthetic natural law' remained remarkably robust in the age of liberal nationalism.[69] This should not be surprising in light of the gradual narrowing of the universalism of natural law that had taken place in Europe in the decades since the French Revolution. It had become a particularistic universalism, based on principles idiomatic to only one self-defined civilisation which increasingly claimed a mission for itself to export those values to the rest of the world.[70] The imperial roots, and colonial fruits, of that mission would in due course bring all such European universalisms into disrepute. But we should beware of throwing the universalist baby out with the particularist bathwater. Just as it has proved possible to detach Bentham the sceptic about colonialism from his utilitarian followers,[71] so it is feasible to discriminate Bentham the proponent of a universal international law from his more sceptical heirs, like Austin. Deciding whether it was his own evolving universalism, the global conjuncture in which he lived, or a combination of more local circumstances around the world that made him, almost alone among his contemporaries, a figure with worldwide fame and influence will be among the many pressing tasks for any future global history of political thought to pursue.

---

[67] Austin (1995), pp. 112, 124.
[68] Sylvest (2009), pp. 63–8; Rumble (2005); Varouxakis (2009), pp. 119–23.
[69] Fitzmaurice (2009); Sylvest (2009), pp. 77–80, 90–1.
[70] Pitts (2007); Pitts (2012); see also Orakhelashvili (2006).   [71] Pitts (2005b); Pitts (2011).

PART IV

Building on the foundations: making states since 1776

The Declaration of Independence and international law

Perhaps the most momentous but least widely understood development in modern history is the long transition from a world of empires to a world of states. Until at least the late nineteenth century, and in many places for decades after, most of the world's population lived in the territorially expansive, internally diverse, hierarchically organised political communities called empires. It is a striking feature of our political world that humanity is now divided into so many states but it is equally significant that there are no longer any self-styled empires. Although many commentators argued that the United States acted like an empire during the presidency of George W. Bush, 'empire' was not a name formally adopted or publicly promoted by even the most committed proponents of an aggressive American foreign policy after 2001. Indeed, the last *soi-disant* empire died in 1979 when French forces overthrew Jean-Bédel Bokassa, the Napoleonic emperor of the Central African Empire, now the Central African Republic.

In order to understand this great transformation of a world of empires into our world of states, it is essential to go back to the late eighteenth and early nineteenth centuries. This was a period in which empires competed aggressively and expanded successfully, from China under the Qing dynasty to Great Britain under the Hanoverian monarchy. But it was also a century in which other empires were under challenge, from the Mughals in South Asia to the Bourbons and Habsburgs in Europe and the Atlantic world. The number of polities we might recognise to be sovereign states was relatively small and many of them, especially in Europe, sought the greater prestige and resources that came with being, or having, an empire and ruling over diverse and far-flung peoples. It would be anachronistic to see the origins of a world defined by states as early as 1648 and the Peace of Westphalia which is often held to have inaugurated a 'Westphalian order' of mutually acknowledged independent states; it might even be anachronistic to find the roots of a state-based international order even

200 years later in the mid nineteenth century when empires were still on the rise and on the march across the world from Mexico to Russia in the late nineteenth century. Yet it is not inappropriate to see events of the late eighteenth-century and early nineteenth-century Atlantic world as an anticipation of what would come to much of the rest of the globe 200 years later. This chain of events began with the American Revolution.

The American Revolution was a crisis of sovereignty that began as a series of fairly commonplace provincial tax revolts. It later became an imperial civil war and after 1776, at least in the eyes of former British colonists in mainland North America, it changed yet again into an international conflict between the United Kingdom and the United States, soon joined by allies from among the great powers of Europe.[1] This British 'Atlantic crisis' foreshadowed elements of the even larger and more transformative crisis that engulfed the Iberian Atlantic world after 1808: it contained repeated claims to local autonomy, a crisis of monarchy, rebellion, civil war, the redistribution of sovereignty, assertions of independence and the emergence of a new civil society and political economy in the context of emergent statehood amid a restructured international society within the Atlantic world.[2] To be sure, there were fundamental differences between the crisis of British America and the crises of Iberian America, and not only in their timing, some forty years apart. There was nothing equivalent to the shock of the Napoleonic invasion of Iberia in 1808. There was no change of monarchy and no fundamental reorganisation of the political constitution in the metropole. And the British Empire did not dissolve and in fact emerged from its Atlantic crisis stronger and more globally expansive than ever before. The creation of the first successful republican government on the western side of the Atlantic did not immediately inspire other American populations to secure their independence from both monarchy and empire. Yet the American Revolution did prove, for the first time in modern history, that it was possible for new states to emerge, even if they left the bulk of the original host empire intact. And the document that in retrospect seemed to prove to a wider world that this was indeed possible was the American Declaration of Independence of July 1776.

The US Declaration of Independence is among the most heavily interpreted and fiercely discussed documents in modern history: among other secular texts only statutes and constitutions have generated greater

---

[1] Armitage (2011).   [2] I take the term 'Atlantic crisis' from Portillo Valdes (2006).

amounts of commentary upon comparable numbers of words. Yet the Declaration was neither a statute nor a constitution, and was thus originally irrelevant to domestic law, however often its ideals may have since been invoked.[3] It was, 'like the Gettysburg address, another piece of war propaganda with no legal force',[4] and could not therefore be part of the fundamental law of the United States. It may have helped to constitute American ideals of 'life, liberty and the pursuit of happiness', but it was not intended to become a document of constitutional law, despite its popular association (reaching back at least to Abraham Lincoln) with the Constitution and in particular with the Bill of Rights as a statement of basic political principle. It is therefore inappropriate to call it 'America's most fundamental constitutional document', 'the real preamble to the Constitution of the United States', or even the key to constitutional interpretations in light of a natural-rights philosophy, if by that it is understood to be a document equivalent in legal standing to the Constitution itself.[5]

The Declaration would seem to be a unique and unclassifiable text, without historical precedent for its enduring principles and with few contemporary parallels for its place within a national mythology. This is an illusion generated by traditions of interpreting the Declaration that do not reflect the intentions of its framers and would have been largely incomprehensible to its original audiences. Those aims and audiences have been revealed by the historical study of the Declaration, which began only at the turn of the twentieth century.[6] Studies of the Declaration's reception, the various histories of how it was made and re-made in 1776 and thereafter, have excavated the changing status of the Declaration within American life.[7] However, they have done little to examine its reception beyond the United States, whether in 1776 or since. The parts of the Declaration that have been found most compelling in the United States for the last half-century – above all, the 'self-evident truths' of its second paragraph regarding individual rights 'to life, liberty, and the pursuit of happiness' – have been taken as the core of its meaning for its drafters and as its enduring contribution to political philosophy. This may seem obvious or unavoidable to commentators living amidst the resurgence of 'rights talk' since the Second World War and the 1948

---

[3] Reid (1981), pp. 46–89; Larson (2001).   [4] Wills (1978), p. 362.
[5] Mahoney (1987), pp. 54, 65; Gerber (1995), p. 17; C. L. Black, Jr (1997), pp. 6–10.
[6] Friedenwald (1904); Hazelton (1906); Becker (1922).
[7] Desbler (1892); Detweiler (1962); *We, the Other People* (1976); Peterson (1991); Jayne (2007); Dyer (2011); Tsesis (2012).

Universal Declaration of Human Rights, but that does not mean it has always been so.[8] In fact, the Declaration only became an object of reverent exegesis in the early nineteenth century, when a civil religion of national patriotism sanctified it as 'American scripture', a status it has held consistently and continuously only since the Civil War.[9] That status is unique to its place in American national life. The Declaration has, of course, also been excerpted, imitated and even occasionally revered in places other than the United States, but nowhere else does it possess such an aura of sanctity.

Historians of the Declaration's composition have generally looked to Europe for its inspiration. Their studies have produced vigorous disagreement over the sources of the Declaration's doctrine, whether derived from constitutionalist theories of resistance, the natural-rights theories of John Locke, the broader tradition of natural law, the common-sense epistemology of the Scottish Enlightenment, the heterodox theology of Viscount Bolingbroke or the English language of classical republicanism.[10] There has also been much controversy regarding the Declaration's form. Perhaps it was a typical exercise in mid-eighteenth-century logic, indebted to William Duncan's textbook which Jefferson almost certainly studied as a student at the College of William and Mary.[11] Maybe it was modelled on the opening of a bill of indictment in a civil pleading.[12] It may have been a script for declamation, marked up and composed as if a score for public performance, and hence meant to persuade by rhetoric rather than to convince by logical proof, or it may have formed the typographical expression of a collective identity, a truly democratic artefact of the age of mechanical reproduction.[13] The Declaration's language and genre could in fact have been indebted to all these sources at once. Its lasting appeal and its susceptibility to interpretation and appropriation might therefore derive not from the self-evidence of the 'truths' it professed to have discovered but rather from its eclecticism, and hence its ability to appeal simultaneously to many different audiences.

Disagreement about the Declaration's sources and character has created confusion about its original purpose, whether as a text for internal or

---

[8] Haskell (1987); Lacey and Haakonssen (1991); Primus (1999), ch. 5, 'Rights after World War II'. On the crucial discontinuities within these traditions, see Moyn (2010).

[9] P. Maier (1997), ch. 4, 'American Scripture'.

[10] Angermann (1965); Becker (1922); White (1978); Gerber (1993); Zuckert (1996); Wills (1978); Hamowy (1979); Reck (1991); Jayne (1998); Alvis (1998).

[11] Howell (1961).   [12] Anastaplo (1965), pp. 391–4; Ferguson (1984), p. 63.

[13] Fliegelman (1993); T. Starr (1998).

international consumption; as the enactment of independence itself or the justification of independence after the fact; as a contingent and strategic document or as a universal statement of 'self-evident truths' regarding the 'inalienable rights' of all human beings. This chapter offers an interpretation that situates the Declaration within two overlapping contexts that most commentary had tended to slight: law and international relations. As John Phillip Reid has noted, historians of the Declaration generally avoid its legal context in order to search for its meaning and genesis in more intellectually fashionable sources.[14] However, law in Reid's sense means domestic or municipal law, the enactments of Congress and the judgments of courts. This chapter proposes a different legal context for both the immediate composition and the longer-term reception of the Declaration. That context can be found in what was called at the time 'the law of nature and of nations' and which was just coming to be called international law. Such law both provided norms for the behaviour of states and was derived from an empirical observation of that behaviour: in the first mode, it was close to classical conceptions of natural law, and in the second to what was coming to be called 'positive' law in the international realm. This chapter locates the Declaration within these two conceptions of international law and argues that its place within these conceptions can partly account for its form and for its early reception in Europe.

The Declaration should thus be interpreted as 'a document performed in the discourse of the *jus gentium* [law of nations] rather than *jus civile* [civil law]', and hence as a statement of the powers and capacities of states as much as of the rights and duties of individuals.[15] The interpretation of the Declaration of Independence offered here comprises four parts. First, it treats the argument of the Declaration, in an attempt to answer the question: 'What Did the Declaration Declare?'[16] Second, it reconstructs the early reception of the Declaration in Europe. Third, it examines the context of the Declaration's composition and argues that it arose from a transitional and eclectic moment within the history of international law when both natural law and the positive law of nations could be appealed to equally (as they were in the Declaration), a moment that in retrospect came to be seen as crucial in a shift away from naturalism to positivism in the realm of international law. Finally, it concludes with a brief assessment of the implications of such a recontextualisation of the Declaration of Independence for a historical understanding of the American

[14] Reid (1981).   [15] Pocock (1995), p. 281.   [16] Ellis (1999).

Revolution. Such an approach emphasises the assertions of autonomy the Declaration made for the United States within the international order rather than the claims made on behalf of individuals in relation to their governments. To interpret the Declaration in this way is to draw it out of its traditional American setting as the foundation of a 'national compact', the birth-certificate of a nation or the secular scripture of a self-chosen people;[17] instead, it puts it into the more cosmopolitan contexts of international law and of the relations between states.

The argumentative structure of the Declaration falls into five parts.[18] The first paragraph outlines the immediate statement of purpose, the necessity of declaring the causes that compelled one people to dissolve the political bands that had connected them with another. The second paragraph states the principles upon which legitimate government rests, and for the violation of which it might be justifiable to 'throw off such Government, and to provide new Guards for ... future security'. The following bill of grievances lists the alleged 'injuries and usurpations' by George III that had justified separation from that government.[19] The fourth section narrates the response to colonial complaints in order to show that, the grievances having gone unredressed, and the Americans' 'Brittish brethren' being 'deaf to the voice of justice and consanguinity', 'necessity ... denounces our Separation'. On this basis, the Declaration concludes in its fifth part that 'these United Colonies are, and of Right ought to be Free and Independent States': this was what Congress had resolved on 2 July 1776 and, once Congress had restored these words to the final draft, this was what the Declaration declared.[20]

The logical structure of the Declaration provides a conclusion, based upon a major premise, a minor premise and two proofs. The major premise, stated in the opening paragraph, is that causes of separation must be declared; the minor premise, in the second paragraph, is that there can be violations of principle that would justify separation. The first proof consists in the evidence that such violations have repeatedly taken place; the second proof, that no redress or remission for such violations has

---

[17] *Pace* Lutz (1989).   [18] Jones (1976), p. 55.

[19] Fisher (1907); Wills (1978), pp. 65–75; P. Maier (1997), pp. 105–23.

[20] 'The Declaration of Independence as Adopted by Congress' (4 July 1776), in Jefferson (1950–), 1, pp. 429–32. The phrase 'these United Colonies are, and of Right ought to be Free and Independent States' was added by Congress to the final draft of the Declaration: Boyd (1999), p. 35; P. Maier (1997), p. 148.

been offered. On these grounds, the conclusion follows that separation can be justified in 'the opinions of mankind'.[21] Within this logical structure, the statement of 'self-evident' truths in the second paragraph of the Declaration – the paragraph that has, after all, attracted most modern commentary and which has come to guarantee the Declaration's place in American national mythology – was strictly subordinate to the necessity of proving the grounds for the freedom and independence of the United States. As Abraham Lincoln shrewdly noted in 1857, '[t]he assertion that "all men are created equal" was of no practical use to our effecting separation from Great Britain; and it was placed in the Declaration, not for that, but for future use'.[22]

Almost all commentary has nonetheless focused on the second paragraph of the Declaration and its natural-rights philosophy. This is in spite of the fact that it provided the minor premises, not the major premises, for separation, and was logically equivalent to the tabulation of grievances among the justifications for declaring independence. In concentrating on that paragraph, commentators have generally ignored the first and last paragraphs which together form its irreducible logical skeleton.[23] Those paragraphs contained the major premise and the conclusion; they thus affirmed the two indispensable statements that constitute the Declaration a declaration of *independence*: that the United States were now among 'the Powers of the earth' and that they were 'Free and Independent States'. *Quod erat demonstrandum.*

The Declaration of Independence was a declaration in three senses. The first was that understood by Sir William Blackstone and other eighteenth-century common lawyers – that is, 'the *declaration, narratio,* or *count* ... in which the plaintiff sets forth his cause of complaint at length': its third section approximated to such an account.[24] It was also a document 'in the traditions of declarations as a genre of British political discourse ... in a line of descent from the revolutionary parliamentary declarations of the seventeenth century'.[25] It was moreover a declaration in the sense understood by international lawyers: that is, an expression of 'will, ... intent or ... opinion when acting in the field of international relations',

[21] As also argued by Zuckert (1996), pp. 16–17; compare the alternative accounts of the Declaration's logical structure in Howell (1961), pp. 480–1, and Lucas (1989), p. 91.
[22] Abraham Lincoln, 'Speech at Springfield, Illinois' (26 June 1857), in Lincoln (1953–5), II, p. 406.
[23] The exceptions are Dumbauld (1950), pp. 34–44, 153–5; Marshall (1974), pp. 8–9, 19; Dumbauld (1976); Wills (1978), pp. 325–32; Pocock (1988a), pp. 13–15; Pocock (1988b); Pocock (1995), pp. 280–2; P. Maier (1997), pp. 132–3, 142; P. S. Onuf (1998), pp. 71–2, 82–3.
[24] Blackstone (1765–9), III, p. 293.   [25] Lucas (1998), p. 151.

such as a declaration of war, which could be made 'either by a general manifesto, published to all the world; or by a note to each particular court, delivered by an ambassador'.[26] This particular 'general manifesto' began by announcing the arrival of new actors on the international stage, and expressed a duty to account for their emergence:

> When in the Course of human events, it becomes necessary for one people to dissolve the political bands which have connected them with another, and to assume among the powers of the earth the separate and equal station to which the Laws of Nature and of Nature's God entitle them, a decent respect to the opinions of mankind requires that they should declare the causes which impel them to the separation.[27]

The Declaration's audience was the whole of 'mankind', not only those who might call themselves Americans by virtue of the fact that they had cast off their allegiance to the British Crown and who could thus voluntarily engage themselves as citizens of an independent state or states.[28]

The final substantive sentence of the Declaration now defined more precisely what it would mean to take the part of one of 'the powers of the earth':

> as Free and Independent States, they have full Power to levy War, conclude Peace, contract Alliances, establish Commerce, and to do all other Acts and Things which Independent States may of right do.[29]

Congress had been exercising most of the rights it now formally claimed – negotiating with Britain; appointing agents to work on its behalf abroad; corresponding with foreign powers; seeking aid – for almost two years before the Declaration.[30] Among those rights was the ability to make meaningful declarations to 'the candid world'. The Declaration itself was just such an act. It was in fact a speech-act which not only *communicated* the fact of the independence of the United States to the world but by so doing also *performed* the independence it declared.[31]

The opening and closing statements of the Declaration have been taken for granted because they seemed, in retrospect, to have successfully and enduringly confirmed American independence by performing an

---

[26] Carl-August Fleischhauer, 'Declaration', in Bernhardt (1992–2003), VII, p. 67; R. Ward (1805), p. 3.
[27] 'The Declaration of Independence', in Jefferson (1950–), I, p. 429; 'separate and equal' replaced 'equal and independent' in Jefferson's Rough Draft: Boyd (1999), p. 67.
[28] Kettner (1978), ch. 7, 'The Idea of Volitional Allegiance'.
[29] 'The Declaration of Independence', in Jefferson (1950–), I, p. 432.
[30] Marston (1987), pp. 206–23.
[31] For the speech-act theory of 'locutionary' (that is, communicative) and 'illocutionary' (performative) force, see Austin (1962).

independent declaration. This may account for the relative lack of commentary these passages have received. Yet they are, after all, the most prominent sentences in the document, the statements of what the United States intended to become – that is, 'to assume among the powers of the earth the separate and equal station to which the Laws of Nature and of Nature's God entitle them' – and of what they could do once they had achieved that goal – that is, to 'to levy War, conclude Peace, contract Alliances, establish Commerce, and to do all other Acts and Things which Independent States may of right do'. The rest of the Declaration provided only a statement of the abstract principles upon which the assertion of such standing within the international order rested, and an accounting of the grievances that had compelled the assumption of that status.

The diplomatic, strategic and international purpose of declaring independence partly explained the logical structure of the Declaration, and accounted for the necessity of declaring independence at all. As the concluding (and conclusive) sentence of the Declaration put it, the precise intention was to 'levy war' and 'contract alliances' against Great Britain. This had become increasingly urgent since the King had declared the colonists to be rebels in August 1775, and as the colonists then began their search for allies against Great Britain.[32] In order to turn a civil war into a war between states, and thus to create legitimate corporate combatants out of individual rebels and traitors, it was essential to declare war and to obtain recognition of the legitimacy of such a declaration. In October 1775 John Adams wondered whether independent American ambassadors might not be rebuffed by foreign powers: 'Would not our Proposals and Agents be treated with Contempt?'[33] Richard Henry Lee likewise noted in April 1776 that 'no state in Europe will either Treat or Trade with us for so long as we consider ourselves subjects of G[reat]. B[ritain]. Honor, dignity, and the customs of states forbid them until we rank as an independant people.'[34] Fear of a partition treaty among the European powers made it yet more urgent for the colonies to constitute themselves as independent actors within the international order.[35] The likely partitioners were the Catholic monarchies of Europe in concert with Britain. John Dickinson warned that '[a] PAR[TI]T[I]ON of these Col[onie]s will take Place if G[reat] B[ritain] cant conq[uer] Us'.[36] In retrospect, and in

---

[32] The transition from colonists to rebels is traced on the British side in Conway (2002).

[33] John Adams to James Warren, 7 October 1775, in Warren and Adams (1917–25), I, pp. 127–8.

[34] Richard Henry Lee to Patrick Henry, 20 April 1776, in Lee (1911–14), I, p. 178.

[35] Hutson (1971–2); Wandycz (1980).   [36] Dickinson (1941), p. 478.

light of the French alliance of 1778, such fears appear groundless, but they were real enough in the years following the division of North America between Britain and Spain in the aftermath of the Seven Years' War, in the wake of the French capture of Corsica in 1768 and after the first Partition of Poland in 1772, in which Prussia, Austria and Russia had partially dismembered Europe's largest state. As Lee warned, '[a] slight attention to the late proceedings of many European Courts will sufficiently evince the spirit of partition, and the assumed right of disposing of Men & Countries like live stock on a farm ... Corsica, & Poland indisputably prove this'.[37]

It was therefore necessary for the colonists to create juridical bodies with which the European powers could make alliances and conduct commerce. Thomas Paine had ended *Common Sense* (9 January 1776) with the most extensive statement of this argument for independence, on the grounds of the 'custom of Nations' (by which a mediator might negotiate peace between warring states), the necessity of foreign alliances and the desire to avoid the imputation of rebellion. Above all, Paine, like Lee, noted the need for a 'manifesto to be published, and dispatched to foreign Courts'; until such a manifesto or declaration was produced, Paine concluded, 'the custom of all Courts is against us, and will be so, until by an Independance we take rank with other Nations'.[38] The same point had been repeated frequently in the local instructions, addresses and resolutions addressed to the delegates to the Continental Congress, 'to concur with the Delegates of the other Colonies in declaring Independency, and forming foreign alliances', 'to cast off the *British* yoke, and to enter into a commercial alliance with any nation or nations friendly to our cause', 'to beware of any other than commercial alliances with foreigners', to express 'the ardent wish of our souls that *America* may become a free and independent State', and hence 'to declare the United Colonies free and independent States'.[39] Lee's motion of 7 June to declare '[t]hat these United Colonies are and of right, ought to be, free and independent states ... That it is expedient forthwith to take the most effectual measures

---

[37] Richard Henry Lee to Patrick Henry, 20 April 1776, in Lee (1911–14), I, p. 176; Simms (2007), pp. 569–71.
[38] Paine (1776), pp. 77–8.
[39] North Carolina Instructions (12 April 1776); Instructions for the Delegates of Charlotte County, Virginia (23 April 1776); Address and Instructions of the Freeholders of [Buckingham] County, Virginia (n. d.); Virginia Instructions (15 May 1776); 'Meeting of the Inhabitants of the Town of Malden' (27 May 1776); Connecticut Instructions (14 June 1776), in *American Archives* (1833–46), V, pp. 1322, 1035, 1208; VI, pp. 461, 602, 868.

for forming alliances' and '[t]hat a plan of confederation be prepared and transmitted to the respective Colonies' led Congress to set up three overlapping committees: to compose a declaration of independence, to draft a model treaty and to draw up articles of confederation.[40] In debate on 1 July, John Dickinson made last-ditch arguments against any declaration, and warned against any general manifesto because 'for[eign] Pow[ers] will not rely on Words', recommending instead private negoti- ations with European powers (especially France): '[w]e must not talk gen [eral]ly of for[eign] Pow[ers] but [only] of those We expect to fav[o]r. Us'. However, envoys had already been sent to Europe, and Congressional sentiment was overwhelmingly in favour of the Declaration. Lee's reso- lution passed on 2 July without any dissenting vote, thanks to the abstention of the Pennsylvania delegation.[41]

Among the sources deployed by the overlapping committees were some of the basic documents of eighteenth-century international relations. Benjamin Franklin argued in December 1775 that 'the circumstances of a rising State make it necessary frequently to consult the law of nations';[42] accordingly, he distributed copies obtained from France of the 1775 Amsterdam edition of Emer de Vattel's *Droit des gens* (1758) to the Library Company of Philadelphia, the Harvard College Library and Congress itself.[43] He also supplied John Adams with 'a printed volume of treaties' which he marked up in pencil.[44] The Congressional commit- tees thus had available to them the most up-to-date tools of contemporary diplomacy: Vattel's French compendium of the law of nations (an instant classic on its publication in 1758) and one of the treaty-collections that had become indispensable to diplomats and statesmen since they had first been compiled in the late seventeenth century.[45] In the latter, Adams certainly found the templates for a model treaty, in the Anglo-French commercial alliances of 1686 and 1713; in the former, Jefferson and his colleagues possessed the common wisdom of mid-eighteenth-century

---

[40] *Journals of the Continental Congress* (1904–6), v, pp. 425–6; Wills (1978), pp. 326–9.
[41] Dickinson (1941), pp. 471, 474; Flower (1983), pp. 161–6; Calvert (2009), ch. 6.
[42] Benjamin Franklin to Charles Dumas, December 1775, in *Revolutionary Diplomatic Correspondence* (1889), II, p. 64.
[43] Vattel (1775), Library Company of Philadelphia, call-number Rare E Vatt 303. Q; Houghton Library, Harvard University, call-number *AC7. F8545. Zz775V. Congress's copy has not been located.
[44] John Adams, *Autobiography*, in Adams (1850–6), II, p. 516; Gilbert (1961), p. 50. The volume of treaties was *Compleat Collection* (1760), Houghton Library, Harvard University, call-number *EC7 Ed596 741; Adams (1977–), IV, pp. 262–3.
[45] Toscano (1966), I, pp. 47–66.

European diplomacy that 'independence is ever necessary to each state' to secure which 'it is sufficient that nations conform to what is required of them by the natural and general society, established among all mankind'.[46] Such materials could easily have remedied the deficiencies in Jefferson's own knowledge of the law of nations, hardly any trace of which in the decades before 1776 can be found in his legal commonplace book.[47] Out of them, Jefferson, his fellow committee-members, and Congress itself created a document calculated to appeal equally to audiences at home and abroad.

Despite the careful drafting of the Declaration for domestic and foreign consumption, the immediate response from abroad was a deafening diplomatic silence, in Britain, France and more generally across Europe.[48] Four copies of the Declaration made their way into the British State Papers in the summer and autumn of 1776.[49] Lord Howe's secretary, Ambrose Serle, privately expressed his horror at the Declaration in his diary on 13 July – 'A more impudent, false and atrocious Proclamation was never fabricated by the Hands of Man' – but none of his superiors registered any such sentiments as they dispatched their copies back to London.[50] It appeared in London newspapers in mid-August 1776,[51] was printed in Edinburgh on 20 August 1776 (five days before David Hume's death),[52] in Dublin on 24 August,[53] Leiden on 30 August,[54] Copenhagen on 2 September,[55] Florence by mid-September[56] and in a German translation (by the Swiss disciple of Rousseau, Isaak Iselin) that appeared in Basel in October;[57] news of independence had also reached Warsaw by

---

[46] Vattel (1760), p. xi.   [47] LC, Jefferson Papers, ser. V, vol. 13; Jefferson (1926).

[48] Van Alstyne (1965), pp. 96, 100, 106, 108–10; Kite (1928); Peckham (1976); Palmer (1976); Dippel (1977), pp. 29, 36, 100–5, 276, 347; Nordholt (1982); Venturi (1991), pp. 13, 17 (Italy); Melero (1977), pp. 297–8. More generally, see Adams (1999); Armitage (2007a).

[49] TNA ADM 1/487/34; CO 5/40/252; CO 5/177/29; CO 5/1353/401. Only one of these four copies is recorded in Walsh (1949).

[50] Serle (1940), p. 31.

[51] *Morning Chronicle* (London), 14 August 1776; *British Chronicle* (London), 14–16 August 1776; *St James's Chronicle* (London), *General Evening Post* (London), 15 August 1776; *Annual Register* (London) (1776), pp 261–4; D. D. (1898), pp. 127–8; Lutnick (1967), pp. 75–6.

[52] *Caledonian Mercury* (Edinburgh), 20 August 1776; *Scots Magazine* (Edinburgh), 38 (1776), pp. 433–6; Livingston (1990), p. 133.

[53] *Freeman's Journal* (Dublin), 24 August 1776.

[54] *Gazette de Leyde* (Leiden), 30 August 1776; Popkin (1989), p. 151.

[55] *Berlingske Tidende* (Copenhagen), 2 September 1776, reproduced in *Independence Documents of the World* (1977), I, p. 187.

[56] *Gazzetta Universale o Sieno Notizie Istoriche, Politiche, di Scienze, Arti, Agricoltura* (Florence) and *Notizie del Mondo* (Florence), 14 September 1776; Venturi (1991), I, p. 50.

[57] *Ephemeriden der Menschheit* (Basel), October 1776, pp. 96–106; Dippel (1977), p. 29.

11 September, though the Declaration itself was only briefly summarised there.[58] Along its path through Europe, it split the radical movement in England between supporters and opponents of independence (as pro-Ministerial writers had predicted); excited admiration but not imitation in Ireland; merited refutation in Scotland; but received little or no direct comment in Italy, Germany, Poland, Switzerland or Spain.[59] The most worrying silence as far as the Americans were concerned came from France, the original object of the United States's overtures for an alliance. The first of two copies of the Declaration sent to the American representative in Paris, Silas Deane, was lost, while the second arrived only in November 1776, after the news of American independence had been circulating for at least three months elsewhere in Europe. When France did eventually enter into alliance with the United States in February 1778, following the watershed of the American defeat of British forces at the battle of Saratoga, it was 'to maintain effectually the liberty, Sovereignty and independence absolute and unlimited of the said United States'.[60] This was, of course, what Congress had hoped for all along, at least since it had simultaneously created committees for drafting the Declaration and a model treaty of alliance and commerce.

The British government could not respond officially to the Declaration for that 'would be to recognise that equality and independence, to which subjects, persisting in revolt, cannot fail to pretend ... This would be to recognise the right of other states to interfere in matters, from which all foreign interposition should for ever be precluded.'[61] Lord North's Ministry did, however, commission a rebuttal of the Declaration (from which these words came). This comprised mostly a point-by-point examination and refutation of the charges against the King. Five hundred copies were sent from London to America, to instruct British troops and to rebut the arguments of the rebels.[62] The author of this *Answer to the Declaration of the American Congress* (1776) was John Lind, a young lawyer and pamphleteer who had come to the administration's notice with the publication of his *Remarks on the Principal Acts of the Thirteenth Parliament* (1775) and *Three Letters to Dr Price, Containing Remarks on*

[58] *Gazeta Warszawska* (Warsaw), 11 September 1776; Sokol (1967), p. 8.
[59] TNA CO 5/177/113; York (1994), p. 103; 'An Answer to the Declaration of Independence', *Scots Magazine*, 38 (1776), pp. 652–5; 39 (1777), pp. 65–74, 121–8, 177–86, 233–42, 289–93 (reprinting extracts from [Lind and Bentham] (1776)); Swinfen (1976), p. 71; Venturi (1991), I, p. 50.
[60] Treaty of Alliance, 6 February 1778, Article 2, in *Treaties and Other International Acts* (1931–48), II, pp. 36–7; Stinchcombe (1969), pp. 8–13.
[61] [Lind and Bentham] (1776), p. 5.   [62] TNA CO 5/93/290.

his Observations on the Nature of Civil Liberty, the Principles of Government, and the Justice and Policy of the War with America (1776).[63] Lind denied that the Americans were still anything other than treacherous individuals, rather than states, and hence rebels rather than legitimate corporate belligerents. To do otherwise would have been to make a mockery of the idea of allegiance, let alone legality: after all, if the colonists were acknowledged to be independent citizens of a foreign state, what could have prevented a pirate like Captain Kidd from just as easily protecting himself from criminal prosecution by declaring himself independent? 'Instead of the guilty pirate, he would have become the *independent* prince; and taken among the "*maritime*" powers – "*that separate and equal station, to which*" – he too might have discovered – "*the laws of nature and of nature's God entitled him*".' Finally, Lind mocked the colonists for their hypocrisy in announcing the natural equality of all mankind while failing to free their slaves: such rights were hardly inalienable, and clearly not natural, if they were denied to 'these wretched beings'.[64]

The *Answer to the Declaration* was almost the only foreign publication to comment on the natural-rights claims of the Declaration.[65] It was accompanied by a 'Short Review of the Declaration' that exposed the logical fallacies of the principles upon which the Americans claimed their independence, and judged them to be tautologous, redundant, inconsistent and hypocritical. 'If to what they now demand they were entitled by any law of God', thundered the reviewer, 'they had only to produce that law, and all controversy was at an end. Instead of this, what do they produce? What they call self-evident truths ... At the same time, to secure these rights, they are content that Governments should be instituted. They perceive not, or will not seem to perceive, that nothing which can be called government ever was, or ever could be, in any instance, exercised, but at the expence of one or other of those rights' to life, liberty or the pursuit of happiness.[66]

The precocious attack on the language of individual natural rights in *The Answer to the Declaration* was a significant contribution to counter-revolutionary discourse. In particular, the 'Short Review' formed a link between the American and French Revolutions because its author was not Lind but his friend Jeremy Bentham. Though American historians have

---

[63] Lind (1775); Lind (1776); Avery (1978). [64] [Lind and Bentham] (1776), pp. 6–7, 95, 107.
[65] Compare the passing remarks in Hutchinson (1776), pp. 9–10, the only other full-length British pamphlet devoted to answering the Declaration; Bailyn (1974), pp. 357–9.
[66] [Jeremy Bentham,] 'Short Review of the Declaration', in [Lind and Bentham] (1776), p. 120; printed in Armitage (2007a), p. 174.

generally remained unaware of this fact, it has been known since 1968 and has received ample commentary by Bentham scholars.[67] Bentham had earlier collaborated on Lind's *Remarks* and had prepared a devastating critique of the concept of 'negative liberty' (as he was almost the first to call it) for inclusion in Lind's *Three Letters to Dr Price*.[68] Bentham remained consistently critical of the principles that underlay the American Declaration to the end of his life. 'Who can help lamenting that so rational a cause should be rested upon reasons, so much fitter to beget objections, than to remove them?' he complained in 1780, referring to the Virginia Declaration of Rights, the Massachusetts Declaration and the Declaration itself; half a century later he still called the Virginia Declaration 'a hodge-podge of confusion and absurdity, in which the thing to be proved is all along taken for granted'.[69] The basis of his critique remained the same: only the positive acts of an identifiable legislator could be called laws, and only from such laws could any defensible rights be derived. To ascribe laws to nature, and to derive natural rights from such laws, was therefore not simply nonsense, it was doubly incoherent: 'Natural rights is simple nonsense: natural and impre-scriptible rights, rhetorical nonsense, nonsense upon stilts', as he called it in his demolition of the French Declaration of the Rights of Man and the Citizen almost twenty years after his earlier reply to the American Declaration.[70]

The modern tradition of natural law had arisen in the early seventeenth century and derived moral and political norms from nature, God or human nature, rather than the acts of particular legislators or the con-tractual agreements of peoples and sovereigns. This theory had formed the dominant – if not unchallenged – theory of morality and politics for at least a century and a half, but by the third quarter of the eighteenth century its ascendancy in Britain, France and Germany was beginning to waver. It was therefore ironic that the language of individual natural rights which had sprung in its modern form from this tradition should have become so prominent during the era of the American and French Revolutions: it was only as the philosophical underpinnings which had

---

[67] BL Add. MS 33551, ff. 359r–60v, printed in Bentham (1968–), I, pp. 341–4; D. G. Long (1977), pp. 51–4; Hart (1982), pp. 63–5; Onuf and Onuf (1990), p. 77.

[68] Jeremy Bentham, 'Hey' (1776), UCL Bentham LXIX, pp. 57–68, replying to Hey (1776); D. G. Long (1977), pp. 57–9; Molivas (1999); Elazar (2012).

[69] Bentham (1996), p. 311, n. c.; Bentham (1838–43), X, p. 63.

[70] Jeremy Bentham, 'Nonsense upon Stilts' (1792), in Bentham (2002), p. 330.

made sense of it were beginning to shift that it gained a temporary, though far from permanent, hegemony over political discourse.[71]

In retrospect, it came to appear that the lifetime of the generation of lawyers, politicians and philosophers born in the mid eighteenth century had encompassed an epochal transition in international norms. It would not be complete by the time that generation passed, but its progress was evident, and many thought it should be hastened. After all, asked Jefferson in 1784, 'Why should not this law of nations go on improving: Ages have intervened between its several steps; but as knowledge of late increases rapidly, why should not these steps be quickened?'[72] A standard narrative of the history of the law of nations began to emerge in this period that described a gradual waning of naturalism and a consequent rise in positivism in the law of nations. None of the commentators who compiled that narrative argued that the transition had entailed the abrupt and exclusive substitution of positive international law in place of a law of nations (*ius gentium*) identified with the law of nature (*ius naturae*).[73] However, they did acknowledge that the eighteenth century had seen the increasing ascendancy of positive law.

Their accounts implied the supremacy of the international agreements, treaties and customs derived from the consent of states and their sovereigns; its sources could be found in the mammoth collections of treaties which began publication in the late seventeenth century (and which continue to this day), in the history of the relations between states and in the works of the great international publicists. Grotius and Vattel agreed that the *jus belli ac pacis* or the *droit des gens* was derived both from the law of nature and from the consent of states. However, it was 'hardly possible that the simple law of nature should be sufficient, even between individuals, and still less between nations, when they come to frequent and carry on commerce with each other'; instead, states had to temper the law of nature in practice and by consent: 'The whole of the rights and obligations thus established between two nations, form the positive law of nations between them. It is called *positive*, particular or arbitrary, in opposition to natural, universal and

---

[71] On the history of this tradition, see especially Haakonssen (1996); Haakonssen (1999); Hochstrasser (2000); and, on its perceived late eighteenth-century 'crisis', especially in Germany, Tang (2010).
[72] Thomas Jefferson, 'Reasons in Support of the New Proposed Articles in the Treaties of Commerce' (10 March 1784), in *Diplomatic Correspondence* (1837), I, pp. 532–4, quoted in Lint (1977), p. 34.
[73] Moser (1778–80); Neyron (1783); G. F. Martens (1785); Ompteda (1785); Günther (1787–92); R. Ward (1795); Klüber (1819); Eden (1823); Wheaton (1836), pp. 1–29; Wheaton (1841), English translation: Wheaton (1845).

necessary law.'[74] Jefferson himself encapsulated contemporary wisdom when he stated in 1793 that '[t]he Law of Nations ... is composed of three branches. 1. the Moral law of our nature. 2. the Usages of nations. 3. their special Conventions'.[75]

Before the mid eighteenth century, the laws of nations had been almost completely assimilated to the laws of nature, as Thomas Hobbes and his later followers in the tradition of natural jurisprudence had proposed. These universal norms, accessible to all rational creatures, applied equally to individuals and their societies. States were therefore not simply analogous to persons (as in later conceptions of international law), but morally equivalent to them in their autonomy, rationality and duty to obey the dictates of natural law.[76] However, the increasingly bloody wars of eighteenth-century Europe, and the extension of that bloodshed to the rest of the globe, made it ever more obvious to commentators that deriving the law of nations from the law of nature had offered no guarantees against aggression and may only have served to increase international instability and bloodshed. As David Hume had noted ominously in 1751, '[t]he observance of justice, though useful among [nations], is not guarded by so strong a necessity as it is among individuals; and the *moral obligation* holds proportion with the *usefulness*'.[77] In 1795, Robert Ward declared unequivocally that 'the argument concerning a particular System of Morality for *all* mankind, enjoined by the Law of Nature, as far as it is drawn from the *Universality* of its reception, must be given up'.[78] In the same year, Immanuel Kant condemned the greatest representatives of the modern tradition of natural law, 'Hugo Grotius, Pufendorf, Vattel and the rest', as 'sorry comforters' (*leidige Tröster*) because 'their philosophically and diplomatically formulated codes do not and cannot have the slightest *legal* force'.[79] No less pointedly, Bentham later ridiculed 'the professors of natural law ... the Grotiuses and the Pufendorfs, the legislators of the human race' who wanted to achieve the universalist ambitions of Alexander and Tamburlane 'each one sitting in his armchair'.[80] Both Kant and Bentham proposed replacing

---

[74] G. F. Martens (1795), pp. 3–4.
[75] Thomas Jefferson, 'Opinions on the French Treaties' (28 April 1793), in Jefferson (1950–), xxv, p. 609.
[76] See generally Tuck (1999).   [77] Hume (1998), p. 100.   [78] R. Ward (1795), I, p. 63.
[79] Immanuel Kant, 'Zum Ewigen Frieden. Ein philosophischer Entwurf' (1795), in Kant (1964), I, p. 210; English translation in Kant (1991), p. 103.
[80] 'Voila professeurs de la droit naturel qu'ils avoient rêvé voila les Grotius et les Puffendorf legislateur, et legislateur du genre humain. Ce qui les Alexandres et les Tamerlan voulaiont faire en traversant le globe, les Grotius et le Puffendorf faisaient assis chacun dans son fauteuil':

the ineffective norms of natural law in international affairs with positive, enforceable agreements between nations, Kant in his proposed articles of perpetual peace, Bentham in his long-imagined digest of laws, the *Pannomion.* Such proposals were characteristic of the fifty years around the turn of the nineteenth century, when the shift from the natural-jurisprudential foundations of the law of nations towards a conception of positive international law became generally observable.

The international reception of the Declaration and the response to American independence itself were symptomatic of the jurisprudential eclecticism of the late eighteenth century. The naturalist claims of the Declaration's second paragraph elicited almost no comment from contemporaries, but the Declaration itself became a central exhibit in debates within the positive law of nations. The central question of international law raised by the Declaration was deceptively simple, but revealingly controversial: how did the Declaration declare independence? With his characteristic perceptiveness, Bentham, in the 'Short Review of the Declaration', had noted that 'it is one thing for them to *say*, the connection, which bound them to us, is *dissolved,* another to *dissolve* it; ... to *accomplish* their *independence* is not quite so easy as to *declare* it'.[81] Though Bentham did not elaborate the point, this problem was the nub of the international legal argument regarding the Declaration – or any document with similar intent – as it unfolded in the two generations immediately after 1776: how could independence be declared, except by a body that was already independent, in the sense understood by the law of nations?

A mere declaration could not constitute independence; it could only announce what had already been achieved by other means.[82] Only upon joining in the Franco-American alliance did the United States formally enter the international system; only thenceforth could the question of American independence be treated as a positive, albeit contested, fact of international law. Yet the fact of independence was one thing; the basis on which the opening of the Declaration had asserted it, quite another, for only positive acts could constitute statehood. If the Declaration's purpose was to enable the rebellious colonies to enter into diplomatic and commercial alliances with other powers, as Paine, Richard Henry Lee, the local declarations and the drafting committee of the Continental

---

Bentham, 'Pannomial Fragments' (1820s), BL Add. MS 33550, f. 92r, translated in Bentham (1838–43), III, p. 220.

[81] [Bentham,] 'Short Review of the Declaration', in [Lind and Bentham] (1776), p. 131; printed in Armitage (2007a), p. 186.

[82] Derrida (1984), pp. 13–32; English translation, Derrida (1986); Honig (1991).

Congress intended, at what point did the colonies become states, and the rebels acquire legitimacy? If a mere declaration were insufficient, and the acknowledgement of independence by Britain were inconceivable, would recognition of independence by a third power, such as France, be necessary to ensure legitimacy? Or, indeed, would even recognition by third parties be inadequate until the metropolitan government had conceded independence as it did only by the Treaty of Paris in 1783?[83]

These questions concerning independence, statehood and recognition were at the heart of the positive law of nations, and the Declaration – like American independence itself – was particularly received in this light after 1783 and in Europe. These aspects of the Declaration became the focus of the rapidly evolving argument in this early positivist period over the theory of the legal recognition of states. To claim an equal station for the United States among 'the powers of the earth' more was needed than the bare assertion that those states were entitled to their independence by virtue of the 'laws of nature and of nature's God'. The modern exponents of naturalism, like Grotius and Vattel, agreed that states did, indeed, possess a natural right to existence, independence and equality; however, the means by which new states might acquire that right, if they had not previously possessed it, only became a central topic of international legal argument in the late eighteenth century, partly in response to the issues of recognition raised by the Declaration of Independence itself.[84]

The American Declaration became a prominent exhibit in the earliest discussion of the recognition of states. This came from the German jurist and belletrist J. C. W. von Steck in 1783. His approach was original in that he treated the recognition and legitimation of states *per se*, rather than of princes; previously, discussions of recognition had been confined to the acknowledgement of the rights of succession of individual rulers. His account accordingly focused on republics like the United Provinces and the United States. In the latter case, Steck denied that American independence had had any international meaning until it was formally and positively recognised by Britain. He wrote in the immediate aftermath of the Treaty of Paris, and deemed French recognition in 1778 to have been premature, and hence without constructive force, because not accompanied by any renunciation of rights by Britain.[85] In 1789,

[83] On the contemporary context of these issues, see Goebel, Jr (1915), ch. 3, 'Intervention and Recognition in the American Revolution'.

[84] Alexandrowicz (1958); Crawford (2006), pp. 6–14; Grewe (2000), pp. 343–8.

[85] J. C. W. von Steck, 'Versuch von Erkennung der Unabhängigkeit einer Nation, und eines Staats', in Steck (1783), pp. 49–56; Alexandrowicz (1958), pp. 180–4; Frowein (1971).

G. F. von Martens pressed Steck's point further to argue that, 'when once obedience has been formally refused, and the refusing party has entered into the possession of the independence demanded, the dispute becomes the same as those which happen between independent states', subject to the major proviso that the offended party could legitimately construe any aid or succour offered to the newly independent state as an act of war: 'The conduct that Great Britain observed ... after the Colonies of North America declared themselves independent, may serve to illustrate this subject.'[86] By 1843, the question of recognition raised by American independence had become one of the great *causes célèbres* of international law as it passed into a more positivist phase.[87]

The success of the French alliance, and the victory of the Americans in the War of Independence, changed the status of the Declaration as a document. Soon after the official British recognition of American independence by Article I of the Treaty of Paris, publicists recognised the Declaration as part of the modern positive law of nations. For example, Charles Jenkinson's collection of treaties (1785) included it, and indeed used it to mark the most recent moment in the period in international affairs that had begun with the recognition of the independence of the United Provinces by the Treaty of Munster in 1649: 'By the Treaties made at Paris in 1783, another Revolution was acknowledged and confirmed, viz. that of the United States of America.' The Declaration appeared between the Spanish declaration concerning the Falkland Islands of 1771 and the Franco-American treaty of 1778, as an equivalent document within the positive law of nations.[88] Martens's *Précis du droit des gens moderne de l'Europe* (1789) listed it, along with the Articles of Confederation, which these same European commentators also construed as an international agreement.[89]

By 1783, there could be no question of the independence of the American states. The Declaration's purpose had been served, and arguments over the difference between *de facto* and *de jure* independence were now beside the point as far as the United States were concerned. British recognition of American independence in 1783 meant the United States could legitimately do all the things that free and independent states may of right do, as they had been doing at least since 1774. They had therefore

[86] Martens (1795), p. 80 and note; Alexandrowicz (1958), pp. 184–7.
[87] C. Martens (1843), I, pp. 113–209, 370–498.   [88] Jenkinson (1785), I, p. iii; III, pp. 237–41.
[89] 'List of the Principal Treaties ... Between the Different Powers of Europe since the Year 1748 down to the Present Time', in G. F. Martens (1795), p. 362; Martens (1791–1807), I, p. 580; Martens (1817–35), II, pp. 481–5 (Declaration), pp. 486–502 (Articles of Confederation).

attained statehood, in the international order; the acquisition of nation-hood – defined as an internal self-consciousness of identicality through shared history, traditions and institutions – was a separate process, to which the Declaration would only be definitively harnessed after the Civil War. The Fourth of July could be adopted as the birthday of the nation, but the Declaration itself remained the object of partisan dispute and competitive appropriation. The earliest citations of the Declaration by white Americans 'were usually drawn from its final paragraph' – declaring independence – but from the 1820s the natural-rights claims of the second paragraph 'gradually eclipsed altogether the document's assertion of the right to revolution'.[90] Only African Americans seem to have rapidly taken up the Declaration's message of liberation: as early as 1776 the free black former minuteman Lemuel Haynes precociously discerned a charter for abolition in the Declaration's second paragraph.[91]

The first generation of lawyers in the new Republic observed that the United States had entered the international system at a peculiarly propitious time in the history of the law of nations. For example, when James Kent produced the first digest of American law in 1826, he not only began his *Commentaries* with a chapter on the law of nations, but opened that chapter with the assertion that '[w]hen the United States ceased to be a part of the British empire, and assumed the character of an independent nation, they became subject to that system of rules which reason, mora-lity, and custom, had established among the civilised nations of Europe, as their public law'. He acknowledged that opinions differed over the foundation of the law of nations, whether as 'a mere system of positive institutions' or as 'essentially the same as the law of nature, applied to the conduct of nations'. Like the majority of his contemporaries, Kent concluded that neither was exclusively true: 'There is a natural and a positive law of nations.'[92]

The Declaration of Independence was a product of the jurisprudential eclecticism of the late eighteenth century. Neither wholly naturalist nor exclusively positivist, it appealed to the 'Laws of Nature, and of Nature's God' to empower the United States 'to do all other acts and things which

---

[90] L. Travers (1997), pp. 21–3, 161, 206; Waldstreicher (1997), pp. 30–5, 99–102, 206–7, 219–29, 240, 311–13; P. Maier (1997), pp. 160, 191 (quoted).

[91] Bay (2006); Slauter (2009); Lemuel Haynes, 'Liberty Further Extended...' (1776?), Houghton Library, Wendell Family Papers, bMS Am 1907 (608); printed in Bogin (1983), pp. 93–105.

[92] Kent (1828), I, p. 2; Janis (1992), pp. 38–9. On the relationship of American municipal law to international law in this period see Jay (1989), and the debate between Yoo (1999a) and Flaherty (1999), with the reply by Yoo (1999b). More generally, see now Golove and Hulsebosch (2010).

independent states may of right do'. Its argument rested on natural law, but ended with a statement of the positive powers of states. The international reception of the Declaration concentrated on the latter at the expense of the former; the domestic reception, on individual rights rather than the capacities of states. Beyond the United States, appeals to natural rights competed throughout the western world for much of the nineteenth century with more compellingly collective political languages such as corporatism and socialism, or the sceptical calculations of utilitarianism. These languages were variously hostile to the individualism of modern theories of natural rights, and none proved hospitable to the naturalistic claims to 'life, liberty, and the pursuit of happiness'. Utilitarianism and collectivism held less appeal in American intellectual life, and this in itself may account for the divergence in European and American perceptions of the Declaration's central message. Yet even after its appropriation into an exclusively American civil religion, the Declaration could still be read as a document of positive international law, detailing the collective rights of states rather than the particular rights of individuals. Thus James Brown Scott suggested in 1917 that the federal structure of the United States could be the model for a larger pacific world federation, with the Declaration as the charter for a new league of nations, the Articles of Confederation as its blueprint and the United States Constitution as its guiding set of principles.[93] That such a proposal now seems merely quaint is a sign that the individualistic, natural-rights interpretation of the Declaration has become unavoidable, while its prescriptions for the rights of states as international actors have been almost entirely forgotten.

To return the Declaration to its immediate international context reveals the Janus-faced nature of the American Revolution itself. It has been seen both as a belated episode in the history of early modern rebellions and as the prototype for modern decolonisation movements, thus harking back to the sixteenth century and laying foundations for the twentieth.[94] Though the Declaration has been called 'the first national independence document in the world', that honour is perhaps better accorded to the Dutch Act of Abjuration, the *Plakkaat van Verlatinge* (1581), in which the leaders of the Dutch Revolt cast off their allegiance to the Spanish

---

[93] Scott (1917), pp. xvii–xix; Scott (1920), pp. x, 467–9.

[94] On the former, see for example Clark (1995); on the latter, Lipset (1963); Barrow (1968); Morris (1970); Burrows and Wallace (1972), pp. 167, 279–80; Boyce (1999), pp. 21–8.

Habsburgs.[95] The Irish Confederation of Kilkenny had achieved *de facto* independence from England (with recognition by the papacy) between 1641 and 1649.[96] Closer in time to the American Revolution, Corsican rebels had proclaimed their independence from Genoa in 1735, only to be absorbed by France in 1762, while the Crimean Tartars had cast off their allegiance to Turkey in 1772, to find themselves almost immediately a dependency of Catherine the Great's Russia.[97] By the late eighteenth century, the American Revolution became assimilated within histories of international affairs to the rebellions and independence movements of the Dutch Republic, Corsica and the Crimea.[98] Yet, within a generation, the 1770s could be held to have signalled the 'total abandonment of public no less than private morality which marked the latter portion of the 18th century ... from this inauspicious moment may be dated the decline of the International system of Europe', marked especially by the Partitions of Poland and by the Franco-American alliance of 1778.[99]

The American colonists were not colonised peoples; this basic fact renders any facile assimilation of the American Revolution to the decolonisation movements of the second half of the twentieth century implausible.[100] Nor was the American Revolution a nationalist revolt, in the sense that a self-conscious 'people' recovered a suppressed collective identity as the motive for a rebellion against their colonial masters. The American revolutionaries were forced to create states out of colonies as they also began to recognise themselves as members of the same nation. They had to become independent in order to realise their interdependence. They could only declare that independence to a 'candid world' in the available languages of the law of nations; by so doing, they offered themselves as willing participants in an international system created by common norms, customs and agreements. Unlike the French Revolution, the American Revolution was not a nationalistic affront to international stability: as Friedrich Gentz noted in 1800, its aims were more limited, and its maxims not so plainly destructive to the law of nations, because the Americans had requested admission to the international order with their Declaration of Independence rather

[95] *Independence Documents of the World* (1977), II, p. 733; *Dutch Declaration* (1896); Coopmans (1983); Lucas (1994); Lucas (1998), pp. 159–69.
[96] Ohlmeyer (1995).   [97] T. Hall (1971); A. W. Fisher (1970).
[98] For example, Moser (1777–80), VI, pp. 126–47 (Corsica, Crimea, the United States); Steck, 'Versuch von Erkennung der Unabhängigkeit einer Nation, und eines Staats', in Steck (1783), pp. 49–56 (the United Provinces, Crimea, the United States).
[99] Eden (1823), pp. 81–2.   [100] Compare Greene (2007); Armitage (2007b).

than threatened its overthrow.[101] The successful incorporation of the United States into that international order obscured the fact that the American Revolution was as much about the creation of states (in the international sense) as it was about the birth of a nation. The Declaration of Independence aimed to achieve the one, but gradually came to be assimilated to the other, as what originated as a document characteristic of the eclecticism of contemporary international law became instead a talisman within a specifically national mythology.

Rainbolt (1973), pp. 430–3; Gentz (1800). Armstrong (1995), pp. 42–112, 204–25, illuminatingly compares the American and French Revolutions in this regard.

CHAPTER 12

Declarations of independence, 1776–2012

The process of extinguishing the legitimacy of empires would take more than two more centuries and was generally 'conflictual and contingent', though never quite complete. Our world is still marked by post-imperial legacies: for example, 'the fiction of sovereign equivalence, and ... the reality of inequality within and among states'. And imperial practices still remain – for example, in the treatment of indigenous peoples or in the promotion of multiculturalism – but now they are the policies of states, not the procedures of the empires they have universally replaced. The first Atlantic crisis, better known as the American Revolution, foreshadowed many of the complexities and conflicts in Iberian America and then later in the creation of a world of states that now encompasses the whole globe.[1]

Conjuring states out of colonies had been the single most radical act of the American Revolution: indeed, that process began the transformation of the Atlantic world into an arena hospitable, first, to independent states on its western shores, then to republicanism (in the sense of non-monarchical government), and finally to the creation of federal republics – the United States, Venezuela and Mexico, for instance – on a scale undreamed of by classical and early modern thinkers. It may therefore be instructive to consider the American Revolution not as an isolated process, of little relevance causally or comparatively to the revolutions in Spanish and Portuguese America, but as their precursor in the Atlantic world.[2]

The practice of declaring independence was common to all these movements and can therefore provide a useful synecdoche for parallels and divergences in the reconstruction of sovereignty and autonomy. The years between roughly 1809 and 1830 witnessed the first – but hardly the

---

[1] Wimmer and Min (2006); Tully (2008); Cooper and Burbank (2010), p. 458 (quoted).
[2] Rodríguez O. (2010) has emphatically denied that there was any connection between the British Atlantic crisis and that of the Iberian Atlantic world.

last – great age of declaring independence in world history. Almost all the declarations of independence issued in these decades came from Iberian America. From Texas in the north to Chile in the south, *juntas* and *congresos*, *pueblos* and emperors, announced the freedom and independence of their respective *ciudades, provincias, estados, naciones* or *imperios*. These claims appeared in a variety of genres: in the formal *actas* of representative bodies; in printed declarations, manifestos, *pronunciamentos* and plans; and in verbal proclamations and shouted *gritos*. In some cases, the declarations were later enshrined as foundational documents or pivotal events in national histories which have lasted to this day; in others, they led to the creation of states or nations that disappeared because they broke into smaller units or were absorbed into larger federations. And many other declarations simply failed to secure independence or were subsequently lost or forgotten, unknown and uncelebrated. The multiplicity of media in which independence was declared, the different languages in which it was expressed and the divergent outcomes of the declarations themselves defy easy categorisation. For all these reasons, there has never been a comprehensive collection of these texts, though more selective compilations do exist.[3] Without a firm documentary base, it has been difficult to analyse declarations of independence comparatively or collectively.[4]

The bicentennial celebrations of Latin American 'independence' – for example, those of 2010 in Venezuela, Colombia, Argentina, Mexico and Chile – focused attention on these fundamental documents. The commemorations marked points of origin and national beginnings, as if such moments were as clearly identifiable in their own time as they appeared to have become in retrospect. Nationalist historians have always constructed narratives in which such clean breaks, anchored in specific dates or particular acts, signified the passage from colonial dependence to national independence. Post-nationalist historians, and those who have taken Atlantic and imperial perspectives on the processes set in motion by the Napoleonic invasion of Spain in 1808, insist instead that all such stories are artificial because the processes of imperial implosion, reconstruction and dissolution led only accidentally and tortuously, not inevitably and teleologically, to political independence. Independence, in the sense of autonomy from interference by outside powers, was only one

---

[3] *Las actas de independencia de América* (1955); *Textos fundamentales de la independencia centroamericana* ([1971]); *Textos insurgentes* (2007); *La Independencia de Hispanoamérica* (2005); *Actas de formación* (2008).

[4] Though see Armitage (2007a); Kaempfer (2009); Ávila, Dym, Galvarriato and Pani (2012).

solution among many to imperial crisis: 'it was not so much separation from empire that was at stake, but how to reconstitute it on new foundations, even by giving it a new centre, or multiple centres'. In an 'age of imperial revolutions', sovereignty was less a source of jurisdictional certainty than a site of ferocious contestation.[5] Discussion of sovereignty and its sites raged incessantly in the empires and colonies of the Atlantic world from the 1760s onwards: 'I am quite sick of this *our Sovereignty*', exclaimed Benjamin Franklin as early as 1770.[6]

The western hemisphere's multiple transitions from empire to state (and, in some cases, from one empire to another) were never smooth or uncontested, in part because the legal and political sources of sovereignty were eclectic and plural.[7] As recent scholars have shown, in most cases it was not the first option embraced by actors in Iberian America: it was usually the last.[8] The *juntas* created after 1808 spoke on behalf of *naciones* or *pueblos*; they did so not to claim their independence from Spain but to affirm the independence of all Spaniards from Napoleon, and to support a Spanish war of independence against the French invaders. Expressions of loyalty to Ferdinand VII united the transatlantic Spanish Monarchy in the face of a power vacuum in the metropolis.

Only after 1810 did conceptions of independence begin to emerge in ways that betokened a loosening of bonds between the various parts of the Spanish Monarchy and then led to an efflorescence of local autonomy. Yet even these claims were initially made in the language of loyalty and a conservative idiom of the recovery of sovereignty, as when the *junta* of Quito in December 1811 declared its inhabitants 'absolutely free from all dependence, subjection and will of any other foreign government, subject only to the supreme and legitimate authority of King Ferdinand VII'.[9] It is also now clear that, in most of Iberian America, independence was achieved *de facto* and recognised *de jure* only in the 1820s and 1830s, while in Central America the process continued

[5] Adelman (2008); Adelman (2010), p. 76 (quoted).
[6] Benjamin Franklin, 'Marginalia in *An Inquiry*, an Anonymous Pamphlet' (1770), quoted in Rothschild (2004), p. 5.
[7] For important introductions, see Chiaramonte (2004); Chiaramonte (2010); and, more generally, Frederick Cooper, 'States, Empires, and Political Imagination', in Cooper (2005), pp. 153–203; Benton (2010).
[8] Rodríguez O. (1996); Guerra (2009); Portillo Valdes (2006); Ávila and Pérez Herrero (2008); Paquette (2009); Lucena Giraldo (2010); Pérez Vejo (2010).
[9] '[A]bsolutamente libres de toda dependencia, sujeción y arbitrio de cualquiera otro Gobierno extraño; sujetándose únicamente a la autoridad supreme y legitima de nuestro Rey el Señor Fernando Séptimo de Borbón': 'Acta de del gobierno de Quito en que se constituye soberano y sanciona su independencia de España' (December 1811), quoted in Morelli (2012).

to 1838 and beyond.[10] This suggests that many of the recent bicentennial celebrations in Latin America may have been premature, to say the least.

The gap between popular perceptions of independence as an event and historians' understandings of it as a process raises a series of pressing questions: What did independence mean in the late eighteenth and early nineteenth centuries? How was it secured politically and juridically? And what part did declarations of independence play in its achievement? Close examination of the fundamental texts of independence in the Americas, of their origins and their outcomes, can help to answer such questions, as can putting these documents into broader comparative contexts of both time and space. I hope such wider perspectives might make it easier both to discern what was distinctive about these fundamental Iberian American texts and also how they fit within larger historical patterns down to the present day.

In March 1815, the former President of the United States, John Adams, looked back over the second half of his eighty-year life and saw a world of unparalleled upheaval on both sides of the Atlantic. Unusually among English-speaking observers in his own time and since, Adams included the movements in Spanish America among the revolutions of the age;[11] indeed, it was memories of the stirrings there in 1798 under Francisco de Miranda that inspired his reflections. 'The last twenty-five years of the last century, and the first fifteen of this', he wrote, 'may be called the age of revolutions and constitutions. We [that is, the inhabitants of the United States] began the dance, and have produced eighteen or twenty models of constitutions.' Perhaps if Adams had not still been smarting at the prominence given to his rival Thomas Jefferson as author of the US Declaration of Independence (on which he had also collaborated), he might with equal justice have called it 'an age of revolutions, constitutions, *and declarations of independence*'.[12]

By the time Adams wrote, well over twenty declarations of independence had appeared in the Americas, sixteen in Venezuela and New Granada alone;[13] many more would be issued in the following two decades. On both sides of the Atlantic and increasingly also elsewhere around the globe in

[10] Fabry (2010), pp. 49–70; Dym (2009); Dym (2012).

[11] Compare Palmer (1959–64); Albertone and De Francesco (2009); Armitage and Subrahmanyam (2010).

[12] John Adams to James Lloyd, 29 March 1815, in Adams (1850–6), x, p. 149; McGlone (1998). On the Iberian American constitutions of this period, see Dealy (1968); Gargarella (2010).

[13] Martínez Garnica (2011); Martínez Garnica (2012).

the late eighteenth and early nineteenth centuries, patriots and liberators appealed to the people, to the nation and to various conceptions of rights to inspire their compatriots and give substance to their political claims.[14] They used both traditional and novel political genres to achieve their aims and consolidate their incremental victories within and against existing empires. In this regard, Iberian American actors possessed at least one major advantage over their predecessors in the American and French Revolutions: they could draw promiscuously and creatively upon the legacies of the earlier revolutions as well as on their own political and philosophical traditions.

For example, one major instrument for inculcating the values of independence in Spanish America was the political catechism. That genre had risen to prominence in the French Revolution and then became a vital instrument of political education for American populations who had been raised on its religious antecedents.[15] Other features of the revolutionary repertoire, from tricolor flags and republican festivals to federalism and imperial monarchies, would also be domesticated and hybridised. This is not to argue that revolutionary practices and discourse were derivative; rather, that Iberian Americans could improvise and select from a wide array of precedents, depending on the audiences they appealed to and the claims they wished to make. It is certainly true to say that 'neither the independence of the United States nor the French Revolution *persuaded* the inhabitants of Spanish America to cut their links with the Spanish Monarchy', as Jaime Rodríguez O. has argued. However, it would be a mistake to throw the baby out with the bathwater by denying the utility and attractiveness in Iberian America of elements of the earlier revolutionary repertoire, including declarations of independence.[16]

Declarations of independence were born in the Americas. They were more characteristic of the Age of Revolutions than the constitutions Adams had picked out for praise. Written constitutions had become increasingly prominent, first in the flood of state constitutions in the United States, and then throughout the world, but they had a history prior to the late eighteenth century. They cross-bred generically with declarations of independence because both forms appealed to domestic and international audiences, and were designed as much to secure external recognition

[14] Bayly (2004), pp. 106–14; Bayly (2007).
[15] *De la colonia a la república* (2009); Ocampo López (1988); Tanck de Estrada (1992).
[16] Rodríguez O. (2010), p. 698 (my emphasis).

as to promote internal cohesion.[17] Some constitutions incorporated declarations of independence; others functioned as such declarations in themselves: for example, the 1784 constitution of the abortive 'new and independent state' of Franklin (now Tennessee), which lasted for less than five years after the American Revolution.[18] However, declarations of independence were more truly original in taking on these functions and in providing a model for other fundamental political and legal texts.

The first such document, the US Declaration of Independence (4 July 1776), had included various features drawn from earlier documentary traditions and that would recur in later revolutionary instruments. The first was the famous assertion of inalienable rights among the 'self-evident' truths laid out in its second paragraph, among them the rights to life, liberty and the pursuit of happiness, as well as a people's right to throw off a tyrannical government. The main drafter of the Declaration, Thomas Jefferson, took much of this language from George Mason's draft declaration of rights for Virginia (May 1776), notably from Mason's opening lines, which spoke in the familiar terms of the natural-law tradition: 'all Men are born equally free and independent, and have certain inherent natural Rights ... among which are the Enjoyment of Life and Liberty, with the Means of acquiring and possessing Property, and pursueing and obtaining Happiness and Safety'.[19]

The US Declaration also had precedents within English traditions of 'regime change': for example, the public documents issued on the deposition, replacement or execution of a monarch between the fourteenth and the seventeenth centuries. The charges against George III, which made up the bulk of the US Declaration, followed these earlier models.[20] Most of the specific charges had also appeared in Jefferson's *Summary View of the Rights of British America* (1774) and in the preamble to the Virginia Constitution, which Jefferson had also drafted. Bills of rights and lists of grievances would become optional rather than obligatory features of later declarations of independence. In later documents, the association of enumerated rights with French Revolutionary republicanism made them potentially dangerous and to be shunned; elsewhere, they would be reserved for separate documents, often attached to constitutions rather than independence documents. Similarly, listings of historical grievances

---

[17] Golove and Hulsebosch (2010), pp. 934–46, 1061–6.
[18] 'The Constitution of the State of Franklin' (17 December 1784), in S. C. Williams (1933), p. 339.
[19] George Mason, 'First Draft of the Virginia Declaration of Rights' (c. 20–6 May 1776), in Mason (1970), I, p. 277.
[20] P. Maier (1997), pp. 50–9.

and arguments for independence would often be made in separate *manifiestos*, a genre more prevalent in Spanish America than anywhere else.[21]

What cannot be found before 1776 is the combination of the traditional English legal and constitutional model of a declaration along with the relatively new political language of 'independence', meaning the defining attribute of a state or nation among other states and nations. The term 'declaration of independence' was not used in print in English until 1776, and the cognate phrase 'declaration of independency' appeared only twice. Only one of those uses was political, as a disapproving description of the radical protest issued by Suffolk County, Massachusetts (17 September 1774) in response to the British ministry's Coercive Acts against Massachusetts earlier that year.[22] There was therefore something self-consciously novel about a declaration of independence from the rebellious colonies of British America in the summer of 1776. No other people had ever previously used the language of independence to assert that they were absolved of their allegiance to a monarch or seceding from an existing polity. Among all the various acts, addresses, bills, charges, charters, declarations, petitions and other formal documents known to Britons, none had ever been used to announce a new form of statehood as independence. The closest model was the Dutch Act of Abjuration (26 July 1581) in which the Spanish Netherlands threw off Habsburg rule, but this document did not use the language of independence and, in its search for a new ruler, was more a prospective declaration of *dependence*.[23] Where, then, did the avant-garde language of independence come from in 1776?

The authors of the US Declaration had picked up the idiom of independence from three sets of sources, local, polemical and legal, which stretched back genealogically to the late 1750s. Most immediately, they drew it from the various instructions, addresses and resolutions local bodies had sent in the summer of 1776 to the Continental Congress. These documents are the nearest equivalent in British America to the *actas* issued by *juntas* throughout Spanish America in 1808 and 1810, or by municipalities across Central America in the closing months of 1821,

---

[21] For example, *Manifiesto* (1811); Bárcena (1821). On the genre of the manifesto more generally, see Puchner (2006).

[22] Warburton (1756), p. 312 ('For what is a *Kingdom*, but a *Society*? And what is the *not being of this World*, but a declaration of *independency*?'); Chandler (1775), p. 23 ('a DECLARATION of INDEPENDENCY made by the *Suffolk* Committees').

[23] 'Edict of the States General of the United Netherlands' (26 July 1581), in *Texts Concerning the Revolt of the Netherlands* (1974), pp. 216–31.

for example.[24] These texts did not declare the independence of towns or colonies, from each other or from the British Crown, but they did urge delegates to Congress to unite 'in declaring Independency' and 'to declare the United Colonies free and independent states'.[25]

Behind these exhortations lay the arguments of Thomas Paine, who had urged in *Common Sense* (January 1776) that 'nothing can settle our affairs so expeditiously as an open and determined declaration for Independance', after which the former colonies, now independent states, could properly 'take rank with other Nations'.[26] Paine firmly linked his argument for independence to a non-monarchical regime for the newly independent colonies. This equation of independence with anti-monarchical republicanism proved to be contingent rather than necessary in later struggles. In 1811, Manuel García de Sena edited translations of Paine's works, along with the first Spanish translation of the US Declaration and versions of various state constitutions, to encourage the independence of Venezuela;[27] he included Paine's attacks on monarchy and hereditary government, and Venezuela's declaration of independence (5 July 1811) did throw off loyalty to Ferdinand VII and the Bourbons.[28] However, independence would be quite compatible with monarchy in Haïti after 1804,[29] in the Mexican empire between 1821 and 1823, and in Dom Pedro's Brazil after 1822. The globalisation of republican conceptions of sovereignty was one story whose beginnings can be found in the Age of Revolutions; the globalisation of independent statehood was another. The two often intersected but they were quite distinct and detachable from one another. External independence therefore did not imply a commitment to any particular constitution or internal structure of authority, though it generally entailed a claim to popular sovereignty vested in an emerging or identifiable nation.

The major source for the language of independence in the second half of the eighteenth century, Vattel's *Le Droit des gens* (1758), adopted a similar constitutional agnosticism. The circulation of this book in Protestant Europe and the wider world made its author perhaps the single most globally influential moral and political writer of the decades between roughly 1760 and 1840.[30] In 1776, Joaquín Marín y Mendoza,

---

[24] P. Maier (1997), pp. 59–90; Dym (2006), pp. 159–93.   [25] Quoted in Armitage (2007a), p. 37.
[26] Paine (1776), pp. 77, 78.   [27] Paine (1811); Grases and Harkness (1953).
[28] 'Acta [de independencia]' (5 July 1811), in *Interesting Official Documents* (1812), pp. 2–20; Leal Curiel (2008); Martínez Garnica (2012).
[29] Geggus (2012); Cheesman (2007).
[30] On Vattel's global circulation see, for example, Isabella (2009), pp. 99–100; Ford (2010), pp. 9, 210.

professor of natural law in the Reales Estudios de San Isidro, hailed Vattel's book as 'the best work to have treated the Law of Nations' for its 'good order and abundance of modern examples'.[31] However, Iberian America would remain mostly immune to Vattel's direct impact. *Le Droit des gens* would not be translated into Spanish until 1820, and the Venezuelan jurist Andrés Bello's critical remarks about him in the 1830s and 1840s, alongside his frequent citations from the work, suggest Vattel's ambiguous position within Hispanic legal culture.[32] Vattel was popular elsewhere not least because he communicated divergent messages to different audiences: for example, in favour of colonial settlement and the dispossession of indigenous peoples on the one hand, and seemingly against empire or composite monarchy and in favour of secession or the creation of new states on the other. He could be read in multiple ways to support both republican and monarchical, metropolitan and creole, causes.[33] Yet what secured his initial popularity was the prominence of independence in his definition of statehood.

Vattel developed his central conception of independence out of the natural-law tradition of the seventeenth and eighteenth centuries. Over the course of that tradition, conceptions of the capacities of individuals in an interpersonal state of nature converged with those of states within an international state of nature. In the opening pages of his work, Vattel defined the law of nations as the science of rights and duties between nations or states, and almost immediately proposed an analogy between human beings living under the law of nature and the existence of states in a similar condition:

Nations being composed of people naturally free and independent [*libres & indépendans*], and who, before the establishment of civil societies, lived together in a state of nature, – nations or sovereign states are to be considered as so many free persons living together in the state of nature.[34]

States take on the primary characteristics of those who compose them: because humans were originally 'free and independent', then so are the political communities they create through their consent and agreement. If those originally free and independent humans lived under the law of nature before they made civil societies for themselves, then states, too, must exist under something quite similar: 'consequently', Vattel wrote, in Hobbesian terms, 'the *law of nations* is originally no other than the *law of*

---

[31] Marín y Mendoza (1950), p. 48.   [32] Vattel (1820); Bello (1844), pp. 22–3.   [33] Hunter (2010).
[34] Vattel (2008), p. 68 (I. i. 3).

nature applied to nations'.[35] If humans were free and independent then, logically, the defining characteristics of the states they created were likewise freedom and independence: freedom to act as they wish, including entering into agreements voluntarily to limit their own freedom (for instance, through treaties), and an absence of dependence upon all other states and external authorities.

The language of independence had its roots in the seventeenth century, though mostly with negative associations of insubordination and resistance to natural hierarchy. In this vein, the authors of the *Encyclopédie* argued shortly before Vattel published his work, independence was 'the philosopher's stone of human pride; the chimera which self-love blindly pursues'.[36] The concept of independence was however positively transvalued in the late eighteenth century to take on the primary political meaning it still possesses: the autonomy of a political community among other political communities, sometimes within federal or confederal systems.[37] This quality was nicely captured by the Spanish jurist Jose Olmeda y León in 1771: 'The right of independence is nothing other than the ability to prevent other nations from interfering in one's own business and to fend off insults, blocking whatever might be prejudicial to one's interests.'[38] Questions of honour were not so prominent in subsequent conceptions of independence, but Olmeda's definition reflected the Vattelian understanding of the term. So great was Vattel's impact on positive conceptions of independence that we might call the late eighteenth and early nineteenth centuries a 'Vattelian moment'.

The US Declaration of Independence was the most enduring product of that Vattelian moment. When in June 1776 Richard Henry Lee proposed a resolution in favour of independence from Great Britain, he did so in strikingly Vattelian language: 'That these United Colonies are, and of right ought to be, free and independent States'. Thomas Jefferson then imported these words into his draft of the Declaration of Independence, which concluded, in its final published version:

That these United Colonies are, and of Right ought to be, FREE AND INDEPENDENT STATES . . . and that as FREE AND INDEPENDENT STATES, they have full Power to

---

[35] Vattel (2008), p. 68 (Preliminaries, 6).

[36] '[L]a pierre philosophale de l'orgeuil humain; la chimere après laquelle l'amour-propre court en aveugle': *Encyclopédie* (1754–72), VIII, p. 671, *s.v.*, 'Indépendance'.

[37] Fernández Sebastian (2012); Fernández Sebastian and Suárez Cabral (2010); Morelli (2012).

[38] 'El Derecho de independencia no es otra cosa, que la facultad de impedir à las demàs Naciones el mezclarse en negocios propios, y defenderse de sus insultos, estorvando quanto pueda ser perjudicial à sus interesos': Olmeda y Léon (1771), I, p. 249.

levy War, conclude Peace, contract Alliances, establish Commerce, and to do all other Acts and Things which INDEPENDENT STATES may of right do.[39]

With these words, the Declaration announced that the United States was – or, rather, were – open for business and available for alliances. It was therefore not just a declaration of independence from Great Britain but a declaration of *inter*-dependence with the other 'powers of the earth'. To reassure those other European powers of the United States' good intentions, it spoke in Vattel's familiar contemporary language of sovereignty as independence. The conclusion of the Declaration affirmed that independence was inextricable from interdependence: it was the quality of a state among states, or a nation among nations, not in isolation but in the context of both competitive and cooperative interaction.

The success of the American Revolution and the circulation of the US Declaration greatly helped to domesticate and disseminate the language of independence. In this way, the *intendente* of Venezuela, José de Ábalos, in 1781 and the Conde de Aranda in 1783 used the term to describe earlier uprisings and prospectively to forecast the possible break-up of the Spanish Monarchy on the model of the North American revolt.[40] This would be the meaning of independence used, for example, in José María Morelos's 'Sentimientos de la Nación' (September 1813), where he declared America 'free and independent of Spain and of every other nation'; a few weeks later a patriotic catechism published in the Chilean *Monitor Araucano* in November 1813 argued similarly that 'national liberty is independence: that is, that the nation does not depend upon Spain, England, Turkey, etc., but governs itself'; and a later Mexican independence catechism (1821), where it explained independence as 'the right of every people or nation to be governed by their own laws and customs, without submitting to another'.[41] In such examples, we can see the early cementing of the principle by which independence came to be 'the central criterion for statehood' among international lawyers, prior even to the possession of territory, rule over a population or the capacity to govern.[42]

[39] Richard Henry Lee, 'Resolution of Independence' (7 June 1776), in *Journals of the Continental Congress* (1904–6), v, pp. 425–6; *Declaration of Independence* (1776).
[40] Ábalos and Aranda (2003), pp. 58, 64, 67 (Ábalos), pp. 75–9 (Aranda).
[41] José María Morelos, 'Sentimientos de la Nación' (14 September 1813), in *Textos insurgentes* (2007), p. 133; Camilo Henríquez, 'El catecismo de los patriotas', *El Monitor Araucano* (27 November 1813) and *Catecismo de la independencia* (México, 1821), in *De la colonia a la república* (2009), pp. 97, 137; San Francisco (2012).
[42] Crawford (2006), p. 62.

The association of independence with popular self-determination was, however, still contingent in the early nineteenth century. In the Americas, this was a period not only of movements for the reorganisation of sovereignty and assertion of various conceptions of freedom but also an age of filibusters and corsairs, meddlesome freelancers and itinerant idealists. These self-styled liberators and chartered opponents of empire often used declarations of independence and constitutions as weapons in their plots to weaken Spain, expand the territory of the United States or disseminate republicanism. In this manner, American plotters encouraged a wave of secessionism in Spanish Florida, Louisiana and Texas after 1810. They declared the independence of West Florida on 26 September 1810 and maintained it as the first 'lone-star state' for seventy-two days; one observer, a veteran of the American Continental Congress, justified West Florida's independence and US protection of it with extensive citations of Vattel.[43] Also in imitation of North American models, in 1817 first the Venezuelan patriot and Scottish adventurer Gregor MacGregor and then the French republican freebooter Louis-Michel Aury captured Amelia Island off the coast of Florida and led an independent 'República de las Floridas' under a draft constitution until the US invaded in December of that year.[44] Five years later, in October 1822, the former Napoleonic general, later Simon Bolívar's biographer, H. L. V. Ducoudray Holstein, declared the independence of the *República Boricua* or Republic of Boriguen, to be established in present-day Puerto Rico. In these same years, North American filibusters relentlessly propagated schemes to break chunks of territory and groups of settlers from the Spanish Monarchy and paid lip-service to legitimacy by declaring their independence from Spain.[45]

There were many similar examples of secessionism and republicanism in the Gulf of Mexico and the Caribbean in the years between the 1810s and the 1830s.[46] This proliferating separatism was inspired by the crisis of the Spanish Monarchy and anticipated the fissiparousness of the Río de la Plata and Central America as, for example, different groups of settlers in

---

[43] 'The [West Florida] Declaration of Independence' (26 September 1810), in Arthur (1935), pp. 113–14; Gould (2012), pp. 192–5; Thomas Rodney, 'Treatise on Florida and Louisiana' (October 1810), University of Virginia, MS 5178. Rodney's brother, Caesar Rodney, was a signer of the US Declaration of Independence.

[44] Wyllys (1928); *La República de las Floridas* (1986).

[45] On the filibusters see Owsley and Smith (1997); Shields (2007); Stagg (2009); on the itinerant European republicans in the Americas, including Aury and Ducoudray Holstein, see Mongey (2009).

[46] Reséndez (2010).

Mexico drew upon Spanish legal and constitutional traditions to declare their independence in April 1813, or upon American models to declare, along with local Cherokees, the short-lived republic of Fredonia on 21 December 1826 and, later, the more famous lone-star republic of Texas (1836–45).[47] These efforts, some sincere, others hostile, are often forgotten as a context and consequence of the declarations of independence that emerged from Central and South America in the first third of the nineteenth century. Whatever their motivations, they all affirmed the transformative potential of the language of independence during these turbulent years.

Independence became a defining political value during the Age of Revolutions. Yet why did it have to be *declared*? And why did so many different forms of political community, at every level from the transatlantic *Nación Española* to towns and municipalities across Spanish America, feel the need to announce their independence publicly? The answer is that their causes needed both publicity and legitimacy to succeed. Publicity in the late eighteenth and nineteenth centuries could take many forms. Within communities whose politics were derived from traditions of natural law, especially in its Thomistic version, among the defining features of any legitimate pronouncement was that it had to be promulgated. Moreover, an increasing republican aversion to the secrecy of cabinet government associated with unrestrained and competitive monarchies complemented an enlightened desire to communicate and circulate information, particularly in printed form, to shape opinion among both domestic and international publics.

Publicity *informed* people; just as importantly, it formed *peoples*. Observers became participants in political communities both long-established and freshly formed, as the recovery or recreation of sovereignty turned them into bearers of authority and wielders of public opinion.[48] In such situations, the portable printing-press increasingly became an indispensable engine of revolution. That was why the Continental Congress ordered the Philadelphia printer John Dunlap to run off a now unknown number of copies of the US Declaration of Independence over the night of 4–5 July 1776. This was why Francisco de Miranda brought a

---

[47] Guedea (2001); 'Declaration of the Republic of Fredonia' (21 December 1826), quoted in Reséndez (2005), p. 44; 'The Unanimous Declaration of Independence Made by the Delegates of the People of Texas' (2 March 1836), in *The Papers of the Texas Revolution* (1973), IV, pp. 493–7.

[48] See Uribe-Uran (2000); Goldman (2009); Fatima Sá (2009).

printing-press, 'a portable factory of words about liberty and sovereignty', with him to Venezuela in September 1806. And this was why in August 1816 the congress of the provinces of the Río de la Plata ordered 3,000 printed copies of its *acta de independencia* – 1,500 in Spanish, 1,000 in Quechua and 500 in Aymará.[49] Yet printing was not the only means to affirm independence, and scenes like José de San Martín's entry into Lima on 28 July 1821, when he verbally announced Peruvian independence, waved the new country's flag and led the population in shouts of '¡Viva la patria! ¡Viva la independencia! ¡Viva la libertad!', were played out across the continent.[50]

With the desire for publicity came the need for legitimacy. Its most acute form arose in the context of civil war, as in the British Atlantic empire in 1776, in New Spain in 1812 or the Río de la Plata in 1816, for example. In each case, and many similar ones, rebels could not claim the status of belligerents without the legitimacy conferred by independence and its recognition. Paine had stated this point forcefully in *Common Sense*: 'we must in the eyes of foreign Nations be considered as Rebels' before declaring independence.[51] Facing viceregal charges of rebellion in 1812, José María Cos similarly sought to transform a 'war between brothers and citizens' into a war of independence by asserting the legitimate equality of New Spain with Spain and by subjecting their contentions to the 'law of nations and of war'.[52] Four years later, in April 1816, San Martín might have been quoting Paine when he urged the congress convened in Tucumán to declare independence speedily: 'Our enemies, and with good reason, treat us as insurgents, while we declare ourselves vassals. You can be sure no-one will aid us in such a situation.'[53] The effort to transform these struggles shifted the source of relevant norms and sanctions from domestic law to the laws of war and the law of nations. Yet that could only work if other powers recognised the belligerents, a problem faced by every insurgent movement in its quest for legitimacy.

By the late eighteenth century, doctrines of recognition were still confined mostly to matters of dynastic succession, not to judging the emergence of new (usually republican) states.[54] Independence and its recognition had become questions for the law of nations with the challenge thrown down by the US Declaration, as the infant United States

[49] Goff (1976); Adelman (2008), p. 319; Ternavasio (2012).
[50] B. Hall (1824), p. 193; Sobrevilla (2012).   [51] Paine (1776), pp. 77, 78.
[52] José María Cos, 'Plan de guerra' (10 June 1812), in *Textos insurgentes* (2007), pp. 52–5.
[53] José de San Martín to Tomás Godoy Cruz (12 April 1816), quoted in Lynch (2009), p. 131.
[54] Alexandrowicz (1958).

sought foreign aid from France, Spain and the Dutch Republic, among others. After France entered into a treaty of amity and commerce in 1778, there was general agreement among other European powers that this recognition had been premature; indeed, it became the cause of a global war between Europe's major empires. Britain's recognition of the independence of the United States in 1783 opened the way for all the powers of the earth to acknowledge their legitimacy: as the Treaty of Paris put it, 'His *Britannick* Majesty acknowledges the said *United States* . . . to be Free, Sovereign, and Independent States', *de jure*, and not just *de facto*.[55] From this moment until the Congress of Vienna in 1815, the general understanding within the law of nations was 'that new states could be formed only with the free consent of their legitimate parent sovereign, regardless of how a new state might actually justify its establishment'.[56] That did not deter unilateral declarations of independence, of course, but it did make them less likely to be successful in the short term. The later example of the US Civil War would show that unilateral secession has historically been more often the cause of civil conflict than a road to successful state-building.[57]

The lack of settled rules for declaring independence may account for the paucity of such declarations in the quarter-century after Britain's acknowledgement of American independence. In those years, declarations of independence came from Vermont (1777), Flanders (1790) and Haïti (1803–4). Like the US Declaration, those from Vermont and Flanders marked the beginning of a process of secession. The inhabitants of Vermont announced their independence of both New York state and Great Britain in January 1777, and did not join the United States until 1791. Europe's first declaration of independence, the manifesto issued by the estates of Flanders in 1790 to declare their separation from the Habsburg monarchy of Joseph II, was also the first outside America to draw language directly from the US Declaration.[58] Haïti's declaration of 1 January 1804 was anomalous in many ways. It marked the end, not the beginning, of the process of independence; it was initially spoken rather than printed;[59] and it was the third instance of such a declaration, after another issued in November 1803 in the name of Saint-Domingue (not yet

---

[55] *The Definitive Treaty of Peace and Friendship* (1783), p. 4.
[56] Fabry (2010), p. 41.   [57] Armitage (2010).
[58] *Records of the Governor and Council of the State of Vermont* (1873–80), I, pp. 40–4 (15 January 1777); Rohaert (1790); Armitage (2007a), pp. 113–14.
[59] A unique printed copy of Haïti's declaration was recently discovered in the British National Archives: TNA CO 137/III, ff. 113–17.

Haïti) and a rejected declaration which had been patterned more closely on the US document.[60] These different iterations of independence anticipated some of the multiple declarations issued in parts of Spanish America. The form in which Jean-Jacques Dessalines announced the declaration on New Year's Day 1804 also foreshadowed the oral delivery of Mexico's *Grito de Dolores* in 1810 or of Dom Pedro's declaration that he would not return to Portugal from Brazil in September 1822.[61]

The practice of declaring independence gradually became routine for the wider world in large part because of events in Iberian America. There, a common legal and political culture, emergent public spheres throughout the continent and the experience of political imitation reinforced and multiplied the instances of independence. Yet declaring independence would not, of course, always be confined to the Americas. Over the past two centuries a contagion of sovereignty has swept across the world; declarations of independence were among its major symptoms. Remarkably few declarations of independence appeared in the decades between 1860 and 1918, a period often seen as the high tide of nationalism, at least in Europe. However, they clustered throughout the twentieth century at key moments in the break-up of empires: for example, in the aftermath of the First World War, with the collapse of the Ottoman, Romanov, Habsburg and Hohenzollern empires; during the process of decolonisation in Africa and Asia in the 1950s and 1960s; and amid the break-up of the Soviet Union and the Yugoslav Federation after 1989.[62]

Declarations of independence have returned in the early twenty-first century as instruments of national self-determination and as a focus of international controversy. For example, as part of the long-drawn-out dissolution of Yugoslavia, Montenegro peacefully declared its independence from the Serbian Republic in June 2006, but when Kosovo followed suit in February 2008 Serbia protested that its action was illegal and demanded an advisory opinion on the matter from the International Court of Justice (ICJ) at The Hague. The Assembly of Kosovo's declaration of independence (17 February 2008) had explicitly denied that it could be taken as a precedent for any other acts of secession,[63] but Serbia and its allies – notably Russia – alleged that it would only encourage further secessionist movements in regions such as South

---

[60] Manigat (2005); Mentor (2003), pp. 168–9; Geggus (2012).   [61] Herrejón Peredo (2009).

[62] Armitage (2005); Armitage (2007a), pp. 107–12.

[63] 'Observing that Kosovo is a special case arising from Yugoslavia's non-consensual breakup and is not a precedent for any other situation': *Kosovo Declaration of Independence* (2008).

Ossetia and Chechnya. In July 2010, the ICJ concluded that Kosovo's declaration was in accordance with international law because 'general international law contains no applicable prohibition of declarations of independence'.[64]

This ruling affirmed the legitimacy of Kosovo's declaration but could not ensure its efficacy. By January 2011, fewer than half of the member-states of the United Nations had recognised Kosovo's independence. The lesson from the example of Kosovo is that a declaration of independence may be necessary for the achievement of statehood but is not in itself sufficient. That fact did not deter an overwhelming majority of the population of southern Sudan from voting to secede from the existing Sudanese state that same month. This paved the way for South Sudan's declaration of independence (9 July 2011),[65] a move that had implications for secessionist movements across Africa, from the Western Sahara to Somaliland. Within less than a year, in April 2012, the National Movement for the Liberation of Azawad (NMLA) had declared the independence of a new state in the northern region of Mali, though this bid for statehood was immediately rejected by Mali, the African Union and the international community.[66] Such otherwise quite distinct events in the Balkans and in Africa indicate that the world is entering a new era of declaring independence.

The forms and meanings of the earliest declarations of independence were strikingly diverse and often quite different from those we might expect today. The greatest change in the past two centuries is in the different sources of legal authority to which these declarations appealed. When the delegates to the Second Continental Congress convened in Philadelphia in 1776 announced that the 'United Colonies' of British America were now 'FREE AND INDEPENDENT STATES', they did so by appealing first to 'the Laws of Nature and of Nature's God'. By contrast, when the members of the Assembly of Kosovo promulgated their declaration of independence in 2008, they noted that '[w]ith independence comes the duty of responsible membership in the international community. We accept fully this duty and shall abide by the principles of the United Nations Charter, the Helsinki Final Act, other acts of the Organization on Security and Cooperation in Europe, and the international legal obligations and principles of international

---

[64] International Court of Justice (2010), § 84; Orakhelashvili (2008); Fierstein (2009); Christakis and Corten (2011).
[65] *South Sudan Independence Declaration* (2011).
[66] *Déclaration d'Indépendance de l'Azawad* (2012).

comity that mark the relations among states.'[67] In the twenty-first century, only a declaration made in accordance with the prevailing norms and customs of the international community can hope to attract external recognition or legal legitimacy.

Declarations of independence are now more closely tied to positive international law and must abide by certain prescriptions. They cannot be accompanied by violence. They must enjoy majority support within the territory for which independence is claimed (hence the need for a referendum in Southern Sudan). And they must acknowledge, often explicitly, prevailing international norms, agreements and often institutions like the United Nations or the European Union (as the Kosovo declaration repeatedly did). Moreover, their scope has narrowed so that independence could never be declared by a province, city or town (hence the rejection of Azawad's bid for statehood). As the United States argued in its submission to the ICJ on the question of Kosovo's declaration, '[a] declaration of independence is an expression of a will or desire by an entity to be accepted as a state by the members of the international community'.[68] As the practice of declaring independence became more widespread, the meaning of independence narrowed, so that it is now identified wholly and exclusively with statehood.

Despite these developments, declarations of independence in the early twenty-first century often follow a script first rehearsed in the Americas in the late eighteenth and early nineteenth centuries. Familiar elements of the repertoire common to both eras include the ceremonial pronouncement of the declaration, the address to a wider world and an appeal to the authority of the sovereign people.[69] Such similarities are sufficient to encourage comparisons between the worlds of the early nineteenth century and the early twenty-first century. Attention to the composition, circulation and reception of the first wave of declarations of independence can therefore shed light on the conditions for success or failure of claims to independence in our own time. They all arose from moments of imperial reconstitution or dissolution similar to those that marked the moments of independence across the twentieth century. In this regard, the age of imperial revolutions in the Americas anticipated some of the crucial processes in the making of the modern world.[70]

---

[67] *Kosovo Declaration of Independence* (2008).   [68] United States of America (2009), p. 51.
[69] For modern examples, see Holland, Williams and Barringer (2010).
[70] Adelman (2008); Anderson (1991), ch. 4, classically presented a rather different argument for the priority of Spanish America's 'creole pioneers'.

Bibliography

MANUSCRIPT SOURCES

BAKEWELL, DERBYSHIRE, CHATSWORTH HOUSE

Hardwick MS 51: Francis Bacon, 'Aphorismi de Jure gentium maiore sive de fontibus Justiciae et Juris'

Hobbes MS 73.Aa: Fulgenzio Micanzio, letters to the second Earl of Devonshire on foreign affairs (1615–26), trans. Thomas Hobbes

CAMBRIDGE, MASSACHUSETTS, HARVARD UNIVERSITY ARCHIVES, HARVARD UNIVERSITY

Acs. 14990, box 12: John Rawls, lecture-notes (1968–9)

CAMBRIDGE, MASSACHUSETTS, HOUGHTON LIBRARY, HARVARD UNIVERSITY

Wendell Family Papers, bMS Am 1907 (608): Lemuel Haynes, 'Liberty Further Extended . . .' (1776?)

CHARLOTTESVILLE, VIRGINIA, ALBERT AND SHIRLEY SMALL SPECIAL COLLECTIONS LIBRARY, UNIVERSITY OF VIRGINIA

MS 5178: Thomas Rodney, 'Treatise on Florida and Louisiana' (October 1810)

COLUMBIA, SOUTH CAROLINA, SOUTH CAROLINA DEPARTMENT OF ARCHIVES AND HISTORY

Recital of Grants, AD120, pt. II

GENEVA, BIBLIOTHÈQUE DE GENÈVE

Dumont MSS 60: Étienne Dumont, untitled manuscript treatise on international law.

KEW, THE NATIONAL ARCHIVES

ADM 1/487/34
C 66/3136/45
CO 268/1/11
CO 5/40/252
CO 5/93/290
CO 5/177/29
CO 5/177/113
CO 5/286
CO 5/287, ff. 24–32: 'Fourth' *Fundamental Constitutions of Carolina* (17 August 1682)
CO 5/1116
CO 5/1353/401
CO 137/111, ff. 113–17: Haïtian Declaration of Independence (1803–4)
CO 324/6
CO 388/5
CO 391/9
CO 391/10
CO 391/11
CO 391/12
CO 391/13
PRO 30/24/47
PRO 30/24/47/3: 'The Fundamental Constitutions of Carolina' (21 July 1669)
PRO 30/24/47/35: John Locke, 'Observations on Wine, Olives, Fruit and Silk' (1 February 1680)
PRO 30/24/48
PRO 30/24/49

LONDON, BRITISH LIBRARY

Add. MS 5253
Add. MS 11309
Add. MS 15640
Add. MS 16272

Add. MS 29125
Add. MS 30151
Add. MS 33550
Add. MS 33551
Add. MS 33564
Add. MS 48190: [Richard Zouche], *Iuris Faecialis. Sive Juris et Judicii inter Gentes Explicatio*
Add. MS 72854: Sir William Petty, 'A Treatise of Navall Philosophy in Three Parts'
Add. MS 78781: James Mackintosh, 'Extracts for Lectures on the Law of Nat: & Nations Begun Cambridge Augt 7th 1799'
Add. MS 78784A

LONDON, UNIVERSITY COLLEGE LONDON
LIBRARY (BENTHAM PAPERS)

XIV
XXV
XXVII
XXXIII
LXIX
XCVII
CIX

NEW YORK, NEW YORK PUBLIC LIBRARY

Ford Collection: 'Coppy Of the modell of Government prepared for the Province of Carolina &c' (21 July 1669)

OXFORD, BODLEIAN LIBRARY

MS Locke b. 2
MS Locke b. 5/9: Locke's landgrave patent (4 April 1671)
MS Locke c. 1
MS Locke c. 25
MS Locke c. 28
MS Locke c. 30
MS Locke c. 34: 'Critical Notes' on Stillingfleet (1681)
MS Locke c. 35
MS Locke d. 3

MS Locke e. 9, ff. 1–39: 'Some of the Cheif Greivances of the present
Constitution of Virginia with an Essay towards the Remedies thereof'
(1697)
MS Locke e. 9, ff. 39–43: 'Queries to be put to Colonel Henry Hartwell or
any other discreet person that knows the Constitution of Virginia'
(1697)
MS Locke e. 18
MS Locke f. 2
MS Locke f. 5
MS Locke f. 6
MS Locke f. 9
MS Locke f. 10
MS Locke f. 15
MS Locke f. 17
MS Locke f. 28

SHEFFIELD, SHEFFIELD ARCHIVES

Wentworth-Woodhouse Muniments BkP 10/27

TAUNTON, SOMERSET RECORD OFFICE

Sanford (Clarke) Papers

WASHINGTON, DC, THE LIBRARY OF CONGRESS

Jefferson Papers, ser. V, vol. 13, 'Miscellaneous Papers: Jefferson's [Legal]
Common-place Book'
Phillipps MS 8539, pt. 1: Journals of the Council for [Trade and] Foreign
Plantations, 1670–4

WINCHESTER, HAMPSHIRE RECORD OFFICE

Malmesbury Papers 7M54/232: Articles of Agreement of the Bahamas
Adventurers (4 September 1672)

PRINTED PRIMARY SOURCES

Ábalos, José de and Aranda, Conde de (2003). *Premoniciones de la independencia
de Iberoamérica. Las reflexiones de José de Ábalos y el Conde de Aranda sobre la
situación de la América española a finales del siglo XVIII*, ed. Manuel Lucena
Giraldo, Madrid.

Actas de formación (2008). *Actas de formación de juntas y declaraciones de independencia (1809–22), Reales Audiencias de Quito, Caracas y Santa Fé*, ed. Inés Quintero Montiel and Armando Martínez Garnica, 2 vols., Bucaramanga.

Las actas de independencia de América (1955). *Las actas de independencia de América*, ed. Javier Malagón, Washington, DC.

Adams, John (1850–6). *The Works of John Adams*, ed. Charles Francis Adams, 10 vols., Boston.

(1977–). *The Papers of John Adams*, gen. ed. Robert J. Taylor, 15 vols. to date, Cambridge, Mass.

D'Aguesseau, Henri François (1771). *Discours et œuvres mêlées de M. Le Chancellier D'Aguesseau*, 2 vols., Paris.

Altera secretissima instructio (1626). *Altera secretissima instructio Gallo-Britanno-Batava*, The Hague.

American Archives (1833–46). *American Archives: Fourth Series. Containing a Documentary History of the English Colonies in North America, From the King's Message to Parliament, of March 7, 1774, to the Declaration of Independence by the United States*, ed. Peter Force, 6 vols., Washington, DC.

Angell, Norman (1921). *The Fruits of Victory: A Sequel to 'The Great Illusion'*, London.

Ascham, Anthony (1648). *A Discourse: Wherein is Examined What is Particularly Lawful during the Confusions and Revolutions of Government*, London.

(1689). *A Seasonable Discourse, Wherein is Examined What is Particularly Lawful during the Confusions and Revolutions of Government*, London.

Austin, John (1995). *The Province of Jurisprudence Determined*, ed. Wilfrid E. Rumble, Cambridge.

Bárcena, Manuel de la (1821). *Manifiesto al mundo. La justicia y la necesidad de la independencia de la Nueva España*, Puebla.

Beddoe, John (1872). 'Anniversary Address', *Journal of the Anthropological Institute of Great Britain and Ireland* 1: xxiv–xxvii.

Bello, Andrés (1844). *Principios de derecho de gentes*, new edn, Madrid.

Bentham, Jeremy (1802). *Second Letter to Lord Pelham … in Continuation of the Comparative View of the System of Penal Colonization in New South Wales, and the Home Penitentiary System*, London.

(1803). *A Plea for the Constitution: Shewing the Enormities Committed to the Oppression of British Subjects, Innocent as well as Guilty … in and by the Design, Foundation and Government of the Penal Colony of New South Wales*, London.

(1830). *Principles of Legislation: From the MS. of Jeremy Bentham … By M. Dumont*, ed. and trans. John Neal, Boston.

(1838–43). *The Works of Jeremy Bentham*, ed. John Bowring, 11 vols., Edinburgh.

([1842?]). *Auto-Icon; Or, Farther Uses of the Dead to the Living*, n.p., n.d., [London?].

(1968–). *The Correspondence of Jeremy Bentham*, 12 vols. to date, ed. T. L. S. Sprigge, et al., London and Oxford.

(1988). *A Fragment on Government*, ed. J. H. Burns and H. L. A. Hart, introd. Ross Harrison, Cambridge.

(1990). *Securities Against Misrule and Other Constitutional Writings for Tripoli and Greece*, ed. Philip Schofield, Oxford.

(1996). *An Introduction to the Principles of Morals and Legislation (1780/89)*, ed. J. H. Burns and H. L. A. Hart, introd. F. Rosen, Oxford.

(1998). *'Legislator of the World': Writings on Codification, Law and Education*, ed. Philip Schofield and Jonathan Harris, Oxford.

(2002). *Rights, Representation, and Reform: Nonsense upon Stilts and Other Writings on the French Revolution*, ed. Philip Schofield, Catherine Pease-Watkin and Cyprian Blamires, Oxford.

Blackstone, Sir William (1765–9). *Commentaries on the Laws of England*, 4 vols., London.

(1766–9). *Commentaries on the Laws of England*, 2nd edn, 4 vols., Oxford.

[Blount, Charles] (1689). *The Proceedings of the Present Parliament Justified by the Opinion of the Most Judicious and Learned Hugo Grotius*, London.

Bogin, Ruth (1983). '"Liberty Further Extended": A 1776 Antislavery Manuscript by Lemuel Haynes', *William and Mary Quarterly*, 3rd ser., 40: 85–105.

Bolingbroke, Henry St John, Viscount (1932). *Bolingbroke's Defence of the Treaty of Utrecht*, ed. G. M. Trevelyan, Cambridge.

Boucher, Jonathan (1797). *A View of the Causes and Consequences of the American Revolution*, London.

Bourne, Randolph (1916). 'Trans-National America', *Atlantic Monthly* 118: 86–97.

[Brown, Robert?] (1790). *An Essay on the Law of Nations as a Test of Manners*, London.

Browne, Sir Thomas (1977). *The Major Works*, ed. C. A. Patrides, Harmondsworth.

Bryce, James (1922). *International Relations*, New York.

Burke, Edmund (1793). *Remarks on the Policy of the Allies*, London.

(1803–27). *The Works of the Right Honourable Edmund Burke*, 16 vols., London.

(1949). *Burke's Politics: Selected Writings and Speeches of Edmund Burke on Reform, Revolution, and War*, ed. Ross J. Hoffman and Paul Levack, New York.

(1958–78). *The Correspondence of Edmund Burke*, ed. Thomas W. Copeland, 10 vols., Cambridge.

(1989). *The Writings and Speeches of Edmund Burke*, VIII: *The French Revolution, 1790–1794*, ed. L. G. Mitchell, Oxford.

(1991). *The Writings and Speeches of Edmund Burke*, IX: *1: The Revolutionary War, 1794–1797; 2: Ireland*, ed. R. B. McDowell, Oxford.

(1992). *Further Reflections on the Revolution in France*, ed. Daniel E. Ritchie, Indianapolis.

(1993). *Burke: Pre-Revolutionary Writings*, ed. Ian Harris, Cambridge.

(1997). *The Writings and Speeches of Edmund Burke,* I: *The Early Writings,* ed. T. O. McLoughlin and James T. Boulton, Oxford.

(1998). *The Writings and Speeches of Edmund Burke,* VII: *India: The Hastings Trial 1789–1794,* ed. P. J. Marshall, Oxford.

(1999). *Empire and Community: Edmund Burke's Writings and Speeches on International Relations,* ed. David P. Fidler and Jennifer M. Welsh, Boulder, Colo.

Burlamaqui, Jean-Jacques (1748). *The Principles of Natural Law,* trans. Thomas Nugent, London.

(1763). *The Principles of Natural and Politic Law,* English translation, 2 vols., London.

[Butel-Dumont, Georges Marie] (1755). *Histoire et commerce des colonies angloises,* London.

Carolina Described (1684). *Carolina Described More Fully than Heretofore . . . ,* Dublin.

Cases in Equity (1741). *Cases in Equity During the Time of the Late Lord Chancellor Talbot,* The Savoy [London].

Cavendish, William (1620). *Horae Subsecivae. Observations and Discourses,* London.

Chambers, Sir Robert (1986). *A Course of Lectures on the English Law: Delivered at the University of Oxford 1767–1773,* ed. Thomas M. Curley, 2 vols., Madison, Wis.

Chandler, Thomas Bradbury (1775). *What Think ye of the Congress Now? Or, An Inquiry, How Far Americans are Bound to Abide by, and Execute the Decisions of, the Late Congress?,* New York.

Collet, Joseph (1933). *The Private Letter Books of Joseph Collet,* ed. H. H. Dodwell, London.

De la colonia a la república (2009). *De la colonia a la república: los catecismos políticos americanos, 1811–1827,* ed. Rafael Sagredo Baeza, Madrid.

Compleat Collection (1760). *A Compleat Collection of All the Articles and Clauses which Relate to the Marine, in the Several Treaties Now Subsisting Between Great Britain and Other Kingdoms and States,* ed. Henry Edmunds and William Harris, London.

Cooper, Anthony Ashley, Third Earl of Shaftesbury (1981–). *Standard Edition/ Sämtliche Werke,* ed. Wolfram Benda, Christine Jackson-Holzberg, Friedrich A. Uehlein and Erwin Wolff, 2 vols. to date, Stuttgart-Bad Cannstatt.

Cumberland, Richard (2005). *A Treatise of the Laws of Nature,* ed. Jon Parkin, Indianapolis.

Davenant, Charles (1701). *An Essay upon Universal Monarchy,* London.

Déclaration d'Indépendance de l'Azawad (2012): *Mouvement Nationale de libération de l'Azawad, 'Déclaration d'Indépendance de l'Azawad'* (7 April 2012): http:// www.mnlamov.net/component/content/article/169-declaration-dindependance-de-lazawad.html, accessed 15 April 2012.

Declaration of Independence (1776). *Declaration of the Representatives of the United States of America,* Philadelphia.

The Definitive Treaty of Peace and Friendship (1783). *The Definitive Treaty of Peace and Friendship Between His Britannick Majesty, and the United States of America. Signed at Paris, the 3d of September, 1783*, London.

[Defoe, Daniel] (1705). *Party Tyranny, Or An Occasional Bill in Miniature*, London.

Dickinson, Edwin DeWitt (1916–17). 'The Analogy Between Natural Persons and International Persons in the Law of Nations', *Yale Law Journal* 26: 564–91.

Dickinson, John (1941). 'Speech of John Dickinson Opposing the Declaration of Independence, 1 July, 1776', ed. J. H. Powell, *Pennsylvania Magazine of History and Biography* 61: 458–81.

Digest (1985). *The Digest of Justinian*, ed. Theodor Mommsen and Paul Krueger, trans. Alan Watson, 4 vols., Philadelphia.

Diplomatic Correspondence (1837). *Diplomatic Correspondence of the United States from the Signing of the Definitive Treaty of Peace, 10th September 1783, to the Adoption of the Constitution, March 4, 1789*, 3 vols., Washington, DC.

Dumont, Étienne (1829a). Review of Jean Jacques Burlamaqui, *Principes du droit de la nature et des gens*, nouvelle edn. (1820), *Bibliothèque Universelle, des Sciences, Belles-Lettres et Arts* 40, Geneva, pp. 20–29.

(1829b). 'Origine des notions morales, des lois civiles et du droit des gens', *Bibliothèque Universelle, des Sciences, Belles-Lettres et Arts* 40, Geneva, pp. 337–51.

Dutch Declaration (1896). *The Dutch Declaration of Independence, Old South Leaflets* 72, Boston.

Eden, Frederick (1823). *An Historical Sketch of the International Policy of Modern Europe, as Connected with the Principles of the Law of Nature and of Nations*, London.

Encyclopédie (1754–72). *Encyclopédie, ou Dictionnaire raisonné des sciences, des arts et des métiers*, 28 vols., [Paris and Neuchâtel].

F., R. (1682). *The Present State of Carolina with Advice to the Settlers*, London.

Farr, James and Roberts, Clayton (1985). 'John Locke on the Glorious Revolution: A Rediscovered Document', *Historical Journal* 28: 385–98.

Fox, Charles James (1815). *The Speeches of the Right Honourable Charles James Fox in the House of Commons*, 6 vols., London.

Fundamental Constitutions ([1672?]). *The Fundamental Constitutions of Carolina* (1 March 1670), n. p., [London], n. d.

(1682). *The Fundamental Constitutions of Carolina* (12 January 1682), n. p.

Galsworthy, John (1923). *International Thought*, Cambridge.

Garner, James W. (1925). 'Limitations on National Sovereignty in International Relations', *American Political Science Review* 19: 1–24.

Gentz, Friedrich (1800). *The Origins and Principles of the American Revolution, Compared with the Origins and Principles of the French Revolution*, trans. John Quincy Adams, Philadelphia.

Goldie Mark, (ed.) (1999). *The Reception of Locke's Politics: From the 1690s to the 1830s*, 6 vols., London.

Gordon, George (1794). *A Sermon, Preached in the Cathedral Church of St. Peter, Exeter, On Friday, February 28, 1794*, Exeter.

Grotius, Hugo (1928–2001). *Briefwisseling van Hugo Grotius*, ed. P. C. Molhuysen, B. L. Meulenbroek and H. J. M. Nellen, 17 vols., The Hague.

(2004). *The Free Sea*, ed. David Armitage, Indianapolis.

(2006). *Commentary on the Law of Prize and Booty*, ed. Martine van Ittersum, Indianapolis.

Günther, Karl Gottlob (1787–92). *Europäisches Völkerrecht in Friedenszeiten nach Vernunft, Verträgen und Herkommen*, 2 vols., Altenburg.

Hall, Basil (1824). *Extracts from a Journal, Written on the Coasts of Chili, Peru, and Mexico, in the Years 1820, 1821, 1822*, Philadelphia.

Halsbury's Statutes (1985–). *Halsbury's Statutes of England and Wales*, 4th edn, London.

Hamilton, Alexander, Madison, James and Jay, John (1982). *The Federalist Papers*, ed. Garry Wills, New York.

Hardy, Thomas (1978–88). *The Collected Letters of Thomas Hardy*, ed. Richard Little Purdy and Michael Millgate, 7 vols., Oxford.

Hazlitt, William (1825). *The Spirit of the Age; or, Contemporary Portraits*, London.

Heeren, A. H. L. (1857). *A Manual of the History of the Political System of Europe and Its Colonies*, 5th edn, English translation, New York.

Henry, Jabez (1823). *The Judgment of the Court of Demerara, in the Case of Odwin v. Forbes, On the Plea of the English Certificate of Bankruptcy in Bar, in a Foreign Jurisdiction*, London.

([1825?]). *Outline of a Plan of an International Bankrupt Code for the Different Commercial States of Europe*, London.

Hewatt, Alexander (1779). *Historical Account of the Rise and Progress of South Carolina and Georgia*, 2 vols., London.

[Hey, Richard] (1776). *Observations, on the Nature of Civil Liberty, and the Principles of Government*, London.

Hill, David Jayne (1911). *World Organization as Affected by the Nature of the Modern State*, New York.

Hobbes, Thomas (1651). *Leviathan, or the Matter, Form and Power of a Commonwealth, Ecclesiastical and Civil*, London.

(1679). *Behemoth, or, An Epitome of the Civil Wars of England, from 1640 to 1660*, London.

(1969). *The Elements of Law, Natural and Politic*, ed. Ferdinand Tönnies, 2nd edn, introd. M. M. Goldsmith, London.

(1983). *De Cive: The Latin Version*, ed. Howard Warrender, Oxford.

(1995). *Three Discourses: A Critical Modern Edition of a Newly Identified Work of the Young Hobbes*, ed. Noel B. Reynolds and Arlene W. Saxonhouse, Chicago.

(1998). *On the Citizen*, ed. Richard Tuck and Michael Silverthorne, Cambridge.

(2005). *Writings on Common Law and Hereditary Right*, ed. Alan Cromartie and Quentin Skinner, Oxford.

(2012). *Leviathan*, ed. Noel Malcolm, 3 vols., Oxford.

Holland, Thomas Erskine (1874). *An Inaugural Lecture on Albericus Gentilis Delivered at All Souls College November 7, 1874*, Oxford.

Horne, George (1800). *The Scholar Armed Against the Errors of the Time: Or, A Collection of Tracts on the Principles and Evidences of Christianity, the Constitution of the Church, and the Authority of Civil Government*, 2nd edn, 2 vols., London.

Hume, David (1987). *Essays: Moral, Political and Literary*, ed. Eugene F. Miller, Indianapolis.

(1998) *An Enquiry concerning the Principles of Morals*, ed. Tom L. Beauchamp, Oxford.

(2000). *A Treatise of Human Nature*, ed. David Fate Norton and Mary Norton, Oxford.

[Hutchinson, Thomas] (1776). *Strictures upon the Declaration of the Congress at Philadelphia*, London.

Independence Documents of the World (1977). *Independence Documents of the World*, ed. Albert P. Blaustein, Jay Sigler and Benjamin R. Breede, 2 vols., New York.

La Independencia de Hispanoamérica (2005). *La Independencia de Hispanoamérica. Declaraciones y Actas*, ed. Haydée Miranda Bastidas and Hasdrúbal Becerra, Caracas.

Interesting Official Documents (1812). *Interesting Official Documents Relating to the United Provinces of Venezuela*, London.

International Court of Justice (2010). 'Accordance with International Law of the Unilateral Declaration of Independence in Respect of Kosovo' (22 July 2010): www.icj-cij.org/docket/files/141/15987.pdf, accessed 31 January 2012.

Jefferson, Thomas (1926). *The Commonplace Book of Thomas Jefferson: A Repository of His Ideas on Government*, ed. Gilbert Chinard, Johns Hopkins Studies in Romance Literatures and Languages, extra vol. 2, Baltimore.

(1950–). *The Papers of Thomas Jefferson*, gen. ed. Julian P. Boyd, 38 vols. to date, Princeton.

Jenkinson, Charles (1785). *A Collection of All the Treaties of Peace, Alliance, and Commerce between Great-Britain and Other Powers, From the Treaty Signed at Munster in 1649, to the Treaties Signed at Paris in 1783*, 3 vols., London.

Journals of the Continental Congress (1904–6). *Journals of the Continental Congress, 1774–1789*, ed. Worthington Chauncey Ford, 5 vols., Washington, DC.

Junius (1978). *The Letters of Junius*, ed. John Cannon, Oxford.

Kant, Immanuel (1964). *Schriften zur Anthropologie, Geschichtsphilosophie, Politik und Pädagogik*, ed. Wilhelm Weischedel, 2 vols., Frankfurt.

(1991). *Political Writings*, ed. Hans Reiss, trans. H. B. Nisbet, 2nd edn, Cambridge.

Kent, James (1828). *Commentaries on American Law*, 4 vols., New York.

King, Walker (1793). *Two Sermons, Preached at Gray's-Inn Chapel; On Friday, April 19, 1793*, London.

Klüber, Jean Louis (1819). *Droit des gens moderne de l'Europe*, 2 vols., Stuttgart.

Knox, Robert (1680). *An Historical Relation of the Island of Ceylon*, London.

Kosovo Declaration of Independence (2008). Assembly of Kosovo, 'Declaration of Independence' (17 February 2008): http://.news.bbc.co.uk/1/hi/world/europe/7249677.stm, accessed 22 June 2012.

Laski, H. J. (1927). *The Problems of Peace*, 1st ser., London.

Leacock, Stephen (1906). *Elements of Political Science*, Boston.

Lederer, John (1672). *The Discoveries of John Lederer*, trans. Sir William Talbot, London.

[Lee, Arthur] (1764). *An Essay in Vindication of the Continental Colonies of America*, London.

Lee, Richard Henry (1911–14). *The Letters of Richard Henry Lee*, ed. James Curtis Ballagh, 2 vols., New York.

Leibniz, G. W. (1988). *Leibniz: Political Writings*, ed. Patrick Riley, 2nd edn, Cambridge.

Letters Illustrative of Public Affairs (1851). *Letters Illustrative of Public Affairs in Scotland, Addressed ... to George, Earl of Aberdeen ... MDCLXXXI–MDCLXXXIV*, Aberdeen.

Lincoln, Abraham (1953–5). *The Collected Works of Abraham Lincoln*, ed. Roy P. Basler, 9 vols., New Brunswick.

[Lind, John] (1775). *Remarks on the Principal Acts of the Thirteenth Parliament of Great Britain*, London.

(1776). *Three Letters to Dr Price, Containing Remarks on his Observations on the Nature of Civil Liberty, the Principles of Government, and the Justice and Policy of the War with America*, London.

[Lind, John and Bentham, Jeremy] (1776). *An Answer to the Declaration of the American Congress*, London.

Lipsius, Justus (1585). *Saturnalium Sermonum libri duo, qui de gladiatoribus*, Antwerp.

Locke, John (1690). *A Second Letter Concerning Toleration*, London.

(1698). *Two Treatises of Government*, 3rd edn, London.

(1720). *A Collection of Several Pieces of Mr John Locke*, ed. Pierre Desmaizeaux, London.

(1823). *The Works of John Locke*, 10 vols., London.

(1953). *Locke's Travels in France, 1675–9: As Related in his Journals, Correspondence and Other Papers*, ed. John Lough, Cambridge.

(1954). *Essays on the Law of Nature and Associated Writings*, ed. W. von Leyden, Oxford.

(1975). *An Essay Concerning Human Understanding*, ed. Peter H. Nidditch, Oxford.

(1976–). *The Correspondence of John Locke*, ed. E. S. de Beer, 8 vols. to date, Oxford.

(1988). *Two Treatises of Government*, ed. Peter Laslett, rev. edn, Cambridge.

(1989). *Political Writings*, ed. David Wootton, Harmondsworth.

(1990–). *Drafts for the 'Essay Concerning Human Understanding' and Other Philosophical Writings*, ed. Peter H. Nidditch and G. A. J. Rogers, 3 vols. projected, Oxford.

(1991). *Locke on Money*, ed. Patrick Hyde Kelly, 2 vols., Oxford.

(1997). *Political Essays*, ed. Mark Goldie, Cambridge.

(2000). *Of the Conduct of the Understanding*, ed. Paul Schuurman, Keele.

(2002). *John Locke: Selected Correspondence*, ed. and introd. Mark Goldie, Oxford.

(2005). *Carnet de voyage à Montpellier et dans le sud de la France: 1676–1679. Inédit*, ed. Guy Boisson, Montpellier.

(2010). *'A Letter Concerning Toleration' and Other Writings*, ed. Mark Goldie, Indianapolis.

(in press). *Colonial Writings*, ed. David Armitage, Oxford.

[Locke, John] (1766). *Observations upon the Growth and Culture of Vines and Olives*, ed. G. S., London.

[Long, Thomas] (1689). *The Historian Unmask'd*, London.

Mackintosh, James (1799). *A Discourse on the Study of the Law of Nature and Nations, &c.*, London.

(2006). *Vindiciae Gallicae and Other Writings on the French Revolution*, ed. Donald Winch, Indianapolis.

Mackintosh, R. J. (1835). *Memoirs of the Life of the Right Honourable Sir James Mackintosh*, 2 vols., London.

Manifiesto (1811). *Manifiesto que hace al mundo al confederación de Venezuela de las razones en que ha fundado su absoluta independencia de la España*, Caracas.

Marín y Mendoza, Joaquin (1950). *Historia del derecho natural y de gentes*, ed. Manuel García Pelayo, Madrid.

Martens, Charles de (1843). *Nouvelles causes célèbres du droit des gens*, 2 vols., Leipzig.

Martens, Georg Friedrich von (1789). *Précis du droit des gens moderne de l'Europe*, 2 vols., Göttingen.

(1791–1807). *Recueil des principaux traités d'alliance, de paix, de trève, de neutralité, de commerce*, 5 vols., Göttingen.

(1795). *Summary of the Law of Nations, Founded on the Treaties and Customs of the Modern Nations of Europe*, trans. William Cobbett, Philadelphia.

(1817–35). *Recueil de traités d'alliance, de paix, de trève . . . et de plusieurs autres actes servant à la connaissance des relations étrangères des puissances et états de l'Europe*, 2nd edn, 8 vols., Göttingen.

Martyn, Henry (1701). *Considerations upon the East-India Trade*, London.

Marx, Karl and Engels, Friedrich (2002). *The Communist Manifesto*, ed. Gareth Stedman Jones, London.

Mason, George (1970). *The Papers of George Mason, 1725–1792*, ed. Robert A. Rutland, 3 vols., Chapel Hill.

Maurice, F. D. (1862). *Modern Philosophy*, London.

Micanzio, Fulgenzio (1987). *Lettere a William Cavendish (1615–1628) nella versione inglese di Thomas Hobbes*, ed. Roberto Ferrini, Rome.

Mill, James (1825). *Essays on Government, Jurisprudence, Liberty of the Press, and Law of Nations*, London.

Mill, J. S. (1838). 'Bentham', *London and Westminster Review* 29 (August): 467–506.

Montesquieu, Charles-Louis de Secondat, baron de (1973). *L'Esprit des Lois*, ed. Robert Derathé, 2 vols., Paris.

 (1989). *The Spirit of the Laws*, trans. and ed. Anne Cohler, Basia Miller and Harold Stone, Cambridge.

Moser, Johann Jacob (1777–80). *Versuch des neuesten Europäischen Völkerrechts*, 10 vols., Frankfurt am Main.

 (1778–80). *Beyträge zu dem neuesten Europäischen Völkerrecht in Friedenszeiten*, 5 vols., Tübingen.

[Murray, William, et al.] (1753). *The Duke of Newcastle's Letter, by His Majesty's Order, to Monsieur Michell*, London.

Neyron, Pierre Joseph (1783). *Principes du droit des gens Européen conventionnel et coutumier*, Brunswick.

Nicole, Pierre (2000). 'Treatise Concerneing the Way of Preserveing Peace with Men', trans. John Locke, in Jean S. Yolton (ed.), *John Locke as Translator: Three of the Essais of Pierre Nicole in French and English*, Oxford, pp. 115–259.

North Carolina Charters and Constitutions (1963). *North Carolina Charters and Constitutions, 1578–1698*, ed. M. E. E. Parker, Raleigh, NC.

[Ogilby, John] (1671). *America: Being the Latest, and Most Accurate Description of the New World*, London.

Old Oligarch (2008). *The 'Old Oligarch': The Constitutions of the Athenians Attributed to Xenophon*, ed. and trans. J. L. Marr and P. J. Rhodes, Oxford.

Olmeda y Léon, José (1771). *Elementos del Derecho público de la paz, y de la guerra*, 2 vols., Madrid.

von Ompteda, D. H. L. (1785). *Litteratur des gesammten sowohl natürlichen als positiven Völkerrechts*, 2 vols., Regensburg.

Paine, Thomas (1776). *Common Sense: Addressed to the Inhabitants of America*, Philadelphia.

 (1811). *La Independencia de la Costa Firme justificada por Thomas Paine treinta años há*, ed. Manuel García de Sena, Philadelphia.

The Papers of the Texas Revolution (1973). *The Papers of the Texas Revolution, 1835–1836*, ed. John H. Jenkins, 10 vols., Austin, Tex.

Parkes, Joseph and Merivale, Herman (1867). *Memoirs of Sir Philip Francis, K.C. B.*, 2 vols., London.

Parliamentary History (1806–20). *Cobbett's Parliamentary History of England from the Earliest Times to 1803*, ed. William Cobbett, 36 vols., London.

Phipps, Edmund (1850). *Memoirs of the Political and Literary Life of Robert Plumer Ward, Esq.*, 2 vols., London.

[Plowden, Francis] (1784). *An Investigation of the Native Rights of British Subjects*, London.

(1785). *A Supplement to the Investigation of the Native Rights of British Subjects*, London.

Poems on Affairs of State (1968). *Poems on Affairs of State: Augustan Satirical Verse, 1660–1714*, III: *1682–1685*, ed. Howard H. Schless, New Haven.

Portalis, Joseph-Marie (1841). 'Rapports sur les mémoires adressés au Concours pour le prix sur la question du Droit des gens', *Mémoires de l'Académie royale des sciences morales et politiques de l'Institut de France* 2nd ser., 3, Paris: 399–453.

Pownall, Thomas (1803). *Memorial Addressed to the Sovereigns of Europe and the Atlantic*, London.

Price, Richard (1789). *A Discourse on the Love of our Country*, 3rd edn, London.

Pufendorf, Samuel (1690). *The Present State of Germany*, trans. Edmund Bohun, London.

(1729). *Of the Law of Nature and Nations*, trans. Basil Kennett, 4th edn, London.

Rachel, Samuel (1676). *De Jure Naturae et Gentium Dissertationes*, Kiel.

Rawls, John (1993). 'The Law of Peoples', in Stephen Shute and Susan Hurley (eds.), *On Human Rights: The Oxford Amnesty Lectures 1993*, New York, pp. 41–82.

(1999a), *The Law of Peoples: with 'The Idea of Public Reason Revisited'*, Cambridge, Mass.

(1999b). *A Theory of Justice*, rev. edn, Cambridge, Mass.

(2007). *Lectures on the History of Political Philosophy*, ed. Samuel Freeman, Cambridge, Mass.

Raynal, Guillaume-Thomas (1777). *A Philosophical and Political History of the Settlements and Trade of the Europeans in the East and West Indies*, trans. J. Justamond, 5 vols., London.

Records of the Governor and Council of the State of Vermont (1873–80). *Records of the Governor and Council of the State of Vermont*, ed. E. P. Walton, 8 vols., Montpelier, Vt.

Reddie, James (1842). *Inquiries in International Law*, Edinburgh.

Reports of Cases (1771–80). *Reports of Cases Adjudged in the Court of King's Bench Since the Time of Lord Mansfield's Coming to Preside in it*, ed. James Burrow, 5 vols., London.

La República de las Floridas (1986). *La República de las Floridas: Texts and Documents*, ed. David Bushnell, Mexico, DF.

Revolutionary Diplomatic Correspondence (1889). *The Revolutionary Diplomatic Correspondence of the United States*, ed. Francis Wharton, 6 vols., Washington, DC.

[Rivers, W. J.] (1856). *A Sketch of the History of South Carolina to the Close of the Proprietary Government by the Revolution of 1719*, Charleston, SC.

Robertson, George Croom (1886). *Hobbes*, Edinburgh.

Rohaert, J. F. (1790). *Manifeste de la Province de Flandre*, Ghent.

Rousseau, Jean-Jacques (1997). *The Social Contract and Other Later Political Writings*, ed. Victor Gourevitch, Cambridge.

(2005). *'The Plan for Perpetual Peace', 'On the Government of Poland', and Other Writings on History and Politics*, ed. Christopher Kelly, Hanover, NH.
Ryder, Nathaniel (1969). 'Parliamentary Diaries of Nathaniel Ryder, 1764–7', ed. P. D. G. Thomas, *Camden Miscellany*, 23, Camden Society 4th ser., 7: 229–351.
Savile, George, Marquis of Halifax (1989). *The Works of George Savile Marquis of Halifax*, ed. Mark N. Brown, 3 vols., Oxford.
Schmitt, Carl (1942). *Land und Meer, eine weltgeschichtliche Betrachtung*, Leipzig.
   (1996). *The Leviathan in the State Theory of Thomas Hobbes: Meaning and Failure of a Political Symbol*, trans. George Schwab and Erna Hilfstein, Westport, Conn.
   (2003). *The Nomos of the Earth in the International Law of the Jus Publicum Europaeum*, trans. G. L. Ulmen, New York.
Scott, James Brown (1920). *The United States of America: A Study in International Organization*, Washington, DC.
   (ed.) (1917). *The Declaration of Independence, The Articles of Confederation, The Constitution of the United States*, New York.
Seeley, J. R. (1883). *The Expansion of England*, London.
Serle, Ambrose (1940). *The American Journal of Ambrose Serle, Secretary to Lord Howe, 1776–1778*, ed. Edward H. Tatum, Jr, San Marino, Calif.
Shaftesbury Papers (2000). *The Shaftesbury Papers, Collections of the South Carolina Historical Society* 5, ed. Langdon Cheves, introd. Robert M. Weir, Charleston, SC.
Sharrock, Robert (1660). *Hypothesis Ethike, De Officiis Secundum Naturae Ius*, Oxford.
Smith, Adam (1976). *An Inquiry into the Nature and Causes of the Wealth of Nations*, ed. R. H. Campbell and A. S. Skinner, 2 vols., Oxford.
   (1978). *Lectures on Jurisprudence*, ed. R. L. Meek, D. D. Raphael and P. G. Stein, Oxford.
South Sudan Independence Declaration (2011). *South Sudan Legislative Assembly, 'South Sudan Independence Declaration'* (9 July 2011): http://republicofsouthsudan.blogspot.com/2011/07/south-sudan-independence-declaration.html, accessed 31 January 2012.
Stawell, F. Melian (1929). *The Growth of International Thought*, London.
Steck, J. C. W. von (1783). *Versuche über verschiedene Materien politischer und rechtlicher Kenntnisse*, Berlin.
Stephen, James Fitzjames (1892). *Horae Sabbaticae*, 2nd ser., London.
Stephen, Leslie (1904). *Hobbes*, London.
Suárez, Francisco (1612). *Tractatus de legibus ac Deo legislatore*, Coimbra.
Sutton, Charles Manners (1794). *A Sermon Preached Before the Lords Spiritual and Temporal in the Abbey Church of St Peter, Westminster, on Friday, February 28, 1794*, London.
Textos fundamentales de la independencia centroamericana ([1971]). *Textos fundamentales de la independencia centroamericana*, ed. Carlos Meléndez, San José, Costa Rica.

Textos insurgentes (2007). *Textos insurgentes (1808–1821)*, ed. Virginia Guedea, Mexico, DF.

Texts Concerning the Revolt of the Netherlands (1974). *Texts Concerning the Revolt of the Netherlands*, ed. E. H. Kossman and A. F. Mellink, Cambridge.

Thucydides (1629). *Eight Bookes of the Peloponnesian Warre*, trans. Thomas Hobbes, London.

[Toland, John] (1701). *The Art of Governing by Partys*, London.

Tönnies, Ferdinand (1896). *Hobbes, Leben und Lehre*, Stuttgart.

(1912). *Thomas Hobbes, der Man und der Denker*, Osterwieck.

Treaties and Other International Acts (1931–48). *Treaties and Other International Acts of the United States of America*, ed. Hunter Miller, 8 vols., Washington, DC.

True Description ([1682]). *A True Description of Carolina*, London.

[Tucker, Josiah] (1776). *A Series of Answers to Certain Popular Objections, Against Separating the Rebellious Colonies, and Discarding them Entirely*, Gloucester.

(1781). *A Treatise Concerning Civil Government, In Three Parts*, London.

(1783). *Four Letters on Important National Subjects, Addressed to the Right Honourable the Earl of Shelburne*, Gloucester.

United States of America (2009). 'Advisory Opinion on Accordance with International Law of the Unilateral Declaration of Independence by the Provisional Institutions of Self-Government of Kosovo' (17 April 2009): www.icj-cij.org/docket/files/141/15640.pdf, accessed 31 January 2012.

Vattel, Emer de (1760). *The Law of Nations, or, Principles of the Law of Nature, Applied to the Conduct and Affairs of Nations and Sovereigns*, London.

(1775). *Le Droit des gens*, ed. Charles Dumas, Amsterdam.

(1820). *El Derecho de gentes*, trans. Manuel Maria Pascual Hernández, 4 vols., Madrid.

(2008). *The Law of Nations, or, Principles of the Law of Nature, Applied to the Conduct and Affairs of Nations and Sovereigns, with Three Early Essays on the Origin and Nature of Natural Law and on Luxury*, ed. Béla Kapossy and Richard Whatmore, Indianapolis.

Voltaire, François-Marie Arouet de (2000). *Traité de la tolérance*, ed. John Renwick, Oxford.

Warburton, William (1756). *A View of Lord Bolingbroke's Philosophy, Compleat, In Four Letters to a Friend*, 3rd edn, London.

Ward, Robert [Plumer] (1795). *An Enquiry into the Foundation and History of the Law of Nations in Europe, From the Time of the Greeks and Romans, to the Age of Grotius*, 2 vols., London.

(1805). *An Enquiry into the Manner in which the Different Wars in Europe Have Commenced, During the Last Two Centuries: To which Are Added the Authorities upon the Nature of a Modern Declaration*, London.

Warren, James and Adams, John (1917–25). *The Warren-Adams Letters: Being Chiefly a Correspondence among John Adams, Samuel Adams, and James Warren*, ed. Worthington C. Ford, 2 vols., Boston.

We, the Other People (1976). *We, the Other People: Alternative Declarations of Independence by Labor Groups, Farmers, Woman's Rights Advocates, Socialist, and Blacks, 1829–1975*, ed. Philip S. Foner, Lincoln, Nebr.

Weber, Max (1991). *From Max Weber: Essays in Sociology*, ed. H. H. Gerth and C. Wright Mills, new edn, London.

Wheaton, Henry (1836). *Elements of International Law, with a Sketch of the History of the Science*, Philadelphia.

(1841). *Histoire des progrès du droit des gens en Europe*, Leipzig.

(1845). *History of the Law of Nations in Europe and America; From the Earliest Times to the Treaty of Washington, 1842*, English translation, New York.

Whewell, William (1852). *Lectures on the History of Moral Philosophy in England*, London.

Willoughby, Westel Woodbury (1918). 'The Juristic Conception of the State', *American Political Science Review* 12: 192–208.

Wilson, James (1967). *The Works of James Wilson*, ed. Robert Green McCloskey, 2 vols., Cambridge, Mass.

[Wilson, Samuel] (1682). *An Account of the Province of Carolina in America*, London.

Witsen, Nicolaes (1671). *Aeloude en Hedendaegsche Scheeps-bouwen Bestier: Waer in Wijtloopigh wert Verhandelt, de Wijze van Scheeps-timmeren, by Grieken en Romeynen*, Amsterdam.

Wolcott, Roger (1725). *Poetical Meditations, Being the Improvement of Some Vacant Hours*, New London.

Woolhouse, Roger (2003). 'Lady Masham's Account of Locke', *Locke Studies* 3: 167–93.

Woolsey, Theodore D. (1860). *Introduction to the Study of International Law, Devised as an Aid in Teaching, and in Historical Studies*, Boston.

Zouche, Richard (1650). *Iuris et Iudicii Fecialis, sive, Iuris Inter Gentes*, Oxford.

SECONDARY SOURCES

Abbattista, Guido (2008). 'Edmund Burke, the Atlantic American War and the "Poor Jews at St. Eustatius": Empire and the Law of Nations', *Cromohs* 13: 1–39.

Abulafia, David (2004) 'Mediterraneans', in Harris (2004), pp. 64–93.

Adair, E. R. (1928). 'The Law of Nations and the Common Law of England: A Study of 7 Anne Cap. 12', *Cambridge Historical Journal* 2: 290–97.

Adams, Willi Paul, et al. (1999). 'Round Table: Interpreting the Declaration of Independence by Translation', *Journal of American History* 85, no. 4 (March): 1283–454

Adelman, Jeremy (2008). 'An Age of Imperial Revolutions', *American Historical Review* 113: 319–40.

(2010). 'Iberian Passages: Continuity and Change in the South Atlantic', in Armitage and Subrahmanyam (2010), pp. 59–82.

Agamben, Giorgio (2005). *State of Exception*, trans. Kevin Attell, Chicago.
Ahn, Doohwan (2008). 'Xenophon and the Greek Tradition in British Political Thought', in James Moore, Ian Macgregor Morris and Andrew J. Bayliss (eds.), *Reinventing History: The Enlightenment Origins of Ancient History*, London, pp. 33–55.
　(2011). 'From "Jealous Emulation" to "Cautious Politics": British Foreign Policy and Public Discourse in the Mirror of Ancient Athens (ca. 1730–ca. 1750)', in David Onnekink and Gijs Rommelse (eds.), *Ideology and Foreign Policy in Early Modern Europe (1650–1750)*, Farnham, pp. 93–130.
Ahn, Doohwan and Simms, Brendan (2010). 'European Great Power Politics in British Public Discourse, 1714–1763', in William Mulligan and Brendan Simms (eds.), *The Primacy of Foreign Policy in British History, 1660–2000: How Strategic Concerns Shaped Modern Britain*, Basingstoke, pp. 79–101.
Airaksinen, Timo and Bertman, Martin A. (eds.) (1989). *Hobbes: War Among Nations*, Aldershot.
Akashi, Kinji (2000). 'Hobbes's Relevance to the Modern Law of Nations', *Journal of the History of International Law* 2: 199–216.
Albertone, Manuela and De Francesco, Antonino (eds.) (2009). *Rethinking the Atlantic World: Europe and America in the Age of Democratic Revolutions*, Basingstoke.
Alcock, Susan E., D'Altroy, Terence N., Morrison, Kathleen D. and Sinopoli, Carla M. (eds.) (2001). *Empires: Perspectives from Archaeology and History*, Cambridge.
Alexandrowicz, C. H. (1958). 'The Theory of Recognition *In Fieri*', *British Year Book of International Law* 34: 176–98.
　(1961). 'Doctrinal Aspects of the Universality of the Law of Nations', *British Year Book of International Law* 37: 506–15.
　(1967). *An Introduction to the History of the Law of Nations in the East Indies (16th, 17th and 18th Centuries)*, Oxford.
　(1973). *The European-African Confrontation: A Study in Treaty Making*, Leiden.
Allain, Jean (2007). 'The Nineteenth Century Law of the Sea and the British Suppression of the Slave Trade', *British Yearbook of International Law* 78: 342–88.
Alvis, John (1998). 'Milton and the Declaration of Independence', *Interpretation* 25: 367–405.
Anastaplo, George (1965). 'The Declaration of Independence', *St Louis University Law Journal* 9: 390–415.
Anderson, Benedict (1991). *Imagined Communities: Reflections on the Origin and Spread of Nationalism*, rev. edn, London.
Anderson, M. S. (1993). *The Rise of Modern Diplomacy, 1450–1919*, London.
Andrew, Edward (2009). 'A Note on Locke's "The Great Art of Government"', *Canadian Journal of Political Science/Revue canadienne de science politique* 42: 511–19.
Angermann, Erich (1965). 'Ständische Rechtstraditionen in der Amerikanischen Unabhängigkeitserklärung', *Historische Zeitschrift* 200: 61–91.

Anghie, Anthony (1996). 'Francisco de Vitoria and the Colonial Origins of International Law', *Social and Legal Studies* 5: 321–36.

(2005). *Imperialism, Sovereignty and the Making of International Law*, Cambridge.

Anstey, Peter R. (2011). *John Locke and Natural Philosophy*, Oxford.

Anstey, Peter R. and Harris, Stephen A. (2006). 'Locke and Botany', *Studies in History and Philosophy of Biological and Biomedical Sciences* 37: 151–71.

Aravamudan, Srinivas (2009) 'Hobbes and America', in Daniel Carey and Lynn Festa (eds.), *The Postcolonial Enlightenment: Eighteenth-Century Colonialism and Postcolonial Theory*, Oxford, pp. 37–70.

Armitage, David (2000). *The Ideological Origins of the British Empire*, Cambridge.

(2004). 'The Fifty Years' Rift: Intellectual History and International Relations', *Modern Intellectual History* 1: 97–109.

(2005). 'The Contagion of Sovereignty: Declarations of Independence since 1776', *South African Historical Journal* 52: 1–18.

(2007a). *The Declaration of Independence: A Global History*, Cambridge, Mass.

(2007b). 'From Colonial History to Postcolonial History: A Turn Too Far?', *William and Mary Quarterly*, 3rd ser., 64: 251–4.

(2010). 'Secession and Civil War', in Don H. Doyle (ed.), *Secession as an International Phenomenon: From America's Civil War to Contemporary Separatist Movements*, Athens, Ga., pp. 37–55.

(2011). 'The American Revolution in Atlantic Perspective', in Nicholas Canny and Philip Morgan (eds.), *The Oxford Handbook of the Atlantic World, 1450–1850*, Oxford, pp. 516–32.

(2012). 'What's the Big Idea? Intellectual History and the *Longue Durée*', *History of European Ideas*, 38.

(in press). *Civil War: A History in Ideas*, New York.

(ed.) (1998). *Theories of Empire, 1450–1800*, Aldershot.

(2006). *British Political Thought in History, Literature and Theory, 1500–1800*, Cambridge.

Armitage, David and Subrahmanyam, Sanjay (eds.) (2010). *The Age of Revolutions in Global Context, c. 1760–1840*, Basingstoke.

Armstrong, David (1995). *Revolution and World Order: The Revolutionary State in International Society*, Oxford.

Arneil, Barbara (1996). *John Locke and America: The Defence of English Colonialism*, Oxford.

(2007). 'Citizens, Wives, Latent Citizens and Non-Citizens in the *Two Treatises*: A Legacy of Inclusion, Exclusion and Assimilation', *Eighteenth-Century Thought* 3: 207–33.

Arthur, Stanley Clisby (1935). *The Story of the West Florida Rebellion*, St Francisville, La.

Ashcraft, Richard (1969). 'Political Theory and Political Reform: John Locke's Essay on Virginia', *Western Political Quarterly* 22: 742–58.

(1986). *Revolutionary Politics and Locke's 'Two Treatises of Government'*, Princeton.

Ashworth, Lucian M. (2009). 'Interdisciplinarity and International Relations', *European Political Science* 8: 16–25.

Avery, Margaret E. (1978). 'Toryism in the Age of the American Revolution: John Lind and John Shebbeare', *Historical Studies* 18: 24–36.

Ávila, Alfredo and Pérez Herrero, Pedro (eds.) (2008). *Las Experiencias de 1808 en Iberoamérica*, Madrid.

Ávila, Alfredo, Dym, Jordana, Galvarriato, Aurora Gómez and Pani, Erika (eds.) (2012). *La era de las declaraciónes. Textos fundamentales de las independencias en América*, Mexico, DF.

Austin, J. L. (1962). *How to Do Things with Words*, Oxford.

Aydin, Cemil (2007). *The Politics of Anti-Westernism in Asia: Visions of World Order in Pan-Islamic and Pan-Asian Thought*, New York.

Bailyn, Bernard (1974). *The Ordeal of Thomas Hutchinson*, Cambridge, Mass.

Baker, J. H. (1999). 'The Law Merchant as a Source of English Law', in William Swadling and Gareth Jones (eds.), *The Search for Principle: Essays in Honour of Lord Goff of Chieveley*, Oxford, pp. 79–96.

Baldwin, Thomas (1992). 'The Territorial State', in Hyman Gross and Ross Harrison (eds.), *Jurisprudence: Cambridge Essays*, Oxford, pp. 207–30.

Ballantyne, Tony (2002). *Orientalism and Race: Aryanism in the British Empire*, Basingstoke.

Barrow, Thomas C. (1968). 'The American Revolution as a War of Colonial Independence', *William and Mary Quarterly* 3rd ser., 25: 452–64.

Bartelson, Jens (1995). *A Genealogy of Sovereignty*, Cambridge.
  (2009). *Visions of World Community*, Cambridge.

Bay, Mia (2006). '"See Your Declaration Americans!!!": Abolitionism, Americanism, and the Revolutionary Tradition in Free Black Politics', in Michael Kazin and Joseph A. McCartin (eds.), *Americanism: New Perspectives on the History of an Ideal*, Chapel Hill, pp. 25–52.

Bayly, C. A. (1998). 'The First Age of Global Imperialism, c. 1760–1830', *Journal of Imperial and Commonwealth History* 26: 28–47.
  (2004). *The Birth of the Modern World, 1780–1914: Global Connections and Comparisons*, Oxford.
  (2007). 'Rammohan Roy and the Advent of Constitutional Liberalism in India, 1800–30', *Modern Intellectual History* 4: 25–41.
  (2011a). 'European Political Thought and the Wider World during the Nineteenth Century', in Gareth Stedman Jones and Gregory Claeys (eds.), *The Cambridge History of Nineteenth-Century Political Thought*, Cambridge, pp. 835–63.
  (2011b). 'History and World History', in Ulinka Rublack (ed.), *A Concise Companion to History*, Oxford, pp. 3–25.
  (2012). *Recovering Liberties: Indian Thought in the Age of Liberalism and Empire*, Cambridge.

Bayly, C. A., Beckert, Sven, Connelly, Matthew, Hofmeyr, Isabel, Kozol, Wendy and Seed, Patricia (2006). '*AHR* Conversation: On Transnational History', *American Historical Review* 111: 1441–64.

Bayly, C. A. and Biagini, Eugenio (eds.) (2008). *Giuseppe Mazzini and the Globalization of Democratic Nationalism, 1830–1920*, Oxford.

Beaulac, Stéphane (2004). *The Power of Language in the Making of International Law: The Word 'Sovereignty' in Bodin and Vattel and the Myth of Westphalia*, Leiden.

Becker, Carl (1922). *The Declaration of Independence: A Study in the History of Political Ideas*, New York.

Bederman, David J. (1995–6). 'Reception of the Classical Tradition in International Law: Grotius's *De Jure Belli ac Pacis*', *Grotiana* 16–17: 3–34.

Behr, Hartmut (2010). *A History of International Political Theory: Ontologies of the International*, Basingstoke.

Beitz, Charles R. (1999). *Political Theory and International Relations*, new edn, Princeton.

Bell, David A. (2001). *The Cult of the Nation in France: Inventing Nationalism, 1680–1800*, Cambridge, Mass.

Bell, Duncan (2002a). 'International Relations: The Dawn of a Historiographical Turn', *British Journal of Politics and International Relations* 3: 115–26.

   (2002b). 'Language, Legitimacy, and the Project of Critique', *Alternatives* 27: 327–50.

   (2005). 'Dissolving Distance: Technology, Space, and Empire in British Political Thought, c. 1770–1900', *Journal of Modern History* 77: 523–63.

   (2007a). *The Idea of Greater Britain: Empire and the Future of World Order, 1860–1900*, Princeton.

   (2007b). 'Victorian Visions of Global Order: An Introduction', in Duncan Bell (ed.), *Victorian Visions of Global Order: Empire and International Relations in Nineteenth-Century Political Thought*, Cambridge.

   (2009a). 'Writing the World: Disciplinary History and Beyond', *International Affairs* 85: 3–22.

   (2013). 'Making and Taking Worlds', in Moyn and Sartori (2013).

   (ed.) (2007c). *Victorian Visions of Global Order: Empire and International Relations in Nineteenth-Century Political Thought*, Cambridge.

   (2009b). *Political Thought and International Relations: Variations on a Realist Theme*, Oxford.

   (2010). *Ethics and World Politics*, Oxford.

Bellatalla, Luciana (1983). *Atlantis: Spunti e appunti su un inedito lockiano*, Lucca.

Bély, Lucien (2007). *L'art de la paix en Europe: Naissance de la diplomatie moderne, XVIᵉ–XVIIIᵉ siècle*, Paris.

Ben-Ghiat, Ruth (ed.) (2009). *Gli imperi. Dall'antichità all'età contemporanea*, Bologna.

Benton, Lauren (2002). *Law and Colonial Cultures: Legal Regimes in World History, 1400–1900*, Cambridge.

   (2005). 'Legal Spaces of Empire: Piracy and the Origins of Oceanic Regionalism', *Comparative Studies in Society and History* 47: 700–24.

   (2010). *A Search for Sovereignty: Law and Geography in European Empires, 1400–1900*, Cambridge.

Bernhardt, Rudolf (gen. ed.) (1992–2003). *Encyclopedia of Public International Law*, 5 vols. Amsterdam.

Bieber, Ralph Paul (1925). 'The British Plantation Councils of 1670–4', *English Historical Review* 40: 93–106.

Black, Antony (2009). 'Toward a Global History of Political Thought', in Takashi Shōgimen and Cary J. Nederman (eds.), *Western Political Thought in Dialogue with Asia*, Lanham, Md., pp. 25–42.

Black, Charles L., Jr (1997). *A New Birth of Freedom: Human Rights, Named and Unnamed*, New York.

Black, Jeremy (1991). 'A Parliamentary Foreign Policy? The "Glorious Revolution" and the Conduct of British Foreign Policy', *Parliaments, Estates and Representation* 11: 69–80.

(1992). 'Parliament and Foreign Policy 1739–1763', *Parliaments, Estates and Representation* 12: 121–42.

(1993). 'Parliament and Foreign Policy 1763–1793', *Parliaments, Estates and Representation* 13: 153–71.

(1994). *British Foreign Policy in an Age of Revolutions, 1783–1793*, Cambridge.

(1997). 'Gibbon and International Relations', in Rosamond McKitterick and Roland Quinault (eds.), *Edward Gibbon and Empire*, Cambridge, pp. 217–46.

(2000). *A System of Ambition? British Foreign Policy 1660–1793*, 2nd edn, Stroud.

(2004). *Parliament and Foreign Policy in the Eighteenth Century*, Cambridge.

(2011). *Debating Foreign Policy in Eighteenth-Century Britain*, Farnham.

Blamires, Cyprian (2008). *The French Revolution and the Creation of Benthamism*, Basingstoke.

Bobbitt, Philip (2002). *The Shield of Achilles: War, Peace, and the Course of History*, New York.

Boralevi, Lea Campos (1984). *Bentham and the Oppressed*, Berlin.

Borgwardt, Elizabeth (2005). *A New Deal for the World: America's Vision for Human Rights*, Cambridge, Mass.

Borschberg, Peter (2011). *Hugo Grotius, the Portuguese and Free Trade in the East Indies*, Singapore.

Borstelmann, Thomas (2012). *The 1970s: A New Global History from Civil Rights to Economic Inequality*, Princeton.

Bose, Sugata (2006). *A Hundred Horizons: The Indian Ocean in the Age of Global Empire*, Cambridge, Mass.

Bose, Sugata and Manjapra, Kris (eds.) (2010). *Cosmopolitan Thought Zones: South Asia and the Global Circulation of Ideas*, Basingstoke.

Boucher, David (1991). 'The Character of the History of Philosophy of International Relations and the Case of Edmund Burke', *Review of International Studies* 17, 127–48.

(1998). *Political Theories of International Relations: From Thucydides to the Present*, Oxford.

(2006). 'Propriety and Property in International Relations: The Case of John Locke', in Beate Jahn (ed.), *Classical Theory in International Relations*, Cambridge, pp. 156–77.

Bourdieu, Pierre (1990). 'Les conditions sociales de la circulation internationale des idées', *Romanistische Zeitschrift für Literaturgeschichte / Cahiers d'Histoire des Littératures Romanes* 14, 1–10.

Bourguignon, Henry J. (1987). *Sir William Scott, Lord Stowell: Judge of the High Court of Admiralty, 1798–1828*, Cambridge.

Bourke, Richard (2009). 'Edmund Burke and International Conflict', in Hall and Hill (2009), pp. 91–116.

Bourquin, Maurice (1948). 'Grotius est-il le père du droit des gens?', in Bourquin, *Grandes figures et grandes œuvres juridiques*, Geneva, pp. 77–99.

Bowen, H. V. (1991). *Revenue and Reform: The Indian Problem in British Politics 1757–1773*, Cambridge.

(1998). 'British Conceptions of Global Empire, 1756–83', *Journal of Imperial and Commonwealth History* 26: 1–27.

Bowersock, Glen (2004). 'The East-West Orientation of Mediterranean Studies and the Meaning of North and South in Antiquity', in Harris (2004), pp. 167–78.

Boyce, D. George (1999). *Decolonisation and the British Empire, 1775–1997*, Basingstoke.

Boyd, Julian P. (1999). *The Declaration of Independence: The Evolution of the Text*, ed. Gerard W. Gawalt, Washington, DC.

Boyle, Joseph (1992). 'Natural Law and International Ethics', in Terry Nardin and David R. Mapel (eds.), *Traditions of International Ethics*, Cambridge, pp. 112–35.

Brett, Annabel S. (1997). *Liberty, Right and Nature: Individual Rights in Later Scholastic Thought*, Cambridge.

(2002). 'What is Intellectual History Now?', in David Cannadine (ed.), *What is History Now?*, London, pp. 113–31.

(2011). *Changes of State: Nature and the Limits of the City in Early Modern Natural Law*, Princeton.

Brierly, J. L. (1963). *The Law of Nations: An Introduction to the International Law of Peace*, ed. Humphrey Waldock, 6th edn, Oxford.

Brown, Chris, Nardin, Terry and Rengger, Nicholas (eds.) (2002). *International Relations in Political Thought: Texts from the Ancient Greeks to the First World War*, Cambridge.

Brown, Louise Fargo (1933). *The First Earl of Shaftesbury*, New York.

Brubaker, Rogers and Cooper, Frederick (2000). 'Beyond "Identity"', *Theory and Society* 29: 1–47.

Buchanan, J. E. (1989). 'The Colleton Family and the Early History of South Carolina and Barbados', PhD thesis, University of Edinburgh.

Buckle, Stephen (2001). 'Tully, Locke and America', *British Journal for the History of Philosophy* 9: 245–81.

Bull, Hedley (1966). 'Society and Anarchy in International Relations', in Herbert Butterfield and Martin Wight (eds.), *Diplomatic Investigations: Essays in the Theory of International Politics*, London, pp. 35–50.

(1976). 'Martin Wight and the Theory of International Relations', *British Journal of International Studies* 2: 101–16.

(1977). *The Anarchical Society: A Study of Order in World Politics*, New York.

(1981). 'Hobbes and the International Anarchy', *Social Research* 48: 717–38.

Bull, Hedley, Kingsbury, Benedict and Roberts, Adam (eds.) (1990). *Hugo Grotius and International Relations*, Oxford.

Burke, Peter (2002). 'Context in Context', *Common Knowledge* 8: 152–77.

Burrows, Edwin G. and Wallace, Michael (1972). 'The American Revolution: The Ideology and Psychology of National Liberation', *Perspectives in American History* 6: 167–305.

Cairns, John W. (1995). 'Scottish Law, Scottish Lawyers and the Status of the Union', in John Robertson (ed.), *A Union for Empire: Political Thought and the British Union of 1707*, Cambridge, pp. 243–68.

Calvert, Jane (2009). *Quaker Constitutionalism and the Political Thought of John Dickinson*, Cambridge.

Carey, Daniel (1996). 'Locke, Travel Literature, and the Natural History of Man', *The Seventeenth Century* 11: 259–80.

(2006). *Locke, Shaftesbury, and Hutcheson: Contesting Diversity in the Enlightenment and Beyond*, Cambridge.

Carey, Daniel and Trakulhun, Sven (2009). 'Universalism, Diversity, and the Postcolonial Enlightenment', in Daniel Carey and Lynn Festa (eds.), *The Postcolonial Enlightenment: Eighteenth-Century Colonialism and Postcolonial Theory*, Oxford, pp. 240–80.

Carstairs, Charles and Ware, Richard (eds.) (1991). *Parliament and International Relations*, Buckingham.

Castilla Urbano, Francisco (1986). 'El Indio Americano en la Filosofia Politica de John Locke', *Revista de Indias* 46: 421–51.

Cavallar, Georg (2002). *The Rights of Strangers: Theories of International Hospitality, the Global Community, and Political Justice since Vitoria*, Aldershot.

(2011). *Imperfect Cosmopolis: Studies in the History of International Legal Theory and Cosmopolitan Ideas*, Cardiff.

Caws, Peter (ed.) (1989). *The Causes of Quarrel: Essays on Peace, War, and Thomas Hobbes*, Boston.

Chakrabarty, Dipesh (2008). *Provincializing Europe: Postcolonial Thought and Historical Difference*, new edn, Princeton.

de Champs, Emmanuelle (2006). 'La postérité des idées de Jeremy Bentham: la notion d'influence à l'épreuve', *Cromohs* 11: 1–17.

de Champs, Emmanuelle and Cléro, Jean-Pierre (eds.) (2009). *Bentham et la France: fortune et infortunes de l'utilitarisme*, Oxford.

Charlesworth, Hilary (1992). 'The Public/Private Distinction and the Right to Development in International Law', *Australian Yearbook of International Law* 12: 190–204.

(1997). 'The Sex of the State in International Law', in Ngaire Naffine and R. J. Owens (eds.), *Sexing the Subject of Law*, North Ryde, NSW, pp. 251–68.

Charlesworth, Hilary and Chinkin, Christine (2000). *The Boundaries of International Law: A Feminist Analysis*, Manchester.

Chase-Dunn, Christopher and Hall, Thomas D. (2002). 'Paradigms Bridged: Institutional Materialism and World-Systemic Evolution', in Sing C. Chew and J. David Knottnerus (eds.), *Structure, Culture, and History: Recent Issues in Social Theory*, Lanham, Md., pp. 197–216.

Cheesman, Clive (ed.) (2007). *The Armorial of Haiti: Symbols of Nobility in the Reign of Henry Christophe*, London.

Cheney, Paul (2010). *Revolutionary Commerce: Globalization and the French Monarchy*, Cambridge, Mass.

Chiaramonte, José Carlos (2004). *Nación y estado en Iberoamérica: el lenguaje político en tiempos de las independencias*, Buenos Aires.

(2010). *Fundamentos intelectuales y políticos de las independencias. Notas para una nueva historia intelectual de Iberoamérica*, Buenos Aires.

Childs, St Julien R. (1942). 'The Petit-Guérard Colony', *South Carolina Historical and Genealogical Magazine* 43: 2–3.

(1963). 'Honest and Just at the Court of Charles II', *South Carolina Historical Magazine* 64: 27.

Christakis, Theodore and Corten, Olivier (eds.) (2011). 'Kosovo Symposium: The ICJ Advisory Opinion on the Unilateral Declaration of Independence of Kosovo', *Leiden Journal of International Law* 24: 71–161.

Christov, Theodore (2008). 'Beyond International Anarchy: Political Theory and International Relations in Early Modern Political Thought', PhD thesis, University of California, Los Angeles.

Claeys, Gregory (2010). *Imperial Sceptics: British Critics of Empire, 1850–1920*, Cambridge.

Clark, Ian (1996). 'Traditions of Thought and Classical Theories of International Relations', in Ian Clark and Iver B. Neumann (eds.), *Classical Theories of International Relations*, Basingstoke, pp. 1–19.

Clark, J. C. D. (1995). *The Language of Liberty 1660–1832: Political Discourse and Social Dynamics in the Anglo-American World*, Cambridge.

Clavin, Patricia (2005). 'Defining Transnationalism', *Contemporary European History* 14: 421–39.

Clossey, Luke (2008). *Salvation and Globalization in the Early Jesuit Missions*, Cambridge.

Coates, Benjamin Allen (2010). 'Trans-Atlantic Advocates: American International Law and US Foreign Relations, 1898–1919', PhD thesis, Columbia University.

Coli, Daniela (2009). *Hobbes, Roma e Machiavelli nell'Inghilterra degli Stuart*, Florence.

Colley, Linda (2010). 'Gendering the Globe: The Political and Imperial Thought of Philip Francis', *Past and Present* 209 (November): 117–48.

Cone, Carl B. (1957–64). *Edmund Burke and the Nature of Politics*, 2 vols., Lexington, Ky.

Connery, Christopher L. (2001). 'Ideologies of Land and Sea: Alfred Thayer Mahan, Carl Schmitt, and the Shaping of Global Myth Elements', *Boundary 2* 28: 173–201.

Conway, Stephen (1987). 'Bentham versus Pitt: Jeremy Bentham and British Foreign Policy 1789', *Historical Journal* 30: 791–809.

(1989). 'Bentham on Peace and War', *Utilitas* 50: 82–101.

(1991). 'John Bowring and the Nineteenth-century Peace Movement', *Historical Research* 64: 344–58.

(2002). 'From Fellow-Nationals to Foreigners: British Perceptions of the Americans, circa 1739–1783', *William and Mary Quarterly* 3rd ser., 59: 65–100.

Cook, Harold J. (2007). *Matters of Exchange: Commerce, Medicine, and Science in the Dutch Golden Age*, New Haven.

Cooper, Frederick (2005). *Colonialism in Question: Theory, Knowledge, History*, Berkeley.

Cooper, Frederick and Burbank, Jane (2010). *Empires in World History: Power and the Politics of Difference*, Princeton.

Cooper, Robert (2003). *The Breaking of Nations: Order and Chaos in the Twenty-First Century*, London.

Coopmans, J. P. A. (1983). 'Het Plakkaat van Verlatinge (1581) en de Declaration of Independence (1776)', *Bijdragen en Mededelingen betreffende de Geschiedenis der Nederlanden* 98: 540–67.

Covell, Charles (2004). *Hobbes, Realism and the Tradition of International Law*, Basingstoke.

(2009). *The Law of Nations in Political Thought: A Critical Survey from Vitoria to Hegel*, Basingstoke.

Cox, Richard H. (1960). *Locke on War and Peace*, Oxford.

Cranston, Maurice (1957). *John Locke: A Biography*, London.

Crawford, James (2006). *The Creation of States in International Law*, 2nd edn, Oxford.

Crimmins, James E. (2002). 'Bentham and Hobbes: An Issue of Influence', *Journal of the History of Ideas* 63: 677–96.

Cunliffe, Barry (2001). *Facing the Ocean: The Atlantic and Its Peoples, 8000 BC–AD 1500*, Oxford.

D., D. (1898). 'London Newspapers of 1776 and the Declaration of Independence', *The Nation* 66 (17 February): 127–8.

Darnton, Robert (1980). 'Intellectual History and Cultural History', in Michael Kammen (ed.), *The Past Before Us: Contemporary Historical Writing in the United States*, Ithaca, NY, pp. 327–54.

(2005). 'Discourse and Diffusion', *Contributions to the History of Concepts* 1: 21–28.

Darnton, Robert and Daskalova, Krassimira (1994). 'Book History, the State of Play: An Interview with Robert Darnton', *SHARP News* 3, 3 (Summer): 2–4.

Darwin, John (2007). *After Tamerlane: The Rise and Fall of Global Empire*, London.

Davis, David Brion (1998). *The Problem of Slavery in the Age of Revolution, 1770–1823*, rev. edn, New York.

Dealy, Glen (1968). 'Prolegomena on the Spanish American Political Tradition', *Hispanic American Historical Review* 48: 37–58.

Delbrück, Jost (1993). 'A More Effective International Law or a New "World Law"? Some Aspects of the Development of International Law in a Changing Economic System', *Indiana Law Journal* 68: 705–25.

Derman, Joshua (2011). 'Carl Schmitt on Land and Sea', *History of European Ideas* 37: 181–89.

Derrida, Jacques (1984). *Otobiographies: L'enseignement de Nietzsche et la politique du nom propre*, Paris.

(1986). 'Declarations of Independence', *New Political Science* 15: 7–17.

Desbler, Charles D. (1892). 'How The Declaration Was Received in the Old Thirteen', *Harper's New Monthly Magazine* 85 (July): 165–87.

Detweiler, Philip F. (1962). 'The Changing Reputation of the Declaration of Independence: The First Fifty Years', *William and Mary Quarterly* 3rd ser., 19: 557–74.

Devetak, Richard (2011). 'Law of Nations as Reason of State: Diplomacy and the Balance of Power in Vattel's *Law of Nations*', *Parergon* 28: 105–28.

Dinwiddy, John (1974). 'Utility and Natural Law in Burke's Thought: A Reconsideration', *Studies in Burke and His Time* 16: 105–28.

Dippel, Horst (1977). *Germany and the American Revolution, 1770–1800*, trans. Bernhard A. Uhlendorf, Chapel Hill.

Doyle, Michael W. (1997). *Ways of War and Peace: Realism, Liberalism, and Socialism*, New York.

Doyle, Michael W. and Carlson, Geoffrey S. (2008). 'Silence of the Laws? Conceptions of International Relations and International Law in Hobbes, Kant, and Locke', *Columbia Journal of Transnational Law* 46: 648–66.

Doyle, William (2000). 'The [British-Irish] Union in a European Context', *Transactions of the Royal Historical Society* 6th ser., 10: 167–80.

Drescher, Seymour (1988). 'On James Farr's "So vile and miserable an estate"', *Political Theory* 16: 502–3.

Droit, Roger-Pol (2005). *L'Humanité toujours à construire: regard sur l'histoire intellectuelle de l'UNESCO, 1945–2005*, Paris.

Duara, Prasenjit (1995). *Rescuing History from the Nation: Questioning Narratives of Modern China*, Chicago.

Dumbauld, Edward (1950). *The Declaration of Independence And What It Means Today*, Norman, Okla.

(1976). 'Independence under International Law', *American Journal of International Law* 70: 425–31.

Dunn, John (1969). *The Political Thought of John Locke: An Historical Account of the Argument of the 'Two Treatises of Government'*, Cambridge.

(2008). 'Why We Need a Global History of Political Thought', unpublished lecture, Helsinki Collegium for Advanced Studies.

Dunne, Timothy (1993). 'Mythology or Methodology? Traditions in International Theory', *Review of International Studies* 19: 305–18.

(1998). *Inventing International Society: A History of the English School*, Basingstoke.

Dyer, Justin Buckley (ed.) (2011). *American Soul: The Contested Legacy of the Declaration of Independence*, Lanham, Md.

Dym, Jordana (2006). *From Sovereign Villages to National States: City, State, and Federation in Central America, 1759–1839*, Albuquerque.

(2009). 'Actas de independencia: De la Capitanía General de Guatemala a la República Federal de Centroamérica', in Marco Palacios (ed.), *Las independencias hispanoamericanas: interpretaciones 200 años después*, Bogotá, pp. 339–66.

(2012). 'Declarando independencia: la evolución de la independencia centroamericana, 1821–1864', in Ávila, Dym, Gómez Galvarriato and Pani (2012), pp. 299–330.

Dziembowski, Edmond (1998). *Un nouveau Patriotisme français, 1750–1770: la France face à la puissance anglaise à l'époque de la guerre de Sept Ans*, Oxford.

Easley, Eric S. (2004). *The War over Perpetual Peace: An Exploration into the History of a Foundational International Relations Text*, Basingstoke.

Elazar, Yiftah (2012). 'The Liberty Debate: Richard Price and His Critics on Civil Liberty, Free Government, and Democratic Participation', PhD thesis, Princeton University.

Elliott, J. H. (2007). *Spain, Europe and the Wider World, 1500–1800*, New Haven.

(2009). 'Atlantic History: A Circumnavigation', in David Armitage and Michael J. Braddick (eds.), *The British Atlantic World, 1500–1800*, 2nd edn, Basingstoke, pp. 253–70.

Ellis, Joseph J. (ed.) (1999). *What Did the Declaration Declare?*, Boston.

Elshtain, Jean Bethke (2008). *Sovereignty: God, State, and Self*, New York.

Enenkel, Karl E. (2001). 'Strange and Bewildering Antiquity: Lipsius' Dialogue *Saturnales Sermones* on the Gladiatorial Games (1582)', in Karl E. Enenkel, Jan L. De Jong and Jeannine De Landtsheer (eds.), *Recreating Ancient History: Episodes from the Greek and Roman Past in the Arts and Literature of the Early Modern Period*, Leiden, pp. 75–99.

Fabry, Mikulas (2010). *Recognizing States: International Society and the Establishment of New States*, Oxford.

Farr, James (1986). '"So vile and miserable an estate": The Problem of Slavery in Locke's Political Thought', *Political Theory* 14: 263–90.

(1989). '"Slaves bought with money": A Reply to Drescher', *Political Theory* 17: 471–4.

(2008). 'Locke, Natural Law, and New World Slavery', *Political Theory* 36: 495–522.

(2009). 'Locke, "Some Americans", and the Discourse on "Carolina"', *Locke Studies* 9: 19–77.

Fatima Sá e Melo Ferreira, Maria de, et al. (2009). 'Pueblo/pueblos', in Javier Fernández Sebastian (gen. ed.), *Diccionario político y social del mundo iberoamericano, 1: La era de las revoluciones, 1750–1850*, Madrid, pp. 1117–250.

Felski, Rita, and Tucker, Herbert F. (eds.) (2011). 'Context?', *New Literary History* 42, no. 4 (Autumn): vii–xii, 557–756.

Ferguson, Niall, Maier, Charles S., Manela, Erez and Sargent, Daniel J. (eds.) (2010). *The Shock of the Global: The 1970s in Perspective*, Cambridge, Mass.

Ferguson, Robert A. (1984). *Law and Letters in American Culture*, Cambridge, Mass.

Fernández-Armesto, Felipe (2002). Review of Hopkins (2002), *History Today* 52, 5 (May): 76.

Fernández-Sebastián, Javier (2012). 'La independencia de España y otras independencias. La transformación radical de un concepto er la crisis del mundo hispano', in Ávila, Dym, Gómez Galvarriato and Pani (2012), pp 41–78.

Fernández Sebastián, Javier and Suárez Cabral, Cecilia (2010). 'El concepto de "independencia" y otras nociones conexas en la España de los siglos XVIII y XIX', *Bicentenario. Revista de historia de Chile y América* 9: 5–26.

Fierstein, Daniel (2009). 'Kosovo's Declaration of Independence: An Incident Analysis of Legality, Policy and Future Implications', *Boston University International Law Journal* 26: 417–42.

Findlen, Paula (ed.) (2004). *Athanasius Kircher: The Last Man Who Knew Everything*, New York.

Finnegan, Diarmid A. (2008). 'The Spatial Turn: Geographical Approaches to the History of Science', *Journal of the History of Biology* 41: 369–88.

Fisher, Alan W. (1970). *The Russian Annexation of the Crimea, 1772–1783*, Cambridge.

Fisher, Sydney George (1907). 'The Twenty-Eight Charges Against the King in the Declaration of Independence', *Pennsylvania Magazine of History and Biography* 31: 257–303.

Fitzmaurice, Andrew (2009). 'The Resilience of Natural Law in the Writings of Sir Travers Twiss', in Hall and Hill (2009), pp. 137–59.

(2012). 'Liberalism and Empire in Nineteenth-century International Law', *American Historical Review* 117: 122–40.

Flaherty, Martin S. (1999). 'History Right? Historical Scholarship, Original Understanding, and Treaties as "Supreme Law of the Land"', *Columbia Law Review* 99: 2095–153.

Fliegelman, Jay (1993). *Declaring Independence: Jefferson, Natural Language, and the Culture of Performance*, Stanford.

Flower, Milton E. (1983). *John Dickinson, Conservative Revolutionary*, Charlottesville.

Flynn, Dennis O. and Giráldez, Arturo (1995). 'Born with a "Silver Spoon": The Origin of World Trade in 1571', *Journal of World History* 6: 201–21.

(2002). 'Cycles of Silver: Global Economic Unity through the Mid-Eighteenth Century', *Journal of World History* 13: 391–427.

(2010). *China and the Birth of Globalization in the 16th Century*, Farnham.

Flynn, Dennis O., Giráldez, Arturo and von Glahn, Richard (eds.) (2003). *Global Connections and Monetary History, 1470–1800*, Aldershot.

Force, Pierre (1997). 'Self-love, Identification, and the Origin of Political Economy', *Yale French Studies* 92: 45–64.

Ford, Lisa (2010). *Settler Sovereignty: Jurisdiction and Indigenous Peoples in America and Australia, 1788–1836*, Cambridge, Mass.

Foreign and Commonwealth Office (2004). Departmental Report, 1 April 2003–31 March 2004: www.fco.gov.uk/resources/en/pdf/departmental-report-04, accessed 31 January 2012.

Forsyth, Murray (1979). 'Thomas Hobbes and the External Relations of States', *British Journal of International Studies* 5: 196–209.

Fortier, John C. (1997). 'Hobbes and "A Discourse of Laws": The Perils of Wordprint Analysis', *Review of Politics* 59: 861–87.

Foucault, Michel (1976). 'Questions à Michel Foucault sur la géographie', *Hérodote* 1: 71–85.

Francis, Mark (1980). 'The Nineteenth-Century Theory of Sovereignty and Thomas Hobbes', *History of Political Thought* 1: 517–40.

Franck, Thomas M. (2001). 'Are Human Rights Universal?' *Foreign Affairs*, 80, 1 (January–February): 191–204.

Frey, Linda S. and Frey, Marsha L. (1999). *The History of Diplomatic Immunity*, Columbus, OH.

Friedenwald, Herbert (1904). *The Declaration of Independence, An Interpretation and an Analysis*, New York.

Friedrich, Carl (1957). *Constitutional Reason of State: The Survival of the Constitutional Order*, Providence, RI.

Frowein, J. A. (1971). 'Transfer or Recognition of Sovereignty – Some Early Problems in Connection with Dependent Territories', *American Journal of International Law* 65: 568–71.

Fryer, Linda (1998). 'Documents Relating to the Formation of the Carolina Company in Scotland, 1682', *South Carolina Historical Magazine* 99: 110–34.

Fuerst, James W. (2000). 'Mestizo Rhetoric: The Political Thought of El Inca Garcilaso de la Vega', PhD thesis, Harvard University.

Galgano, Francesco (2007). 'John Locke azionista delle compagnie coloniali (una chiave di lettura del *Secondo trattato del governo*)', *Contratto e impresa* 23: 327–41.

Gallie, W. B. (1978). *Philosophers of Peace and War: Kant, Clausewitz, Marx, Engels and Tolstoy*, Cambridge.

Games, Alison, Horden, Peregrine, Purcell, Nicholas, Matsuda, Matt and Wigen, Kären (2006). '*AHR* Forum: Oceans of History', *American Historical Review* 111: 717–80.

Gargarella, Roberto (2010). *The Legal Foundations of Inequality: Constitutionalism in the Americas, 1776–1860*, Cambridge.

Garton Ash, Timothy (2007). 'Commentary', in Anthony Seldon (ed.), *Blair's Britain, 1997–2007*, Cambridge, pp. 633–8.

Gauthier, David (1969). *The Logic of 'Leviathan': The Moral and Political Theory of Thomas Hobbes*, Oxford.

Geggus, David (2012). 'La declaración de independencia de Haití', in Ávila, Dym, Gómez Galvarriato and Pani (2012), pp. 121–33.

Gellner, Ernest (1996). 'Reply: Do Nations Have Navels?', *Nations and Nationalism* 2: 365–70.

Gerber, Scott D. (1993). 'Whatever Happened to the Declaration of Independence: A Commentary on the Republican Revisionism in the Political Thought of the American Revolution', *Polity* 26: 214–19.

(1995). *To Secure These Rights: The Declaration of Independence and Constitutional Interpretation*, New York.

Geyer, Michael and Bright, Charles (1995). 'World History in a Global Age', *American Historical Review* 100: 1034–60.

Gibbs, G. C. (1970). 'Laying Treaties before Parliament in the Eighteenth Century', in Ragnhild Hatton and M. S. Anderson (eds.), *Studies in Diplomatic History: Essays in Memory of David Bayne Horn*, London, pp. 118–37.

Gilbert, Felix (1961). *To the Farewell Address: Ideas of Early American Foreign Policy*, Princeton.

Glausser, Wayne (1990). 'Three Approaches to Locke and the Slave Trade', *Journal of the History of Ideas* 51: 199–216.

Glaziou, Yves (1993). *Hobbes en France au XVIII͏ᵉ siècle*, Paris.

Gluck, Carol and Tsing, Anne Lowenhaupt (eds.) (2009). *Words in Motion: Toward a Global Lexicon*, Durham, NC.

Goebel, Julius, Jr (1915). *The Recognition Policy of the United States*, New York.

Goff, Frederick R. (1976). *The John Dunlap Broadside: The First Printing of the Declaration of Independence*, Washington, DC.

Goldie, Mark (1977). 'Edmund Bohun and *Jus Gentium* in the Revolution Debate, 1689–1693', *Historical Journal* 20: 569–86.

(1978a). 'Charles Blount's Intention in Writing *King William and Queen Mary Conquerors* (1693)', *Notes and Queries* 223: 527–32.

(1978b). 'Tory Political Thought, 1689–1714', PhD thesis, Cambridge University.

Goldman, Noemí, et al. (2009). 'Opinión pública', in Javier Fernández Sebastian (gen. ed.), *Diccionario político y social del mundo iberoamericano, 1: La era de las revoluciones, 1750–1850*, Madrid, pp. 981–1113.

Goldstein, Thomas (1972). 'The Renaissance Concept of the Earth in Its Influence upon Copernicus', *Terrae Incognitae* 4: 19–51.

Golove, David and Hulsebosch, Daniel J. (2010). 'A Civilized Nation: The Early American Constitution, the Law of Nations, and the Pursuit of International Recognition', *New York University Law Review* 85: 932–1066.

Gong, Gerrit W. (1984). *The Standard of 'Civilization' in International Society*, Oxford.

Gordon, Peter E. (2013). 'Contextualism and Criticism in the History of Ideas', in McMahon and Moyn (2013).

Goto-Jones, Chris (2009). 'The Kyoto School, the Cambridge School, and the History of the Political Philosophy in Wartime Japan', *Positions: East Asia Cultures Critique* 17: 13–42.

Gould, Eliga H. (1997). 'American Independence and Britain's Counter-Revolution', *Past and Present* 154 (February): 107–41.

(1999). 'A Virtual Nation: Greater Britain and the Imperial Legacy of the American Revolution', *American Historical Review* 104: 476–89.

(2012). *Among the Powers of the Earth: The American Revolution and the Making of a New World Empire*, Cambridge, Mass.

Grafton, Anthony (2006). 'The History of Ideas: Precept and Practice, 1950–2000 and Beyond', *Journal of the History of Ideas* 67: 1–32.

(2009). *Worlds Made by Words: Scholarship and Community in the Modern West*, Cambridge, Mass.

Graham, David (2001). 'Discovering Jabez Henry: Cross-Border Insolvency Law in the 19th Century', *International Insolvency Review* 10: 153–66.

(2005). 'In Search of Jabez Henry – Part II: The Readership of *Foreign Law*', *International Insolvency Review* 14: 223–34.

Grases, Pedro and Harkness, Albert (1953). *Manuel García de Sena y la independencia de Hispanoamérica*, Caracas.

Gray, Lewis Cecil and Thompson, Esther Katherine (1941). *History of Agriculture in the Southern United States to 1860*, 2 vols., New York.

Greene, Jack P. (2007). 'Colonial History and National History: Reflections on a Continuing Problem', *William and Mary Quarterly* 3rd ser., 64: 235–50.

(ed.) (2010). *Exclusionary Empire: English Liberty Overseas, 1600–1900*, Cambridge.

Greengrass, Mark (1991). 'Introduction: Conquest and Coalescence', in Mark Greengrass (ed.), *Conquest and Coalescence: The Shaping of the State in Early Modern Europe*, London, pp. 1–24.

Greenleaf, W. H. (1975). 'Burke and State Necessity: The Case of Warren Hastings', in Roman Schnur (ed.), *Staatsräson: Studien zur Geschichte eines politischen Begriff*, Berlin, pp. 549–67.

Greer, Allan (2012). 'Commons and Enclosure in the Colonization of North America', *American Historical Review* 117: 365–86.

Grew, Raymond (2006). 'Expanding Worlds of World History', *Journal of Modern History* 78: 878–98.

Grewe, Wilhelm G. (1984). 'Grotius – Vater der Völkerrechts?', *Der Staat* 23: 161–78.

(1988). *Epochen der Völkerrechtsgeschichte*, 2nd edn, Baden-Baden.

(2000). *The Epochs of International Law*, rev. and trans. Michael Byers, Berlin.

Gruzinski, Serge (2004). *Les Quatre Parties du monde. Histoire d'une mondialisation*, Paris.

Guedalla, Philip (1931). *The Duke*, London.

Guedea, Virginia (2001). 'Autonomía e independencia en la provincia de Texas', in Virginia Guedea (ed.), *La independencia de México y el proceso autonomista novohispano, 1808–1824*, Mexico, DF, pp. 135–83.

Guerra, François-Xavier (2009). *Modernidad e independencias: ensayos sobre las revoluciones hispánicas*, Madrid.

Guha, Ranajit (1996). *A Rule of Property for Bengal: An Essay on the Idea of Permanent Settlement*, 2nd edn., Durham, NC.

Guilhot, Nicolas (ed.) (2011). *The Invention of International Relations Theory: Realism, the Rockefeller Foundation, and the 1954 Conference on Theory*, New York.
Guillot, Armand (2011a). 'Jeremy Bentham et la théorie des relations internationales', in Malik Bozzo-Rey and Guillaume Tusseau (eds.), *Bentham juriste: L'utilitarisme juridique en question: actes du colloque international des 5 et 6 février 2009*, Paris, pp. 213–28.
   (2011b). 'Bentham et le droit international', in Malik Bozzo-Rey and Guillaume Tusseau (eds.), *Bentham juriste: L'utilitarisme juridique en question: actes du colloque international des 5 et 6 février 2009*, Paris, pp. 229–49.
Guldi, Jo (2011). 'What is the Spatial Turn?': http://spatial.scholarslab.org/spatial-turn, accessed 31 January 2012.
Gunn, J. A. W. (1999). 'Eighteenth-Century Britain: In Search of the State and Finding the Quarter Sessions', in John Brewer and Eckhart Hellmuth (eds.), *Rethinking 'Leviathan': The Eighteenth-Century State in Britain and Germany*, Oxford, pp. 99–125.
Haakonssen, Knud (1996). *Natural Law and Moral Philosophy: From Grotius to the Scottish Enlightenment*, Cambridge.
   (ed.) (1999). *Grotius, Pufendorf and Modern Natural Law*, Aldershot.
Haley, K. H. D. (1968). *The First Earl of Shaftesbury*, Oxford.
Hall, Catherine (1994). 'Rethinking Imperial Histories: The Reform Act of 1867', *New Left Review* 208: 3–29.
Hall, Catherine, McClelland, Keith and Rendall, Jane (2000). *Defining the Victorian Nation: Class, Race, Gender and the Reform Act of 1867*, Cambridge.
Hall, Ian (2006). *The International Thought of Martin Wight*, Basingstoke.
Hall, Ian and Hill, Lisa (eds.) (2009). *British International Thinkers from Hobbes to Namier*, Basingstoke.
Hall, Thadd E. (1971). *France and the Eighteenth-Century Corsican Question*, New York.
Halliday, Fred (1994). *Rethinking International Relations*, London.
Hallmark, Terrell L. (1998). 'John Locke and the Fundamental Constitutions of Carolina', PhD thesis, Claremont Graduate University.
Hamowy, Ronald (1979). 'Jefferson and the Scottish Enlightenment: A Critique of Garry Wills's *Inventing America: Jefferson's Declaration of Independence*', *William and Mary Quarterly* 3rd ser., 36: 503–23.
Hampsher-Monk, Iain (1998). 'Burke and the Religious Sources of Skeptical Conservatism', in Johan Van der Zande and Richard H. Popkin (eds.), *The Skeptical Tradition Around 1800: Skepticism in Philosophy, Science, and Society*, Dordrecht, pp. 235–59.
   (2005). 'Edmund Burke's Changing Justification for Intervention', *Historical Journal* 48: 65–100.
   (2010). 'Rousseau, Burke's *Vindication of Natural Society*, and Revolutionary Ideology', *European Journal of Political Theory* 9: 245–66.
Hampton, Timothy (2009). *Fictions of Embassy: Literature and Diplomacy in Early Modern Europe*, Ithaca, NY.

Hanson, Donald W. (1984). 'Thomas Hobbes's "Highway to Peace"', *International Organization* 38: 329–54.

Harle, Vilho (1990). 'Burke the International Theorist – or the War of the Sons of Light and the Sons of Darkness', in Vilho Harle (ed.), *European Values in International Relations*, London, pp. 58–79.

Harris, Steven J. (1998). 'Long-Distance Corporations, Big Sciences, and the Geography of Knowledge', *Configurations* 6: 269–304.

Harris, W. V. (ed.) (2004). *Rethinking the Mediterranean*, Oxford.

Hart, H. L. A. (1982). 'The United States of America', in Hart, *Essays on Bentham: Jurisprudence and Political Theory*, Oxford, pp. 53–78.

Harvey, David (1990). *The Condition of Postmodernity: An Enquiry into the Origins of Cultural Change*, Oxford.

Haskell, Thomas (1987). 'The Curious Persistence of Rights Talk in the "Age of Interpretation"', *Journal of American History* 74: 984–1012.

Hazelton, John (1906). *The Declaration of Independence: Its History*, New York.

Head, J. W. (1994). 'Supranational Law: How the Move Toward Multilateral Solutions is Changing the Character of "International Law"', *University of Kansas Law Review* 42: 606–66.

Headley, John M. (2007). *The Europeanization of the World: On the Origins of Human Rights and Democracy*, Princeton.

Heller, Mark A. (1980). 'The Use and Abuse of Hobbes: The State of Nature in International Relations', *Polity* 13: 21–32.

Henning, Basil Duke (ed.) (1983). *The House of Commons, 1660–1690*, 3 vols., London.

Hepp, John (2008). 'James Brown Scott and the Rise of Public International Law', *Journal of the Gilded Age and Progressive Era* 7: 151–79.

Herrejón Peredo, Carlos (2009). 'Versiones del grito de dolores y algo más', *20/10. Memoria de las revoluciones de México* 5: 39–53.

Hevia, James L. (1995). *Cherishing Men from Afar: Qing Guest Ritual and the Macartney Embassy of 1793*, Durham, NC.

Hexter, J. H. (1952). *More's 'Utopia': The Biography of an Idea*, Princeton.

Hill, Christopher L. (2008). *National History and the World of Nations: Capital, State, and the Rhetoric of History in Japan, France, and the United States*, Durham, NC.

Hilliard, Chris (2006). *To Exercise Our Talents: The Democratization of Writing in Britain*, Cambridge, Mass.

Hinshelwood, Bradley A. (in press). 'The Carolinian Context of John Locke's Theory of Slavery', *Political Theory*.

Hinsley, F. H. (1986). *Sovereignty*, 2nd edn, Cambridge.

Hobsbawm, Eric (1992). *Nations and Nationalism since 1780: Programme, Myth, Reality*, 2nd edn, Cambridge.

Hochstrasser, T. J. (2000). *Natural Law Theories in the Early Enlightenment*, Cambridge.

Hoekstra, Kinch (2007). 'The Natural Condition of Mankind', in Patricia Springborg (ed.), *The Cambridge Companion to Hobbes's 'Leviathan'*, Cambridge, pp. 109–27.

Hoekstra, S. J. (1998). 'The Savage, the Citizen, and the Foole: The Compulsion for Civil Society in the Philosophy of Thomas Hobbes', DPhil. thesis, University of Oxford.

Hoffmann, Stanley (1977). 'An American Social Science: International Relations', *Daedalus* 106: 41–60.

Hoffmann, Stefan-Ludwig (ed.) (2010). *Human Rights in the Twentieth Century*, Cambridge.

Hofman, Amos (1988). 'The Origins of the Theory of the *Philosophe* Conspiracy', *French History* 2: 152–72.

Holdsworth, Sir William (1937–72). *A History of the English Law*, ed. A. L. Goodhart and H. G. Hanbury, 17 vols., London.

Holland, Robert, Williams, Susan and Barringer, Terry A. (eds.) (2010). *The Iconography of Independence: 'Freedoms at Midnight'*, London.

Holland, Thomas Erskine (1898). *Studies in International Law*, Oxford.

Holmes, Geoffrey (1973). *The Trial of Dr Sacheverell*, London.

Holzgrefe, J. L. (1989). 'The Origins of Modern International Relations Theory', *Review of International Studies* 15: 11–26.

Honig, Bonnie (1991). 'Declarations of Independence: Arendt and Derrida on the Problem of Founding a Republic', *American Political Science Review* 85: 97–113.

Hont, Istvan (2005). *Jealousy of Trade: International Competition and the Nation-State in Historical Perspective*, Cambridge, Mass.

Hoogensen, Gunhild (2005). *International Relations, Security and Jeremy Bentham*, Abingdon.

Hooker, William (2009). *Carl Schmitt's International Thought: Order and Orientation*, Cambridge.

Hopkins, A. G. (ed.) (2002). *Globalization in World History*, London.

(2006). *Global History: Interactions between the Universal and the Local*, Basingstoke.

Horden, Peregrine and Purcell, Nicholas (2000). *The Corrupting Sea: A Study of Mediterranean History*, Oxford.

Howell, Wilbur Samuel (1961). 'The Declaration of Independence and Eighteenth-Century Logic', *William and Mary Quarterly* 3rd ser., 18: 463–84.

Howsam, Leslie and Raven, James (2011). 'Introduction', in Leslie Howsam and James Raven (eds.), *Books between Europe and the Americas: Connections and Communities, 1620–1860*, Basingstoke, pp. 1–22.

Hsueh, Vicki (2010). *Hybrid Constitutions: Challenging Legacies of Law, Privilege, and Culture in Colonial America*, Durham, NC.

Hundert, E. J. (1972). 'The Making of *Homo Faber*: John Locke between Ideology and History', *Journal of the History of Ideas* 33: 3–22.

Hüning, Dieter (1999). '"Inter arma silent leges": Naturrecht, Staat und Völkerrecht bei Thomas Hobbes', in Rüdiger Voigt (ed.), *Der Leviathan*, Baden-Baden, pp. 129–63.

Hunt, Lynn (2007). *Inventing Human Rights: A History*, New York.

Hunt, Peter (2006). 'Arming Slaves and Helots in Classical Greece', in Christopher L. Brown and Philip D. Morgan (eds.), *Arming Slaves: From Classical Times to the Modern Age*, New Haven, pp. 14–39.

Hunter, Ian (2010). 'Vattel's Law of Nations: Diplomatic Casuistry for the Protestant Nation', *Grotiana* 31: 108–40.

Hurst, Ronald (1996). *The Golden Rock: An Episode of the American War of Independence, 1775–1783*, London.

Hutson, James H. (1971–2). 'The Partition Treaty and the Declaration of American Independence', *Journal of American History* 58: 875–96.

Huxley, Andrew (2004). 'The *Aphorismi* and *A Discourse of Laws*: Bacon, Cavendish, and Hobbes 1615–1620', *Historical Journal* 47: 399–412.

Innes, Joanna (2003). 'Legislating for Three Kingdoms: How the Westminster Parliament Legislated for England, Scotland and Ireland, 1707–1830', in Julian Hoppit (ed.), *Parliaments, Nations and Identities in Britain and Ireland, 1660–1850*, Manchester, pp. 15–47.

Iriye, Akira (2002a). *Global Community: The Role of International Organizations in the Making of the Contemporary World*, Berkeley.

(2002b). 'Internationalizing International History', in Thomas Bender (ed.), *Rethinking American History in a Global Age*, Berkeley, pp. 47–62.

Iriye, Akira, Goedde, Petra and Hitchcock, William I. (eds.) (2011). *The Human Rights Revolution: An International History*, Oxford.

Isabella, Maurizio (2009). *Risorgimento in Exile: Italian Émigrés and the Liberal International in the Post-Napoleonic Era*, Oxford.

Israel, Jonathan (2006a). *Enlightenment Contested: Philosophy, Modernity, and the Emancipation of Man, 1670–1752*, Oxford.

(2006b). 'Enlightenment! Which Enlightenment?', *Journal of the History of Ideas* 67: 523–45.

Ivison, Duncan (2002). *Postcolonial Liberalism*, Cambridge.

(2003). 'Locke, Liberalism and Empire', in Peter R. Anstey (ed.), *The Philosophy of John Locke: New Perspectives*, London, pp. 86–105.

(2006). 'The Nature of Rights and the History of Empire', in David Armitage (ed.), *British Political Thought in History, Literature and Theory, 1500–1800*, Cambridge, pp. 191–211.

Jackson, Robert (2005). *Classical and Modern Thought on International Relations: From Anarchy to Cosmopolis*, Basingstoke.

Jahn, Beate (ed.) (2006). *Classical Theory in International Relations*, Cambridge.

James, Harold (2001). *The End of Globalization: Lessons from the Great Depression*, Cambridge, Mass.

Janis, Mark Weston (1984). 'Jeremy Bentham and the Fashioning of "International Law"', *American Journal of International Law* 78: 405–18.

(1992). 'American Versions of the International Law of Christendom: Kent, Wheaton and the Grotian Tradition', *Netherlands International Law Review* 39: 37–61.

(2010). *America and the Law of Nations, 1776–1939*, Oxford.

Jay, Stewart (1989). 'The Status of the Law of Nations in Early American Law', *Vanderbilt Law Review* 42: 819–49.

Jayne, Allen (1998). *Jefferson's Declaration of Independence: Origins, Philosophy and Theology*, Lexington, Ky.

(2007). *Lincoln and the American Manifesto*, Amherst, NY.
Jeffery, Renée (2005). 'Tradition as Invention: The "Traditions Tradition" and the History of Ideas in International Relations', *Millennium* 34: 57–84.
(2009). 'Moral Sentiment Theory and the International Thought of David Hume', in Hall and Hill (2009), pp. 49–69.
Jessup, Philip (1956). *Transnational Law*, New Haven.
Johnson, Laurie M. (1993). *Thucydides, Hobbes, and the Interpretation of Realism*, DeKalb, Ill.
Jolly, Richard, Emmerij, Louis and Weiss, Thomas G. (2009). *UN Ideas that Changed the World*, Bloomington.
Jones, Howard Mumford (1976). 'The Declaration of Independence: A Critique', *Proceedings of the American Antiquarian Society* n. s., 85: 55–74.
Jouannet, Emmanuelle (1998). *Emer de Vattel et l'émergence doctrinale du droit international classique*, Paris.
Kaempfer, Alvaro (2009). *Relatos de soberanía, cohesión y emancipación: las declaraciones de las Provincias Unidas en Sud-America (1816), Chile (1818) y Brasil (1822)*, Santiago de Chile.
Kaino, Michihiro (2008). 'Bentham's Concept of Security in a Global Context: The Pannomion and the Public Opinion Tribunal as a Universal Plan', *Journal of Bentham Studies* 10 (2008): http://discovery.ucl.ac.uk/1322984/1/010_Kaino__2008_.pdf, accessed 31 January 2012.
Kalmo, Hent and Skinner, Quentin (eds.) (2010). *Sovereignty in Fragments: The Past, Present and Future of a Contested Concept*, Cambridge.
Kammen, Michael (1966). 'Virginia at the Close of the Seventeenth Century: An Appraisal by James Blair and John Locke', *Virginia Magazine of History and Biography* 74: 141–69.
Kapila, Shruti (ed.) (2010). *An Intellectual History for India*, Cambridge.
Kapila, Shruti and Devji, Faisal (eds.) (2010). 'Forum: The Bhagavad Gita and Modern Thought', *Modern Intellectual History* 7: 269–457.
Karsten, Peter (1975–76). 'Plotters and Proprietaries, 1682–83: The "Council of Six" and the Colonies: Plan for Colonization or Front for Revolution?', *Historian* 38: 474–84.
Kaser, Max (1993). *Ius gentium*, Cologne.
Kayaoğlu, Turan (2010). *Legal Imperialism: Sovereignty and Extraterritoriality in Japan, the Ottoman Empire, and China*, Cambridge.
Keene, Edward (2002). *Beyond the Anarchical Society: Grotius, Colonialism and Order in World Politics*, Cambridge.
(2005). *International Political Thought: A Historical Introduction*, Cambridge.
(2007). 'A Case Study of the Construction of International Hierarchy: British Treaty-Making Against the Slave Trade in the Early Nineteenth Century', *International Organization* 61: 311–39.
Kelley, Donald R. (1987). 'Horizons of Intellectual History: Retrospect, Circumspect, Prospect', *Journal of the History of Ideas* 48: 143–69.

(2002). *The Descent of Ideas: The History of Intellectual History*, Aldershot.

Kelley, Donald R., Levine, Joseph, Megill, Allan, Schneewind, J. B. and Schneider, Ulrich Johannes (2005). 'Intellectual History in a Global Age', *Journal of the History of Ideas* 66: 143–200.

Kennedy, David (1986). 'Primitive Legal Scholarship', *Harvard International Law Journal* 27: 1–98.

Kettner, James H. (1976). 'Subjects or Citizens: A Note on British Views Respecting the Legal Effects of American Independence', *Virginia Law Review* 22: 945–67.

(1978). *The Development of American Citizenship, 1608–1870*, Chapel Hill.

Kidd, Colin (1999). *British Identities Before Nationalism: Ethnicity and Nationhood in the Atlantic World, 1600–1800*, Cambridge.

Kidder, Frederick E. (1965). 'The Fundamental Constitutions in the Light of John Locke's Political Theory', *Atenea* (Mayaguez, P.R.) 2: 47–60.

Kingsbury, Benedict and Straumann, Benjamin (eds.) (2010). *The Roman Foundations of the Law of Nations: Alberico Gentili and the Law of Nations*, Oxford.

Kinsella, Helen (2011). *The Image before the Weapon: A Critical History of the Distinction between Combatant and Civilian*, Ithaca, NY.

Kite, Elizabeth S. (1928). 'How the Declaration of Independence Reached Europe', *Daughters of the American Revolution Magazine* 62 (July): 405–13.

Klausen, Jimmy Casas (2007). 'Room Enough: America, Natural Liberty, and Consent in Locke's *Second Treatise*', *Journal of Politics* 69: 760–9.

Klein, Bernhard and Mackenthun, Gesa (eds.) (2004). *Sea Changes: Historicizing the Ocean*, New York.

Knutsen, Torbjørn L. (1992). *A History of International Relations Theory: An Introduction*, Manchester.

Koselleck, Reinhart (1988). *Critique and Crisis: Enlightenment and the Pathogenesis of Modern Society*, English translation, Cambridge, Mass.

(2004). '*Neuzeit*: Remarks on the Semantics of Modern Concepts of Movement', in Reinhart Koselleck, *Futures Past: On the Semantics of Historical Time*, trans. Keith Tribe, New York, pp. 222–54.

Koskenniemi, Martti (2002). *The Gentle Civilizer of Nations: The Rise and Fall of International Law, 1870–1960*, Cambridge.

(2005). *From Apology to Utopia: The Structure of International Legal Argument*, reissue with a new epilogue, Cambridge.

(2008). 'Into Positivism: Georg Friedrich Martens (1756–1821) and Modern International Law', *Constellations* 15: 189–207.

(2009). 'The Advantage of Treaties: International Law in the Enlightenment', *Edinburgh Law Review* 13: 27–67.

(2010a). 'Colonization of the "Indies": The Origin of International Law?', in Yolanda Gamarra Chopo (ed.), *La idea de América en el pensamiento ius internacionalista del siglo XXI*, Zaragoza, pp. 43–63.

(2010b). 'International Law and *raison d'état*: Rethinking the Prehistory of International Law', in Kingsbury and Straumann (2010), pp. 297–339.

Krasner, Stephen D. (1999). *Sovereignty: Organized Hypocrisy*, Princeton.

Kratochwil, Friedrich (1989). *Rules, Norms and Decisions: On the Conditions of Practical and Legal Reasoning in International Relations and Domestic Affairs*, Cambridge.

Lacey, Michael J. and Haakonssen, Knud (eds.) (1991). *A Culture of Rights: The Bill of Rights in Philosophy, Politics, and Law, 1791 and 1991*, Cambridge.

LaCroix, Alison (2010). *The Ideological Origins of American Federalism*, Cambridge, Mass.

Lang, Michael (2003). 'Mapping Globalization or Globalizing the Map: Heidegger and Planetary Discourse', *Genre: Forms of Discourse and Culture* 36: 239–50.

(2006). 'Globalization and Its History', *Journal of Modern History* 78: 899–931.

Larson, Carlton F. (2001). 'The Declaration of Independence: A 225th Anniversary Re-Interpretation', *Washington Law Review* 76: 701–91.

Laslett, Peter (1969). 'John Locke, the Great Recoinage and the Origins of the Board of Trade, 1695–1698', in John Yolton (ed.), *John Locke: Problems and Perspectives*, Cambridge, pp. 137–64.

(ed.) (1956). *Philosophy, Politics, and Society*, 1st ser., Oxford.

Lauterpacht, Hersh (1940). 'Is International Law a Part of the Law of England?', *Transactions of the Grotius Society* 25: 51–88.

Lazier, Benjamin (2011). 'Earthrise; or, The Globalization of the World Picture', *American Historical Review* 116: 602–30.

Leal Curiel, Carole, (2008). '¿Radicales o timoratos? La declaración de la Independencia absoluta como una acción teórica-discursiva (1811)', *Politeia. Revista de la Facultad de Ciencias Juricas y Polícas de la Universidad Central de Venezuela* 31, 40: 1–18.

Lebovics, Herman (1986). 'The Uses of America in Locke's Second Treatise on Government', *Journal of the History of Ideas* 47: 567–82.

Lebow, Richard Ned (2008). *A Cultural Theory of International Relations*, Cambridge.

Legg, Stephen (ed.) (2011). *Spatiality, Sovereignty and Carl Schmitt: Geographies of the Nomos*, London.

Leng, Tom (2011). 'Shaftesbury's Aristocratic Empire', in John Spurr (ed.), *Anthony Ashley Cooper, First Earl of Shaftesbury, 1621–1683*, Aldershot, pp. 101–25.

Lesaffer, Randall (ed.) (2004). *Peace Treaties and International Law in European History: From the Late Middle Ages to World War One*, Cambridge.

Lesser, Charles H. (1995). *South Carolina Begins: The Records of a Proprietary Colony, 1663–1721*, Columbia, SC.

Leung, Man To (1998). 'Extending Liberalism to Non-European Peoples: A Comparison of John Locke and James Mill', DPhil. thesis, University of Oxford.

Liddel, Peter (2008). 'William Young and the *Spirit of Athens*', in James Moore, Ian Macgregor Morris and Andrew J. Bayliss (eds.), *Reinventing History: The Enlightenment Origins of Ancient History*, London, pp. 57–85.

Lieberman, David (1989). *The Province of Legislation Determined: Legal Theory in Eighteenth-Century Britain*, Cambridge.

  (1999a). 'Codification, Consolidation, and Parliamentary Statute', in John Brewer and Eckhart Hellmuth (eds.), *Rethinking Leviathan: The Eighteenth-Century State in Britain and Germany*, Oxford, pp. 359–90.

  (2000). 'Economy and Polity in Bentham's Science of Legislation', in Stefan Collini, Richard Whatmore and Brian Young (eds.), *Economy, Polity and Society: British Intellectual History, 1750–1950*, Cambridge.

Lieberman, Victor (2003). *Strange Parallels: Southeast Asia in Global Context, c. 800–1830*, I: *Integration on the Mainland*, Cambridge.

Lint, Gregg L. (1977). 'The American Revolution and the Law of Nations, 1776–1789', *Diplomatic History* 1: 20–34.

Lintott, Andrew (1981). 'What Was the "Imperium Romanum"?', *Greece and Rome* 28: 53–67.

Lipset, Seymour Martin (1963). *The First New Nation: The United States in Historical and Comparative Perspective*, New York.

Liu, Lydia H. (1999a). 'Legislating the Universal: The Circulation of International Law in the Nineteenth Century', in Liu (1999b), pp. 127–64.

  (2004). *The Clash of Empires: The Invention of China in Modern World Making*, Cambridge, Mass.

  (ed.) (1999b). *Tokens of Exchange: The Problem of Translation in Global Circulations*, Durham, NC.

Livingston, Donald W. (1990). 'Hume, English Barbarism and American Independence', in Richard B. Sher and Jeffrey R. Smitten (eds.), *Scotland and America in the Age of Enlightenment*, Princeton, pp. 133–47.

Livingstone, David and Withers, Charles W. J. (eds.) (1999). *Geography and Enlightenment*, Chicago.

Lodge, Paul (ed.) (2004). *Leibniz and His Correspondents*, Cambridge.

Long, David and Wilson, Peter (eds.) (1995). *Thinkers of the Twenty Years' Crisis: Inter-War Idealism Reassessed*, Oxford.

Long, Douglas G. (1977). *Bentham on Liberty: Jeremy Bentham's Idea of Liberty in Relation to his Utilitarianism*, Toronto.

Long, Philip (1959). *A Summary Catalogue of the Lovelace Collection of the Papers of John Locke in the Bodleian Library*, Oxford.

Lorca, Arnulf Becker (in press). *Mestizo International Law: A Global Intellectual History, 1850s–1950s*, Cambridge.

Lovejoy, Arthur O. (1940). 'Reflections on the History of Ideas', *Journal of the History of Ideas* 1: 3–23.

  (1948). 'The Historiography of Ideas', in Lovejoy, *Essays in the History of Ideas*, Baltimore, pp. 1–13.

Lucas, Stephen E. (1989). 'Justifying America: The Declaration of Independence as a Rhetorical Document', in Thomas W. Benson (ed.), *American Rhetoric: Context and Criticism*, Carbondale, pp. 67–130.

(1994). 'The *Plakkaat van Verlatinge*: A Neglected Model for the American Declaration of Independence', in Rosemarijn Hoefte and Johanna C. Kardux (eds.), *Connecting Cultures: The Netherlands in Five Centuries of Transatlantic Exchange*, Amsterdam, pp. 187–207.

(1998). 'The Rhetorical Ancestry of the Declaration of Independence', *Rhetoric and Public Affairs* 1: 143–84.

Lucena Giraldo Manuel, (2010). *Naciones de Rebeldes. Las revoluciones de independencia latinoamericanos*, Madrid.

Lutnick, Solomon (1967). *The American Revolution and the British Press, 1775–1783*, Columbia, Mo.

Lutz, Donald S. (1989). 'The Declaration of Independence as Part of an American National Compact', *Publius: The Journal of Federalism* 19: 41–58.

Lynch, John (2009). *San Martín. Soldado argentino, héroe americano*, trans. Alejandra Chaparro, Barcelona.

Macalister-Smith, Peter and Schweitzke, Joachim (1999). 'Literature and Documentary Sources relating to the History of Public International Law: A Bibliographical Survey', *Journal of the History of International Law* 1: 136–212.

Mack, Mary P. (1963). *Jeremy Bentham: An Odyssey of Ideas, 1748–1792*, New York.

Macmillan, Ken (2011). 'Benign and Benevolent Conquest?: The Ideology of Elizabethan Atlantic Expansion Revisited', *Early American Studies* 9: 59–99.

Mahoney, Dennis J. (1987). 'The Declaration of Independence as a Constitutional Document', in Leonard W. Levy and Dennis J. Mahoney (eds.), *The Framing and Ratification of the Constitution*, New York, pp. 54–68.

Maier, Charles S. (1980). 'Marking Time: The Historiography of International Relations', in Michael Kammen (ed.), *The Past Before Us: Contemporary Historical Writing in the United States*, Ithaca, NY, pp. 355–87.

(2000). 'Consigning the Twentieth Century to History: Alternative Narratives for the Modern Era', *American Historical Review* 105: 807–31.

(2006). *Among Empires: American Ascendancy and its Predecessors*, Cambridge, Mass.

Maier, Pauline (1997). *American Scripture: Making the Declaration of Independence*, New York.

Maitland, F. W. (1908). *The Constitutional History of England*, ed. H. A. L. Fisher, Cambridge.

Malcolm, Noel (2002). *Aspects of Hobbes*, Oxford.

(2007a). 'The Name and Nature of Leviathan: Political Symbolism and Biblical Exegesis', *Intellectual History Review* 17: 21–39.

(2007b). *Reason of State, Propaganda, and the Thirty Years' War: An Unknown Translation by Thomas Hobbes*, Oxford.

Malnes, Raino (1993). *The Hobbesian Theory of International Conflict*, Oslo.

Mandler, Peter (2006). 'What is "National Identity"? Definitions and Applications in Modern British Historiography', *Modern Intellectual History* 3: 271–97.

Manela, Erez (2007). *The Wilsonian Moment: Self-Determination and the International Origins of Anticolonial Nationalism*, Oxford.

Manigat, Leslie F. (2005). 'Une brève analyse-commentaire critique d'un document historique', *Revue de la Société haïtienne d'histoire et de géographie* 221: 44–56.

Manning, Susan and Cogliano, Frank D. (eds.) (2008). *The Atlantic Enlightenment*, Aldershot.

Mantena, Karuna (2010). *Alibis of Empire: Henry Maine and the Ends of Liberal Imperialism*, Princeton.

de Marchi, Ernesto, (1955). 'Locke's *Atlantis*', *Political Studies* 3: 164–5.

Marino, James F. (1998). 'Empire and Commerce: A History of the Modern States-System', PhD thesis, Johns Hopkins University.

Marks, Susan (2000). *The Riddle of All Constitutions: International Law, Democracy, and the Critique of Ideology*, Oxford.

Marshall, Charles Burton (1974). *American Foreign Policy as a Dimension of the American Revolution*, Washington, DC.

Marshall, John (1994). *John Locke: Resistance, Religion and Responsibility*, Cambridge.
  (2006). *John Locke, Toleration and Early Enlightenment Culture: Religious Intolerance and Arguments for Religious Toleration in Early Modern and 'Early Enlightenment' Europe*, Cambridge.

Marshall, P. J. (1998). 'Britain and the World in the Eighteenth Century: I, Reshaping the Empire', *Transactions of the Royal Historical Society*, 6th ser., 8: 1–18.

Marshall, P. J. and Williams, Glyndwr (1982). *The Great Map of Mankind: British Perceptions of the World in the Age of Enlightenment*, London.

Marston, Jerrilyn Greene (1987). *King and Congress: The Transfer of Political Legitimacy, 1774–1776*, Princeton.

Martin, T. S. (1991). '*Nemo potest exuere patriam*: Indelibility of Allegiance and the American Revolution', *American Journal of Legal History* 35: 205–18.

Martinez, Jenny S. (2012). *The Slave Trade and the Origins of International Humanitarian Law*, Oxford.

Martínez Garnica, Armando (2012). 'Las declaraciones de independencia en Venezuela y la Nueva Granada', in Ávila, Dym, Gómez Galvarriato and Pani (2012), pp. 155–82.
  et al. (2011). 'Simposio sobre la Declaracion de Independencia de Cartagena', *Economía & Región* (Cartagena, Colombia) 5: 201–72.

Masters, Roger D. (1967a). 'The Lockean Tradition in American Foreign Policy', *Journal of International Politics* 21: 253–77.
  (1967b). *The Nation Is Burdened: American Foreign Policy in a Changing World*, New York.

Mattingly, Garrett (1955). *Renaissance Diplomacy*, New York.

Mazlish, Bruce (1993). 'An Introduction to Global History', in Bruce Mazlish and Ralph Buultjens (eds.), *Conceptualizing Global History*, Boulder, Colo., pp. 1–26.

Mazower, Mark (2009). *No Enchanted Palace: The End of Empire and the Ideological Origins of the United Nations*, Princeton.

McClure, Ellen M. (2006). *Sunspots and the Sun King: Sovereignty and Mediation in Seventeenth-century France*, Urbana.

McCormick, Ted (2009). *William Petty and the Ambitions of Political Arithmetic*, Oxford.

McGlone, Robert E. (1998). 'Deciphering Memory: John Adams and the Authorship of the Declaration of Independence', *Journal of American History* 85: 411–38.

McGuinness, Celia (1989). 'The *Fundamental Constitutions of Carolina* as a Tool for Lockean Scholarship', *Interpretation* 17: 127–43.

McMahon, Darrin M. (2001). *Enemies of the Enlightenment: The French Counter-Enlightenment and the Making of Modernity*, Oxford.

   (2013). 'The Return of the History of Ideas?', in McMahon and Moyn (2013).

McMahon, Darrin M. and Moyn, Samuel (eds.) (2013). *Rethinking Modern European Intellectual History*, New York.

Mehta, Uday Singh (1990). 'Liberal Strategies of Exclusion', *Politics and Society* 18: 427–54.

   (1999). *Liberalism and Empire: A Study in Nineteenth-Century British Liberal Thought*, Chicago.

Meinecke, Friedrich (1970). *Cosmopolitanism and the Nation State*, trans. Robert B. Kimber, Princeton.

   (1998). *Machiavellism: The Doctrine of Raison d'État and Its Place in Modern History*, trans. Douglas Scott, introd. Werner Stark, New Brunswick.

Melero, Luis Ángel García (1977). *La Independencia de los Estados Unidos de Norteamérica a través de la Prensa Española ... Los Precedentes (1763–1776)*, Madrid.

Ménager, Daniel (2001). *Diplomatie et théologie à la Renaissance*, Paris.

Menozzi, Luciano (1974). *Studi sul pensiero etico politici di Locke. Le relazioni internazionali*, Rome.

Mentor, Gaétan (2003). *Les Fils noir de la veuve. Histoire de la franc-maçonnerie en Haïti*, Pétionville.

Michael, Mark A. (1998). 'Locke's *Second Treatise* and the Literature of Colonization', *Interpretation* 25: 407–27.

Middleton, Richard (1985). *The Bells of Victory: The Pitt-Newcastle Ministry and the Conduct of the Seven Years' War, 1757–1762*, Cambridge.

Miller, Peter N. (1994). *Defining the Common Good: Empire, Religion and Philosophy in Eighteenth-Century Britain*, Cambridge.

Milton, J. R. (1990). 'John Locke and the Fundamental Constitutions of Carolina', *Locke Newsletter* 21: 111–33.

   (1995). 'Dating Locke's *Second Treatise*', *History of Political Thought* 16: 356–90.

Milton, Philip (2000). 'John Locke and the Rye House Plot', *Historical Journal* 43: 647–68.

(2007a). 'Locke the Plotter? Ashcraft's *Revolutionary Politics* Reconsidered', *Locke Studies* 7: 51–112.

(2007b). 'Pierre Des Maizeaux, *A Collection of Several Pieces of Mr. John Locke*, and the Formation of the Locke Canon', *Eighteenth-Century Thought* 3: 255–91.

Mishra, Pramod Kumar (2002). '"[A]ll the World was America": The Transatlantic (Post)Coloniality of John Locke, William Bartram, and the Declaration of Independence', *CR: The New Centennial Review* 2: 215–58.

Molivas, G. I. (1999). 'A Right, Utility and the Definition of Liberty as a Negative Idea: Richard Hey and the Benthamite Conception of Liberty', *History of European Ideas* 25: 75–92.

Moloney, Pat (2011). 'Hobbes, Savagery, and International Anarchy', *American Political Science Review* 105: 189–204.

Momigliano, Arnaldo (1944). 'Sea-Power in Greek Thought', *Classical Review* 58: 1–7.

Mongey, Vanessa (2009). 'Les vagabonds de la république: les révolutionnaires européens aux Amériques, 1780–1820', in Federica Morelli, Clément Thibaud and Geneviève Verdo (eds.), *Les Empires atlantiques des Lumières au libéralisme (1763–1865)*, Rennes, pp. 67–82.

Moore, John Alexander (1991). 'Royalizing South Carolina: The Revolution of 1719 and the Evolution of Early South Carolina Government', PhD thesis, University of South Carolina.

Morefield, Jeanne (2005). *Covenants without Swords: Idealist Liberalism and the Spirit of Empire*, Princeton.

Morelli, Federica (2012). 'Las declaraciones de independencia en Ecuador: de una Audiencia a múltiples Estados', in Ávila, Dym, Gómez Galvarriato and Pani (2012), pp. 135–54.

Morris, Ian and Scheidel, Walter (eds.) (2009). *The Dynamics of Ancient Empires: State Power from Assyria to Byzantium*, Cambridge.

Morris, Richard B. (1970). *The Emerging Nations and the American Revolution*, New York.

Moseley, Alexander (2005). 'John Locke's Morality of War', *Journal of Military Ethics* 4: 119–28.

Moyn, Samuel (2010). *The Last Utopia: Human Rights in History*, Cambridge, Mass.

Moyn, Samuel and Sartori, Andrew (eds.) (2013). *Global Intellectual History*, New York.

Murison, Barbara C. (2007). 'The Talented Mr Blathwayt: His Empire Revisited', in Nancy L. Rhoden (ed.), *English Atlantics Revisited: Essays Honouring Professor Ian K. Steele*, Montreal and Kingston, pp. 33–58.

Muthu, Sankar (2003). *Enlightenment Against Empire*, Princeton.

(2008) 'Adam Smith's Critique of International Trading Companies: Theorizing Globalization in the Age of Enlightenment', *Political Theory* 36: 185–212.

(2011). 'Diderot's Theory of Global (and Imperial) Commerce: An Enlightenment Account of "Globalization"', in Jacob T. Levy and Iris Marion Young (eds.), *Colonialism and its Legacies*, Lanham, Md., pp. 1–19.

(ed.) (2012). *Empire and Modern Political Thought*, Cambridge.

Nadelmann, Kurt H. (1961). 'An International Bankruptcy Code: New Thoughts on an Old Idea', *International and Comparative Law Quarterly* 10: 70–82.

Nakhimovsky, Isaac (2007). 'Vattel's Theory of the International Order: Commerce and the Balance of Power in the *Law of Nations*', *History of European Ideas* 33: 157–73.

Nardin, Terry and Mapel, David R. (eds.) (1992). *Traditions of International Ethics*, Cambridge.

Navari, Cornelia (1982). 'Hobbes and the "Hobbesian Tradition" in International Thought', *Millennium: Journal of International Studies* 11: 203–22.

Neem, Johann N. (2011). 'American History in a Global Age', *History and Theory* 50: 41–70.

Neustadt, Mark S. (1987). 'The Making of the Instauration: Science, Politics, and Law in the Career of Francis Bacon', PhD thesis, Johns Hopkins University.

Niesen, Peter (2006). 'Varieties of Cosmopolitanism: Bentham and Kant on International Politics', in Luigi Caranti (ed.), *Kant's Perpetual Peace: New Interpretive Essays*, Rome, pp. 247–88.

(2007). 'The "West Divided"? Bentham and Kant on Law and the Ethics in Foreign Policy', in David Chandler and Volker Heins (eds.), *Rethinking Ethical Foreign Policy: Pitfalls, Possibilities and Paradoxes*, London, pp. 93–115.

Nordholt, J. W. Schulte (1982). *The Dutch Republic and American Independence*, trans. Herbert R. Rowen, Chapel Hill.

Novick, Peter (1988). *That Noble Dream: The 'Objectivity Question' and the American Historical Profession*, Cambridge.

Nussbaum, Arthur (1947). *A Concise History of the Law of Nations*, New York.

Nys, Ernest (1885). 'Notes inédites de Bentham sur le droit international', *Law Quarterly Review* 1: 225–31.

O'Brien, Conor Cruise (1972). *The Suspecting Glance*, London.

(1992). *The Great Melody: A Thematic Biography and Commented Anthology of Edmund Burke*, London.

O'Brien, Karen (1997). *Narratives of Enlightenment: Cosmopolitan History from Voltaire to Gibbon*, Cambridge.

Ocampo López, Javier (1988). *Los catecismos políticos en la independencia de hispanoamerica: de la monarquía a la república*, Tunja.

Odysseos, Louiza and Petito, Fabio (eds.) (2007). *The International Political Thought of Carl Schmitt: Terror, Liberal War and the Crisis of Global Order*, London.

Ohlmeyer, Jane (1995). 'Ireland Independent: Confederate Foreign Policy and International Relations during the Mid-Seventeenth Century', in Jane Ohlmeyer (ed.), *Ireland from Independence to Occupation, 1641–1660*, Cambridge, pp. 89–112.

O'Keefe, Roger (2008). 'The Doctrine of Incorporation Revisited', *British Yearbook of International Law* 79: 7–85.

Olivieri, Marco (2006). 'Bentham, Lind e il dibattito sulla Dichiarazione d'Independenza degli Stati Uniti', *Il Pensiero Politico* 39: 36–48.

Onuf, Nicholas G. (1989). *World of Our Making: Rules and Rule in Social Theory and International Relations*, Columbia, SC.

Onuf, Peter S. (1998). 'A Declaration of Independence for Diplomatic Historians', *Diplomatic History* 22: 71–83.

Onuf, Peter S. and Onuf, Nicholas G. (1990). 'American Constitutionalism and the Emergence of a Liberal World Order', in George Athan Billias (ed.), *American Constitutionalism Abroad: Selected Essays in Comparative Constitutional History*, Westport, Conn., pp. 65–90.

(1993). *Federal Union, Modern World: The Law of Nations in an Age of Revolutions, 1776–1814*, Madison, Wis.

Onuma, Yasuaki (2000). 'When was the Law of International Society Born? – An Inquiry of the History of International Law from an Intercivilizational Perspective', *Journal of the History of International Law* 2: 1–66.

Ophir, Adi and Shapin, Steven (1991). 'The Place of Knowledge: A Methodological Survey', *Science in Context* 4: 3–21.

Orakhelashvili, Alexander (2006). 'The Idea of European International Law', *European Journal of International Law* 17: 315–47.

(2008). 'Statehood, Recognition and the United Nations System: A Unilateral Declaration of Independence in Kosovo', *Max-Planck Yearbook of United Nations Law* 12: 1–44.

(ed.) (2011). *Research Handbook on the Theory and History of International Law*, Cheltenham.

O'Rourke, Kevin H. and Williamson, Jeffrey G. (1999). *Globalization and History: The Evolution of a Nineteenth-Century Atlantic Economy*, Cambridge, Mass.

(2002). 'When Did Globalisation Begin?', *European Review of Economic History* 6: 23–50.

(2004). 'Once More: When did Globalisation Begin?', *European Review of Economic History* 8: 109–17.

Osiander, Andreas (2001). 'Sovereignty, International Relations, and the Westphalian Myth', *International Organization* 55: 251–87.

Owens, Patricia (2007). *Between War and Politics: International Relations and the Thought of Hannah Arendt*, Oxford.

Owsley, Frank Lawrence and Smith, Gene A. (1997). *Filibusters and Expansionists: Jeffersonian Manifest Destiny, 1800–1821*, Tuscaloosa.

Pagden, Anthony (1986). *The Fall of Natural Man: The American Indian and the Origins of Comparative Ethnology*, rev. edn, Cambridge.

(1995). *Lords of All the World: Ideologies of Empire in Spain, Britain and France c. 1500–c. 1800*, New Haven.

(1998). 'The Struggle for Legitimacy and the Image of Empire in the Atlantic to *c.* 1700', in Nicholas Canny (ed.), *The Oxford History of the British Empire*, I: *The Origins of Empire*, Oxford, pp. 34–54.

(2000). 'Stoicism, Cosmopolitanism, and the Legacy of European Imperialism', *Constellations* 7: 3–22.

(2003). 'Human Rights, Natural Rights, and Europe's Imperial Legacy', *Political Theory* 31: 171–99.

(2008). *Worlds at War: The 2,500-Year Struggle between East and West*, New York.

(2010). 'Gentili, Vitoria, and the Fabrication of a "Natural Law of Nations"', in Kingsbury and Straumann (2010), pp. 340–61.

Palmer, R. R. (1959–64). *The Age of the Democratic Revolution: A Political History of Europe and America, 1760–1800*, 2 vols., Princeton.

(1976). 'The Declaration of Independence in France', *Studies on Voltaire and the Eighteenth Century* 154: 1569–79.

Pangle, Thomas L. and Ahrensdorf, Peter J. (1999). *Justice Among Nations: On the Moral Basis of Power and Peace*, Lawrence, Kans.

Panizza, Diego (1997). *Genesi di una ideologia. Il conservatorismo moderno in Robert Ward*, Milan.

Paquette, Gabriel (2009). 'The Dissolution of the Spanish Atlantic Monarchy', *Historical Journal* 52: 175–212.

Parekh, Bhikhu (1994a) 'Decolonizing Liberalism', in Aleksandras Shtromas (ed.), *The End of 'Isms'?: Reflections on the Fate of Ideological Politics after Communism's Collapse*, Oxford, pp. 85–103.

(1994b). 'Superior People: The Narrowness of Liberalism from Mill to Rawls', *Times Literary Supplement* 4743 (25 February): 11–13.

(1995). 'Liberalism and Colonialism: A Critique of Locke and Mill', in Jan Nederveen Pieterse and Bhikhu Parekh (eds.), *The Decolonization of Imagination: Culture, Knowledge and Power*, London, pp. 81–98.

Parkin, Jon (2007). *Taming the Leviathan: The Reception of the Political and Religious Ideas of Thomas Hobbes in England, 1640–1700*, Cambridge.

Patapan, Haig (2009). 'The Glorious Sovereign: Thomas Hobbes on Leadership and International Relations', in Hall and Hill (2009), pp. 11–31.

Peckham, Howard H. (1976). 'Independence: The View from Britain', *Proceedings of the American Antiquarian Society* n. s. 85: 387–403.

Pérez Vejo, Tomás (2010). *Elegía Criolla. Una reinterpretación de las guerras de independencia hispanoamericanas*, Mexico, DF.

Pérotin-Dumont, Anne (1991). 'The Pirate and the Emperor: Power and Law on the Seas, 1450–1850', in James D. Tracy (ed.), *The Political Economy of Merchant Empires: State Power and World Trade, 1350–1750*, Cambridge, pp. 196–227.

Peterson, Merrill D. (1991). *'This Grand Pertinacity': Abraham Lincoln and the Declaration of Independence*, Fort Wayne.

Picciotto, Cyril M. (1915). *The Relation of International Law to the Law of England and of the United States*, London.

Piirimäe, Pärtel (2010). 'The Westphalian Myth of Sovereignty and the Idea of External Sovereignty', in Hent Kalmo and Quentin Skinner (eds.), *Sovereignty in Fragments: The Past, Present and Future of a Contested Concept*, Cambridge, pp. 64–80.

Pitts, Jennifer (2005a). *A Turn to Empire: The Rise of Imperial Liberalism in Britain and France*, Princeton.

(2005b). 'Jeremy Bentham: Legislator of the World?', in Bart Schultz and Georgios Varouxakis (eds.), *Utilitarianism and Empire*, Lanham, Md., pp. 57–91.

(2007). 'Boundaries of Victorian International Law', in Duncan Bell (ed.), *Victorian Visions of Global Order: Empire and International Relations in Nineteenth-Century Political Thought*, Cambridge, pp. 67–88.

(2010). 'Political Theory of Empire and Imperialism', *Annual Review of Political Science* 13: 211–35.

(2011). '"Great and Distant Crimes": Empire in Bentham's Thought', in Jeremy Bentham, *Selected Writings*, ed. Stephen G. Engelmann, New Haven, pp. 478–99.

(2012). 'Empire and Legal Universalisms in the Eighteenth Century', *American Historical Review* 117: 92–121.

Pocock, J. G. A. (1985). 'Josiah Tucker on Burke, Locke, and Price: A Study in the Varieties of Eighteenth-Century Conservatism', in J. G. A. Pocock, *Virtue, Commerce, and History: Essays on Political Thought and History, Chiefly in the Eighteenth Century*, Cambridge, pp. 157–92.

(1987). *The Ancient Constitution and the Feudal Law: A Reissue with Retrospect*, Cambridge.

(1988a). *The Politics of Extent and the Problems of Freedom*, Colorado College Studies 25, Colorado Springs.

(1988b). 'States, Republics, and Empires: The American Founding in Early Modern Perspective', in Terence Ball and J. G. A. Pocock (eds.), *Conceptual Change and the Constitution*, Lawrence, Kans., pp. 55–77.

(1995). 'Political Thought in the English-Speaking Atlantic: I, The Imperial Crisis', in J. G. A. Pocock (ed.), *The Varieties of British Political Thought, 1500–1800*, Cambridge, pp. 246–82.

(1996). *La ricostruzione di un impero: sovranità britannica e federalismo Americano*, Manduria.

(1999a). *Barbarism and Religion*, I: *The Enlightenments of Edward Gibbon, 1737–1764*, Cambridge.

(1999b). *Barbarism and Religion*, II: *Narratives of Civil Government*, Cambridge.

(2005). *Barbarism and Religion*, IV: *Savages and Empires*, Cambridge.

Popkin, Jeremy D. (1989). *News and Politics in the Age of Revolution: Jean Luzac's 'Gazette de Leyde'*, Ithaca, NY.

Porter, Andrew (1999). 'From Empire to Commonwealth of Nations', in Franz Bosbach and Hermann Hiery (eds.), *Imperium / Empire / Reich. Ein Konzept politischer Herrschaft im deutsch-britischen Vergleich*, Munich, pp. 167–78.

Porter, Brian (1978). 'Patterns of Thought and Practice: Martin Wight's "International Theory"', in Michael Donelan (ed.), *The Reason of States: A Study in International Political Theory*, London, pp. 64–74.

Portillo Valdes, José M. (2006). *Crisis atlántica. Autonomia e independencia en la crisis de la monarquía hispana*, Madrid.

Powell, William S. (1964). 'Carolina in the Seventeenth Century: An Annotated Bibliography of Contemporary Publications', *North Carolina Historical Review* 41: 74–104.

Prest, Wilfrid (2008). *William Blackstone: Law and Letters in the Eighteenth Century*, Oxford.

Primus, Richard A. (1999). *The American Language of Rights*, Cambridge.

Prokhovnik, Raia and Slomp, Gabriella (eds.) (2011). *International Political Theory after Hobbes: Analysis, Interpretation and Orientation*, Basingstoke.

Puchner, Martin (2006). *Poetry of the Revolution: Marx, Manifestos, and the Avant-Gardes*, Princeton.

Putterman, Ethan (2010). *Rousseau, Law and the Sovereignty of the People*, Cambridge.

Rainbolt, John C. (1973). 'Americans' Initial View of Their Revolution's Significance for Other Peoples, 1776–1788', *Historian* 35: 418–33.

Reck, Andrew J. (1991). 'The Enlightenment in American Law: I, The Declaration of Independence', *Review of Metaphysics* 44: 549–73.

Reid, John Phillip (1981). 'The Irrelevance of the Declaration', in Hendrik Hartog (ed.), *Law in the American Revolution and the American Revolution in the Law*, New York, pp. 46–89.

Reinert, Sophus (2011). *Translating Empire: Emulation and the Origins of Political Economy*, Cambridge, Mass.

Reséndez, Andres (2005). *Changing National Identities at the Frontier: Texas and New Mexico, 1800–1850*, Cambridge.

  (2010). 'Texas and the Spread of the Troublesome Secessionist Spirit through the Gulf of Mexico Basin', in Don H. Doyle (ed.), *Secession as an International Phenomenon: From America's Civil War to Contemporary Separatist Movements*, Athens, Ga., pp. 193–213.

Reynolds, Noel B. and Hilton, John L. (1993). 'Thomas Hobbes and the Authorship of the *Horae Subsecivae*', *History of Political Thought* 14: 361–80.

Richards, Peter G. (1967). *Parliament and Foreign Affairs*, London.

Richardson, John (2008). *The Language of Empire: Rome and the Idea of Empire from the Third Century BC to the Second Century AD*, Cambridge.

Ritchie, Robert C. (1986). *Captain Kidd and the War Against the Pirates*, Cambridge, Mass.

Roberts, Sir Ivor (ed.) (2009). *Satow's Guide to Diplomatic Practice*, 6th edn, Oxford.

Roberts, J. M. (1971). 'The Origins of a Mythology: Freemasons, Protestants and the French Revolution', *Bulletin of the Institute of Historical Research* 44: 78–97.

Robertson, John (1993). 'Universal Monarchy and the Liberties of Europe: David Hume's Critique of an English Whig Doctrine', in Nicholas Phillipson and Quentin Skinner (eds.), *Political Discourse in Early Modern Britain*, Cambridge, pp. 349–76.

    (1995a). 'Empire and Union: Two Concepts of the Early Modern European Political Order' in John Robertson (ed.), *A Union for Empire: Political Thought and the British Union of 1707*, Cambridge, pp. 3–36.

    (1995b). 'An Elusive Sovereignty: The Union Debate in Scotland 1698–1707', in John Robertson (ed.), *A Union for Empire: Political Thought and the British Union of 1707*, Cambridge, pp. 198–227.

Rodríguez O., Jaime E. (1996). *La independencia de la América española*, Mexico, DF.

    (2010). 'Sobre la supuesta influencia de la independencia de los Estados Unidos en las independencias hispanoamericanas', *Revista de Indias* 70: 691–714.

Rodrik, Dani, Obstfeld, Maurice, Feenstra, Robert C. and Williamson, Jeffrey G. (1998). 'Globalization in Perspective', *Journal of Economic Perspectives* 12: 1–72.

Roper, L. H. (2004). *Conceiving Carolina: Proprietors, Planters, and Plots, 1662–1729*, Basingstoke.

Rose, Jonathan (2010). *The Intellectual Life of the British Working Classes*, 2nd edn, New Haven.

Rosen, Frederick (1992). *Bentham, Byron, and Greece: Constitutionalism, Nationalism, and Early Liberal Political Thought*, Oxford.

Rothschild, Emma (1999). 'Globalization and the Return of History', *Foreign Policy* 115 (Summer): 106–16.

    (2001). 'The Politics of Globalization circa 1773', *The OECD Observer* 228 (September): 12–14.

    (2004). 'Global Commerce and the Question of Sovereignty in the Eighteenth-Century Provinces', *Modern Intellectual History* 1: 3–26.

    (2005). 'Language and Empire, c. 1800', *Historical Research* 78: 208–29.

    (2006). 'Arcs of Ideas: International History and Intellectual History', in Gunilla Budde, Sebastian Conrad and Oliver Janz (eds.), *Transnationale Geschichte: Themen, Tendenzen und Theorien*, Göttingen, pp. 217–26.

    (2008). 'The Archives of Universal History', *Journal of World History* 19: 375–401.

    (2009). 'The Atlantic Worlds of David Hume', in Bernard Bailyn and Patricia L. Denault (eds.), *Soundings in Atlantic History: Latent Structures and Intellectual Currents, 1500–1830*, Cambridge, Mass., pp. 405–48.

    (2011a). *The Inner Life of Empires: An Eighteenth-Century History*, Princeton.

(2011b). 'Political Economy', in Gareth Stedman Jones and Gregory Claeys (eds.), *The Cambridge History of Nineteenth-Century Political Thought*, Cambridge, pp. 748–79.

Rudan, Paola (2007). 'Dalla constituzione al governo. Jeremy Bentham e le Americhe', PhD thesis, Università di Bologna.

Rumble, Wilfrid E. (2005). *Doing Austin Justice: The Reception of John Austin's Philosophy of Law in Nineteenth-Century England*, London.

Runciman, David (1997). *Pluralism and the Personality of the State*, Cambridge.

Ryan, Dermot (2010). '"A New Description of Empire": Edmund Burke and the Regicide Republic of Letters', *Eighteenth-Century Studies* 44: 1–19.

Sachsenmaier, Dominic (2011). *Global Perspectives on Global History: Theories and Approaches in a Connected World*, Cambridge.

San Francisco, Alejandro (2012). 'Chile y su independencia. Los hechos, los textos y la declaración de 1818', in Ávila, Dym, Gómez Galvarriato and Pani (2012), pp. 183–214.

Sartori, Andrew (2006). 'The British Empire and Its Liberal Mission', *Journal of Modern History* 78: 623–42.

(2008). *Bengal in Global Concept History: Culturalism in the Age of Capital*, Chicago.

Saunier, Pierre-Yves (2009). 'Transnational', in Akira Iriye and Pierre-Yves Saunier (eds.), *The Palgrave Dictionary of Transnational History*, Basingstoke, pp. 1047–55.

Scattola, Merio (2003). 'Before and After Natural Law: Models of Natural Law in Ancient and Modern Times', in T. J. Hochstrasser and Peter Schröder (eds.), *Early Modern Natural Law Theories: Contexts and Strategies in the Early Enlightenment*, Dordrecht, pp. 1–30.

Schaffer, Simon (2009). 'Newton on the Beach: The Information Order of *Principia Mathematica*', *History of Science* 47: 243–76.

Schaffer, Simon, Roberts, Lissa, Raj, Kapil and Delbourgo, James (eds.) (2009). *The Brokered World: Go-Betweens and Global Intelligence, 1780–1820*, Sagamore Beach, Calif.

Schmidt, Brian C. (1998). *The Political Discourse of Anarchy: A Disciplinary History of International Relations*, Albany, NY.

(2002). 'Together Again: Reuniting Political Theory and International Relations Theory', *British Journal of Politics and International Relations* 4: 115–40.

Schofield, Philip (2006). *Utility and Democracy: The Political Thought of Jeremy Bentham*, Oxford.

Schröder, Peter (1999). 'The Constitution of the Holy Roman Empire after 1648: Samuel Pufendorf's Assessment in his *Monzambano*', *Historical Journal* 42: 961–83.

(2002). 'Natural Law, Sovereignty and International Law: A Comparative Perspective', in Ian Hunter and David Saunders (eds.), *Natural Law and*

Civil Sovereignty: Moral Right and State Authority in Early Modern Political Thought, Basingstoke, pp. 204–18.

Schroeder, Paul W. (1994). *The Transformation of European Politics, 1763–1848*, Oxford.

Schwarzenberger, Georg (1948). 'Bentham's Contribution to International Law and Organisation', in George W. Keeton and Georg Schwarzenberger (eds.), *Jeremy Bentham and the Law: A Symposium*, London, pp. 152–84.

Scott, James Brown (1928). *The Spanish Origin of International Law*, Washington, DC.

Scott, Jonathan (2010). 'Maritime Orientalism, or the Political Theory of Water', Inaugural Lecture, University of Auckland, www.artsfaculty.auckland.ac.nz/special/lectures/?view=1#JohnathanScott, accessed 31 January 2012.

(2011). *When the Waves Ruled Britannia: Geography and Political Identities, 1500–1800*, Cambridge.

Shapin, Steven (1998). 'Placing the View from Nowhere: Historical and Sociological Problems in the Location of Science', *Transactions of the Institute of British Geographers* n. s. 23: 5–12.

Shields, David (2007). '"We declare you independent whether you wish it or not": The Print Culture of Early Filibusterism', in Caroline Fuller Sloat (ed.), *Liberty! Égalité! ¡Independencia!: Print Culture, Enlightenment, and Revolution in the Americas, 1776–1838*, Worcester, Mass., pp. 13–39.

Simms, Brendan (2007). *Three Victories and a Defeat: The Rise and Fall of the First British Empire, 1714–1783*, London.

(2011). '"A False Principle in the Law of Nations": Burke, State Sovereignty, [German] Liberty, and Intervention in the Age of Westphalia', in Brendan Simms and D. J. B. Trim (eds.), *Humanitarian Intervention: A History*, Cambridge, pp. 89–110.

Simons, Penelope (2003). 'The Emergence of the Idea of the Individualized State in the International Legal System', *Journal of the History of International Law* 5: 293–335.

Sirmans, Eugene M. (1966). *Colonial South Carolina: A Political History, 1663–1763*, Chapel Hill, NC.

Skinner, Quentin (1969). 'Meaning and Understanding in the History of Ideas', *History and Theory* 8: 3–53.

(1978). *The Foundations of Modern Political Thought*, 2 vols., Cambridge.

(1998). *Liberty before Liberalism*, Cambridge.

(2002a). 'Classical Liberty and the Coming of the English Civil War', in Martin van Gelderen and Quentin Skinner (eds.), *Republicanism: A Shared European Heritage, ii: The Values of Republicanism in Early Modern Europe*, Cambridge, pp. 9–28.

(2002b). *Visions of Politics*, 3 vols., Cambridge.

(2005). 'On Intellectual History and the History of Books', *Contributions to the History of Concepts* 1: 29–36.

(2007). 'Hobbes on Persons, Authors and Representatives', in Patricia Springborg (ed.), *The Cambridge Companion to Hobbes's 'Leviathan'*, Cambridge, pp. 157–80.

Slate, Nico (2011). *Colored Cosmopolitanism: The Shared Struggle for Freedom in the United States and India*, Cambridge, Mass.

Slauter, Eric (2009). 'The Declaration of Independence and the New Nation', in Frank Shuffelton (ed.), *The Cambridge Companion to Thomas Jefferson*, Cambridge, pp. 12–34.

Sluga, Glenda and Amrith, Sunil (2008). 'New Histories of the United Nations', *Journal of World History* 19: 251–74.

Smith, Steve, Booth, Ken and Zalewski, Marysia (eds.) (1996). *International Theory: Positivism and Beyond*, Cambridge.

Smith, T. B. (1962). 'The Union of 1707 as Fundamental Law', in T. B. Smith, *Studies Critical and Comparative*, Edinburgh, pp. 1–27.

Sobrevilla Perea, Natalia (2012). 'Entre proclamas, actas y una capitulación: la independencia peruana vista en sus actos de fundación', in Ávila, Dym, Gómez Galvarriato and Pani (2012), pp. 243–76.

Sokol, Irene M. (1967). 'The American Revolution and Poland: A Bibliographical Essay', *Polish Review* 12: 3–17.

Sorell, Tom (2006). 'Hobbes on Trade, Consumption and International Order', *Monist* 89: 245–58.

de Sousa, Norberto (1992). 'Societas civilis: Classical Roman Republican Theory on the Theme of Justice', PhD thesis, Cambridge University.

Stagg, J. C. A. (2009). *Borderlines in Borderlands: James Madison and the Spanish-American Frontier, 1776–1821*, New Haven.

Stanlis, Peter J. (1953). 'Edmund Burke and the Law of Nations', *American Journal of International Law* 67: 397–413.

Stanton, Tim (2003). 'John Locke, Edward Stillingfleet, and Toleration', PhD thesis, University of Leicester.

(2011). 'Hobbes and Schmitt', *History of European Ideas* 37: 160–67.

Starobinski, Jean (1993). 'The Word *Civilization*', in Starobinski, *Blessings in Disguise: On the Morality of Evil*, Cambridge, Mass., pp. 1–35.

Starr, Chester G. (1978). 'Thucydides on Sea Power', *Mnemosyne* 31: 343–50.

Starr, Thomas (1998). 'American Relations: Fabricating the Image of the Declaration of Independence', *AIGA Journal of Graphic Design* 16, no. 3 (December): 18–23.

Steinberg, Philip E. (2001). *The Social Construction of the Ocean*, Cambridge.

Stern, Philip J. (2011). *The Company-State: Corporate Sovereignty and the Early Modern Foundations of the British Empire in India*, Oxford.

Stinchcombe, William C. (1969). *The American Revolution and the French Alliance*, Syracuse, NY.

Strang, David (1991). 'Global Patterns of Decolonization, 1500–1987', *International Studies Quarterly* 35: 429–54.

Straumann, Benjamin (2007). *Hugo Grotius und die Antike: römisches Recht und römische Ethik im frühneuzeitlichen Naturrecht*, Baden-Baden.

(2008). 'The Peace of Westphalia as a Secular Constitution', *Constellations* 15: 173–88.

Strauss, Barry S. (1996). 'The Athenian Trireme, School of Democracy', in Josiah Ober and Charles Hedrick (eds.), *Demokratia: A Conversation on Democracies, Ancient and Modern*, Princeton, pp. 313–25.

Subrahmanyam, Sanjay (2005). 'On World Historians in the Sixteenth Century', *Representations* 91: 26–57.

Suganami, Hidemi (1978). 'A Note on the Origin of the Word "International"', *British Journal of International Studies* 4: 226–32.

    (2002). 'On Wendt's Philosophy: A Critique', *Review of International Studies* 28: 23–37.

Surkis, Judith, Wilder, Gary, Cook, James W., Ghosh, Durba, Thomas, Julia Adeney and Perl-Rosenthal, Nathan (2012). '*AHR* Forum: Historiographic "Turns" in Critical Perspective', *American Historical Review* 117: 698–813.

Sutherland, Lucy S. (1968). 'Edmund Burke and the Relations Between Members of Parliament and Their Constituents', *Studies in Burke and His Time* 10: 1005–21.

Swinfen, D. B. (1976). 'The American Revolution in the Scottish Press', in Owen Dudley Edwards and George Shepperson (eds.), *Scotland, Europe and the American Revolution*, Edinburgh, pp. 66–74.

Sylvest, Casper (2008). '"Our Passion for Legality": International Law and Imperialism in Late Nineteenth-Century Britain', *Review of International Studies* 34: 403–23.

    (2009). *British Liberal Internationalism, 1880–1930: Making Progress?*, Manchester.

Talbot, Ann (2010). '*The Great Ocean of Knowledge': The Influence of Travel Literature on the Work of John Locke*, Leiden.

Tanck de Estrada, Dorothy (1992). 'Los catecismos políticos: de la revolución francesa al México independiente', in Solange Alberro, Alicia Hernández Chévez and Elías Trabulse (eds.), *La revolución francesa en México*, Mexico, DF, pp. 65–80.

Tang, Chenxi (2008). *The Geographic Imagination of Modernity: Geography, Literature, and Philosophy in German Romanticism*, Stanford.

    (2010). 'Re-imagining World Order: From International Law to Romantic Poetics', *Deutsche Vierteljahrsschrift für Literaturwissenschaft und Geistesgeschichte* 84: 526–79.

Taylor, Charles (1989). *Sources of the Self: The Making of the Modern Identity*, Cambridge, Mass.

Taylor, Miles (2003a). 'Colonial Representation at Westminster, 1800–60', in Julian Hoppit (ed.), *Parliaments, Nations and Identities in Britain and Ireland, 1660–1850*, Manchester, pp. 206–19.

    (2003b). 'Empire and Parliamentary Reform: The 1832 Reform Act Reconsidered', in Arthur Burns and Joanna Innes (eds.), *Rethinking the Age of Reform: Britain and Ireland c. 1780–1850*, Cambridge, pp. 295–311.

Ternavasio, Marcela (2012). 'Los laberintos de la libertad. Revolución e independencias en el Río de la Plata', in Ávila, Dym, Gómez Galvarriato and Pani (2012), pp. 215–42.

Teschke, Benno (2003). *The Myth of 1648: Class, Geopolitics and the Making of Modern International Relations*, London.

Thompson, Kenneth W. (1994). *Fathers of International Thought: The Legacy of Political Theory*, Baton Rouge.

Thompson, Martyn P. (1977). 'The Idea of Conquest in the Controversies over the 1688 Revolution', *Journal of the History of Ideas* 38: 33–46.

Tierney, Brian (1997). *The Idea of Natural Rights: Studies on Natural Rights, Natural Law, and Church Law, 1150–1625*, Atlanta.

Todd, David (2008). 'John Bowring and the Global Dissemination of Free Trade', *Historical Journal* 51: 373–97.

Tombs, Robert and Tombs, Isabelle (2006). *That Sweet Enemy: The French and the British from the Sun King to the Present*, London.

Toscano, Mario (1966). *The History of Treaties and International Politics*, 2 vols., Baltimore.

Travers, Len (1997). *Celebrating the Fourth: Independence Day and the Rites of Nationalism in the Early Republic*, Amherst.

Travers, Robert (2007). *Ideology and Empire in Eighteenth Century India: The British in Bengal*, Cambridge.

Tresch, John (2013). 'Bringing Back the Lovejoy: History of Science and Intellectual History', in McMahon and Moyn (2013).

Trevor-Roper, H. R. (1957). *Historical Essays*, London.

Tricaud, François (1969). '"Homo homini Deus", "Homo homini Lupus": Recherche des Sources des deux Formules de Hobbes', in Reinhart Koselleck and Roman Schnur (eds.), *Hobbes-Forschungen*, Berlin, pp. 61–70.

Tsesis, Alexander (2012). *For Liberty and Equality: The Life and Times of the Declaration of Independence*, New York.

Tsing, Anna (2000). 'The Global Situation', *Cultural Anthropology* 15: 327–60.

Tuck, Richard (1979). *Natural Rights Theories: Their Origin and Development*, Cambridge.

(1987). 'The "Modern" Theory of Natural Law', in Anthony Pagden (ed.), *The Languages of Political Theory in Early-Modern Europe*, Cambridge, pp. 99–119.

(1989). *Hobbes*, Oxford.

(1993). *Philosophy and Government, 1572–1651*, Cambridge.

(1994). 'Rights and Pluralism', in James Tully (ed.), *Philosophy in an Age of Pluralism: The Philosophy of Charles Taylor in Question*, Cambridge, pp. 159–70.

(1999). *The Rights of War and Peace: Political Thought and the International Order from Grotius to Kant*, Oxford.

Tuckness, Alex (2008). 'Punishment, Property, and the Limits of Altruism: Locke's International Asymmetry', *American Political Science Review* 102: 467–79.

Tully, James (1993). 'Rediscovering America: The *Two Treatises* and Aboriginal Rights', in James Tully, *An Approach to Political Philosophy: Locke in Contexts*, Cambridge, pp. 137–76.

(1995). *Strange Multiplicity: Constitutionalism in an Age of Diversity*, Cambridge.

(2008). *Public Philosophy in a New Key*, ii: *Imperialism and Civic Freedom*, Cambridge.

(2009). 'Lineages of Contemporary Imperialism', in Duncan Kelly (ed.), *Lineages of Empire: The Historical Roots of British Imperial Thought*, Oxford, pp. 3–29.

Turner, Frederick Jackson (1938). 'The Significance of History', in *The Early Writings of Frederick Jackson Turner*, ed. Everett E. Edwards, Madison, Wis., pp. 41–68.

Turner, Jack (2011). 'John Locke, Christian Mission, and Colonial America', *Modern Intellectual History* 8: 267–97.

Twining, William (2000). *Globalisation and Legal Theory*, London.

Unwin, Tim (1998). 'Locke's Interest in Wine', *Locke Newsletter* 29: 119–51.

(2000). 'The Viticultural Geography of France in the 17th Century according to John Locke', *Annales de Géographie* 614–15: 395–414.

(2001). 'From Montpellier to New England: John Locke on Wine', in Iain Black and Robin A. Butlin (eds.), *Place, Culture and Identity: Essays in Historical Geography in Honour of Alan R. H. Baker*, Saint-Nicholas, pp. 69–90.

Uribe-Uran, Victor M. (2000). 'The Birth of a Public Sphere in Latin America during the Age of Revolution', *Comparative Studies in Society and History* 42: 425–57.

Uzgalis, William (1998). '". . . the Same Tyrannical Principle": Locke's Legacy on Slavery', in Tommy Lee Lott (ed.), *Subjugation and Bondage: Critical Essays on Slavery and Social Philosophy*, Lanham, Md., pp. 49–77.

Vagts, Alfred and Vagts, Detlev F. (1979). 'The Balance of Power in International Law: A History of an Idea', *American Journal of International Law* 73: 555–80.

Valentini, Monica (1993). 'Bentham sull'independenza delle colonie americane', *Il Pensiero Politico* 26: 356–81.

Van Alstyne, Richard W. (1965). *Empire and Independence: The International History of the American Revolution*, New York.

van Ittersum, Martine Julia (2006). *Profit and Principle: Hugo Grotius, Natural Rights Theories and the Rise of Dutch Power in the East Indies, 1595–1615*, Leiden.

(2010). 'The Long Goodbye: Hugo Grotius and the Justification of Dutch Expansion Overseas (1604–1645)', *History of European Ideas* 36: 386–411.

Varouxakis, Georgios (2009). 'The International Political Thought of John Stuart Mill', in Hall and Hill (2009), pp. 117–36.

Vaughan, Alden T. (2006). *Transatlantic Encounters: American Indians in Britain, 1500–1776*, Cambridge.

Venturi, Franco (1972). *Italy and the Enlightenment: Studies in a Cosmopolitan Century*, trans. Susan Corsi, ed. S. J. Woolf, London.

(1991). *The End of the Old Regime in Europe, 1776–1789*, i: *The Great States of the West*, trans. R. Burr Litchfield, Princeton.

Vigezzi, Brunello (2005). *The British Committee on the Theory of International Politics (1954–1985): The Rediscovery of History*, Milan.

Vincent, R. J. (1984). 'Edmund Burke and the Theory of International Relations', *Review of International Studies* 10: 205–18.

Vincitorio, Gaetano L. (1969). 'Edmund Burke and the First Partition of Poland: Britain and the Crisis of 1772 in the "Great Republic"', in Gaetano L. Vincitorio (ed.), *Crisis in the 'Great Republic': Essays Presented to Ross J. Hoffman*, New York, pp. 14–46.

Viroli, Maurizio (1992). *From Politics to Reason of State: The Acquisition and Transformation of the Language of Politics 1250–1600*, Cambridge.

Wahrman, Dror (2004). *The Making of the Modern Self: Identity and Culture in Eighteenth-Century England*, New Haven.

Waldron, Jeremy (2002). *God, Locke, and Equality: Christian Foundations in Locke's Political Thought*, Cambridge.

Waldstreicher, David (1997). *In the Midst of Perpetual Fetes: The Making of American Nationalism, 1776–1820*, Chapel Hill.

Walker, R. B. J. (1993). *Inside/Outside: International Relations as Political Theory*, Cambridge.

(2010). *After the Globe, Before the World*, London.

Wallace, John M. (1968). *Destiny His Choice: The Loyalism of Andrew Marvell*, Cambridge.

Walsh, M. J. (1949). 'Contemporary Broadside Editions of the Declaration of Independence', *Harvard Library Bulletin* 3: 31–43.

Walzer, Michael (2006). *Just and Unjust Wars: A Moral Argument with Historical Illustrations*, 4th edn, New York.

Wandycz, Piotr S. (1980). 'The American Revolution and the Partitions of Poland', in Jaroslaw Pelenski (ed.), *The American and European Revolutions, 1776–1848: Sociopolitical and Ideological Aspects*, Iowa City, pp. 95–110.

Ward, Lee (2006). 'Locke on the Moral Basis of International Relations', *American Journal of Political Science* 50: 691–705.

(2009). 'A Note on a Note on Locke's "Great Art of Government"', *Canadian Journal of Political Science/Revue canadienne de science politique* 42: 521–3.

(2010). *John Locke and Modern Life*, Cambridge.

Warren, Christopher N. (2009). 'Hobbes's Thucydides and the Colonial Law of Nations', *The Seventeenth Century* 24: 260–86.

Welchman, Jennifer (1995). 'Locke on Slavery and Inalienable Rights', *Canadian Journal of Philosophy* 25: 67–81.

Wellek, René (1955). *A History of Modern Criticism, 1750–1950, IV: The Later Nineteenth Century*, New Haven.

Welsh, Jennifer M. (1995). *Edmund Burke and International Relations*, London.

(1996). 'Edmund Burke and the Commonwealth of Europe: The Cultural Bases of International Order', in Ian Clark and Iver B. Neumann (eds.), *Classical Theories of International Relations*, Basingstoke, pp. 173–92.

Wendt, Alexander (1999). *Social Theory of International Politics*, Cambridge.

Weston, J. C., Jr (1958). 'The Ironic Purpose of Burke's *Vindication* Vindicated', *Journal of the History of Ideas* 19: 435–41.

Whatmore, Richard (2007). 'Étienne Dumont, the British Constitution and the French Revolution', *Historical Journal* 50: 23–47.
Whelan, Frederick G. (1995). 'Robertson, Hume, and the Balance of Power', *Hume Studies* 21: 315–32.
  (1996). *Edmund Burke and India: Political Morality and Empire*, Pittsburgh.
White, Morton (1978). *The Philosophy of the American Revolution*, New York.
Whitehead, Judith (2012). 'John Locke, Accumulation by Dispossession and the Government of Colonial India', *Journal of Contemporary Asia* 42: 1–21.
Wight, Martin (1966). 'Why Is There No International Theory?', in Herbert Butterfield and Martin Wight (eds.), *Diplomatic Investigations: Essays in the Theory of International Politics*, London, pp. 17–34.
  (1987). 'An Anatomy of International Thought', *Review of International Studies* 13: 221–7.
  (1991). *International Theory: The Three Traditions*, ed. Gabriele Wight and Brian Porter, Leicester.
Williams, Howard (1990). *International Relations in Political Theory*, Basingstoke.
  (1996). *International Relations and the Limits of Political Theory*, New York.
  (2003). *Kant's Critique of Hobbes: Sovereignty and Cosmopolitanism*, Cardiff.
Williams, Michael C. (2006). 'The Hobbesian Theory of International Relations: Three Traditions', in Beate Jahn (ed.), *Classical Theory in International Relations*, Cambridge, pp. 253–76.
Williams, Samuel Cole (1933). *History of the Lost State of Franklin*, New York.
Wills, Garry (1978). *Inventing America: Jefferson's Declaration of Independence*, New York.
Wilson, Jon (2008). *The Domination of Strangers: Modern Governance in Eastern India, 1780–1835*, Basingstoke.
Wimmer, Andreas and Schiller, Nina Glick (2003). 'Methodological Nationalism, the Social Sciences, and the Study of Migration: An Essay in Historical Epistemology', *International Migration Review* 37: 576–610.
Wimmer, Andreas and Min, Brian (2006). 'From Empire to Nation-State: Explaining Wars in the Modern World, 1816–2001', *American Sociological Review* 71: 867–97.
Winch, Donald (1996). *Riches and Poverty: An Intellectual History of Political Economy in Britain, 1750–1834*, Cambridge.
Winterbottom, Anna (2009). 'Producing and Using the *Historical Relation of Ceylon*: Robert Knox, the East India Company and the Royal Society', *British Journal for the History of Science* 42: 515–38.
Winterer, Caroline (2010). 'Model Empire, Lost City: Ancient Carthage and the Science of Politics in Revolutionary America', *William and Mary Quarterly*, 3rd ser., 67: 3–30.
Withers, Charles W. J. (2007). *Placing the Enlightenment: Thinking Geographically about the Age of Reason*, Chicago.
  (2009). 'Place and the "Spatial Turn" in Geography and in History', *Journal of the History of Ideas* 70: 637–58.
Wood, Neal (1984). *John Locke and Agrarian Capitalism*, Berkeley.

Woolhouse, Roger (2007). *Locke: A Biography*, Cambridge.

Wootton, David (1992). 'John Locke and Richard Ashcraft's *Revolutionary Politics*', *Political Studies* 40: 79–98.

—— (2000). 'Unhappy Voltaire, or "I Shall Never Get Over It as Long as I Live"', *History Workshop Journal* 50: 137–55.

Wyllys, Rufus Kay (1928). 'Filibusters of Amelia Island', *Georgia Historical Quarterly* 12: 297–325.

Yirush, Craig (2011). 'Claiming the New World: Empire, Law, and Indigenous Right in the Mohegan Case, 1704–1743', *Law and History Review* 29: 333–73.

Yoo, John C. (1999a). 'Globalism and the Constitution: Treaties, Non-Self-Execution, and the Original Understanding', *Columbia Law Review* 99: 1955–2094.

—— (1999b). 'Treaties and Public Lawmaking: A Textual and Structural Defense of Non-Self-Execution', *Columbia Law Review* 99: 2218–58.

York, Neil Longley (1994). *Neither Kingdom nor Nation: The Irish Quest for Constitutional Rights, 1698–1800*, Washington, DC.

Zehfuss, Maja (2002). *Constructivism in International Relations: The Politics of Reality*, Cambridge.

Zeiler, Thomas W. (2009). 'The Diplomatic History Bandwagon: A State of the Field', *Journal of American History* 95: 1053–73.

Zuckert, Michael P. (1996). *The Natural Rights Republic: Studies in the Foundation of the American Political Tradition*, Notre Dame.

Zurbuchen, Simone (2010). 'Vattel's "Law of Nations" and the Principle of Non-Intervention', *Grotiana* 31: 69–84.

Index

Ábalos, José de, 225
Académie de France, essay-competition
  of 1836, 11–12
Acosta, José de, 92
Adams, John, 199, 201, 218
  *Defence of the Constitutions . . . of the United
    States*, 96
Age of Revolutions, 174, 218, 219
agriculturalist argument, 125
  cultivation of waste land, 78
  see also Locke, John
D'Aguesseau, Henri-François, Chancellor
  of France, 43
ambergris, 83, 108
America, Central, 221
America, Iberian, 36, 52–3, 192, 215–19, 221–3, 230
  unrest in during nineteenth century, 226–7
  see also America, Central, America, Latin
America, Latin, bicentennial celebrations in, 216–18
American Revolution / War, 123, 176–80, 192,
    212–14, 215
  consequences, 12, 219
  and Parliament, 138, 148–50
  see also colonies, British American
anarchy, discourse of, 71
  see also state of nature, international
ancient constitution, 162
Angell, Norman, 44
Anglo-Dutch Wars, 51, 75
Anne, Queen, 143
Antarctica, 49
Apochancana, King of Virginia, 123
Aquinas, Thomas, 87
Aranda, Pedro Pablo Abarca de Bolea,
    Conde de, 225
archaeology, 46
Arendt, Hannah, 25
d'Argonne, Bonaventure, 19
Aron, Raymond, 25
Ascham, Anthony, 162
Asia, British trade to, 116–18

Athens, 50–2
Atlantic world, 49, 115, 129, 192, 215
Aury, Louis-Michel, 226
Austin, John, 71, 152, 186–7
authority / power, 109, 111–13
  as absolute, 177
Ayala, Balthazar, 26
Azawad, declaration of independence
    (2012), 231

Bacon, Sir Francis, 114
balance of power, 157
Barruel, Augustus, abbé, 169
Beccaria, Cesare, 148
behaviouralism, 25
behemoth / elephant, as land empire, 47–8
Bello, Andrés, 223
Bengal, 185
  see also Permanent Settlement
Bentham, Jeremy, 10, 42, 170
  and American war, 176
  on Sir William Blackstone, 10, 175, 176–8
  coinage of 'international', 42–3, 151, 174
  decontextualised, 174–6
  early life of, 174–5
  and legislation, 181
  on John Locke, 112
  and natural law, 182, 184, 205, 207
  peace proposals of, 181–2
  and principle of utility, 176
  universalist ambition of, 172–4
  works
    Auto-Icon, 184
    'Cabinet no Secresy', 175
    Fragment on Government, 175, 176–8
    *Introduction to the Principles of Morals and
      Legislation*, 179–81
    Pannomion, 208
    'Plan for a Universal and Perpetual Peace',
      150, 175
    Principles of International Law, 181

'*Projet Forme – Entre-gens*', 181
'Short Review of the Declaration', 178–80,
    204–5, 208
Berlin, Sir Isaiah, 3
Blackstone, Sir William, 10, 141–4, 197
    description of Parliament, 139–40
    and natural law, 151
    Commentaries on the Laws of England, 148, 176–7
    see also Bentham, Jeremy
Blair, Tony, 11
Blathwayt, Sir William, 91
Board of Trade, *see* Locke, John, administrative /
    diplomatic experience of
Bokassa, Jean-Bédel, 191
Bolingbroke, Henry St John, Viscount, 159
Bonaparte, Napoleon, 47, 54, 216
books
    distribution of, 23
    history of, 20, 28
    transmission of, 7–8
Bourdieu, Pierre, 23
Bourne, Randolph, 44
Bowring, Sir John, 174, 175
Brandenburg, Frederick William, Elector of, 75
Brazil, 222, 230
Brierly, J. L., 5
Britain, *see* Great Britain
Browne, Sir Thomas, 37
Bull, Hedley, 77
Burke, Edmund, 13, 38, 41, 145, 151
    on French Revolution, 162–4
    and identity, 137
    as international theorist, 154–6
    and Parliament, 138, 151
    and reason of state 157, 159–71
    works
        Appeal from the New to the Old Whigs, 155
        Letters on a Regicide Peace, 159, 167
        Reflections on the Revolution in France,
            160, 163–4
        Remarks on the Policy of the Allies, 167
        Thoughts on French Affairs, 165, 168
        Vindication of Natural Society, 159
Burlamaqui, Jean-Jacques, 69, 149
Bush, George W., 191
Butterfield, Herbert, 12, 25
Buvot v. *Barbuit*, *see* *Triquet* v. *Bath*

Caribbean, British, 111
Carlisle, Frederick Howard, 5th Earl of, 149
Carnegie Endowment for International Peace,
    Classics of International Law series 26
Carolina, 83, 110–11, 120
    migrants to, 103–4
    organisation of, 99–100

Proprietors of, 91
religious toleration in, 96
revisions to, 103–7, 105–7
    Fundamental Constitutions of, 92, 96–101,
        110, 111–13, 128
    see also Locke, John
Carthage, 51–2, 54
cartography, 37
catechism, political, *see* revolution
Cavendish, William, 2nd Earl of Devonshire, 61
Central African Republic, 191
Chambers, Sir Robert, 141
Charles II, King, 100, 106
China, 44–5
Christendom / Christian civilisation, 39, 150,
    169, 184
Cicero, Marcus Tullius, 156, 164
civil war, American Revolution as, 199
    US (1861–5), 139, 194, 211, 229
    see also Glorious Revolution
Clarke, Edward, 108
classism, 30–2
Cold War, 21
Colleton, Sir Peter, 98, 108, 112
Collins, Anthony, 101
colonialism, 23, 40, 78, 114, 216
    English, 76, 112
    see also imperialism, liberalism
colonies, British American, 54, 82, 83, 138, 191
    discovery of, 36
    rights of 198–9
    as *terra nullius*, 110–11, 213
commerce, 36–7, 47, 68, 76, 141
    global, 116–18
    and natural law, 65, 80
    see also reason of state
commonwealth, *see* state
conquest, 110, 164
consent, general, 79–80
    tacit, 82
constitutions, written, 219
constructivism, 5, 77
context, expansion of, 23, 30–2, 213
Continental Congress, US (1774–89), 198,
    200–3, 221
Corsica, 200, 213
Cos, José María, 228
cosmography, 37
cosmopolitanism, 21–3
Cousin, Victor, 19
Cox, Richard, 77
Crimea, 213
Cromwell, Oliver, 79
Cunliffe, Barry, 46
Curtius, Georg, 44

Darnton, Robert, 20, 25
Davenant, Charles, 51, 116
Declaration of Independence, US (1776), 192,
    220–1, 228, 231–2
  audience for, 198
  consequences of, 208–12
  as declaration of inter-dependence, 225
  diplomatic context of, 195
  as document, 210–12
  legal context of, 195–6
  origin and form of, 194–6
  purpose of, 194–6, 199–201
  response to
    British, 203–5
    European, 202
  rhetorical structure of, 196–9
  as speech-act, 197–9
  see also American Revolution/War,
    independence
decolonisation, 21, 114, 212, 230
democracy, 50
deserts, 49
Dickinson, John, 199, 201
diplomacy, 41, 75
diversity, cultural and religious, 119
domestic vs foreign, as realms of the political,
    10–11, 27, 70–2, 73
Dryden, John, 104
Ducoudray Holstein, H. L. V., 226
Dumont, Étienne, 174, 185, 186
Dutch, *see* East India Company, Netherlands

East Florida, 150
East India Company
  Dutch, 22, 117
  English, 116, 130, 136
East Indies, passage to, 36
east vs west, 50
education, legal, 147
Eldon, John Scott, 1st Earl of, Solicitor
    General, 184
elephant, *see* behemoth
empires, 21–4, 114–15
  definition of, 49, 52, 124
  dissolution of, 215–19, 230
  historiography of, 56
  geographic extent of, 191–2
  land vs sea, 49–56
  see also states
empiricism, 114
Encyclopédie, 39, 224
Engels, Friedrich, 36
England, empire of 47, 52
  foreign affairs of 75, 79

'English School' of International Relations,
    2–3, 77
  see also Bull, Hedley, Butterfield, Herbert,
    Wight, Martin
Enlightenment, 23, 33, 34
envoys, free passage of, 65, 80, 143–4
ethics / morality, 25, 29, 38, 71, 155
Europe, 46, 51, 80, 90
  balance of power in, 166–9
  'eurocentrism', 40–2, 114
  international system of, 213
  major powers of, and America, 199–201, 229
  states and polities of, 48–9, 53, 88, 184, 191
Exchequer, 161
Exclusion Crisis, 107
expediency, political, 156
  as necessity, 156–71
  see also reason of state
exploration, 23

federalism, 177
federative power, 84
Fernández-Armesto, Felipe, 35–6
Filmer, Sir Robert, 108, 111, 126
Flanders, 229
Fox, Charles James, 168
Foucault, Michel, 22
foundation myths, 9, 11, 27, 51
France, 85
  as American ally, 203, 208, 229
  Anglo-French commercial treaty, 145
  Directory Government of, 155, 163, 166,
    168–9
  empire of, 93, 180
  Louis XIV, King of, 51, 136, 163, 166
  war with, as holy, 151
  see also French Revolution
Franklin (abortive state), 220
Franklin, Benjamin, 201, 217
French Revolution, 40–1, 167–70, 205, 220
  effects of, 12, 184, 219
Fréron, Élie, 54

Gaius, jurist, *see* Roman law
Gallie, W. B., 4
Galsworthy, John, 26
genealogies, disciplinary, 8, 12
Gentili, Alberico, 9
Gentz, Friedrich, 213
George III, King, 196, 199, 203
  grievances against, 220
Gibbon, Edward, 55
globalisation, 6, 49, 56, 172
  commercial, 55

condition / consciousness of, 37–8
deglobalisation, 38
history of, 35–6
origins, 6–7, 36–7
as process, 33–5
varieties of, 45
Glorious Revolution, 76, 94, 136, 146, 167, 170
Burke's interpretation of, 161–5
as civil war, 164–5
God, 68, 122
concept of, 39, 119
and creation, 47, 110, 122
and divine law, 63, 65, 162, 176
as origin of law, 156, 205
worship of, 99
Godolphin, Sir William, 76
Gordon, Lord George, 169
Great Britain, 135, 136
and America, 199
empire of, 53, 135, 138–41, 148–9, 192
foreign affairs of, 139–41, 145
Protestant succession in, 136
see also England, Scotland
Grotius, Hugo, 12, 26, 60, 65
as authority, 146–8
and natural law, 38, 156
works
De Jure Belli ac Pacis, 9, 155, 162, 183, 206
Mare Liberum, 52–3, 117
Günther, Karl Gottlob, 183

Haïti, 222, 229
Halifax, George Saville, 1st Marquis of, 158
Hardy, Thomas 26
Hartz, Louis, 78
Hastings, Warren, 130, 161
Havana, siege of (1763), 175
see also Seven Years' War
Haynes, Lemuel, 211
Hazlitt, William, 173
Heathfield v. *Chilton*, 144
see also Mansfield
Heeren, Arnold H. L., 41
Hegel, Georg Wilhelm Friedrich, 71
Henry, Jabez, 185
Herodotus, 50
history, 24, 33, 60
European practitioners of, 23
and historiography, 1, 50
pre-history, 35
varieties of
comparative, 18
domestic vs international, 146
early modern, 9, 29
global, 18, 38

imperial, 46–8
intellectual, 1–4, 7–8, 18–21, 24–6, 27–32, 172
international, 6, 18, 24–6, 27–32, 56, 136
maritime, 46–8, 49
material, 8
nationalistic, 17–19, 20
post-colonial, 17, 49
transnational, 18, 56
Hobbes, Thomas, 10, 23, 26, 77, 79, 87
civil science / law, versions of, 62–7
as innovator, 68
as international theorist, 59–63, 67–74
later reputation of, 67
on law of nature / nations, 62, 67
and natural law, 80, 207
and realist theory, 60
reception of works, 60, 62
translations of, 60
works
De Cive, 63–7, 68, 69
Dialogue between a Philosopher and a Student, 67
Discourse of Laws, attributed, 61–2
Elements of Law, 63, 65
Leviathan, 47, 64–7, 73
Hobsbawm, Eric, 173
Holy Roman Empire, 48
Hordern, Peregrine, 46
Horne, George, Bishop of Norwich, 124
human nature, 69
as basis for law, 62, 63, 93, 141, 145, 156
as political, 24
rationality of, 115, 120–3, 129
humans, capacities of, 119, 122–3, 223
as focus of law, 27, 82, 65
Hume, David, 23, 76, 207
and identity, 137
works
Enquiry Concerning the Principles of Morals, 160
Treatise of Human Nature, 160

ideas, audience, for, 23
circulation of 17–18, 20, 21, 28
history of, *see* intellectual history
as innate, 119–20, 122
identity
national, 137, 216
personal, 137
imperialism, *see* colonialism, empires
independence, *see* sovereignty, Vattel
independence, declarations of, 215–22
in twentieth and twenty-first centuries, 230–2
political legitimacy of, 228
precedents for, 220–1

independence, declarations of (cont.)
  as public statements, 227–8
  see also Azawad, Kosovo, Montenegro, South
    Sudan, United States of America
indigenous peoples, 138, 215
  dispossession of, 79, 83, 88, 110, 223
  imperialist concepts of, 124
  see also Native Americans
Institut de Droit international, *see* international
  institutions
intellectual history, *see* history
International Court of Justice, 230
international, origins of term, 42–3, 151, 174
  see also trans-national
international history, *see* history
international institutions, 28–9
international law, 1–2, 9–10, 59, 75, 78
  British contributions to, 150–1
  codification of, 185–7
  and declarations of independence, 231–2
  definitions of, 151–3
  as developing, 206
  discipline of, 8, 70–3, 187
  inter-state law / *jus inter gentes*, 42–3, 68
  moral basis of, 4, 86–7
  as not law, 186
  law of nations / *jus gentium*, 61–9, 79, 80, 163,
    164, 223
  origins of, 38–42
  practitioners of, 6, 24, 27, 197
  and positivism, 11–13, 187
  reform of, 181
  and religion, 184
  and utility, 179–81
  as science, 182
  and transmission of textual authorities, 150
  as trans-national, 43
International Relations, academic discipline of,
    12, 24, 25–6, 74, 75
  history of, 5–6, 9–10, 27–8
  see also 'English School'
international relations, 1–2, 70–3
  and culture, 23
  modern, 21
  and rights, 78
  theory of, 59–60
  see also diplomacy
international thought, 3–4, 7, 24–32, 67, 77–9
  changes in, 206–8
  history of, 60, 86–8
  modern, 8–13
  origins of term, 26
  post-modern, 10, 73
  schools of, 154–6, 171
  textual canon of, 26

inter-War period, 12, 26, 27
Ireland, 136, 213
  independence of, 135
  and Jacobite war, 165
  and Poynings's law (1782), 135

James II, King, 146
  see also Exclusion Crisis, Glorious Revolution
Jefferson, Thomas, 194, 202, 206, 218, 220, 224
  *Summary View of the Rights of British
    America*, 220
  see also Declaration of Independence, US
Jenkinson, Charles, 151, 210
Jessup, Philip, 44
Johnson, Samuel, 175
Justel, Henri, 101

Kant, Immanuel, 8, 26, 38, 115, 184
  and international theory, 60
  and natural law, 207
  works
    Perpetual Peace, 28, 170
    'What is Enlightenment?', 33
Kelley, Donald, 19
Kent, James, 211
Kidd, William, Captain, 204
  see also pirates
King, Walker, 169
Knox, Robert, 95
Koch, Christoph Wilhelm, 41
Koselleck, Reinhart, 37
Koskenniemi, Martti, 5
Kosovo, declaration of independence (2008),
    230, 231

Laertius, Diogenes, 19
language, 52
  importance of, 6
  of independence, 221–7
  and nominalism, 34
Laski, Harold, 72
Laslett, Peter, 3, 94
law, basis of
  agreement / consent, 61, 68
  instinct, 61, 62
  see also human rationality
law, varieties of, 44, 177
  cosmopolitan, 177
  English common, 141–5, 197
  internal as domestic vs external, 146
  globalisation of, 44
  municipal, 61, 71, 205–8
  national, 141
  and naturalism, 67, 68, 71
  normative, 5

public vs private, 61
see also international law, natural law,
	Roman law
League of Nations, 26
see also international institutions
Lee, Richard Henry, 199, 200, 224
Leibniz, G. W., 69
Leon, José Almeda y, 224
leviathan / whale, as sea empire, 47–8
see also Hobbes
liberalism, 112, 114–15, 120, 130–1
	and colonialism, 90–1, 95
	and exclusion, 120
liberty, negative, 205
Lincoln, Abraham, 197
Lind, John, *Answer to the Declaration of the
	American Congress*, 178, 203
linguistic turn, 6
Locke, John, 23, 53, 75
	administrative / diplomatic experience, 75–6,
		79, 91–8, 115, 130
	anti-essentialism, 123
	and Carolina, 101
	correspondence, 75, 101, 105, 108, 118
	exile of, 101, 108
	and Hobbes, 77
	and identity, 137
	on industry / labour, 127
	international theory of, 79, 88
	landgrave of Carolina, 98
	and natural law, 79–82
	political theory of, 96–101
	and property, 78, 93, 109
		as land, 82–3, 126–7
		and labour, 83–5, 126, 127
	reputation of, 77–9, 114
	theory of empire, 115–18, 124–31
	travels of, 118
	and travel literature, 118–19
	on treaties, 84
	works 75, 85, 108–9
		Conduct of Understanding, The, 121
		'Critical Notes on Stillingfleet', 108
		Essay Concerning Human Understanding,
			119, 120, 122
		Essay on the Poor Laws, 127
		Essays on the Law of Nature, 119
		Letter Concerning Toleration, 111, 128
		'Observations on Wine, Olives, Fruit and
			Silk', 102
		'On the Law of Nature', 79
		Second Letter, 116
		Two Treatises of Government, 80–5, 87
			American examples in, 126–7
			biblical references in, 95

colonial reading of, 92–6, 107–13
dating of, 94–6, 102–3
imperialist readings of, 114
as liberal, 30, 100
see also Fundamental Constitutions of
	Carolina, *Shaftesbury, Anthony Ashley
	Cooper, 1st Earl of*
Lovejoy, Arthur O., 20, 30

Macaulay, Thomas Babington, 115
MacGregor, Gregor, 226
Machiavelli, Niccolò, 155
Mackintosh, Sir James, 39
	*Discourse on . . . the Law of Nature and
		Nations*, 150, 182–5
Maier, Charles, 25
manners, 183
Mansfield, William Murray, Lord Chief Justice,
	142, 144, 148, 150
Martyn, Henry, 116
Marx, Karl, 36
Masham, Damaris Cudworth, Lady, 76
Masham, Sir Francis Cudworth, 101
Mason, George, 220
Massachusetts, 221
Matveev, Andrei Artemonovich, 143
Meinecke, Friedrich, 155, 157, 170
Mendoza, Joaquin Marín y, 222
Mexico, 222
	Grito de Dolores (1810), 230
migration, transatlantic, 103
Mill, James, 92, 186
Mill, John Stuart, 31, 174
Milton, J. R., 94
Miranda, Francisco de, 218, 227
Mohegans, 125
money, invention of, 82
	see also Locke, John
Montaigne, Michel de, 120
Montenegro, declaration of independence
	(2006), 120
Montesquieu, Charles-Louis de Secondat,
	39, 51, 84
More, Sir Thomas, *Utopia*, 109, 111
Morelos, José Maria, 225
Morgenthau, Hans, 25
municipal law, distinguished from international
	law, *see* domestic vs foreign
Munster, Treaty of (1648), 210

nationalism, 17–18, 19
Native Americans, 65, 80, 92–6, 100, 109
	as rational beings, 120
	see also indigenous peoples, Locke, John,
		Mohegans

natural law, 156, 176, 198
  Bentham on, 182
  as international, 11, 41, 61–9, 78, 79
  and law of nations, 207
  Locke's conception of, 79–82
  and marriage, 61
  modern concept of, 38–9, 156–71, 205–8
  Thomistic, 227
  tradition of, 223
  see also God, Hobbes, Thomas, law
naval power, 53, 140
Neal, John, 173
Netherlands
  Act of Abjuration (*Plakaat van Verlantinge*,
    1581), 212, 221
  empire of, 47, 52–3, 165
  secession from Spain, 178
'New History', 19
Newcastle, Thomas Pelham-Holles, 1st Duke
  of, 38
New Spain, 228
Newton, Sir Isaac, 22, 118
Nicole, Pierre, 117
Niebuhr, Reinhold, 25
non-citizens
  aliens as, 81
  migrants as, 82
North, Lord Frederick, (later 2nd Earl of
    Guilford), 149, 203–5
  see also Lind, John

O'Brien, Conor Cruise, 160
O'Rourke, Kevin, 36
oceans
  as maritime arenas, 21, 47
  characteristics of, 52–3
  as commons, 82–3
  fishing rights in, 149
  history of, 46
Ogilby, John, 121
Old Oligarch, 50

Paine, Thomas, *Common Sense*, 200, 222, 228
Paris, Treaty of (1783), 209–12, 229
Parliament, British, 135
  Acts of
    Act in Restraint of Appeals (1533), 141
    Act of Settlement, (1701), 140
    7 Anne c 12 (1709), 143–4
    East India Mutiny Bill (1754), 140
    Geo III c. 46 (1782), 149
    Reform Acts (1832 & 1867), 135
    Stamp Act (1765), 141
  and cession of territory, 148–9
  expansion of imperial legislation in, 151–3

and international law, 141–50
  sovereignty / authority of, 135–6, 138–41, 177
Parliament, Irish, *see* Ireland: Poynings's law
Penn, William, *Frame of Government*, 94
Pennsylvania, 93
Permanent Settlement (Bengal), 185
Persia, empire of, 50–1
Peru, 92, 126
Petty, Sir William, 54, 116
piracy, pirates, 116, 151
  see also Kidd, William
Pitt, William the Younger, foreign policy of, 181
Pocock, J. G. A., 3
Poland, 200
political philosophy, death of, *see* Laslett, Peter
political theory, 24, 29, 50, 77, 86
  definition of, 74
  as early modern, 61, 157
  history of, 2–6, 26, 90, 92, 114, 172
  international, 7
  as modern, 13
  as political science, 70–3
Polybius, 50
Pontius the Samnite, 164
Portalis, Joseph-Marie, 11
positivism, 5, 25–6
  international, 73
  and law, 63, 67–8, 71, 206–7
prerogative, royal, 84, 139–41, 143, 148–50
  and *arcana imperii*, 158–9
  see also reason of state
presentism, 30–1
Price, Richard, 161
printing-press, as revolutionary instrument, 227
property, *see* Locke, John
Protestant Association, 161
Pufendorf, Samuel, 53, 62, 68, 69, 94, 117, 150
punishment, as right of sovereign, 81
Purcell, Nicholas, 46

Rawls, John, 3, 4–5, 78, 86–8
  on John Locke, 86–8
Raynal, Guillaume-François-Thomas, abbé,
    51, 53, 55
reason of state, 155–6, 157–71
  commerce as, 52, 53–5
recognition of states, 208–14, 221–7, 228–32
Reformation, Protestant, 168
Reid, John Phillip, 195
reification, 30
religion, Christian, 63
  as destructive of society, 128
  natural, 159
  and toleration, 100, 110
  see also Carolina, *Fundamental Constitutions*

República Boricua, 226
republicanism, 215, 222–3, 227
republic of letters, 19
resistance theory, 158, 162
revolution, practices and discourse of, 219, 225
  see also Age of Revolutions, American
      Revolution / War, French Revolution
rights
  Bill of, US, 220
  defensible, 180, 205
  fundamental, 193–4
  human, 29, 38–9, 42, 44, 194
  inalienable, 220
  of individuals, 78, 205
  natural, 62, 63, 81, 90
  rights-bearing adults, 85
Robertson, William, 38
Robinson, James Harvey, 19
Rockefeller Foundation, New York Conference
      on International Politics, 25
Rodríguez O., Jaime, 219
Roman law, 38
  Digest of, 61, 62, 63, 68
Rome, 51–2, 54
  war against Samnites, 164
Rothschild, Emma, 31
Rousseau, Jean-Jacques, 97, 159
Roy, Rammohan, 30
  see also liberalism
Royal African Company, 91
royal prerogative, *see* prerogative, royal
Royal Society, 114
Russia, 213
  Peter the Great, 143
Rye House Plot, 103

Sacheverell, Dr Henry, 162
Said, Edward, 115
Salamanca, School of, 9
San Martin, José de, 228
Schmitt, Carl, 10, 25, 27, 50, 55, 71
Schroeder, Paul, 167
science, 22–3
  history of, 29
  spatial turn in, 22–4
Scotland
  and common law, 142
  Darien venture of, 147
  independence of, 135
  Union with England, 1707, 136, 146–7
Scott, James Brown, 26, 212
  see also Carnegie Endowment for
      International Peace
self-defence, 156
  see also rights

Sena, Manuel García de, 41
Serbia, 230
Serle, Ambrose, 202
Seven Years' War, 51, 54, 55, 135, 148, 167
Shaftesbury, Anthony Ashley Cooper, 1st Earl
      of, 91, 94, 96–8, 102–6
Shaftesbury, Anthony Ashley Cooper,
      3rd Earl of, 123
Shelbourne, John Dutton, 1st Baron, 138
Skinner, Quentin, 3–4, 8
slavery, 91, 96, 99, 111–12, 152, 204
Smith, Adam, 36, 55
sociability, commercial, *see* Nicole, Pierre
social contract theory, 86–7
Society of Jesus, 22
South Sudan, declaration of independence
      (2011), 231
sovereignty, 'contagion of', *see* independence, state
space, and intellectual history, 21–4, 32
  spatial turn, 22
Spain, 216–18, 225
  Ferdinand VII, King, 217, 222
  monarchy of, 52
  see also America, Iberian
Spanish Succession, war of, 51, 166–7
St Clair, James, 76
St Eustatius, British capture of, 165
Stanley, Thomas, 19
state of nature, 80–2, 87, 146, 223
  fear in, 66–7
  international, 63, 65–7, 69–72, 81–5
  interpersonal, 64, 67
  Locke's conception of, 77–9
  and secession, 178
  see also Hobbes, Thomas
states
  as artificial persons, 63–7, 137, 207
  division of power in, 84
  and federation, 215
  formation of, 215
  as international entities, 70
  nation-states, 13, 17–18, 21, 24, 40, 86
  rights of, 77, 195
  sovereignty of, 27–8, 59, 157, 191, 215–18
  see also recognition of states, empires
Steck J. C. W. von, 209
Stoics, 156
Strange, James Smith-Stanley, Lord, 140
Strauss, Leo, 77
Straw, Jack, 11
Suárez, Francisco, 43
Sutton, Charles Manners, 169

Talbot, Charles, 1st Baron, Lord Chancellor, 142
taxation, 141, 177, 192

technology, 24, 35
Texas, republic of, 227
time-space compression, 37
Toinard, Nicholas, 101, 105
Toland, John, 158
toleration, religious, *see* religion
Tönnies, Ferdinand, 70
trade, *see* commerce
trans-national, origins of term, 42
    see also international
treaties / positive agreements, 81–5, 151, 206–8
Triquet v. *Bath*, 142–4
Tuck, Richard, 5, 90, 94
Tucker, Josiah, 100, 112, 123
Tully, James, 93, 101, 114
Turner, Frederick Jackson, 19
tyranny, *see* democracy

United Nations, 5, 18, 44, 48, 231–2
    see also international institutions
United States of America, 4, 19, 25, 44, 70
    civil unrest in during nineteenth century,
        226–7
    Civil War, 139, 194, 211, 229
    constitution of, 219
    foreign policy of, 49
    *see also individual states by name, Civil War,
        Declaration of Independence, US*
universalism, 23–4, 187
utility / utilitarianism, 71
    consequentialist, 156
    and greatest happiness principle, 181–5
Utrecht, Treaty of (1713), 136, 166–7

Valle, José del, 173
Van Ompteda, D. H. L., 183
Vane, Sir Walter, 75
Vattel, Emer de, 69, 125, 149, 151, 163, 185, 201
    on independence, 223–5
    work: *Le Droit des gens*, 165–8, 206
        reception of, 201, 222
Venezuela, 218, 222, 225
Venturi, Franco, 37

Vermont, 229
Vienna, Congress of (1815), 229
Vietnam War, 4, 86
Virginia, constitution, 220
    Declaration of Rights (1776)
        see Bentham, *Principles of Morals*
Von Martens, G. F., 210
Von Steck, J. C. W., 209

Walpole, Sir Robert, 162
Waltz, Kenneth, 25
Walzer, Michael, 4, 5, 166
war, 4, 68, 81, 140
    causes and prevention of, 182
    just war, 164–7
    justified by tyranny, 165
    laws of, 65
Ward, Robert Plumer, 39–41, 68, 182–5, 207
    Enquiry into . . . the Law of Nations, 150
Wellesley, Arthur, 1st Duke of Wellington, 130
Wendt, Alexander, 77
West Florida, 226
Westminster, *see* Parliament, British
Westminster, Treaty of (1654), 79
Westphalia, Peace of (1648), 9, 11–12, 27–8, 73, 191
    'Westphalian myth', 27–8, 191
whale, *see* leviathan
Wheaton, Henry, 11, 28, 42
Whigs, 158, 162, 169
Wight, Martin, 2–3, 25–6, 77, 154
    see also 'English School'
William III, King (William of Orange), 76, 79,
        84, 85
    and Dutch invasion, 127, 146, 164
Williamson, Jeffrey, 36
Wolff, Christian, 166
Woolsey, Theodore, 70
World War, First, 24
World War, Second, 55

Xenophon, 50–1

Zouche, Richard, 26, 43, 68